The Life and Death of the Shopping City

T0382184

How have British cities changed in the years since the Second World War? And what drove this transformation? This innovative new history traces the development of the post-war British city, from the 1940s era of reconstruction, through the rise and fall of modernist urban renewal, up to the present-day crisis of high street retailing and central area economies. Alistair Kefford shows how planners, property developers, councils and retailers worked together to create the modern shopping city, remaking the physical fabric, economy and experience of cities around this retail-driven developmental model. This book also offers a wider social history of mass affluence, showing how cities were transformed to meet the perceived demands of a society of shoppers, and why this effort was felt to be so urgent in an era of urban deindustrialisation. By bringing the story of the shopping city right up to its present-day crisis and collapse, Kefford makes clear how the historical trajectories traced in this book continue powerfully to shape urban Britain today.

Alistair Kefford is Assistant Professor at Leiden University where he teaches history and urban studies. He was previously a British Academy Postdoctoral Fellow at the Centre for Urban History, University of Leicester, and a Lecturer in Modern British History at the University of Manchester. He worked for a number of years in local government planning and continues to engage with contemporary urban policy and regeneration. His work has appeared in numerous scholarly journals of history and urban studies and his research into 'the death of the high street' has been featured in high-profile publications such as *The Financial Times.*

MODERN BRITISH HISTORIES

Series Editors:

Deborah Cohen, *Northwestern University*
Margot Finn, *University College London*
Peter Mandler, *University of Cambridge*

'Modern British Histories' publishes original research monographs drawn from the full spectrum of a large and lively community of modern historians of Britain. Its goal is to keep metropolitan and national histories of Britain fresh and vital in an intellectual atmosphere increasingly attuned to, and enriched by, the transnational, the international and the comparative. It will include books that focus on British histories within the UK and that tackle the subject of Britain and the world inside and outside the boundaries of formal empire from 1750 to the present. An indicative – not exclusive – list of approaches and topics that the series welcomes includes material culture studies, modern intellectual history, gender, race and class histories, histories of modern science and histories of British capitalism within a global framework. Open and wide-ranging, the series will publish books by authoritative scholars, at all stages of their career, with something genuinely new to say.

A complete list of titles in the series can be found at:
www.cambridge.org/modernbritishhistories

The Life and Death of the Shopping City

Public Planning and Private Redevelopment in Britain since 1945

Alistair Kefford

Leiden University

 CAMBRIDGE
UNIVERSITY PRESS

CAMBRIDGE
UNIVERSITY PRESS

Shaftesbury Road, Cambridge CB2 8EA, United Kingdom

One Liberty Plaza, 20th Floor, New York, NY 10006, USA

477 Williamstown Road, Port Melbourne, VIC 3207, Australia

314–321, 3rd Floor, Plot 3, Splendor Forum, Jasola District Centre, New Delhi – 110025, India

103 Penang Road, #05–06/07, Visioncrest Commercial, Singapore 238467

Cambridge University Press is part of Cambridge University Press & Assessment, a department of the University of Cambridge.

We share the University's mission to contribute to society through the pursuit of education, learning and research at the highest international levels of excellence.

www.cambridge.org
Information on this title: www.cambridge.org/9781108799164

DOI: 10.1017/9781108874502

First published 2022
First paperback edition 2024

A catalogue record for this publication is available from the British Library

Library of Congress Cataloging-in-Publication data
Names: Kefford, Alistair, author.
Title: The life and death of the shopping city : public planning and private redevelopment in Britain since 1945 / Alistair Kefford, Universiteit Leiden.
Description: Cambridge, United Kingdom ; New York, NY : Cambridge University Press, [2022] | Series: Modern British histories | Includes bibliographical references and index.
Identifiers: LCCN 2021055222 (print) | LCCN 2021055223 (ebook) | ISBN 9781108836692 (hardback) | ISBN 9781108799164 (paperback) | ISBN 9781108874502 (ebook)
Subjects: LCSH: City planning – Great Britain – History. | Urban renewal – Great Britain – History. | Shopping centers – Great Britain – History. | BISAC: HISTORY / Europe / Great Britain / General
Classification: LCC HT169.G7 K44 2022 (print) | LCC HT169.G7 (ebook) | DDC 307.1/2160941–dc23/eng/20211209
LC record available at https://lccn.loc.gov/2021055222
LC ebook record available at https://lccn.loc.gov/2021055223

ISBN   978-1-108-83669-2   Hardback
ISBN   978-1-108-79916-4   Paperback

For Laura, who had to live with it.

Contents

Figures

Acknowledgements

This book has been many years in the making, and I have accumulated plenty of debts along the way. The first thanks should go to the two bodies that funded the majority of this work. The doctoral research that formed the original germ of this book was undertaken at the University of Manchester and was generously funded by the Economic and Social Research Council. More recently, I was the recipient of a British Academy (BA) Postdoctoral Fellowship held at the University of Leicester. This fellowship was instrumental in allowing me the time and space to undertake new research and work the book into its current form. I am extremely grateful to the BA for this, along with all the additional support the Academy provided along the way. I was very fortunate to hold my fellowship at Leicester's Centre for Urban History (CUH), which remains one of the foremost centres for the study of the urban past. CUH not only provided the perfect intellectual environment but also offered me an especially warm and friendly welcome. I am grateful to my Leicester colleagues Richard Butler, Sarah Goldsmith, Prashant Kidambi, Mark Rawlinson, Keith Snell and Roey Sweet for making this such a rich and rewarding period. Roey deserves additional thanks for reading substantial chunks of this work and providing perspicacious comments at unparalleled speed. Special mention is due to CUH's Director Simon Gunn. Simon has been a great champion of my work and career, as he has for so many other young scholars, and it was a great pleasure to work closely with him at Leicester. Simon's enthusiasm and generosity towards young scholars like myself mean his imprint on the lively field of modern British urban history stretches far beyond his own important research and writings.

I have benefitted enormously from intellectual engagements and encouragement from a wide range of friends and colleagues. I am grateful to Aaron Andrews, Phil Child, Iain Deas, David Edgerton, Alistair Fair, James Greenhalgh, Ewan Harrison, Michael Hebbert, Leif Jerram, Peter Mandler, Julie Marie-Strange, Sarah Mass, Helen McCarthy, Frank Mort, Guy Ortolano, Richard Rodger, Otto Saumarez Smith,

Rick Trainor, Tim Verlaan, Rosemary Wakeman, Sam Wetherell and Charlotte Wildman. I am also extremely grateful to all those working in the fields of planning and property who took time to meet and talk to me. Their insights and experiences were invaluable, and I thank Grant Butterworth, Chris Miele, Deborah Rose and Justin Webber in this regard. I must also thank Oliver Marriot, whose own book on the British property sector incredibly remains a standard work more than fifty years after it was published, and with whom I spent an enjoyable and enlightening afternoon talking about the post-war property business. At Cambridge University Press, Liz Friend-Smith has been endlessly patient and supportive as an editor, while Peter Mandler's enthusiastic engagement with my work has been a great source of encouragement and sage advice. The Press's reader deserves special credit for his generous and incisive engagement with this work, even as we sometimes diverged on aspects of this history. The book is indebted to him as it is to all the others listed here; all errors and omissions naturally remain my own.

I was grateful to have the chance to present parts of this work to the Cambridge Modern British History Seminar, to Edinburgh's Architectural History Seminar and to Glasgow's Economic and Social History Seminar, and I thank the organisers and participants in all of these sessions. I was also privileged to participate in the New Directions in British Urban History workshop at New York University in September 2019, and I thank Guy Ortolano and Sarah Mass for the invitation and for their hospitality. Simon Gunn and Otto Saumarez Smith's Society for the Promotion of Urban Discussion group has also been a great forum – intellectually and socially – for friendly debate and exchange within our field. When I began this work as a lone doctoral student, I imagined academia as a rather solitary pursuit. I am grateful to all those listed here for showing me otherwise. I should also record my thanks to all the archivists and library staff who have assisted me in the many local record offices and collections I have visited over the past decade. Their work as custodians of our shared history is of great value but sadly often under threat from budgetary pressures. I am also grateful to all the individuals and institutions who have assisted me in the work of obtaining images or granted me permission to reproduce various materials. They are detailed more fully alongside these materials. The final thanks must go to my wife Laura Pennacchietti, who, aside from having to live with the long process of research and writing, is also the first and last person I go to for editorial advice and perspicacious criticism.

Introduction

Britain's town and city centres are in a state of crisis. All over the country, urban centres face a set of challenges caused principally by a marked decline in the business of shopping in the town centre. The evidence of this decline is there for all to see in store closures, vacant shops, mass retail redundancies and underused high streets. Recent years have been a litany of crisis and collapse in high street retailing. In 2018, more than 14,500 stores closed with the loss of more than 117,000 jobs. In 2020, more than 16,000 stores closed and over 182,000 jobs were lost. Some of the medium-term causes of these severe contractions have been building steadily for some time. The proportion of shopping done online, for example, has increased rapidly since the early 2000s, and now makes up around a quarter of all sales. Footfall in town centres has sagged year on year across the same period. Crucially, real wages and household disposable incomes in Britain have stagnated since the 2008 financial crisis – for a sector that relies upon hoovering up consumers' spending money, this is critical. Taken together, these darkening prospects meant that even before the Coronavirus crisis struck in early 2020 the United Kingdom had an estimated oversupply of retail space in the order of 25–30 per cent.[1] In practice, this means a lot of empty shops in a lot of urban centres. The economic dislocation, job losses and forced shop closures of the Coronavirus pandemic have made a very bad situation significantly worse; the contraction of high street retailing and the shift to online purchasing have accelerated markedly, and many shops will never reopen. Today we see government task forces, advisory commissions, industry experts and local authorities searching desperately for new solutions to these problems. The death of the high street and the future of the town centre has become an urgent public policy issue.

---

[1] These details in Centre for Retail Research, *The Crisis in Retailing: Closures and Job Losses*, 2021, available online; Chris Rhodes, *Retail Sector in the UK*, House of Commons Briefing Paper SN06186, 29 October 2018; Helen Thomas, 'Why John Lewis Tells Us This Retail Crisis is Just Beginning', *The Financial Times*, 17 March 2021.

At first glance the causes of these urban woes can seem intensely modern and contemporary; the rise of internet shopping, pandemic-driven dislocation and the dwindling spending power of consumers in post-crash, austerity Britain, are all very much twenty-first century problems. And yet, the current crisis facing town centres has been brewing for a long time. It represents the collapse of an urban developmental model that has held sway in Britain since the 1940s – that of 'the shopping city' – in which urban centres seeking growth and prosperity have competed to establish themselves as the most successful shopping destinations for their region. Since the middle of the twentieth century, retailing has been accepted and promoted as the mainstay of urban economies and, as a result, the demands of the sector have been allowed to dictate the form and function of central areas. The present challenges are so acute precisely because urban centres have come to rely so heavily upon the business of retailing for their economic and social vitality (while, conversely, those places with a more diverse economic structure and a richer mix of social functions face a less existential threat). And it is a very particular form of retailing that has come to dominate Britain's urban centres, specifically the highly organised and efficient multiple retail chains whose sophisticated sales and management techniques enabled them to pay the highest commercial rents. This has produced what one industry expert recently called a 'retail monoculture' in urban Britain, with identikit high streets dominated everywhere by the same nationally organised retail chains.[2] Like all monocultures, this urban economic formation is brittle and vulnerable, lacking resilience and liable to collapse under stress.

The importance of the commercial rents generated by high street retailing points to another critical part of this story, and one that also has a long genesis across the second half of the twentieth century – namely, the transformation of central urban space into a lucrative tradeable commodity and its enlistment in complex financial systems of wealth-holding, investment and accumulation. The dominance of the most efficient and profitable forms of retailing in urban centres has been consistently advanced by the dynamics of property-based wealth-creation, as owners and investors in urban property seek to wring the maximum returns out of this valuable physical asset. Indeed, alongside organised retailing, the commercial property sector also emerged as a mainstay of urban economies from the mid-twentieth century onwards. Commercial property *development* in particular – the 'creative destruction'

---

[2] Jonathan Eley, 'Retail Crisis is the Mother of Urban Centre Reinvention', *The Financial Times*, 23 November 2020.

of the extant urban fabric and its reconstruction as a much more valuable property asset – exploded in size and significance after 1945, and quickly emerged as a significant force within the national economy as a whole. By the early 1960s there were five times as many property companies listed on the London Stock Exchange as there had been before the war, when property development remained a decidedly marginal economic activity. The value of these companies, along with the properties they owned and built and Britain's urban centres, skyrocketed. The property business produced more millionaires in the three decades after the war than any other industry, and the price of urban land soared. Owning and redeveloping valuable central area property became an attractive investment for Britain's sophisticated financial sector, particularly the large financial institutions that became the chief holders of British capital in this era; their annual investments in property went from £8 m in 1946 to over £1bn in 1976.[3] The rise of this dynamic new mode of wealth-creation transformed the physical, economic and social geography of Britain's cities, making redevelopment a profitable end in its own right and conditioning the types of environment and activity that could stand in the town centre. In the period after 1945, the property sector established itself as a major commercial force and a decisive influence on urban form and function.

The life of the shopping city was thus firmly shaped by two important commercial forces – the modern, organised retail sector and the commercial property business – which operated in tandem to overhaul urban economies and environments. By the later decades of the twentieth century, the growth and profitability of both of these sectors in Britain was an internationally recognised business success.[4] Of course, the rise of the shopping city was also inextricable from the societal and structural shift towards mass affluence and a consumer-driven economy which took place in the second half of the twentieth century. This process had long historical genealogies and plenty of pre-war precursors, but the coming of 'the affluent society' – in which the majority saw their real wages and

---

[3] These details in Oliver Marriott, *The Property Boom* (London: Hamish Hamilton, 1967), Appendix 4; 'Property: The Philosopher's Stone', *The Economist*, 18 March 1972, 135–136; Peter Scott, *The Property Masters: A History of the British Commercial Property Sector* (London: E&FN Spon, 1996), Table 10.1.

[4] Carlo Morelli, 'Increasing Value? Modern British Retailing in the Late Twentieth Century', in Richard Coopey & Peter Lyth (eds.), *Business in Britain in the Twentieth Century: Decline and Renaissance?* (Oxford: Oxford University Press, 2009), 271–295; Martin Boddy, 'The Property Sector in Late-Capitalism: The Case of Britain', in Michael Dear & Allen J. Scott (eds.), *Urbanization and Urban Planning in Capitalist Society* (London: Routledge, 1981), 267–286; Alistair Kefford, 'Actually Existing Managerialism: Planning, Politics and Property Development in Post-1945 Britain', *Urban Studies* 58:12 (2021), 2441–2455.

disposable incomes rise significantly – was a post-war phenomenon. In an economy fuelled increasingly by personal consumption, and where traditional sources of urban growth and employment in areas like manufacturing were flagging, towns and cities reoriented themselves towards the dynamic domain of affluent consumerism. Large retailers and commercial property developers were able to operate so successfully in urban Britain, transforming central areas with elaborate and expensive new shopping facilities, because of the new patterns of individual wealth and consumer spending associated with mass affluence.[5]

And yet, despite these new commercial trends and underlying structural dynamics, the reorganisation of urban centres around new modes of retailing and consumption was not a project that unfolded 'naturally' as a result of a free interplay of market forces and commercial development pressures. The life of the shopping city was shaped as much by public planning and initiative as it was by private entrepreneurial endeavour. The period in which the shopping city model was so comprehensively installed in the nation's urban centres was precisely synchronous with the establishment of a modern planning system in Britain, when local authorities were granted much stronger powers over urban land use and redevelopment and took on a heightened responsibility for local economic performance and growth.[6] Local authorities repeatedly deployed these new powers in the service of retail expansion and redevelopment in the town centre, aiming to reinvent their towns as exciting and prosperous shopping destinations. Councils reconfigured and re-zoned central districts, pushing out a wide mix of alternative uses and reorganising the infrastructure and environment of the town centre around the needs of the retail economy. They courted the biggest retailers, hoping to attract the most successful and prestigious retail brands to their towns. And they forged alliances with commercial property developers, who promised to install the latest modern shopping facilities that would secure towns' regional status and future prosperity. Local authorities encouraged and promoted these new modes of commercial urbanism through a variety of means, but the most obvious and effective mechanism was the compulsory public acquisition of central area land, which was assembled into

---

[5] On structural change in the period see Nicholas Crafts, 'The British Economy', in Francesca Carnevali & Julie-Marie Strange (eds.), 20th Century Britain: Economic, Cultural and Social Change (London: Routledge, 2007), 7–25; Avner Offer, 'British Manual Workers: From Producers to Consumers, c. 1950-2000', Contemporary British History 22:4 (2008), 537-571.

[6] For the detailed development of the planning system see Barry Cullingworth & Vincent Nadin, Town and Country Planning in the UK (London: Routledge, 2006); Peter Hall & Mark Tewdwr-Jones, Urban and Regional Planning (London: Routledge, 2019). Both of these classic texts run to many editions.

large plots and delivered to commercial interests for profitable redevelopment. The creation of the modern shopping city thus rested upon a curious union between the newly interventionist planning powers of the post-war polity and the burgeoning commercial domain of retail property development.

This book places this public–private dynamic at the heart of urban transformation since the 1940s, a period that saw successive waves of urban remodelling in Britain from post-war reconstruction, to 1960s-style urban renewal, to late-century urban regeneration. It shows how public planning and private redevelopment came together to reconstitute Britain's towns and cities, remaking urban geographies and economies in the name of efficiency, growth and consumer satisfaction. All over Britain, urban centres large and small were transformed by vast new stores; expanded and beautified shopping districts; supermarkets, precincts and shopping parades; and megalithic new shopping malls. These carefully curated landscapes of consumption amounted to a fundamental restructuring of not just the built environment but of urban public space, culture and experience too. This was a period in which shopping became not just a leading sector of the economy but also a key sphere of post-war social and cultural life – tied to the expanding domains of leisure, pleasure and commercial entertainment, and powerfully connected with individuals' psychosocial worlds, with their identities, and sense of self.[7] New shopping spaces had a cultural resonance and social significance that went far beyond their function within urban economies and local planning strategies. These were the sites in which, for many ordinary Britons, the affluent society was encountered, accommodated and made concrete, and where new cultures of consumption, acquisition and self-curation were most intensively propagated. This book pays close attention to the cultural significance of these projects of urban reinvention, as well as attending to the range of private interests that shaped and profited from these new social and spatial forms – the multiple retailers, property developers, marketing experts, builders and financiers who did so much to steer the course of urban transformation and yet remain almost entirely absent from the many scholarly accounts of British urbanism in this period.

Attending to the way public planning worked in concert with these new commercial forces at the construction of the shopping city raises important questions about the character, aims and impact of 'planning' in post-war

---

[7] Erika Rappaport, Sandra Trudgen Dawson & Mark J. Crowley (eds.), *Consuming Behaviours: Identity, Politics and Pleasure in Twentieth-Century Britain* (London: Routledge, 2015); Daniel Miller, Peter Jackson, Nigel Thrift, Beverley Holbrook & Michael Rowlands (eds.), *Shopping, Place and Identity* (London: Routledge, 1998).

Britain. The creation of a comprehensive public planning system in the 1940s was one element of the wider mid-century reformation of the British polity, in which the state assumed a heightened responsibility for economic management and individual welfare.[8] As a result, the story of planning in this period is frequently subsumed within the familiar narrative of the rise of the welfare state and the coming of social democracy. Indeed, town planning is often understood as the spatial arm of the welfare state – a moralising but meliorist endeavour that cleared slums, rehoused citizens, cleaned up cities and improved the urban environment. These are important stories of course, and town planning – as both a profession and an idea – always contained a strong reformist streak. But, just as recent historical reassessments have stressed that the post-war polity should not be understood solely in terms of welfare statehood, so this work shows that the aims and impact of the post-war planning system are not fully captured by these traditional welfarist terms of reference.[9]

In remaking the nation's urban centres, the planning system as it actually operated was shaped by a complex range of agendas and rationales, some of which were rather less benign than others. In particular, I stress the *developmentalism* of the post-war planning regime – the drive to grow local economies through stimulating and sponsoring the most profitable forms of private enterprise. This was an especially strong impulse within local authorities, who continued to work with their own long traditions of civic boosterism and local growth promotion. Local authorities frequently viewed their expanded post-war planning powers as an opportunity to engage in new forms of urban economic husbandry. In an era of consumer-fuelled growth and – for many places – urban industrial decline, councils focused their developmental efforts on growing the local retail economy. But I also stress the political and financial constraints upon local authorities, particularly when it came to central area redevelopment, where councils were impelled by statute and by necessity to work in partnership with private interests. If they had ever been empowered to do so, local authorities would no doubt have reforged urban centres as an image of civic progress and municipal modernism (as indeed many attempted to do in the reconstruction era). But this was never really the

[8] John Stevenson, 'Planners' Moon? The Second World War and the Planning Movement', in Harold L. Smith (ed.), *War and Social Change: British Society in the Second World War* (Manchester: Manchester University Press, 1986), 58–77.
[9] See, e.g. David Edgerton, *The Rise and Fall of the British Nation: A Twentieth-Century History* (London: Allen Lane, 2018); James Vernon, 'Heathrow and the Making of Neoliberal Britain', *Past & Present* 252:1 (2021), 213–247. Also Sam Wetherell's recent *Foundations: How the Built Environment Made Twentieth-Century Britain* (University of Princeton Press, 2020), which applies Edgerton's notion of a post-war developmental state to British urbanism and planning as an alternative to the conventional welfare state framing.

flavour of redevelopment in the town centre, where local public enterprise was consistently constrained and pared back by the political and legal strictures imposed by central government. In part this was simply a result of the central state's differing view of the importance of urban renewal as a national spending priority, but it was also related to underlying tensions within the new political economy of post-war Britain. This book shows how the post-war redevelopment regime was shaped by continued conflicts over the role of the state and the appropriate balance between public government and private enterprise. In particular, I highlight the continued influence of broadly liberal ideas of political economy and statehood amongst planners, civil servants and politicians (especially those on the right), in which there was unease and hostility to ideas of 'excessive' public intervention and an attempt instead to make planning work with the grain of the market in support of private sector growth.

The upshot of this hybrid and at times confused political economy of planning was an urban redevelopment regime in which new public planning powers were deployed in support of commercial projects of urban renewal and reinvention. This saw the developmentalism of the post-war state harnessed to the expertise of retailers and the entrepreneurial energies of commercial property developers. It produced a curious mode of urban renewal – brash, commercialist and consumer-oriented, and yet imposed arbitrarily upon cities through the use of sweeping state powers of compulsory purchase and comprehensive redevelopment. This book traces the social and economic impact of this mode of redevelopment upon towns and cities all over the country, stressing the deleterious effects it had upon many smaller and less profitable retailers along with the swathes of other small-scale business enterprise that were priced out of redeveloped urban centres. The public–private cultivation of retailing and central area property values also worked to expel many other social activities and patterns of use, and this transformed the social make-up and experience of the town centre. No longer characterised by a rich mix of social functions and experiences, town centres became increasingly monotonous and regimented, with ever-growing portions of central urban space given over to privatised and carefully managed landscapes of consumer seduction.

Far from enriching and revitalising urban social and economic life, these modes of redevelopment quickly came to look exploitative, exclusionary and iniquitous, as the commodified spaces of the city were reworked in the interests of retailers' sales figures and rentiers' investment strategies. And, despite the consuming enthusiasms of the age of affluence, there was never a clear *demand* to remodel cities in this fashion. On the contrary, extravagant new shopping complexes were often widely resisted and a great many failed to live up to their commercial promise. They also failed utterly to arrest the decline and alleviate the severe structural economic woes of many towns and cities in struggling regions. The notion of retail redevelopment as a form of local economic regeneration stretches back far beyond the 1980s. Many of Britain's urban centres were facing signs of industrial collapse as early as the 1920s, and by the mid-century retail-led reinvention was already established as a favoured strategy for local economic and social revitalisation. Yet such struggling locales were also the least likely to successfully relaunch themselves as affluent shopping destinations and the public–private embrace of the shopping city model ultimately did little to address their underlying structural woes. Indeed, many of these same places – Boltons, Blackburns, Grimsbys and Middlesbroughs – have re-emerged at the centre of current policy debates about the death of the high street and the existential collapse of smaller, second-order urban centres, their underlying developmental prospects seemingly little improved by seventy years of state-sponsored urban renewal efforts. The current crisis of the shopping city thus represents the collapse of an urban developmental model whose lifespan stretches back across the second half of the twentieth century to the reconstruction era. It was a model that was pursued vigorously by public policymakers, town planners and property developers, but its installation was deeply contentious and its social and economic impacts were always questionable.

The City and the Affluent Society

Mass affluence, along with the various actors and interests who steered and stimulated consumer expansion, is placed at the heart of urban transformation right across the period under study here. In common with other capitalist democracies, Britain experienced an economic golden age in the post-war decades, in which historically high levels of growth and a worker-friendly economic and employment structure fuelled substantial rises in real wages.[10] Although historians are often keen to highlight the limits of post-war affluence and the persistence of social and economic disadvantage, it remains the case that Britain

---

[10] Nicholas Crafts, 'The British Economy'. Crafts gives the figures for real wage growth in this period in Table 2.5 (3.16% p.a.), which are more than double that of other periods. See also Hugh Pemberton, 'The Transformation of the Economy', in Paul Addison and Harriet Jones (eds.), *A Companion to Contemporary Britain 1939–2000* (Oxford: Blackwell, 2007), 180–202; Robert Millward, 'The Rise of the Service Economy', in Roderick Floud and Paul Johnson (eds.), *Cambridge Economic History of Modern Britain Volume 3: Structural Change and Growth, 1939–2000* (Cambridge: Cambridge University Press, 2004), 238–266.

underwent an unprecedented process of economic transformation in this period, in which the majority of the population saw their living standards and disposable incomes rise significantly.[11] I call this mass affluence, without claiming that all Britons lived lives of luxury and leisure. Mass affluence unleashed a bewildering array of new social forces, as the changed material circumstances of ordinary Britons afforded them new opportunities to participate in, and reshape, the economic, cultural and political life of the nation. The affluent society, and the affluent subject, had to be accommodated, and this meant transformations in economic structure and organisation, in politics and public culture and in the wider cultural currents and collective experiences of British life.[12] Notions of citizenship, for example, were reworked around the figure of the affluent consumer, with their new rights and expectations. Crucially, mass affluence saw a remarkable burgeoning of the dynamic commercial-cultural sphere of personal consumption, which connected the deeply subjective realm of individual identity and experience to the commercial logics and corporate strategies of production, accumulation, distribution and marketing.[13]

The nation's urban centres also had to accommodate mass affluence, and the adaptations were simultaneously physical, economic and cultural. Urban space and society were remodelled around the new demands of an affluent citizenry and an increasingly consumer-driven economy. Large swathes of Britain's towns and cities were reconstructed as

[11] For accounts which stress the social limits of affluence see Pat Thane, *Divided Kingdom: A History of Britain, 1900 to the Present* (Cambridge: Cambridge University Press, 2018); Selina Todd, *The People: The Rise and Fall of the Working Class 1910–2010* (London: John Murray, 2014).
[12] Vernon Bogdanor & Robert Skidelsky (eds.), *The Age of Affluence 1951–1964* (London: Macmillan, 1970); John Benson, *The Rise of Consumer Society in Britain, 1880–1980* (London: Longman, 1994); Arthur Marwick, *British Society since 1945* (London: Penguin, 2003); Lawrence Black & Hugh Pemberton (eds.), *An Affluent Society? Britain's Post-war 'Golden Age' Revisited* (Aldershot: Ashgate, 2004); Lawrence Black, *Redefining British Politics: Culture, Consumerism and Participation, 1954–70* (Basingstoke: Palgrave Macmillan, 2010); Matthew Hilton, *Consumerism in Twentieth-Century Britain: The Search for a Historical Movement* (Cambridge: Cambridge University Press, 2003); Kerstin Brückweh (ed.), *The Voice of the Citizen Consumer: A History of Market Research, Consumer Movements, and the Political Public Sphere* (Oxford: Oxford University Press, 2011); Frank Trentmann (ed.), *The Making of the Consumer: Knowledge, Power and Identity in the Modern World* (Oxford: Berg, 2006).
[13] Frank Mort, 'The Commercial Domain: Advertising and the Cultural Management of Demand', in Peter Jackson, Michelle Lowe, Daniel Miller & Frank Mort (eds.), *Commercial Cultures: Economies, Practices, Spaces* (Oxford: Berg, 2000); Sean Nixon, *Hard Sell: Advertising, Affluence and Transatlantic Relations, c. 1951–69* (Manchester: Manchester University Press, 2013); Daniel Miller, Peter Jackson, Nigel Thrift, Beverley Holbrook & Michael Rowlands (eds.), *Shopping, Place and Identity* (London: Routledge, 1998).

consumer playgrounds, dominated by elaborate shopping facilities and curious new landscapes of consumption. Expensive new shopping spaces, offering new types of consumer experience in increasingly spectacular environments, sprang up rapidly all over the country in the post-war decades. In the earlier post-war period this usually involved the construction of individual large stores in the town centre, or else of modern shopping parades. These new shopping spaces housed Britain's prosperous and expansionary retail chains whose dominance over the town centre and the retail economy had been advancing steadily since the interwar years. In the mid-1950s there were already plenty of retail chains in Britain with a hundred or more stores; by 1970 multiple retailers had captured something like 40 per cent of the total retail trade, and much more in many individual sectors. From the 1960s, individual shop developments were increasingly superseded by the development of various types of holistically planned shopping complex, more elaborate and totalising than what had gone before, housing many different stores arranged together around pedestrianised precincts or in new mall environments. By 1975 around 300 such centres had already been built in Britain's town centres. This process accelerated towards the end of the century, so that by 1993 there were around 800 shopping centres in Britain, and these also now included many ex-urban locations and regional megamalls.[14] The accessibility and mobility of shoppers (particularly 'car-shoppers') was firmly prioritised so that town centres were reworked with major new roads, mammoth car parking facilities and enormous bus stations. Somewhat counterintuitively, the pedestrianisation of urban centres proceeded in tandem with this motorisation of shoppers' mobility, as car-borne shoppers were channelled into the town centre to stroll around the new urban landscapes of affluence.

Shopping was transformed as part of this process and went – albeit with much variation – from being characterised by small, independent shops and more prosaic purchases, to be dominated by nationally organised retail chains retailing high volumes of goods out of large new stores.[15] These changes went hand in hand with a decisive shift from shopping for provisions to shopping for pleasure in which spectacular new shopping environments played a key role. Indeed, shopping was increasingly recast

---

[14] Figures taken from: E. MacFadyen, 'Retailers at the Crossroads', *Building with Steel* 10 (May, 1972), 2–6; John Trafford, 'Shopping Centres: Hiatus for Stocktaking', *The Financial Times*, 2 April 1975, 28; Tony Taylor, 'The British Council of Shopping Centres', *Planning Practice and Research* 8:3 (1993), 43–44.

[15] Michael Winstanley, 'Concentration and Competition in the Retail Sector c.1800-1990', in Maurice W. Kirby & Mary B. Rose (eds.), *Business Enterprise in Modern Britain: From the Eighteenth Century to the Twentieth Century* (London: Routledge, 1994), 236–262.

as an entertaining leisure experience in its own right and a mainstay of urban social life, with new commercial complexes offering bars, restaurants, cafes, dancehalls, nightclubs and bowling alleys as part of the shopping experience. The mundane shopping trip was recast as an exciting leisure experience for all the family, and the design and architecture of new shopping spaces was a key part of this. Urban centres were transformed by the installation of surreal, languorous new landscapes punctuated by entertaining novelties such as fountains, light displays and aviaries, all designed to captivate and amuse the wandering shopper. These were the carefully curated fantasy lands that would later come to be deemed 'hyperreal' 'non-places' by theorists of consumer-driven postmodernity – although, as this book shows, fabricating slick and effective landscapes of seduction was no simple task; it required a long and costly post-war process of trial and error and plenty of abortive experiments.[16] These transformations in the experience of shopping and the nature of the retail economy were enthusiastically encouraged by urban authorities seeking new sources of revenue and new models of growth and prosperity for their towns and cities. In an era of urban deindustrialisation, shopping became ever more critical to the social functions and economic future of cities.

The physical landscape and economic structure of urban Britain was refashioned in the era of mass affluence, and such changes necessarily transformed the public culture and experience of the city. Civic progress and achievement came to be aligned with cities' status and offerings as shopping destinations, and councils bound themselves tightly (at times corruptly) to their private sector partners and the prestigious retail developments they offered. At the same time, the expanding importance of shopping meant that participation in the public spaces and public life of the city came increasingly to mean engagement with the cultures of

[16] The term 'non-place', and its association with 'post-modern' consuming environments, has been adopted from Marc Augé, *Non-Places: Introduction to an Anthropology of Supermodernity* (London: Verso, 2008) [orig. French edition, 1992]. 'Hyperreality' is a term coined by theorist of postmodernity Jean Baudrillard in *Simulacra and Simulation* (Ann Arbor: University of Michigan Press, 1994) [orig. French edition, 1981]. For accounts which treat shopping malls in these terms see David Harvey, *The Condition of Postmodernity: an Enquiry into the Origins of Cultural Change* (Oxford: Blackwell, 1990); Frederic Jameson, *Postmodernism, or, the Cultural Logic of Late Capitalism* (London: Verso, 1991); John Hannigan, *Fantasy City: Pleasure and Profit in the Postmodern Metropolis* (London: Routledge, 1998); David B. Clarke, *The Consumer Society and the Postmodern City* (London: Routledge, 2003); Steven Miles, *Spaces for Consumption: Pleasure and Placelessness in the Post-Industrial City* (London: SAGE, 2010). For longer perspectives on these trends see Kevin Hetherington, *Capitalism's Eye: Cultural Spaces of the Commodity* (London: Routledge, 2007); Geoffrey Crossick & Serge Jaumain (eds.), *Cathedrals of Consumption: the European Department Store, 1850–1939* (Aldershot: Ashgate, 1999).

high-value shopping. On entering the 'temples of frenetic consumption' – as the French situationist Guy Debord described the shopping mall in 1967 – the post-war citizen-shopper could commune with a dynamic culture of acquisition, consumption and leisure, which was itself promulgated most boisterously in the new urban landscapes of mass affluence.[17] This did not mean that all citizens responded enthusiastically to the remodelled urban offering, however, and one of the key themes of this book is the way in which planning powers were used to reshape urban environments and economies in the interests of (large) retailers and rentiers rather than according to the 'demands' of the consuming public. Indeed, it is striking how rarely the views of 'the consumer' were actually canvassed rather than simply invoked in urban redevelopment; this tended to disadvantage many women in particular, who continued to bear primary responsibility for feeding and provisioning their households.[18] As a result, many urban shopping developments fared very poorly in commercial terms, and rolling programmes of regular and wasteful redevelopment were instituted in an effort to draw the crowds. The remodelling of expensive urban retail environments became a continuous process for cities, as poorly performing developments – often little more than a decade old – were reconfigured and refurbished as newer, larger, brighter urban shopping attractions. This frantic refitting of cities' shopping infrastructure was an indication of the limits and failures of the wider developmental model, but the process nonetheless accelerated into the early years of the twenty-first century, driven by massive financial investment in the most expensive retail property. Now the entire system is in a state of collapse and disarray.

As well as offering new models of participation in the public life of the city, the reworked urban environment introduced new codes of behaviour, new conditions of access and new forms of exclusion. 'The right to the city' – understood as both a spatial and a political entitlement – came to be closely tied to one's status as a consuming subject, and the physical and social boundaries of the affluent urban civitas were vigorously policed.[19] Managing and manipulating the shopping citizen in space

---

[17] Guy Debord, *Society of the Spectacle*, 97 (Ken Knabb, Trans., London: Rebel Press, 2002). Original work published 1967.

[18] On the proliferation of market research in this era see Kerstin Brückweh (ed.), *The Voice of the Citizen Consumer: A History of Market Research, Consumer Movements, and the Political Public Sphere* (Oxford: Oxford University Press, 2011). On women in the post-war urban environment see Matrix, *Making Space: Women and the Man-Made Environment* (London: Pluto, 1984).

[19] The concept is Henri Lefebvre's, but has since spawned extensive literatures within urban geography and critical urban studies, e.g. Don Mitchell, *The Right to the City: Social Justice and the Fight for Public Space* (New York: The Guilford Press, 2003); David Harvey, 'The Right to the City', *International Journal of Urban and Regional Research* 27:4 (2003),

became an ever-more precise science, pursued through careful arrangements of selling space and sensory stimuli, and supported by new modes of policing and increasingly sophisticated and psychologised knowledge of consumer behaviour. The public spaces and public culture of Britain's towns and cities were reoriented around affluent consumerism in ways which are instantly recognisable today, but which were novel and untested in the post-war era. Many citizens objected to this commercialisation of the urban public sphere, and powerful critiques of retail-driven urban redevelopment began to emerge by the 1970s. Such criticisms reflected long-standing anxieties about the moral, cultural and political content of 'the consumer society', as well as a rising wave of dissatisfaction with the unusually marketised, money-grubbing thrust of Britain's post-war urban renewal regime, which seemed to have benefitted the booming commercial property sector above all else. Within the academy, from where many of these critiques emanated, a powerful narrative of the privatisation of cities and the neoliberalisation of urban governance began to take shape, which remains hugely influential to this day. Yet, for many of those most proactively involved in contesting urban redevelopment, it was the role of public government, through Britain's developer-friendly public planning regime, in facilitating these commercially driven projects of urban transformation that was most egregious.[20]

The Political Economy of Planning

The character and fate of the British variant of social democracy has become one of the key intellectual concerns of twentieth-century historiography, as evidenced by a remarkable efflorescence of new scholarship on 'post-war Britain', broadly, from the end of the Second World War to the 1970s.[21] Scholarly interest in the social and political forms of the

939–941; Neil Brenner, Peter Marcuse & Margit Mayer (eds.), *Cities for People not for Profit: Critical Urban Theory and the Right to the City* (London: Routledge, 2012).
[20] See for example the searing critique offered by the academics and community activists Peter Ambrose & Bob Colenutt in *The Property Machine* (Harmondsworth: Penguin, 1975).
[21] See *inter alia* Ben Jackson & Robert Saunders (eds.), *Making Thatcher's Britain* (Cambridge: Cambridge University Press, 2012); Jordanna Bailkin, *The Afterlife of Empire* (Berkeley: University of California Press, 2012); Camilla Schofield, *Enoch Powell and the Making of Postcolonial Britain* (Cambridge: Cambridge University Press, 2013); Lawrence Black, Hugh Pemberton & Pat Thane (eds.), *Reassessing 1970s Britain* (Manchester: Manchester University Press, 2013); Aled Davies, *The City of London and Social Democracy: The Political Economy of Finance in Britain, 1959–1979* (Oxford: Oxford University Press, 2017); Florence Sutcliffe-Braithwaite, *Class, Politics and the Decline of Deference in England, 1968–2000* (Oxford: Oxford University Press, 2018); Edgerton, *The Rise and Fall of the British Nation*; Jon Lawrence, *Me, Me, Me: The Search for Community in Post-war England* (Oxford: Oxford University Press, 2019); Guy Ortolano, *Thatcher's*

period has been motivated not least by efforts to wrestle with the transition from post-war social democracy and welfarism to post-1970s Thatcherism and the transformed political economy of neoliberalism which this era is understood to have ushered in (and which, by many accounts, we continue to live with today). Even more than most historians, then, those writing on Britain's post-war experience tend to have more than half an eye on the present; 'telling stories about post-war Britain' has become an important, if implicit, means for historians to engage with the social character and political prospects of contemporary Britain.[22] It was ever thus of course, and one of the first problems facing the historian of post-war Britain was to cut through the intellectual archaeology of earlier rounds of political story-telling – some subtle, some less so – which began in the period itself. Indeed, scholarly approaches to this era often remain responsive to one of the earliest and most nakedly political historicisations of 'post-war Britain' that was offered up by the Thatcherite wing of the Conservative Party as they sought to justify their own political project from the mid-1970s.[23] It was here that the still-recognisable narrative of post-war Britain as a nation in decline, stagnant and sclerotic, and hidebound by corporatist consensus and excessive statism, was most clearly articulated. The fact that much contemporary scholarship remains preoccupied with the important task of debunking these politically motivated myths is a clear indication of their continued purchase.

Urban planning, and the fate of the post-war city, has long been embroiled in these political and historical controversies. In its broadest sense, 'planning' (whether of the physical environment or of the economy) has often served its critics as a useful shorthand for the excessive

---

Progress: From Social Democracy to Market Liberalism through an English New Town (Cambridge: Cambridge University Press, 2019); Otto Saumarez Smith, *Boom Cities: Architect Planners and the Politics of Radical Renewal in 1960s Britain* (Oxford: Oxford University Press, 2019). The swelling corpus of monographs on post-war Britain is underpinned by a particularly lively journal literature, in the pages of *Twentieth Century British History*, *Journal of British Studies*, and other publications.

[22] Emily Robinson, Camilla Schofield, Florence Sutcliffe-Braithwaite & Natalie Thomlinson, 'Telling Stories about Post-war Britain: Popular Individualism and the "Crisis" of the 1970s', *Twentieth Century British History* 28:2 (2017), 268–304. Also, Matthew Hilton, Chris Moores & Florence Sutcliffe-Braithwaite, '*New Times* Revisited: Britain in the 1980s', *Contemporary British History* 31:2 (2017), 145–165; and (forthcoming) Florence Sutcliffe-Braithwaite, Aled Davies and Ben Jackson (eds.), *The Neoliberal Age? Politics, Economy, Society, and Culture in Late Twentieth Century Britain*.

[23] See Bernard Porter, '"Though not an Historian Myself . . . " Margaret Thatcher and the Historians', *Twentieth Century British History* 5:2 (1994), 246–256; Robert Saunders, "Crisis? What Crisis?" Thatcherism and the Seventies', in Jackson & Saunders (eds.), *Making Thatcher's Britain*, (Cambridge University Press, 2012) 25–42.

statism and bureaucracy that supposedly plagued post-war Britain, while Orwellian caricatures of 'the planners' – those faceless, wrong-headed authoritarians – have proved remarkably powerful and enduring.[24] Britain's towns and cities *were* subjected to an unprecedented level of public oversight from the 1940s, when a fully comprehensive planning system was installed for the first time, and the state granted itself the right to determine the form and function of every acre of its territory. These controls were largely negative – the right to withhold permission for new development rather than to proactively remodel extant urban environments – but there was also a surge in positive planning, which reached its peak in the 1960s and 1970s with the verve for comprehensive redevelopment and modernist urban renewal. The period from the mid-1950s to the mid-1970s saw cities remodelled by publicly directed programmes of slum clearance, mass housebuilding, urban motorway construction and central area redevelopment. These projects were made possible by a new willingness on the part of the state to deploy its powers of compulsory purchase to overrule the ancient prerogatives of private property. Once this unusually energetic period of state-sponsored urban rebuilding petered out in the mid-1970s, it became common to lambast the entire endeavour as a classic example of post-war overreach on the part of the state, in which an unwieldy and dysfunctional public sector had been allowed to disfigure the face of urban Britain. Much of the recent upsurge of scholarship on post-war urbanism, architecture and planning has been concerned to debunk these unfair characterisations – to rescue the modernist project from the enormous condescension of posterity – by showing British planners and planning to have been, on the whole, sensible, sensitive and humane.[25]

These insights and revisions are important, and have yielded a far more nuanced and multivalent picture of post-war urbanism and planning. And yet, in rescuing the reputation of welfare state urbanism there is a danger of overstating the progressive credentials and overall character of Britain's planning regime. Historians of town planning have frequently focused their attentions on the most radical and progressive elements within what was in fact a broad spectrum of planning thought and practice.[26] Meanwhile

---

[24] Memorably critiqued at the time in Jon Gower Davies, *The Evangelistic Bureaucrat: A Study of a Planning Exercise in Newcastle upon Tyne* (London: Tavistock, 1972).

[25] For example Saumarez Smith, *Boom Cities*; Ortolano, *Thatcher's Progress*; Barnabus Calder, *Raw Concrete: the Beauty of Brutalism* (London: William Heinemann, 2016); Elaine Harwood, *Space, Hope and Brutalism: English Architecture, 1945–1975* (New Haven: Yale University Press, 2015); John R. Gold, *The Practice of Modernism: Modern Architects and Urban Transformation, 1954–1972* (London: Taylor & Francis, 2007).

[26] For example Gordon E. Cherry, *Town Planning in Britain since 1900: The Rise and Fall of the Planning Ideal* (Oxford: Blackwell, 1996); Gordon Stephenson, *Compassionate Town*

many urban and architectural histories concentrate on the most emblem-
atically 'social democratic' elements of post-war planning endeavour – the
modernist mass housing schemes, New Towns, council estates, schools
and community centres which hold a totemic significance as symbols of
'welfare state Britain'.[27] Beyond the field of history, these characterisations
feed into a tendency to lionise post-war urban governance and planning. In
the adjacent disciplines of urban geography, urban political economy and
contemporary urban studies, post-war 'urban managerialism' – or, sometimes, 'spatial Keynesianism' – is often assumed to have been inherently
progressive, collectivist and redistributive, and regularly serves as a foil with
which to lambast present-day 'entrepreneurial' and 'neoliberal' urban
political and economic regimes. Indeed, such models of the ideological
character and social intent of post-war urbanism underpin a powerful
narrative of epochal political change in British cities and society across
the second half of the twentieth century, in which a collectivist and public-
spirited post-war welfarism collapsed in the 1970s to be replaced by
a ruthlessly economistic, growth-oriented neoliberalism. This narrative
has become so familiar that it has transferred out of academia to occupy
an instantly recognisable place within wider public commentary and
polemic on cities and their recent history.[28]

Planning (Liverpool: Liverpool University Press, 1994); Helen Meller, *Towns, Plans and Society in Modern Britain* (Cambridge: Cambridge University Press, 1997); Stephen V. Ward, *Planning the Twentieth-Century City: The Advanced Capitalist World* (Chichester: John Wiley, 2002); Peter Hall, *Cities of Tomorrow: An Intellectual History of Urban Planning and Design since 1880* (Chichester: John Wiley, 2014).

[27] Andrew Saint, *Towards a Social Architecture: The Role of School-Building* in Post-war England (New Haven: Yale University Press, 1987); Miles Glendenning & Stefan Muthesius, *Tower Block: Modern Public Housing in England, Scotland, Wales and Northern Ireland* (New Haven: Yale University Press, 1994); Mark Clapson, *Invincible Green Suburbs, Brave New Towns: Social Change and Urban Dispersal in Post-war England* (Manchester: Manchester University Press, 1997); Alison Ravetz, *Council Housing and Culture: the History of a Social Experiment* (London: Routledge, 2001); Nicholas Bullock, *Building the Post-war World: Modern Architecture and Reconstruction in Britain* (London: Routledge, 2002); Stephen V. Ward, *The Peaceful Path: Building Garden Cities and New Towns* (Hatfield: Hertfordshire, 2016); James Greenhalgh, *Reconstructing Modernity: Space, Power and Governance in Mid-twentieth century British Cities* (Manchester University Press, 2018); John Boughton, *Municipal Dreams: The Rise and Fall of Council Housing* (London: Verso, 2018). For a sophisticated global history of the New Towns ideal, see Rosemary Wakeman, *Practicing Utopia: An Intellectual History of the New Town Movement* (Chicago: University of Chicago Press, 2016).

[28] The classic account of the neoliberalisation of urban governance remains David Harvey, 'From Managerialism to Entrepreneurialism: The Transformation in Urban Governance in Late Capitalism', *Geografiska Annaler B* 71:(1989), 3–17. This line of argument has since spawned entire sub-fields of study within urban disciplines, and much of Harvey's original historical nuance has often been lost. See Neil Brenner & Nik Theodore (eds.), *Spaces of Neoliberalism: Urban Restructuring in North America and Western Europe* (Oxford: Blackwell, 2002); Helga Leitner, Jamie Peck & Eric S. Sheppard (eds.), *Contesting Neoliberalism: Urban Frontiers* (London: The Guilford Press, 2007); Tim Hall &

This book shows that the classic spatial projects of the welfare state – public housing, New Towns and the like – did not reflect the entirety of post-war planning endeavour. Nor should we read the progressive agendas of some of town planning's most vocal advocates as a straightforward indication of how new planning powers were conceived and deployed by the machinery of government, which – at both the local and the national level – continued to work with a wider range of political aims and administrative imperatives.[29] This study focuses on *the planning system* as it actually existed in Britain, rather than on the ideals and aspirations of leading planners and architects. It traces the complexities, compromises and contradictions of planning in operation, as new ideas about the management of society and space were filtered through the inherited structures and administrative cultures of the British state, and applied in concert with powerful commercial interests. I also prioritise the study of outcomes, rather than aspirations, by closely tracking the experience and impact of scores of different redevelopment projects in towns and cities all over Britain. The focus here is on the planning and redevelopment of Britain's town and city centres, and their transformation at the hands of forces and actors which included, but were not limited to, public planners and officials. Indeed, in the management of urban centres, what is striking is not the rise of an over-mighty public planning apparatus ready to remake the city in its own socially progressive image, but rather how constrained and diluted such reformist programmes were in practice, as they came into contact with the complex machinery and competing administrative imperatives of British statecraft, and rubbed up against the range of powerful commercial forces that were also jostling for position in post-war cities and society.[30]

Phil Hubbard (eds.), *The Entrepreneurial City: Geographies of Politics, Regime and Representation* (Chichester: Wiley, 1998); Brett Christopher, *The New Enclosure: The Appropriation of Public Land in Neoliberal Britain* (London: Verso, 2019). For recent commentary on these established currents of urban thought see the special issue, 'The Neoliberal City – Theory, Evidence, Debates', of *Territory, Politics, Governance* 4:2 in Giles Pinson and Christelle Morel Journel (eds.) (2016).

[29] Indeed, this was something that many of the more progressive voices from within the planning profession regularly complained about: F. J. Mcculloch, 'Physical Planning and Industry', *Town Planning Review* 20:1 (1949), 64–80; H. Myles Wright, 'The First Ten Years: Post-war Planning and Development in England', *Town Planning Review* 26:2 (1955), 73–91; Graeme Shankland, 'Dead Centre – The Crisis of Planning and the Future of Our Cities', *Official Architecture and Planning* 20:3 (1957), 137–140; Peter Ambrose, *Whatever Happened to Planning* (London: Methuen, 1986).

[30] Others have highlighted the importance of new commercial actors alongside public planning in shaping the post-war city, e.g. Saumarez Smith, *Boom Cities*; Frank Mort, 'Fantasies of Metropolitan Life: Planning London in the 1940s', *Journal of British Studies* 43:1 (2004), 120–151; Peter Mandler, 'New Towns for Old: The Fate of the Town Centre', in Becky Conekin, Frank Mort & Chris Waters (eds.), *Moments of Modernity:*

The image of British planning which emerges from this study is developmental, growth promoting, market oriented and business friendly. The more civic-minded currents of planning thought repeatedly fell by the wayside within an overall political economy of planning which placed great emphasis upon local economic performance and private sector growth. Indeed, it is remarkable how far bolstered public planning powers were turned to the ends of private sector profitability. The new planning powers of the post-war state were deployed as instruments of economic management as much as tools of social reform, and the booming retail economy was a key object of intervention. Planning powers were used to adapt deindustrialising cities for the new economic conditions of mass affluence, to service the perceived demands of a society of shoppers and to grow the value of retailing to local economies and the local tax base. The traditionally highly fragmented retail trade was reimagined as an 'industry', which could be made more efficient and more profitable through the creative deployment of planning powers, and shopping was purposely 'rationalised', as inefficient small traders were dispossessed and forced out of Britain's town centres to be replaced by larger, well-capitalised and nationally organised retail businesses. These developmental projects were pursued through powerful new alliances between public planning authorities and selected business interests – most especially commercial property developers – which were conceived and presented in terms of public–private cooperation and 'partnership'. Strategic, growth-promoting, developmental partnerships transformed the landscape and the political economy of urban Britain long before the rise of late-century 'entrepreneurial urbanism'.

The experience of planning and remodelling the nation's urban centres does not therefore support a narrowly welfarist reading of post-war urbanism, and calls into question the extent to which post-1970s 'neoliberal' urban governance should be seen as a radical departure from earlier practice. My emphasis here upon the developmentalism, rather than welfarism, of post-war planning is informed by David Edgerton's suggestive recasting of the wider post-war polity as a 'developmental state', with aims and agendas that are not sufficiently captured within the familiar rubrics of welfare statehood and social democracy.[31] Edgerton's account

Reconstructing Britain 1945–1964 (London: Rivers Oram, 1999), 208–227. Much of the literature on post-war reconstruction also stresses the political and practical constraints upon public planning, e.g. Nick Tiratsoo, 'The Reconstruction of Blitzed British Cities, 1945–55: Myths and Reality', *Contemporary British History* 14:1 (2000), 27–44; Catherine Flinn, *Rebuilding Britain's Blitzed Cities: Hopeful Dreams, Stark Realities* (London: Bloomsbury, 2018).
[31] Edgerton, *The Rise and Fall of the British Nation*, especially 307–308.

is not a specifically urban or spatial one, but Sam Wetherell's recent contribution to the burgeoning field of post-war urban historiography develops similar themes, eschewing the notions of social democracy or welfare statehood in favour of a mid-century 'developmental social politics' that produced a distinctive 'social developmental infrastructure' of state-sponsored industrial estates, mass public housing and municipal shopping precincts.[32] While sharing a great many of their intellectual concerns, my account of the post-war redevelopment of the nation's urban centres draws a much less clear dividing line than either of these authors between the political economy of post-war developmentalism and that of post-Thatcher neoliberalism. Indeed, one important insight of this book is how far the state-sponsored developmentalism of the post-war decades served to foment and nurture many of the very commercial forces and dynamics – the rise of corporate retailing, the explosion of commercial property development and the commodification and financialisation of urban space – that would come to be viewed as quintessential elements of the neoliberal city and challengers to the authority of public sector planning. I also show how – from their very beginnings in the 1940s – Britain's urban developmental projects were complicated and constrained by persistent conflicts both within and beyond the apparatus of government over the role of the state in society and the appropriate balance between public endeavour and private enterprise.

   This book takes issue, then, with the influential narrative of a post-1970s 'neoliberalisation' of British urbanism. It shows instead that the governance of Britain's towns and cities was characterised by growth-oriented, developmental and pro-business agendas right across the period from the 1940s to the 1990s, and that producing new spaces and infrastructures of consumption in partnership with selected private interests was central to this endeavour. Many of the characteristics that are seen as paradigmatic of neoliberalised urban government were powerfully present in British cities between the 1940s and the 1970s. These included an overriding public commitment to pursuing local economic growth; political and financial 'partnerships' between the public and the private sectors; 'entrepreneurial', business-like agendas on the part of local and central government; a deep-rooted commitment to the market mantras of efficiency, profitability and competitiveness; the expulsion of uneconomic or otherwise undesirable patterns of use from valuable urban areas; the commodification, privatisation and financialisation of urban public space; public underwriting of developers' financial risks; and a growing subordination of the shared spaces of the city to the commercial logics of

---

[32] Wetherell, *Foundations*, especially 7–9.

property development and retail capitalism. All of these were prominent features of urban Britain from the 1940s onwards and cannot be ascribed – as they often have been – to an ideologically driven shift in governance which began in the 1970s.

Just as we should not overstate the progressive credentials of post-war urban planning practices, nor should we necessarily endorse the neoconservatives' claims to have successfully 'neoliberalised' the political economy of urbanism in the latter part of the century. Rhetorically, there may have been a heightened emphasis upon releasing entrepreneurial energies by the close of the twentieth century, but the closing chapter of this book shows that in practice the state ceded none of its post-war powers over planning and urban redevelopment. Planning powers came to be wielded more forcefully by the central state rather than by beleaguered and under-funded local authorities, yet – as one of the longest-serving scholars of British planning puts it – the planning system after 1979 was 'in no sense ... dismantled, or even changed in any really significant way'.[33] In the sphere of retail and town centre development, the key change from the 1980s was a new acceptance of large out-of-town retail complexes, which served to turbocharge the financialisation of retail property and exacerbate the damaging competition between urban places for their share of the retail economy (although both financialisation and over-competition were long-established post-war trends). But the rise of out-of-town shopping, along with the location, size and number of regional megamalls, was a process that remained tightly managed by the state, which relinquished none of its authority to determine land use and patterns of development. This book thus presents a picture of urban social and political change across the second half of the twentieth century that is far more evolutionary than epochal and suggests that the dividing lines between post-war and late-century urbanism have often been overdrawn.

Retailing and Regeneration

Another important area of continuity, rather than rupture, across the period studied here was the adoption of retailing as a means of local economic regeneration. The post-war era saw the rise of state-sponsored retail development as a form of urban social policy in Britain, which claimed the capacity to revitalise local economies and improve the economic prospects and material welfare of local populations. These dynamics were central to the agendas of urban regeneration and

---

[33] Cullingworth & Nadin, *Town and Country Planning in the UK*, 28. The first edition of Cullingworth's classic text was issued in 1964.

renaissance which came to the fore within the centrally managed urban policy initiatives of the 1980s and 1990s.[34] At this stage urban scholars and policy analysts were quick to point out the shortcomings of such approaches, in which the material benefits of property-led and consumer-oriented regeneration projects for struggling locales and disadvantaged communities were shown to be highly questionable. Yet such developmental strategies did not originate in the late-twentieth century; they had a long lineage which stretched back through the renewal of struggling industrial towns in the 1960s and 1970s and into the reconstruction era. Even in the moment of post-war reconstruction, it was remarkable how many local authorities viewed their new planning powers as an opportunity to promote retail expansion in the service of local economic regeneration. Reinventing towns and cities as prosperous shopping destinations was central to reconstruction planning in many locales, particularly in traditional industrial regions, and I relate these local efforts to the pre-war experience of municipal enterprise which continued to inspire many urban authorities. Such retail-driven developmental strategies only grew in intensity and significance as the waning of Britain's traditional industries gathered pace and threatened more and more towns with economic redundancy across the later twentieth century.

The adoption of retail development as a form of social and economic policy was always a problematic endeavour. Retailing is a sector which relies on underlying levels of disposable wealth in a society or region, and consumer expenditures are highly susceptible to fluctuations in the wider economy; retail is 'a barometer rather than an engine of change' as one historian of the sector puts it.[35] Thus, while retail may have boomed in the 1950s and 1960s, its prospects as a driver of long-term economic growth and a sustainable basis for urban economies were always doubtful, and there were plenty of signs of stress and insecurity; when the economy dipped in 1962–1963, for example, retail sales immediately stagnated.[36] The geography and distribution of affluence was also highly variable across the country, so that many of the places that were most in need of economic rejuvenation were also least likely to be able to sustain extravagant new shopping facilities. Once again, Britain's light-touch,

[34] Alan Cochrane, *Understanding Urban Policy* (Oxford: Blackwell, 2007); Andrew Tallon, *Urban Regeneration in the UK* (London: Routledge, 2009); Phil Jones & James Evans, *Urban Regeneration in the UK* (Los Angeles: SAGE, 2013); Patsy Healey, Simin Davoudi, Mo O'Toole, Solmaz Tavsanoglu & David Usher (eds.), *Rebuilding the City: Property-led Urban Regeneration* (London: E&FN Spon, 1992); Susan S. Fainstein, *The City Builders: Property, Politics & Planning in London and New York* (Oxford: Blackwell, 1994).
[35] Winstanley, 'Concentration and Competition in the Retail Sector', 237.
[36] National Economic Development Council, *The Growth of the Economy* (London: HMSO, 1964), 125.

liberal-inflected approach to social and territorial administration was important, as policies for regional development and redistribution were partial and patchy and did little to arrest the yawning gap that was opening up between prosperous and struggling regions of the country.[37] Even at the height of the post-war boom, many towns and cities in Britain were struggling with an inherited economic and employment structure which leaned heavily upon industrial sectors that were either in secular decline nationally, or else were relocating themselves away from the traditional urban centres.[38] I focus on numerous smaller industrial towns, particularly in the English North, which were already staring at the prospect of structural economic collapse in the 1950s; in such places, projects of retail-led redevelopment were grasped at desperately as economic lifelines by councils that had few other options.

Despite the evident shortcomings of promoting retailing as a means of holistic social and economic renewal, such practices only intensified as the structural problems facing many urban economies grew steadily worse and spread to some of the major urban conurbations. The 1980s agendas of urban regeneration are here presented as a culmination and a centralisation of these earlier local experiments, but such efforts continued to be hampered by British urbanism's reliance upon private sector investment and market dynamics, as well as by the underlying structural weaknesses of many regional economies. We seem now to have arrived at a point in which the failings of this urban developmental model can no longer be ignored; all over Britain, the shopping city model is in a state of crisis and collapse as retailing's inability to sustain local economies (and vice versa) is glaringly exposed.[39] It is thus a particularly opportune moment to reconsider the history and trajectories of the shopping-centred, public–private reworking of the twentieth-century British city, and I return to these present-day dilemmas and resonances in the book's conclusion.

---

[37] Peter Scott, 'The Worst of Both Worlds: British Regional Policy, 1951-64', *Business History* 38:4 (1996), 41–64; Stephen Rosevear, 'Balancing Business and the Regions: British Distribution of Industry Policy and the Board of Trade, 1945-51', *Business History* 40:1 (1998), 77–99; Ron Martin. 'The Political Economy of Britain's North-South Divide', *Transactions of the Institute of British Geographers* 13:4 (1988), 389–418; Alan Baker and Mark Billinge (eds.), *Geographies of England: The North-South Divide, Material and Imagined* (Cambridge: Cambridge University Press, 2004).

[38] Edgerton's recent account seeks to rescue the reputation of Britain's post-war industrial economy, but the mammoth new industrial installations he points to as signs of productive vigour were generally in ex-urban locations, and thus did little to assist struggling urban centres in traditional manufacturing regions, see *The Rise and Fall of the British Nation*, esp. Ch. 12, 'National Capitalism'.

[39] Alistair Kefford, 'The Death of the High Street', *History & Policy* (2020), available online.

Scope and Structure

Without making any claim to be exhaustive this work ranges widely across the towns and cities of post-war Britain in order to offer as full a picture as possible of planning and redevelopment in practice. London's position as a major financial centre and the hub of Britain's booming development industry is an important element of this history, but the focus is principally upon the major provincial cities of England, Scotland and Wales, along with many smaller urban centres whose history and experience in the twentieth century is lesser known. Questions of political economy, social structure and commercial organisation that operated at a national level are related directly to the urban built forms that were produced in individual towns and cities up and down the country in the period. These physical developments are read both as artefacts of the politics and culture of the era and also as structuring forces in their own right, which decisively reshaped patterns of social life and economic activity in their locales. Indeed, for both the public managers of the post-war urban environment and the private designers of shopping space, gaining a good working knowledge of how precisely the physical environment might influence behaviour and steer the course of future economic development was a key preoccupation. Attending to the microhistory of individual urban projects and their relationship to a broader national picture of planning and redevelopment requires engagement with a wide range of different source materials. These include central government records, legislation and policy directives; local government deliberations and publications; planning agendas as expressed in published plans, professional journals and other literatures; commercially produced material from retailers, advertisers and property firms; and contemporary press reporting.

The book contains seven chapters which move roughly chronologically across the period from the 1940s to the end of the century whilst also being ordered around key themes and arguments. Chapter 1 revisits the 1940s moment of urban and national reconstruction when wartime bomb damage forced government into a much more proactive role with regard to urban redevelopment and the modern planning system emerged out of a tumult of ideas for the reformation of state and society. The 1940s saw the production of a wave of ambitious civic reconstruction plans, and these were often inspired by collectivist visions of social renewal, but the material presented here shows that reconstruction as it was actually practised focused overwhelmingly upon repairing the most valuable commercial districts of blitzed cities – the central shopping districts. I relate this pattern to the intensely productivist vision of reconstruction planning that emanated from central government at this time, as well as an engrained liberalism and administrative economism on the part of central officials. The new Planning Ministry placed supreme emphasis upon business growth and developmental needs while making strenuous efforts to rein in local planning ambitions and public spending commitments. The upshot of these agendas was a mode of reconstruction which aimed to grow the value and enhance the performance of central shopping districts, and planners worked closely with a range of commercial experts and interests to develop planning principles and policies that would maximise the efficiency of local retail environments. Crucially, reconstruction was carried out in close alliance with the powerful and well-organised multiple retail chains, who were invited into the machinery of planning and policy-making as privileged constituents, and extended their dominance over Britain's urban centres as a result. In the process bombed-out small shopkeepers along with many other non-retail users of central urban space were driven out of redeveloped town centres in the interests of capturing the highest possible rental incomes from remodelled and rationalised central shopping districts.

Chapter 2 considers how these developmental, retail-oriented models of planning played out in individual cities across the 1940s and 1950s. It shows that, in both the blitzed cities and elsewhere, many councils embraced the idea of planning as a tool of proactive economic management and enthusiastically bent their powers to the task of promoting valuable new retail development. These activities coincided with a spectacular shops boom in most cities as large retail chains reaped the benefits of full employment and rising wages to embark on major programmes of shop-building and expansion. Councils and retail chains thus worked in tandem to erect huge new stores all over the country and refit urban centres for the affluent age. Local authorities creatively tested the limits of new planning legislation, compulsorily acquiring land and assembling profitable plots for disposal to retailers and property developers. At times, urban authorities even played the part of commercial developer themselves by putting up shops and collecting business rents. I relate these practices to councils' energetic pre-war activities in the field of municipal enterprise and show that post-war planning powers offered a new outlet for these long-standing traditions of civic entrepreneurship. However, this chapter also shows that the 1950s witnessed a decisive recasting of the political economy of planning, in which the newly elected Conservative administration pared back local public enterprise and stripped out many of the more statist elements of Labour's post-war planning regime. Councils were steered firmly towards a more constrained vision of planning, in which the private sector would be encouraged to undertake as much development work as possible. This shift saw the major developmental endeavours of the post-war state opened up to private enterprise and prompted a remarkable boom in the commercial development sector.

Chapter 3 turns to focus upon the unprecedented era of urban rebuilding which took off in the late 1950s and lasted into the 1970s, in which enthusiasm for 'comprehensive' town centre redevelopment and modernist urban renewal was at its peak. It traces the shift from individual large shop developments carried out in alliance with the multiple retail sector, to the increasingly gargantuan shopping complexes that were installed in partnership with property developers from this period. This was the era when shopping malls were imported from the United States and planted at the centre of British towns and cities, and these developments rested upon an unusual alignment between the modernist planning ideals of urban professionals, the developmental agendas of local authorities and the commercial strategies of a handful of development companies. I stress how important the rhetoric of *modernisation* was in uniting these different interests, but also how loosely and variably notions of 'the modern' were defined and applied. I also highlight the importance of the technocratic enthusiasms of the age, particularly in the early 1960s, when the idea of engineering efficient urban environments came to the fore. Planners, policymakers and property developers adopted a deeply Taylorist, mechanistic idea of urban renewal, in which prosperity, efficiency and growth would be precisely engineered while 'obsolescence' would be excised from the modern city with surgical precision. For urban authorities facing darkening economic prospects, these were seductive ideas. And yet the political economy of British planning dictated that, once again, the modern shopping city would be produced by the public and the private sectors working in close partnership. This dynamic saw the expanded planning ambitions and modernising agendas of the 1960s decisively shaped by the commercial strategies and financial imperatives of the development industry, and lent British urban renewal a distinctly commercial and capitalistic flavour.

Chapter 4 focuses upon the politics and the practice of partnership in the urban renewal era. This public–private dynamic was the central political relationship which drove urban transformation; it was codified and mandated explicitly within planning legislation and central policy diktats, and pursued energetically by many individual local authorities eager to remake the image and economy of their towns. At times partnership could cross the line into illegality and become corruption, and the real extent of this is – by definition – hard to ascertain. Yet corruption was by no means a necessary feature of such relationships; instead, close and reciprocal relations between councils and developers were the highly visible, legally enshrined basis for pursuing large-scale urban redevelopment. I show how this hybrid, mixed economy of planning was situated within the wider political economy of post-war Britain, tracking the political influence and connections of the property and construction sectors as well as the attitudes and policy positions of both the Conservative and Labour Parties. I also trace the operation and impact of partnership-based urban renewal on the ground in various cities, focusing in particular on Manchester, Liverpool and Nottingham. Local authorities had a range of motivations for working with the commercial development sector and their experiences were not uniform. The discussion shows that some cities managed to navigate the new terrain of public–private developmentalism more successfully than others, but I also stress the basic asymmetries involved in these relationships, particularly for those places that were struggling most economically.

Chapter 5 considers the production and character of the curious new landscapes of affluence which were installed in Britain's towns and cities in the post-war decades. It shows how new shopping spaces were consciously engineered by designers as entertaining and alluring spectacles, and served as sites in which a new public culture of affluence and acquisition was propagated. I relate this to the powerful political and cultural critiques of new retail environments which emerged in the post-war era and have proliferated since in literatures on the 'postmodern' consumer city. While acknowledging the force of these critiques, I show that retail design was not necessarily all that slick and seductive from the outset and that the techniques of consumer seduction had to be developed and honed through a long and costly process of trial and error. I also stress that, in the 1960s, many public planners felt themselves to be engaged in the production of a new and energising type of *civic* space in the redeveloped shopping landscape and saw this endeavour in light of contemporary ideas about entitlements to mass leisure. For the more high-minded public planners new retail developments were a means of revitalising public space and public culture through uniting the civic with the commercial realms, and thus reflected the wider mingling of the categories of citizen and consumer, of welfare statehood with affluence. Such ideas were reflected both in the physical design of new shopping complexes and in the discourses of social rejuvenation which surrounded them. In practice, however, this attempt to harness commercial retail development with an invigorated urban public sphere was inherently unstable and could not be sustained over the longer term in the face of hostility and obstruction from the new commercial managers of the urban public realm.

Chapter 6 examines some of the public responses to new urban shopping spaces and interrogates the idea of voracious consumer demand which underpinned major retail developments. After delineating the extent of the post-war retail boom in macroeconomic terms, I show that the projections of 'demand' which were put together in support of redevelopment were often extremely questionable and not borne out by the poor trading experience of many new shopping facilities after opening. Indeed, the politically embarrassing failures of high-profile 'white elephants' prompted both government and the development industry to take much more seriously the complexities and limits of 'demand' in the affluent society. The chapter also uses some of the travails of new urban shopping developments to probe some broader questions about the nature of Britain's post-war affluent society. By the later 1960s, it was already clear that projections of inexorably expanding prosperity were misjudged, and the installation of expensive new shopping facilities at the heart of British urban life began to look somewhat misplaced, particularly in regions that were suffering economically. I highlight the rising currents of anxiety and protest against the commercially driven course of urban transformation which became increasingly pronounced at this time. Citizens, activists and academics began to critique the encroachment of the retail economy over ever more of the city's shared spaces, and took aim at the new urban norms and forms which this produced. The chapter concludes by considering the political and behavioural implications of the widespread installation of enclosed, privately owned shopping spaces across the urban centres of post-war Britain, highlighting the new commercially determined regimes of conduct such spaces entailed, and the extent of mistrust and misbehaviour which this provoked.

Chapter 7 examines late twentieth-century trends in city centre management, showing how the models of organising commercial selling space that had been developed within individual shopping complexes came increasingly to be applied to the city centre in its entirety. It also considers the impact of a significant national change in the management of mass consumerism in the 1980s as large and out-of-town shopping centres were allowed to emerge for the first time in Britain. The Conservative administrations that oversaw this shift in policy were keen to talk in terms of a liberalisation of the planning regime, but in practice major development schemes remained closely managed by the state. The rise of out-of-town centres intensified the competitive pressures that were already present within the British urban system, forcing towns and cities to push ever harder for new forms of retail development in their own locales. Smaller urban centres were consistently disadvantaged by these dynamics, and by the 1990s a narrative of 'dying' towns and abandoned high streets had already taken shape. Earlier post-war efforts to adapt waning industrial centres for new, consumer-driven models of growth acquired a renewed urgency and were placed at the centre of the new national policy agendas of 'urban regeneration' and 'renaissance'. The chapter concludes by highlighting the inadequacy of such retail-led regeneration strategies for the most structurally disadvantaged locales.

1   Reconstructing Retail in the 1940s

For historians of twentieth-century Britain, the 1940s have long served as a pivotal moment in the development of state and society. The decade saw the traditionally liberal British polity transformed by the demands of total war and then, in the political flux of the war's aftermath, reconstituted as a social democratic welfare state with new and enlarged responsibilities for the economic health of the nation and the social welfare of the individual. As with all clear-cut historical stories, this is of course much too neat a picture and could be questioned and complicated from many directions.[1] Yet it is a crucial starting point with which to approach the history of British cities in the second half of the twentieth century, both because of the very real transformations in urban governance that took place in the 1940s and because scholarly interpretations of these changes have long been shaped by the instantly recognisable narrative of the coming of the welfare state. Within the annals of planning history (which has traditionally been written almost exclusively from the perspective of town planning professionals), the 1940s mark the crucial moment when the arguments were won, as it were, and town planning finally gained full acceptance as a key competence of the modern British state. The wartime bombing of cities provided the final fillip needed for planning's acceptance, and a slew of landmark pieces of legislation – passed both during and immediately after the war – established a comprehensive system of public planning for the first time in Britain. This extension of public planning powers has often been subsumed within the story of the Britain's post-war rebirth as a social democratic welfare state, underpinned, so the argument goes, by a new politics of collectivism and by the progressive sensibilities of the technocrats who manned the new public planning machinery. Within the many professionally oriented histories of planning, the 1940s were the moment of 'collectivist

---

[1] For a recent retelling, which wrestles with this narrative and its complications, see David Edgerton, *The Rise and Fall of the British Nation: A Twentieth-Century History* (London: Allen Lane, 2018).

advance', ushering in a golden age of 'compassionate town planning' in which reformist urbanism formed a key pillar of the benign meliorism of the post-war polity.[2]

More recent, and more critical, histories have cast some doubt on this narrative, emphasising the brevity and inertia of the 'high moment of planning' in the 1940s, along with the relatively rapid abandonment of bold civic planning ideals in favour of market sovereignty in the 1950s. Plenty of scholars have also offered more nuanced, multivalent and critical accounts of the underlying aims of 'planning', stressing planners' impulses to order and control alongside their genuine reformist intent.[3] This chapter revisits the 1940s experience of reconstruction planning in order to probe these questions of the ideological character and political intent of mid-century planning. It concentrates less upon the reformist ideals of the more radical characters within the wider town planning movement and more upon the way new planning powers were adopted and operationalised by the existing administrative apparatus of the state. I foreground the aims and ideas of the central government officials and experts who were charged with designing the new planning system and who oversaw the reconstruction of bomb-damaged cities. Following the priorities staked out by these figures themselves, I place the rebuilding of cities' central shopping districts at the heart of reconstruction planning and highlight the pragmatic, economistic and developmental imperatives that lay behind this.

Reconstruction planning in Whitehall was focused upon setting local economies (and local authority finances) back on their feet again through the carefully managed rebuilding of cities' most valuable commercial districts: their central shopping areas. This approach to reconstruction required a sophisticated engagement with the unique dynamics of the urban retail trade. New sources of commercial and professional

---

[2] Gordon E. Cherry, *Town Planning in Britain since 1900: The Rise and Fall of the Planning Ideal* (Oxford: Blackwell, 1996); Gordon Stephenson, *Compassionate Town Planning* (Liverpool: Liverpool University Press, 1994).

[3] Frank Mort, 'Fantasies of Metropolitan Life: Planning London in the 1940s', *Journal of British Studies* 43:1 (2004), 120–151, 150. See also John Stevenson, 'Planners' Moon? The Second World War and the Planning Movement', in Harold L. Smith (ed.), *War and Social Change: British Society in the Second World War* (Manchester: Manchester University Press, 1986), 58–77; Peter Mandler, 'New Towns for Old: The Fate of the Town Centre', in Becky Conekin, Frank Mort & Chris Waters (eds.), *Moments of Modernity: Reconstructing Britain 1945–1964* (London: Rivers Oram, 1999), 208–227; Nick Tiratsoo, 'The Reconstruction of Blitzed British Cities, 1945–55: Myths and Reality', *Contemporary British History* 14:1 (2000), 27–44; James Greenhalgh, *Reconstructing Modernity: Space, Power and Governance in Mid-Twentieth Century British Cities* (Manchester: Manchester University Press, 2018); Catherine Flinn, *Rebuilding Britain's Blitzed Cities: Hopeful Dreams, Stark Realities* (London: Bloomsbury, 2018).

expertise – from retailers, commercial architects, property developers, economic geographers and surveyors – were drafted in to assist with this project, and the large-scale organised sections of the retail trade emerged as essential partners for government planners fixated upon urban land values, efficient wealth creation and future growth prospects. I also show that the ambitions of reconstruction planners did not stop at merely reinstating shopping districts, but that the opportunity was seized to reorganise and rationalise urban retailing. Central shopping districts were to be redeveloped along new, more 'efficient' lines in order to ensure the best return on the state's investment in urban rebuilding and to maximise their value to local economies and to a local tax base which rested on central area property values. As a result, the moment of post-war reconstruction was also the beginning of the end for the small shop-keepers in Britain's town and city centres, whose low-value, 'inefficient' business was purposely priced out of central districts by public planners working in concert with large retail concerns. When viewed from the centre, reconstruction planning was a quintessentially growth-oriented endeavour, pursued through new alliances between the state and orga-nised business, and it saw the government begin to concern itself with the micromanagement of the highly lucrative spaces of urban shopping.

The Kernel of Good Planning

In 1937, a book titled *Problems of Town and Country Planning* appeared, authored by an illustrious and influential civil servant Sir Gwilym Gibbon. Gibbon had retired the previous year, but he had enjoyed a stellar civil service career for over thirty years. His biggest impact was in the field of local government and planning, where he spent over a decade as the chief civil servant dealing with planning matters at the Ministry of Health (then the main planning ministry). Here he was instrumental in advancing the case for broader and more systematic planning controls within govern-ment, as well as hammering out some of the finer administrative details. Gibbon had a reputation as a highly effective administrator (he organised conscription during the First World War), a rigorous thinker (he held a Doctorate in Economic Science) and an austere and intimidating char-acter (he lived alone in a hotel in Richmond).[4] Although he was sympa-thetic to the wider planning movement, Gibbon was first and foremost a civil servant – a pragmatic and methodical administrator rather than a planning ideologue. On the opening page of his 1937 book Gibbon

---

[4] Jonathan Bradbury, 'Gibbon, Sir (Ioan) Gwilym (1874–1948), civil servant', *Oxford Dictionary of National Biography*.

derided the simplistic way in which 'the general idea of planning has now become a popular panacea for modern ills . . . advocated without sense of the complication of human affairs or the limits of human foresight'.[5] He was at his most emphatic when setting out what he felt should be the ultimate aims of planning, where support for business, growth and prosperity should always take precedence. This, for Gibbon, was 'the first objective of good planning'. In a chapter titled 'Business the Kernel of Planning', he argued that:

In this country many persons, perhaps most, regard planning as primarily a matter of housing and of open spaces and other amenities. This is woefully wrong. Planning is a matter of life before a matter of life's amenities. A community must live before it can live well. In order to live well it should do all that is possible through planning to help the prosperity of its means of livelihood . . . . Business is the heart (or perhaps stomach would be more correct) of good planning, and to neglect it is as though a man took great thought for raiment and residence and none at all for his means of livelihood.[6]

'Good planning', Gibbon continued, required the 'active cooperation of men of business', who would find in it a route to more efficient and profitable enterprise. He looked approvingly to the United States, 'where business interests were put right in the front and business men themselves in several instances provided funds for the preparation of preliminary plans'. Gibbon's impeccably liberal instincts led him to suggest that 'the best plan' would be one devised and managed by 'a group of business men with a stake in the district'. Nonetheless, he also felt that, at the present juncture, public authorities could usefully be empowered 'to enter into partnership with private enterprise', and may need to initiate projects, put up starting capital and deploy new legal powers – particularly for the compulsory acquisition of land – in support of business growth and development.

Gibbon discussed the publicly sponsored development of industrial estates in Britain and elsewhere in the interwar era (Germany, somewhat surprisingly, was a popular exemplar for British planners in the 1930s, where 'a great deal was done by combined effort of public and private enterprise' as Gibbon put it).[7] He also suggested that the industrial estate

---

[5] Sir Gwilym Gibbon, *Problems of Town and Country Planning* (London: George Allen & Unwin, 1937), 9.

[6] Sir Gwilym Gibbon, 'Business the Kernel of Planning', in *Problems of Town and Country Planning*, 38–53.

[7] Sam Wetherell gives an account of British interwar industrial estate planning in *Foundations: How the Built Environment Made Twentieth-Century Britain* (Princeton: Princeton University Press, 2020), ch. 1. See also Peter Scott, 'Industrial Estates and British Industrial Development 1897–1939', *Business History* 43:2 (2001), 73–98.

model – 'the principle of concentrating businesses in a specially planned estate' – could usefully be turned towards other economic sectors in the city, in particular shops. Gibbon's exploratory reflections on what this might mean anticipated what was to unfold in the reconstruction era and beyond. He noted that the spatial planning of retailing was very much in its infancy with much still to work out, but he was conscious of the growing economic importance of shopping and the new demands which this would place upon the urban environment. He suggested the development of new 'specially planned' shopping areas, dedicated urban shopping environments to be organised around the logistical needs of modern retailers and the efficient seduction of shoppers. 'A well-planned shopping estate', Gibbon maintained, 'where goods could be displayed to far more effect and prospective buyers could inspect temptation with far more comfort and fall the readier victims, should in the long run prove more advantageous to the enterprising retailer'. Indeed, these were the principles that many organised retailers were already applying to their businesses, 'in their long avenues of counters running through their many departments'. Such principles could profitably be applied at scale to the wider reorganisation of shopping in the city. Urban developmental projects like this, Gibbon concluded, were 'just the kind of venture in which public and private parties might join in common endeavour'.

Gibbon's practical suggestions for holistically planned shopping districts, developed via coalitions of public authority and organised retailing, prefigured precisely the character of reconstruction planning as it was conceived and directed by central government officials in the 1940s. Indeed, his ideas serve as a useful guide to the mindset of many of the administrators and experts who manned the central bureaucracy of the British state in the mid-twentieth century. In his fervent support for private enterprise and the business of wealth creation, his mistrust of 'excessive' or overzealous public intervention and his world-weary administrative realism, he represented a set of attitudes towards statehood and political economy which was characteristic of many in the civil service and which shaped the embrace of planning in the 1940s and the course of reconstruction in particular. This was a broadly liberal mindset, in as much as it remained instinctively uneasy about enlarging the remit and expenditures of the state and reluctant to interfere overmuch with the operations of business and commerce. Yet it was a modified, mid-twentieth-century mode of liberal thinking, which accepted that the demands of the age called unavoidably for greater public action and intervention; for social guarantees, for economic development; and for national efficiency, defence and security. In the arena of planning, the circle was squared in the minds of Gibbon and others like him by adopting a vision of planning's purpose which was intensely developmental – growth promoting, efficiency maximising and business oriented. New planning powers could be accepted, even welcomed, as long as they remained judiciously targeted at the goal of efficient economic development and were wielded in concert with the organised business interests that were the guarantors of national prosperity.

In the reformist moment of the 1940s, there were many who would have gone further than this in reconstructing state and society. Many advocates for public planning espoused different visions and ideals, which sought a more decisive break with the past and would happily have taken bolder steps towards the collective public control of economic and social development. And yet figures like Gibbon were far from alone; his was not a lone pro-business voice in a collectivist chorus. Leaving aside his personal stature and influence within British government circles, his ideas resonated strongly with those of other actors involved in reconstruction planning. Not least of these was the important pressure group Political and Economic Planning (PEP), which was established in 1931 as a 'capitalist planning' group financed by businessmen and philanthropists. PEP's founding members were civil servants, financiers, industrialists and intellectuals, and the organisation sought to develop 'a formula of planning that would reconcile the techniques of planning with a private enterprise economy'.[8] Another influential participant in the reconstruction debates of the 1940s was the Association for Planning and Regional Reconstruction, a body which emerged out of the earlier School of Planning and Research for National Development. These two organisations were steered by some of the leading figures in British planning, and they were responsible for much of the training and education of town planners in Britain from the 1930s to the 1950s. Like PEP, these groups were guided firmly by national developmental agendas. The School of Planning and Research for National Development defined its concerns as encompassing 'housing, town planning . . . roads, transport, food production, health, and the economic welfare of the country'. The School was proud to be overseen by 'well-known men in the spheres of administration and industry'.[9] Its successor, the Association for Planning and Regional Reconstruction, intervened in the reconstruction debates in 1945 by publishing an 'atlas' of maps, statistics and geographic data to accompany

---

[8] Daniel Ritschel, *The Politics of Planning: The Debate on Economic Planning in Britain in the 1930s* (Oxford: Oxford University Press, 1997), 145.

[9] Raymond Unwin et al., 'A School for Planning', letter to the editor, *The Times*, 8 December 1937, 12; 'A School for Planning', *The Observer*, 17 February 1935, 19. Also Gordon E. Cherry, *The Evolution of British Town Planning* (Leighton Buzzard: Leonard Hill, 1974), 224.

the major reconstruction reports produced during the war (the Barlow, Scott and Beveridge Reports). This project was sponsored by dozens of commercial and industrial firms, large and small, spanning heavy industrial sectors; construction, power and infrastructure; international trading firms like Imperial Tobacco and Courtaulds; large retailers such as Marks and Spencer and Montague Burton; light consumer industries and food manufacturers; advertisers; and car makers and electrical engineers.[10]

Business interests and business influence were thus integral to the ways in which planning was conceived and adopted by the administrative apparatus of the state in the 1940s. The wartime advance of planning ideas did not entail a wholesale rejection of the British polity's liberal leanings and strong commercial traditions. On the contrary it often involved elevating the influence of selected business interests, who were invited to the machinery of government to assist in devising new models of growth-oriented governance and planning. Reconstruction planning for cities began in earnest in 1940, with the onset of heavy bombing raids, and in October of that year a new Ministry of Works and Building was created with responsibility for managing the rebuilding of bomb-damaged cities. Much has been made of Lord Reith's appointment as the head of this new Ministry, and his exhortation to local councils to 'plan boldly and comprehensively' is often seen as an indication of the new enthusiasm for expansive state-led programmes of reconstruction and renewal. In fact, Reith was fairly quickly dismissed from this position to be replaced by the much less zealous Conservative MP William S. Morrison in 1942.[11] Morrison was a former chairman of the Conservative Party's 1922 Committee, and Harold Macmillan described Morrison's tenure as the nation's first Minister of Town and Country Planning as based upon 'reasonable compromise between the extreme "Letchworthers" [a reference to the Garden City of Letchworth, and the more zealous proponents of town planning] and the extreme defenders of the rights of property'.[12] This is surely an approach which would have resonated with Macmillan, who, as a young Conservative moderniser before the war, had published a centrist agenda for cautiously extending the role of the state titled *The Middle Way: A Study of the Problem of Economic and Social Progress in*

---

[10] Association of Planning and Regional Reconstruction, *Maps for the National Plan: A Background to the Barlow Report, the Scott Report, the Beveridge Report* (London: Lund Humphries, 1945).

[11] Reith's rapid rise and fall are addressed in Stephen V. Ward, 'Gordon Stephenson and the "Galaxy of Talent": Planning for Post-War Reconstruction in Britain 1942–1947', *Town Planning Review* 83:3 (2012), 279–296.

[12] The comment appears in Macmillan's diary entry for 27 June 1944: Harold Macmillan, *War Diaries: The Mediterranean 1943–1945* (London: Macmillan, 1984), 475.

a Free and Democratic Society.[13] Macmillan's throwaway comment is a further reminder that the more radical planning ideas swirling around in the reconstruction moment always existed in a state of tension with powerful alternative poles of opinion – especially on the right – which could be intensely hostile and reactionary.

Within this wide spectrum of opinion on planning, property and statehood, officials at the new Ministry of Town and Country Planning sought to steer a middle course, and in doing so they leaned heavily towards the brand of business-friendly administrative realism espoused by Gwilym Gibbon. The two key figures who led the Ministry's work on bomb-damaged city centres in the 1940s were the planner George Pepler and, tellingly, the retailer Lawrence Neal. Pepler was a long-established figure in British planning, having been a founder member of the Town Planning Institute in 1913, but he was no radical outsider drafted in under the extreme circumstances of war. He had been a civil servant since 1914 and chief planning inspector since 1919, working directly alongside Gwilym Gibbon at the Ministry of Health before he was brought across to the newly formed planning ministry to lead the work on reconstruction. Lawrence Neal was the managing director of a successful chain of children's clothes and shoe stores, a leading figure in the retail industry nationally, and a long-standing member of PEP.[14] He was deputy secretary to the new planning ministry, with an obvious interest in the rebuilding of central business districts. These men were more interested in the rapid reinstatement of cities as functional economic centres than in grandiose schemes of civic reconstruction. They saw it as their role to set local economies working again through restrained and judicious intervention, to rein in the ambitions and the spending plans of overzealous local authorities and to ensure that business interests occupied a privileged place in reconstruction debates. For those tasked with overseeing urban rebuilding within central government, reconstruction was viewed primarily as an economic problem in which the challenge was to return urban economies to productivity and prosperity as quickly as possible and with the minimum of state expenditure.

'The Special Problems' of bomb-damaged cities were set out by the Ministry's reconstruction chiefs in a 1947 *Handbook on the Redevelopment*

---

[13] Harold Macmillan, *The Middle Way: A Study of the Problem of Economic and Social Progress in a Free and Democratic Society* (London: Macmillan, 1938).

[14] For Pepler's career, see Gordon Cherry, 'George Pepler 1882–1959', in Gordon Cherry (ed.), *Pioneers in British Planning* (London: The Architectural Press, 1981); Frederic J. Osborn & Gordon Cherry, 'Pepler, Sir George Lionel (1882–1959), town planner', *Oxford Dictionary of National Biography*, 131–149. For Neal, see Lalage Percival's obituary in *The Independent*, 11 January 1996; Richard C. Whiting, 'Political and Economic Planning (act. 1931–1978)', *Oxford Dictionary of National Biography*.

of Central Areas, which made clear that the issues to be resolved were primarily those of economic dislocation:

[In blitzed cities] the central area has been destroyed by air attack or the buildings damaged beyond repair, and the commercial and civic life of the towns has been suddenly upset, with no chance of restoration to full pre-war vigour for some years ... the damage has both inflicted heavy financial losses on the local authorities and private firms displaced by air attack to find other accommodation ... firms moved to the suburbs or other towns. Similarly, a proportion of shoppers and other persons who had previously relied on the central area to meet some part of their needs, transferred their custom elsewhere. It is of great consequence to the future of war-damaged central areas that business activity in them should be restored to full vigour as soon as possible.[15]

The administrative imperatives for central reconstruction planners revolved around reinstating vital commercial infrastructure and restoring central area economies which hinged upon the business of shopping. Such objectives required close and careful engagement with retail interests. Pepler and Neal engaged the retail industry on reconstruction questions from an early stage, first meeting with the important trade body, the Multiple Shops Federation (MSF), in 1941. The MSF represented the booming retail chains – Boots the Chemist, Marks and Spencer, Woolworths, Sainsbury's, W.H. Smiths, Montague Burtons and suchlike – that had expanded dramatically in the interwar period and which, by the start of the Second World War, had achieved a commanding position in the retail trade in Britain's towns and cities.[16] The MSF, like its constituent members, was energetic, organised and demanding, and inserted itself very effectively into the policy discussions which surrounded reconstruction. The Federation began to petition the new planning ministry as soon as the first major reconstruction report – that of the Barlow Commission in 1940 – became public, when it was clear that new planning legislation would be forthcoming. The MSF began submitting detailed memoranda on the requirements of its members and the implications of specific policy proposals. The Federation's main concern, however, was with the rebuilding of blitzed cities, where many retail chains had had valuable city centre stores destroyed by bombing and where significant changes in the regulatory environment were obviously

---

[15] Ministry of Town and Country Planning, *Advisory Handbook on the Redevelopment of Central Areas* (London: HMSO, 1947), 6–7. Despite being published in 1947, the handbook was put together during the war and completed in 1945, though publication was delayed.

[16] See Peter Scott, 'Learning to Multiply: The Property Market and the Growth of Multiple Retailing in Britain', *Business History* 36:3 (1994), 1–28. Also James B. Jefferys, *Retail Trading in Britain, 1850–1950* (London: Cambridge University Press, 1954), which first traced the multiples' rise.

imminent. Marks and Spencer, for example, whose estates manager was an important point of contact between the Federation and the Ministry, had stores destroyed in Birmingham, Coventry, Bristol, Harlesden, Plymouth, Southampton, Sheffield, Swansea, Wallasey and Great Yarmouth.[17] The Boots retail chain, whose Chairman Lord Trent was president of the MSF, had lost thirty-three shops by 1945 including 'some of [its] largest branches'.[18]

The ideas and arguments of the MSF gained a sympathetic hearing from the Ministry's planners and officials. In particular, both parties were in firm agreement that 'commercial reconstruction and reinstatement' should take priority, 'so as to restore and maintain the economic life of the town concerned', whereas civic building schemes could wait.[19] The Federation clearly saw central government as an important, business-friendly counterweight to some of the visions of civic reconstruction that were being developed by local authorities in individual blitzed cities. Thus, the Federation advised the Ministry to 'curb the ambitions of Local Authorities' and warned against converting large portions of valuable central area land into spacious new 'Civic Centres'. The Federation also assisted the Ministry to flesh out its ideas about *how* city centres should be rebuilt, offering a vision of the city remodelled around the commercial and infrastructural needs of large retail chains. The Federation made detailed suggestions about the appropriate sizes of new building plots, the organisation and layout of shopping districts and their transport and servicing requirements. The retailers' body also sought a more rigid demarcation and enforcement of central shopping zones, which were to be given over to the business of shopping in their entirety, rather than diluted with other uses or wasted on less profitable forms of enterprise. Such arguments for single-use shopping districts chimed with professional planners' contemporary obsession with strict functional segregation and land-use zoning, which was viewed as a pathway to efficiency and order. In the reconstructed city, new public planning powers were to be deployed to expel industrial and residential uses from the valuable central shopping area, which could then be carefully managed and improved 'so as to secure an attractive and important shopping centre'.[20]

The MSF thus offered the wartime Planning Ministry a powerful, business-led model of reconstruction which rested upon new coalitions

---

[17] See 'Multiple Shops', report of a meeting between Pepler and MSF, 2 October 1941, TNA-HLG-71/761.
[18] 'Boots Pure Drug Co. Ltd.', *The Financial Times*, 27 July 1945, 3.
[19] MSF, 'Memorandum', 9 June 1941, TNA-HLG-71/761.
[20] MSF, 'Memorandum', July 1943, TNA-HLG-71/762.

of interest between the state and organised retailing and which seemed to offer a route towards the rapid restoration of urban economic vitality. The Federation's representatives were invited on numerous occasions to the Ministry for detailed discussions on planning policy and assisted in devising model schemes and layouts to guide reconstruction planners. The Federation's call for large doses of fiscal realism and strong business representation in reconstruction planning corresponded closely with the agendas of George Pepler and Lawrence Neal. As soon as bomb-damaged cities like Coventry, Southampton and Hull began to formulate plans for post-war reconstruction, Pepler and Neal put together an 'advisory panel' on city centre redevelopment which would visit individual cities and steer local authorities in the desired directions. The cost, financing and revenue implications of reconstruction schemes were the central issues on which local authorities were challenged. Coventry, for example, was asked how much its reconstruction plan would cost, what the state of the city's finances was, why it had not consulted with local business interests, what effect the plan would have on central area land values and whether, ultimately, 'the plan will pay for itself'.[21] 'Careful consideration of the financial aspects' was required, Coventry's council was told 'so as to ensure that the maximum benefit shall be derived from the plan in the shortest time possible'.[22] The advisory panel toured various blitzed cities from 1943 onwards offering similar fiscally oriented injunctions. In a further illustration of the productivist bent of Ministry thinking, Liverpool's City Architect was told bluntly in 1943 that his civic reconstruction schemes were 'all very well', but 'the important points are (i) restoration of port facilities and (ii) restoration of the shopping centre'.[23]

Pepler and Neal also quietly manoeuvred behind the scenes to amplify the voice of retail businesses in local reconstruction debates. In the summer of 1943, Neal reached out to his contacts across the retail sector to assemble a new advisory group spanning a cross section of the traditionally highly fragmented retail trade. Representatives of the MSF, the National Federation of Grocers' Associations, the Chamber of Drapers, the Chamber of Trade (representing smaller independent traders), the Retail Distributors Association (Neal's own body, representing department stores) and the Co-operative Congress were formed into the 'Retailers Advisory Committee on Town Planning' (RACTP).[24] The

---

[21] 'Questions to be put to Coventry', 12 July 1943. TNA-HLG-79/132.
[22] Letter from MTCP to Coventry Town Clerk, 17 May 1944. TNA-HLG-79/132.
[23] File note, 19 November 1943. TNA-HLG-79/307.
[24] 'Notes of Meeting', 9 August 1943. TNA-HLG-71/762. The Cooperative movement had its own distinctive history and position within the retail economy, see Peter Gurney, '"The Curse of the Co-ops": Co-operation, the Mass Press and the Market in Interwar

Ministry's principal ambition for this body was that it would temper civic ambitions at the local level with a stronger business voice, and thus the RACTP's 'first and most urgent task [was] to secure proper consideration of the retail viewpoint in the formulation of reconstruction plans in heavily bombed towns'.[25] A number of local committees were quickly established, and by early 1944 there were retail committees at work in Bristol, Coventry, Eastbourne, Hastings, Hull, Bath, Exeter, North Shields, Plymouth, Sheffield and Swansea.[26]

George Pepler wrote personally to the town clerks of these towns and cities to commend the retailers' committees to them and encourage consultation and cooperation. Despite his assurances that local retailers' committees were 'entirely independent' and 'in no way connected with the Ministry', it is clear that the bodies were conceived and assembled by Pepler and Neal as vehicles for local business representation.[27] In this they were generally effective, and a number of studies of reconstruction in individual cities have acknowledged the local committees' successful assertion of their interests in the planning process.[28] Indeed, the story of bold civic plans frustrated by local business opposition has become a recurrent theme in assessments of the fate of reconstruction planning at the local level, without necessarily acknowledging the instrumental role of central government in organising and amplifying the voice of business. This political elevation of business interests did not, as is sometimes assumed, reflect a retreat from town planning per se, but rather the pursuit of an alternative, business-centred model of reconstruction – one which was more closely attuned to the dynamics of the market and to economic and fiscal imperatives, and which placed shopping at the centre of cities' economic future in the post-war era.

Rationalising Retail

Pepler and Neal did not envisage their enlistment of retail interests in reconstruction as a rejection of 'planning', although it certainly ran counter to the ideals of municipally led urban renewal that many local authorities were developing, and also to the visions of civic beautification being

---

Britain', *English Historical Review* 130 (2015), 1479–1512; also Gurney, *The Making of Consumer Culture in Modern Britain* (London: Bloomsbury, 2017).

[25] 'Town Planning', file note, March 1944. TNA-HLG-71/762.

[26] Details of local committees in TNA-HLG-71/762.

[27] The wording appears in Pepler's standardised letters to town clerks: TNA-HLG-71/762.

[28] Junichi Hasegawa, *Replanning the Blitzed City Centre* (Buckingham: Open University Press, 1992); Stephen Essex & Mark Brayshay, 'Boldness Diminished? The Post-war Battle to Replan a Bomb-Damaged Provincial City', *Urban History* 35:3 (2008), 437–461.

put forward by celebrated town planners such as Patrick Abercrombie or Edward Lutyens. On the contrary, Ministry officials saw business involvement as a means to refine and improve planning technique and ensure that reconstruction was sensitive above all to practical commercial needs. Thus, the Retailers' Advisory Committee, as well as acting locally, were expected to provide an agreed expert line from the retail trade on planning issues which would inform national policy and practice. There was, it was felt, 'a distinctive retail interest which requires to be advanced' in planning matters, and the RACTP were asked to formulate 'general principles of town planning from the retail standpoint'.[29] This they duly did, and by December 1944 the RACTP had produced a report containing proposals for the complete reorganisation of city centres around retailing, with detailed prescriptions on the design and layout of shopping districts. The *Daily Mail* heralded this 'latest "New Britain" blueprint' as a promise that 'shopping is going to be much easier, speedier and pleasanter in the post-war world' with 'shopping in comfort planned for every town'.[30]

All of this work was undertaken in conversation and collaboration with Pepler and Neal, who, while they were not always complimentary about the results achieved by the Retailers' body, nonetheless demanded information – reliable, expert advice on which effective physical and economic planning could be based. Indeed, their thirst for informed commercial expertise led Ministry officials to meet and consult with a wide range of interested business actors. In 1943, Pepler was taking advice from the important commercial property consultancy – Hillier, Parker, May and Rowden – on the economics of shop development and the commercial performance of different types of shopping schemes.[31] Such discussions enabled Ministry planners to grasp the dramatic and highly uneven economic geography of urban shopping and retail site values, in which, as they were informed by one commercial architect, 'the value of properties in the leading thoroughfares is fabulous'. Values in major shopping streets such as Manchester's Market Street, Birmingham's Corporation Street or Glasgow's Argyle Street exceeded £2,000 *per foot* of shop frontage, while between sites within just fifty yards of each other, the value of shopping space could vary wildly by as much as twenty times.[32] Everything in retail property values depended on the precise location, visibility and attractiveness of sites. These price dynamics had potentially radical fiscal implications, given local authorities' reliance on property

---

[29] 'Town Planning', file note, March 1944. TNA-HLG-71/762.
[30] 'Shopping in Comfort Planned for Every Town', *Daily Mail*, 22 December 1944, 3.
[31] See file note, 'Shops', 15 November 1943. TNA-HLG-71/762.
[32] Comments and figures given in correspondence with N. Martin, developer and architect, 15 July 1949. HLG-TNA-71/615. The figures presumably relate to 1949.

values for their tax revenues, and Ministry officials were quickly impressed by 'the heavy loss which may be incurred by an unwise attempt to interfere with an established shopping centre'.[33]

There were thus multiple impulses at work in the prioritisation of retailing in reconstruction planning. For those figures schooled in Sir Gwilym Gibbon's ideas of planning's purpose, or aligned with the productivist thinking of bodies like PEP or the Association for Planning and Regional Reconstruction (APRR), support for the business of wealth creation was 'the first objective' of planning – an end, indeed the primary end, in itself. An important corollary to this, and one which is most evident in anxieties about land values, was the clear recognition that the business of wealth creation funded the business of administration. Institutional imperatives demanded that officials prioritise the protection of tax revenues when formulating any new policies or regulations. In the case of reconstruction planning, shopping and the associated property values were so critical to local finances that retailers' needs automatically assumed a central place in government thinking. However, the Ministry's careful engagement with the business of retailing was not driven solely by economistic concerns about local growth and tax revenues, important though these issues were. There was also a clear sense of the growing importance of shopping socially, culturally and indeed politically, as planners recognised the increasingly central place which personal consumption was coming to occupy within individuals' social worlds and in the wider public cultures of national life.

The interwar years had witnessed a dramatic expansion of consumer spending in Britain, founded on rising real wages for many, and there had been a corresponding proliferation of new commercial cultures of consumption which in many ways prefigured the post-1945 arrival of 'the affluent society'. The interwar era was a great age of suburban house-building, particularly around London, and thus also for the cultures of domesticity and consumption which such lifestyles entailed. It was also a great age for advertising, branding and consumer research, which became steadily more sophisticated and penetrated ever deeper into society and psyche via the booming mass media of the period, particularly the popular press.[34] All of this amounted to a voluminous expansion of

---

[33] Letter from Pepler to N. Martin, 16 August 1949. HLG-TNA-71/615.

[34] On interwar consumer expansion and lifestyles see Peter Scott, *The Market Makers: Creating Mass Markets for Consumer Durables in Inter-war Britain* (Oxford: Oxford University Press, 2017) & Scott, *The Making of the Modern British Home: The Suburban Semi and Family Life between the Wars* (Oxford: Oxford University Press, 2013); Judy Giles, *The Parlour and the Suburb: Domestic Identities, Class, Femininity and Modernity* (Oxford: Berg, 2004). Kerstin Brückweh (ed.), *The Voice of the Citizen Consumer: A History of Market Research, Consumer Movements, and the Political Public*

the business of shopping, and the associated cultures of consumption, pleasure and self-curation which connected it so powerfully to individuals' psychosocial worlds. Within the biggest cities, the most prestigious shopping streets acquired national reputations: Sauchiehall Street, Glasgow; Market Street, Manchester; Princes Street, Edinburgh; Grey Street, Newcastle and, leading the way, Oxford and Regent Street in London's West End. These were the principal sites in the country for the pursuit of luxury and leisure, in which glamourous art deco department stores vied with the slick new marketing methods of the multiple retailers like Woolworths and Burtons. In the interwar period, as Charlotte Wildman has noted, 'the display and practices of consumer culture became increasingly central to the city's identity'.[35]

Shopping thus assumed a new importance in public life, and therefore also in the calculations of policymakers. The political controversies that were provoked by restricting consumption through rationing in the 1940s and 1950s are well documented, and reconstruction planners clearly understood that a key element of their task was to restore to the consuming public their prestigious shopping facilities.[36] In Coventry in the late 1940s, for example, the Board of Trade worried that, although 'essential' shopping needs had been met by the erection of temporary shop buildings, the destruction of the leading chain and department stores in the city centre meant that the public were still being 'largely deprived of the important entertainment value of shopping'.[37] The cultural and political significance of shopping was further underlined by popular press reporting on bombing raids during the war and reconstruction progress afterward, in which the destruction of landmark shops and shopping streets was frequently lamented while delays in the restoration of shopping districts attracted recurrent criticism.[38] Such complaints made their way into Parliamentary debates, as MPs agitated on behalf of their constituents' shopping needs. In 1953, the newly elected conservative MP for Middlesbrough West, Jocelyn Simon, lamented a 'very great disaster'

Sphere (Oxford: Oxford University Press, 2011) offers useful insight to the early development of marketing. On the popular press see Adrian Bingham, *Gender, Modernity, and the Popular Press in Inter-war Britain* (Oxford: Oxford University Press, 2004).

[35] Charlotte Wildman, *The "Spectacle" of Interwar Manchester and Liverpool: Urban Fantasies, Consumer Cultures and Gendered Identities* (Unpublished PhD Thesis, University of Manchester, 2007), 100.

[36] Ina Zweiniger-Bargielowska, *Austerity in Britain: Rationing, Controls and Consumption, 1939–1955* (Oxford: Oxford University Press, 2000). See page 11 for the figures on interwar consumer expansion.

[37] 'Shopping Facilities – Coventry', report, October 1949. TNA-HLG-79/133.

[38] See for example the *Daily Mail*'s reporting: 'Bond-Street To-Day', 18 September 1940, 6; 'Blitz Town Wants to Smarten Shops', 22 September 1945, 3. Or the provincial press: 'Liverpool's Centre Still Forlorn', *Yorkshire Post and Leeds Mercury*, 28 April 1949.

which had befallen the North East industrial town during the war. Not only had the Middlesbrough Cooperative Society's main store and headquarters been lost during the war, but 'three of the leading departmental stores' had been subsequently destroyed by a teenage arsonist. This had resulted, Simon explained, 'in a loss to Middlesbrough ... of no less than 126,000 square feet of shopping facilities'. The situation was further aggravated by the fact that 'Middlesbrough was not particularly well served for shopping facilities before the war', having been a focus of interwar depression and unemployment. By the early 1950s, the return of population growth and new planned industrial development to the area had led to 'a great increase in demand', and a 'tremendous increase in money incomes which can legitimately be laid out in the shops'. Simon complained that Middlesbrough was not receiving its fair share of reconstruction allocations, particularly when prominent department stores had been rebuilt in nearby Sunderland and Gateshead in the years after the war.[39]

There was therefore a populist and political aspect to reconstruction planners' focus on urban shops and shopping – an imperative to service, new social demands and expectations – which sat alongside more pragmatic administrative concerns with local economic performance and rateable values. The language of consumer demand and desire entered into the calculations of Ministry reconstruction planners who began to seek out new sources of information on the 'preferred tastes of shoppers', recognising the need for 'a sociological point of view' in order to obtain a better understanding of 'consumers' habits'.[40] The Ministry of Planning turned to the Board of Trade (which operated the wartime system of shop licensing) for statistics on shopping habits and the geographies of mass consumerism, enquiring into the catchment areas served by different types of shops and inventing new metrics such as the 'shopping population' of different towns. Just as the Barlow Commission had done, reconstruction planners looked to the increasingly sophisticated field of economic geography to furnish new intellectual and administrative tools with which the urban and regional geographies of consumption could be mapped and managed (Figure 1.1). The leading economic geographer Professor Henry Daysh, for example, who had been drafted into the wartime Board of Trade to assist with the organisation of rationing, became an important source of expertise for Pepler's reconstruction team too. The imperatives of rebuilding central shopping areas also

---

[39] HC Deb. 30 July 1953, vol. 518, cc.1665–1669.
[40] Letter from Pepler to Professor Daysh, 5 April 1944; and McCulloch to Daysh, 4 May 1944. TNA-HLG-71/762.

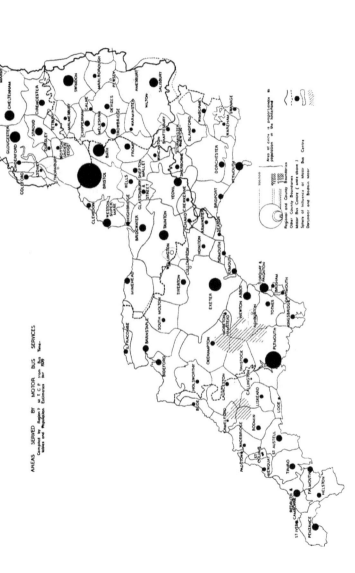

Figure 1.1 Geographical schema to map the importance of various shopping centres in the South West of England, with the dark circles as an indication of the size of the 'hinterlands' served by various towns 'for weekly shopping purposes'. This research was produced for the Planning Ministry and appeared in 1948 in the journal of the Institute of British Geographers. The expanding field of economic geography was a key source of administrative knowledge and planning techniques for the mid-century British state, and government planners maintained close links with leading academics in the discipline. Source: F.H.W. Green, 'Motor-bus Centres in South-West England Considered in Relation to Population and Shopping Facilities', *Transactions and Papers* 14 (1948), 59–68.

stimulated a new administrative interest in shopping, more generally. A recurrent complaint from officials was that they simply did not know enough about the complex socio-economic dynamics of the retail trade to plan with any certainty for future needs. The Board of Trade complained to Pepler's reconstruction unit that 'statistical information about the retail trade is very imperfect', and worried that 'the prospect of bricks and mortar being erected on the scanty foundations of our present knowledge is rather horrifying'.[41]

For its part, the Board of Trade looked to the establishment of the new 'Census of Distribution' as an 'essential preliminary' to the effective planning of consumption.[42] This vast new information-gathering project aimed to survey every single retail business in the country and was established on a decennial basis alongside the conventional census from 1951.[43] Such activities within government were fuelled by a corresponding boom in academic and commercial studies of the retail trade, as shopping began to be talked about as an 'industry' and taken seriously as a vital sector of the national economy. Neal himself – the Ministry's resident retail expert – was a pre-war pioneer in this field but the market for shopping studies experienced a particular glut in the late 1940s as economists began to work through the implications of the new level of national economic management enshrined in the post-war settlement. One late-1940s study by an Oxford economist opened with a warning, 'Distribution is the nation's largest industry [but] it is the one about which we know least'. This study directly referenced the 1944 Employment white paper (which committed the government to full employment) and argued that, given such policy objectives, 'the economics of the distributive trades demand the attention not only of the pure and applied economist but also of every elector'.[44] In this respect the reconstruction of urban shopping districts formed a distinct, localised component of the broader political commitment to

[41] Letter from Board of Trade to Ministry of Town and Country Planning, 12 May 1944. TNA-HLG-71/762.
[42] Letter from Board of Trade to Ministry of Town and Country Planning, 12 May 1944. TNA-HLG-71/762.
[43] For *The Economist*'s reporting on the results of the first, 1951 Census of Distribution, see 'Shops Under a Microscope', 9 October 1954, 143–145. A full account of the genesis and findings of the Census is provided in Dudley A. Clark, 'The Census of Distribution', *Journal of the Royal Statistical Society C (Applied Statistics)* 2:1 (1953), 1–12.
[44] Margaret Hall, *Distributive Trading: An Economic Analysis* (London: William Brendon and Son), vii. The work is undated, but its bibliographic references date it to 1948/49. Neal wrote on these issues in *Retailing and the Public* (George Allen & Unwin, 1933). The glut of late 40s studies include: Hermann Levy, *The Shops of Britain: A Study of Retail Distribution* (London: Kegan Paul, Trench, Trubner, 1947); Henry Smith, *Retail Distribution: A Critical Analysis* (London: Oxford University Press, 1948); James B. Jefferys, *The Distribution of Consumer Goods* (Cambridge: Cambridge University Press, 1950).

managed economic development which emerged in the 1940s with the adoption of Keynesian principles and policy instruments. What was particularly prescient within this aspect of reconstruction planning was the recognition that future economic development might be steered in desirable directions through judicious rearrangements of the physical, geographical and technological parameters in which retail business operated. In an anticipation of later ideas associated with 'the new economic geography', 1940s reconstruction planners understood that the precise manner in which they rebuilt city centres would condition the future modes of business activity and economic growth that developed there.[45] So it was that the Board of Trade wrote again to George Pepler in 1943 noting that:

> One very important immediate question is how far the planned rebuilding of severely bombed areas may limit the number of shop sites, prescribe their location and to some extent the size of business unit and type of business to be carried on.[46]

Armed with this understanding, it became possible to think about using reconstruction planning to not only reinstate urban retail economies but to expand and improve them.

Building on their growing understanding of the urban economic geographies of shopping, reconstruction planners began to formulate proposals for 'improved', more efficient and more valuable shopping districts. They drew upon the ideas and insights which had been provided by the various retail interests they had consulted to develop a set of planning principles which could be applied to grow the value of central shopping districts. These planning approaches were, where necessary, strongly impressed upon recalcitrant local authorities. They were also enforced through the Ministry's role as the ultimate legal authority in planning matters, able to issue standing guidance to all councils and to determine planning decisions on large or controversial development schemes. The approach was codified in the Ministry's *Handbook on the Redevelopment of Central Areas*, which was based upon the principle that 'the future prosperity of the central area will depend in large measure upon its attraction as a shopping centre'.[47] Economic imperatives dictated that the primary and privileged function of the city centre was shopping, and the Handbook advocated a remodelling of urban form, street layouts, traffic planning and circulation in the interests of the retail economy

---

[45] Paul Krugman, 'What's New About the New Economic Geography?', *Oxford Review of Economic Policy* 14:2 (1998), 7–17; and Krugman, 'The New Economic Geography, Now Middle Aged', Paper for Association of American Geographers, 2010, available online.

[46] Letter from A.C. Dice to Pepler, 11 November 1943. TNA-HLG-71/762.

[47] MTCP, *The Redevelopment of Central Areas* (London: HMSO, 1947), 52.

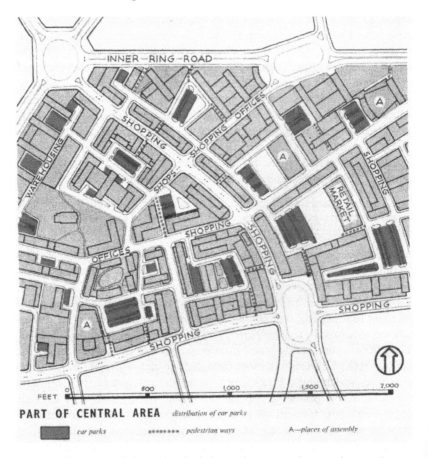

PART OF CENTRAL AREA   *distribution of car parks*

car parks   ●●●●●●●● pedestrian ways   A—places of assembly

Figure 1.2 Schematic depiction of suggested central area layout, showing the dedication of central urban space to shopping and the distribution of small car parks throughout the district. This distribution was designed to deliver lethargic consumers as close to shops as possible. Source: Ministry of Town and Country Planning, *The Redevelopment of Central Areas* (London: HMSO, 1947), 60.

(Figures 1.2 and 1.3). The demands of shopping were firmly prioritised and this was to be achieved through the creation of concentrated, single-purpose shopping districts where citizens would be confronted by nothing but 'continuous shop frontages' lining successive streets. The Handbook instructed that:

A shopping zone should provide the best practicable conditions for shopkeepers and their customers. Permission for other types of development within the

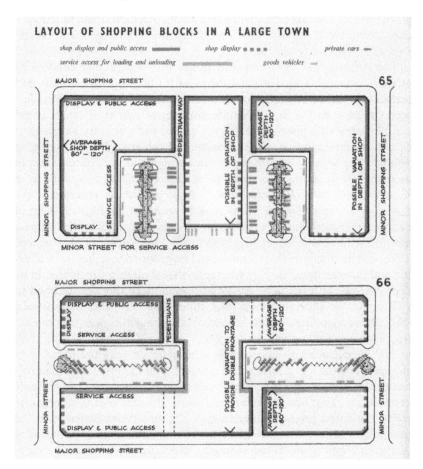

Figure 1.3 Suggested urban arrangements for central shopping districts, designed to accommodate deliveries and customer parking while maximising the alluring display frontages which were crucial for the seduction of shoppers and the promotion of profitability. Source: Ministry of Town and Country Planning, *The Redevelopment of Central Areas* (London: HMSO, 1947), 66.

[shopping] zone should not be granted on a scale or in places which would endanger the shopping character of the zone or its efficiency for its primary purpose.[48]

This was essentially an acceptance of the demands of the MSF and the Retailers' Advisory Committee that the infrastructural needs of their

[48] MTCP, *The Redevelopment of Central Areas* (London: HMSO, 1947), 27.

businesses should take precedence over all other central urban functions – civic, commercial and industrial – to dictate the arrangement and experience of Britain's city centres.

The organisation of streets and traffic was a particular concern to retailers who demanded that all forms of traffic – pedestrian, bus and private car – be afforded maximum ease of access to their stores. Retailers seem to have had remarkably little confidence that their stores could actually attract shoppers on their own merits, and were instead adamant that 'turn-over depends on the numbers of passers-by'. 'The shopping public', they argued, 'is conservative in outlook and undoubtedly lazy in its habits [and] shoppers do not like to have to walk any distance from shop to shop or from a bus stop'.[49] Absorbing these arguments, the guidance drawn up by the Ministry of Planning in the high moment of national reconstruction was designed to deliver unthinking consumers into the arms of waiting retailers with minimum exertion or obstruction. Thus, the instructions that shops should be grouped together, with alluring and uninterrupted display frontages; that shopping streets should be kept narrow, with frequent crossings, lest the lazy shopper declined to visit stores on the other side; that numerous car parks be scattered throughout shopping districts to minimise walking distances; that motorists be able to pull up and wait in front of every store and that 'through traffic' be excluded so that central streets served only the mobility of shoppers and the logistical needs of retailers. Mid-century traffic planning has generally been told as a story of austere policemen and civic planners carefully working out the safest and most efficient means to organise traffic flows and promote circulation.[50] Yet the official advice on traffic planning in city centres in the 1940s was that mobility should be managed in the interests of the retail economy; servicing the business needs of retailers and steering the impulsive movements of shoppers took precedence.

Remaking Blitzed Cities

The Ministry's 1947 handbook provided a set of planning principles and agreed priorities, and offered model street layouts and recommended urban forms to guide local decision making. In most cities this guidance would not be directly translated into built urban forms but served instead

---

[49] RACTP, 'Memoranda Submitted to the Ministry of War Transport', February 1944, 5. TNA-HLG-71/762.

[50] See for example Hall & Tewdwr-Jones, *Urban and Regional Planning*, 39–42. The key figure here was the senior police official H. Alker Tripp, and his 1942 book, *Town Planning and Road Traffic* (London: Edward Arnold).

as the basis for future planning decisions which transformed cities over a longer period. In badly bombed cities, however, extensive rebuilding of whole districts after the war was unavoidable and the blitzed cities became the first sites in which the new ideals for reorganised and rationalised urban shopping centres were put into practice. In Canterbury, which had experienced significant bomb damage during the 1942 'Baedeker' raids, the key task was the restoration of the city's central shopping area around St. George's Street. Following the strictures laid out by central government reconstruction chiefs and their partners in the retail industry, Canterbury's council developed plans for a new and improved central shopping district which would accommodate the largest retailers and the latest retail planning principles. The city's plans for its new shopping district were pursued in collaboration with the most important retail interests in the city, which emerged as the privileged constituents of Canterbury's reconstruction planning. The redevelopment of St. George's Street required public appropriation on a substantial scale and the city council duly applied for compulsory purchase powers over a ten-acre chunk of the central area. The multiple retailer Marks and Spencer, however, was able to secure an exemption from compulsory acquisition for its own three-storey property in the redevelopment area, which remained untouched. The retail chains W.H. Smith and Woolworths also negotiated private arrangements with the council to protect their properties and their interests. The only note of conflict between the council and organised retailing was a clash with the clothing chain Montague Burton's, which was disgruntled enough to hire an expensive planning barrister to contest the compulsory purchase of its site. All was resolved amicably though, with the retailer offering the council an attractive grant of some of its land in return for retaining its key trading site in the redeveloped shopping district.[51]

The redevelopment of Canterbury's central shopping district proceeded on the basis of cooperation between the local planning authority and the largest retailers, who were viewed as the best guarantors of an efficient and economic use of valuable urban real estate. This approach to reconstruction was endorsed wholeheartedly by the centrally appointed planning inspector who oversaw a public inquiry into Canterbury's plans in 1949. The planning inspector was unequivocal, maintaining that 'it is ... evident that this is the most potentially valuable commercial land in Canterbury and should be put to productive use with the least possible delay'. The inspector approved of the council's bid for compulsory purchase powers over the district – so that 'the Corporation ... be enabled to

[51] See the Report of a Public Inquiry, 14 December 1949. TNA-HLG-79/85.

reap the benefit in increased site values' – and yet raised no objection to the exclusion of the most valuable retail properties that had been negotiated with the larger stores. Objections to the city's plans from less favoured constituencies, however, were given short shrift. Many owners and occupiers of pre-existing property in the area contested their forced expulsion from Canterbury's new central district but to no avail. A Quaker meeting house, for example, was banished from the district, as was a local private members' club, where the planning inspector concluded that 'there would be the strongest planning objection to developing the valuable corner ground-floor [site] other than as a shop'. Dispossessed owners were of course compensated for the loss of their property (although in the reconstruction era the compulsory purchase procedure fixed this compensation well below market value) but there was no suggestion that their objections would be allowed to overrule the developmental imperatives of creating 'a 100% shopping area'.[52]

The 1949 inquiry gave Canterbury the official seal of approval from central government, and by the early 1950s the legal powers were in place to allow the council to buy up the necessary plots of land. Numerous new stores were duly erected along St. George's Street, on sites that were provided by the council to retailers and developers on secure long-term leases. The city council continued to bend its new planning powers to the task of retail improvement across the subsequent decade. Canterbury's 1953 Development Plan, for example, instituted a reorganisation of the central area road network 'to improve the road pattern and to provide parking facilities and vehicular access to the rear of all new shops'.[53] Again, such measures closely followed the planning prescriptions developed by the Ministry and its Retailers' Advisory Committee in the 1940s. By the mid-1950s the St. George's Street area had been resurrected as a glamorous shopping district and a showcase for the latest in modern retailing and store design. The district had been redeveloped, as the city's planning chiefs noted in 1958, 'with buildings which are contemporary in character and large in scale'.[54] The most notable of these was a striking modern store built for the grocery chain David Greig on a key site on St. George's Street and completed in 1954 (Figure 1.4). This spectacular showpiece of contemporary retail design housed a David Greig butchers and general store. Its fully glazed ground floor frontage invited passers-by

---

[52] See the Report of a Public Inquiry, 14 December 1949. TNA-HLG-79/85.
[53] John L. Berbiers, 'Canterbury: Reconstruction in the Central Area', *Journal of the Town Planning Institute* 47:2 (1961), 36–39. Berbiers was Canterbury's City Architect and Chief Planner.
[54] J. L. Berbiers, C. W. Gummer, G. Baker & J. L. Grant, 'New Shopping Centre for Longmarket, Canterbury', *Official Architecture and Planning* 21:6 (1958), 266–267.

Figure 1.4 Canterbury's post-war architectural showpiece, the David Greig store on St. George's Street, designed by Robert Paine & Partners and completed in 1954. The almost complete floor-to-ceiling glazing on the ground floor, canopied arcade, and brilliant internal lighting all work to deconstruct the barrier between inside and outside, dragging the gaze – and the customer – into the store. The installation of spectacular new stores like this within blitz reconstruction areas was a clear sign that commercial growth and expansion, rather than mere restoration, was a key aim. Source: RIBAPix.

to gaze in upon the dazzlingly lit retail space within, under the shelter of a distinctive zigzag roof canopy supported by massive pilotis clad with mosaic tiles. This was a touch too much commercial modernity for some in the historic city of Canterbury and the design attracted some critical reaction as a result. The David Greig store was feted by the design and planning professions however. The building received a RIBA award in 1957 and in 1958 the influential architect-planner L. Hugh Wilson also applauded the store. Wilson had been the Chief Architect and Planner at Canterbury in the 1940s, before he took up the same role for Cumbernauld New Town. In a careful consideration of the architectural mechanics of consumer seduction, Wilson explained that 'the well-designed shop front should be an integral part of the conception of the shop'; it was imperative that the shop window be a point of connection, not separation, between 'showroom and shopper'. Canterbury's David Greig store, according to Wilson, represented a harmonious marriage of 'good architecture and good business'.[55]

Each blitzed city's reconstruction scheme had to be signed off by central government, which also controlled the allocation of funds and materials for urban rebuilding. This left the Ministry firmly in control of reconstruction planning and led to repeated conflicts as central government economism clashed with the more radical visions of urban renewal that were being developed locally in many blitzed cities. In places like Coventry and Plymouth, local officials embraced the public rhetoric of bold civic renewal and produced elaborate plans for municipally led urban rebuilding that were decidedly unsatisfactory from the Ministry's point of view. The *Plan for Plymouth* bore the strong imprint of the council's hired consultant, the celebrated town planner Patrick Abercrombie, who was at the same time producing his landmark plans for London.[56] As a key naval port within easy reach of the continental mainland, Plymouth was bombed heavily over a protracted period during the war and its ambitious plan for post-war reconstruction had already been completed and published by 1943. Plymouth's plan was a classic example of the work and politics of the British town planning movement – Macmillan's 'extreme "Letchworthers"' – in which Abercrombie was a leading light. In its obsession with beauty, order and functionality, and its confused blend of technoscientific modernity with prelapsarian fantasies of 'organic' community, this was British town planning at its most creative and cranky.[57]

Abercrombie's vision for Plymouth's centre was a case study in the type of beaux-arts civic monumentality which British town planners had developed at home and across the Empire in the interwar period.[58] Classical allusions, monumental axes, grand vistas and triumphal approaches were the order of the day, as was the creation of an expanded and beautified 'Civic Centre'. The plan rearranged the city into a series of

---

[55] L. Hugh Wilson, 'Civic Design and the Shopping Centre', *Official Architecture and Planning* 21:6 (1958), 271–274. See also Trevor Dannatt, *Modern Architecture in Britain: Selected Examples of Recent Building* (London: Batsford, 1959), 78–80.

[56] Frank Mort, 'Fantasies of Metropolitan Life: Planning London in the 1940s', *Journal of British Studies* 43:1 (2004), 120–151. For more background on Plymouth's reconstruction, see Essex & Brayshay, 'Boldness Diminished'.

[57] The confused cultural and political objectives of British town planning, which overlapped with reactionary ruralist fantasies and quirky haute bourgeois enthusiasms for movements like theosophy and vegetarianism, are dissected in David Matless, *Landscape and Englishness* (London: Reaktion Books, 1998).

[58] For a contemporary manual designed to guide such endeavours across colony and metropole, see Henry Vaughan Lanchester, *The Art of Town Planning* (London: Chapman and Hall, 1932) [first ed. 1925].

functionally distinct zones and, although the new shopping area was naturally to be large and important, the overall balance of land use in the city was to be shifted decisively away from shopping. Whereas before the war shopping had been the dominant land use and occupied 27% of Plymouth's centre, Abercrombie's plan envisaged shops occupying just 12% of the redeveloped city centre. The expanded Civic Centre and a new 'Cultural Precinct' would occupy 17.5% and 42% of central area land would be taken up with the new monumental road axes and grandiose open spaces. The shift in priorities was clear. In addition, the shopping precinct itself had to conform to the overall monumentality of the plan. Thus, an extravagant shopping street 200 feet wide was planned, with 20-foot pavements, imposing colonnaded shop buildings, and enormous, park-like central reservations planted with trees and fountains (Figure 1.5).[59]

Plymouth's plans for a monumental shopping precinct caused predictable anxieties at the Ministry of Planning where, although it was accepted

Figure 1.5 Illustration of Abercrombie's proposed monumental shopping district, with emphasis on classical grandeur, wide open space and civic vistas. Source: J. Paton Watson & Patrick Abercrombie, *A Plan for Plymouth* (Plymouth: Underhill Ltd, 1943).

[59] Detailed in J. Paton Watson & Patrick Abercrombie, *A Plan for Plymouth* (Plymouth: Underhill, 1943), chapter 8: 'The New City Centre'.

that 'the ideal city of the future must be a gracious place', officials felt that 'some of the more workaday considerations do not appear to have been allowed full weight'. The width and scale of the shopping streets was a particular concern, with the Ministry citing its evidence from retailers that 'excessively wide roads' were a hindrance to trade and a waste of the most valuable urban land. The bottom line was how well any planned shopping district would perform as an economic space. 'The central boulevard', the Ministry suggested, 'is a most attractive amenity, and one that would delight visitors; but whether it would be an asset to a shopping centre may be doubted'. For the Ministry, imposing civic vistas were far less important than an appreciation of the psychogeography of shopping – the behavioural responses of shoppers to different types of retail environment, and the corresponding economic implications, were paramount. Thus, it was argued that 'wide streets in a shopping area dispel that intimacy between shops and shoppers and that atmosphere of throng and rivalry which stimulate trade'.[60] Central government's hostility to Plymouth's plan reflected not a lack of enthusiasm for planning per se, but a rejection of the specific models of planning associated with figures like Abercrombie which did not take sufficient account of economic logics and fiscal concerns.

The dilution of local radicalism by centrally mandated economism rapidly emerged as a defining characteristic of reconstruction planning. As early as 1947, such tendencies were being publicly lamented in the pages of *The Observer*, where a special report bemoaned the 'whittling down' of the blitzed cities' 'handsome blueprints', 'in the name of economy, or temporary expediency, or – worst of all – "realistic planning"'. 'The brakes are being put on this local enterprise', the correspondent continued, as 'under the heading of economy and sound finance Ministerial representatives have been getting their way on purely technical matters using a piecemeal and short-sighted approach'.[61] The frustrations in Plymouth were noted, where the Ministry had delayed the approval of key projects for over a year and 'Treasury consent has been withheld for decorative open spaces ... because they are "uneconomic"'. And Plymouth was not alone; in Hull and Norwich and Bristol the story was the same as central government 'carefully cut down on local enterprise'. In Bristol, the Ministry rejected the city's ambitious attempt to obtain compulsory purchase powers over a massive 776 acres of the city (one acre is about the size of a football field; 776 acres represents 1.2 square miles, so easily covering the whole of Bristol's central area and then some). This sort of move was a common gambit on the part of large

[60] 'City of Plymouth', report, 20 March 1945. TNA-HLG-79/532.
[61] 'Out of the Ruins – When?', *The Observer*, 15 June 1947, 4.

urban authorities – Liverpool attempted the same thing – but the whole-sale municipalisation of urban land would never be accepted by central government. The Planning Ministry was also wavering over granting approval for Bristol's plans for an elaborately reconstructed shopping district, 'because no return can be expected on the land for at least 20 years'.[62]

In Coventry, too, local ambition clashed with central government's economism and instinctive mistrust of civic enterprise. The situation here was particularly sensitive however because the severe bombing of Coventry had assumed a powerful place in the collective memory of the blitz. In the immediate post-war years Ministry officials were extremely anxious not to give the impression of reneging on the nation's promises to the city, or watering down the radicalism of local plans, although this was precisely their intention.[63] Locally, Coventry's reconstruction was con-ceived as a pioneering experiment – a 'test-case' of British planning which reflected a growing engagement with modernist architecture and design principles. Within this radical local vision for reconstruction, shopping remained the key to central area form and function but there was much more enthusiasm for innovation and experimentation in urban design. As one of the city's architects, Percy Johnson-Marshall, remembered in 1958, 'the key feature in our plan was the shopping centre' and the scheme was notable in particular for its introduction of a 'completely new building form' – the pedestrianised shopping precinct. Johnson-Marshall suggested the shopping precincts were inspired by his time working in a multiple store, where shoppers 'could buy in comfort and safety [and] get all they wanted under one roof' (although there were a number of important international influences too). Coventry's precincts were an extension of this idea of the curated shopping environment into the open-air spaces of the city centre, as Gwilym Gibbon had envisaged in the 1930s, and designed to recreate shopping as 'a pleasure not a drudge'.[64]

Such enthusiasms for the new realms of consumer pleasure were echoed by no less than Princess Elizabeth, who at Coventry in 1948 began what was to become a long line of employment in cutting ribbons at new shopping centres. The young princess, in faltering but stirring words, hoped that 'the fruits of peace' on offer in Coventry's pedestrian shopping precincts would 'be far richer and far more plentiful than we

[62] 'Out of the Ruins – When?', *The Observer*, 15 June 1947, 4.
[63] Such concerns are stated explicitly in an internal note dated 17 May 1944, in TNA-HLG-79/132.
[64] Percy Johnson-Marshall, 'Coventry: Test-Case of Planning', *The Listener*, 17 April 1958, 654.

have found the fruits of victory to be'. The Princess looked forward to 'a new Broadgate [the main shopping thoroughfare] as fine as modern tastes and craftsmanship can build it'.[65] In the visions of both the young architect and the young princess, the new and exciting realm of modern shopping formed an important plank of the promises of peace and prosperity in the post-war age. This was stirring stuff, but George Pepler's officials at the Ministry of Planning were rather more concerned with practicalities and had taken on board the vehement opposition to pedestrianised precincts from their local retailers' advisory committee. Coventry's council were repeatedly warned by Pepler's team about the 'dangers attached to an experiment in Coventry ... should the closed shopping precinct prove unsuccessful'. They were reminded of the threat to 'the prosperity of shopping interests in Coventry' in a 'highly competitive market'.[66] For the Ministry's reconstruction planners, the risk was that the precincts failed to draw the crowds and trade went elsewhere, leaving the state with an uneconomic proposition on its hands. In the end, Coventry's planners won the argument on precinct planning, and the city's pioneering pedestrianised shopping centre emerged as a much-feted design success. It was also a clear commercial success, as retailers' scepticism about the trading performance of pedestrianised districts proved unfounded. By 1955 a more ambitious proposal to extend 'the "Precinctual" principle ... to the whole commercial area' won easy acceptance from the city's retailers. This was hailed in *The Manchester Guardian* as a 'triumph for radical replanning', although as Chapter 2 shows, by the mid-1950s municipal radicalism in Coventry had been neutered in other less visible but perhaps more significant ways.

Excising Inefficiency

A final key element in the reorganisation of urban retailing in the 1940s was the expulsion of the small trader from the reconstructed centres of blitzed cities. This process went hand-in-hand with the government's clear favouring of the large-scale organised sections of the retail trade. The public prioritisation of large retail chains in part reflected the simple fact that their representatives were well organised, well-funded and able to quickly adapt to the new political and administrative conditions of the 1940s. The Ministry found large retailers able to provide experts in estates management and retail property markets, to agree policy positions and offer detailed information on their business models in ways which

---

[65] The moment is captured in the British Pathé film, 'Princess Elizabeth at Coventry', 1948.
[66] Letter from MTCP to Coventry Town Clerk, 17 May 1944. TNA-HLG-79/132.

independent shopkeepers had no hope of keeping up with. The ability of large retailers to employ expensive legal advocates to fight for their interests in local planning disputes also ensured that they emerged from such contests on favourable terms. But there was a more fundamental set of beliefs and priorities which guaranteed that large retail chains would be the privileged constituents of reconstruction planning. Government planners and civil servants operated with an underlying Taylorist faith in the efficiency and superiority of large-scale corporately organised business.[67] Their most basic administrative impulses were intensely productivist, in line with Gwilym Gibbon's economistic strictures, and planners looked upon the organised sections of the retail industry, with their managerial and marketing innovations, as the surest hope for restoring growth, prosperity and profitability to Britain's damaged cities. Allied to this faith in the inherent superiority of large-scale business was the more immediate concern that reconstruction must always aim at raising urban land values, through the 'improvement' of central districts and the type of businesses which operated there. The prevailing administrative imperatives dictated that, if the state was forced to acquire and rebuild significant tracts of urban land, these should be put to the most profitable use, and disposed of for the highest possible price. It was the multiple stores and retail chains, with their more profitable business models, which could afford to pay more for shop sites, and which would yield more in the way of revenues, rates and wealth creation.

Plymouth again served as a site in which these administrative imperatives came into conflict with local political priorities. In 1946 the city council clashed with the Ministry over the level of ground rents to be charged in their redeveloped shopping district. These were the prices at which publicly acquired land in the city centre would be leased to retailers and developers to put up new shop buildings. Plymouth's council was attempting to keep these land prices low by fixing them at the level of 1939 values – a policy which ignored the significant wartime inflation in land values and discounted any increase in the value of land as a result of replanning. Although this was not in the council's financial interests, Plymouth was a small and isolated city where there were not particularly strong developmental pressures. As a relatively small urban political community, the council felt keenly the pressure from existing local businesses to be reinstated in their shops without paying exorbitant new ground rents. Some indication of this is given in the government regional

---

[67] On Taylorism see Charles S. Maier, 'Between Taylorism and Technocracy: European Ideologies and the Vision of Industrial Productivity in the 1920s', in Maier, *In Search of Stability: Explorations in Historical Political Economy* (Cambridge: Cambridge University Press, 1987), 22–69.

office's suggestion that 'what Plymouth wants is something to tell the tradespeople, many of whom are no doubt on its Council'.[68] Plymouth's insufficiently mercenary approach to its reconstruction brought strong reprimands from the Ministry, which reminded the council that this was 'after all, a commercial transaction between a Lessor and Lessee'. The Ministry's officers acknowledged that 'whatever ground rents are fixed will be in the nature of an experiment', because there was simply no precedent for rebuilding and revaluing an entire shopping district. Yet they were also clear that Plymouth were unjustifiably ignoring market trends and negating the underlying purpose of reconstruction, in which 'the ideal is of course to achieve good planning and increased values'.[69]

The Ministry's instructions to Plymouth give the most explicit indication of the way in which reconstruction was conceived as a judicious, commercially attuned intervention in local economies – a public enterprise which, far from challenging the logics of the market, would see the state successfully harnessing the new economic forces associated with mass consumerism and retail property development. Plymouth was reminded that rental values on shop property in 1946 were 40 per cent higher than in 1939, and that such trends were likely to continue given the anticipated 'rising standard of living, higher wages [and] more equitable distribution of wealth'. These projections of post-war consumer expansion meant that the volume and value of retail trade would expand, land values would rise and businesses could expect to pay ever-higher rents. Aside from these secular trends towards retail expansion, the underlying premise of Ministry thinking was that reconstruction would produce more efficient, more successful and thus more expensive urban shopping centres; it was perfectly natural that this should be reflected and captured in higher rents. Government officials were almost incredulous that Plymouth's council did not accept these logics, writing that:

Surely it cannot be suggested that the redevelopment of the centre of a provincial City on the most modern and efficient lines will have no effect on the overall trade that can be expected after redevelopment ... Obviously the replanned shopping centre will draw more people in from outlying places than an inconvenient and ill-planned city ... [new shoppers] will be attracted into the replanned Plymouth where everything has been done to improve safety, car-parking facilities, simplicity of lay-out, and nature of surroundings. If this were not so it would not commend the scheme very highly.[70]

[68] 'Plymouth Shopping Centre', report from Regional Estate Officer, 6 January 1947. TNA-HLG-79/578.
[69] Comments contained in papers in TNA-HLG-79/578.
[70] 'Plymouth: Shops – Ground Rents', report, 16 December 1946. TNA-HLG-79/578.

Such ideas were a clear illustration that reconstruction was designed to grow the value of city centres as fiscal and economic assets. Indeed, councils all over the country were explicitly directed to expand the size of their lucrative central shopping districts. By breaking up clusters of the most prestigious landmark stores and redistributing them as 'anchors' of higher land values across a wider area, the geographical extent and fiscal yield from each city's key economic asset could, it was hoped, be profitably expanded. Public planners were also surprisingly conscious that shifts in the nature of the shopping experience would translate into economic gains. They envisaged a greater emphasis on spectacle, entertainment and display in post-war shopping environments, and a corresponding expectation that customers would begin to pay more for the experience of shopping. Thus, it was suggested that 'improved shopping facilities particularly elements of show and advertising must affect aggregate shopping value'.[71] This too proved to be a prescient prediction as urban retail developments became progressively more elaborate, spectacular and expensive across the subsequent decades.

It was inevitable that such revenue-maximising approaches to reconstruction would disadvantage many small and independent traders, who found themselves priced out of the city centre in favour of larger stores. This process was politically sensitive, however, due to the wartime promises which had been made to repair and reinstate bomb-damaged businesses, along with the additional complication that many bombed-out small shopkeepers in the 1940s were returning servicemen. Yet such sentimental qualms were not allowed to stand in the way of the rationalisation of the nation's shopping centres. Despite explicit legal commitments that all affected businesses would be guaranteed the opportunity of reinstatement in reconstructed town centres, no promises were made as to the cost of new sites. Small shopkeepers were duly offered new sites at hugely inflated prices which they could ill afford. Once the bombed-out small traders had refused these terms, the new sites could be leased to valuable newcomers, generally multiple stores with profit margins which could stand the rent increases.[72] One of the leading commercial estate agents of this era, Edward Erdman, confirmed that this legally enshrined right of first refusal for displaced traders 'was a token because they couldn't afford to take up the leases at full market rent'.[73]

The voluminous complaints which began to pour into the Ministry from small trader-dominated bodies like the Association of British

---

[71] Comments contained in papers in TNA-HLG-79/578.
[72] This was clearly standard practice: Letter from Valuation Office to MTCP, 21 November 1949. TNA-HLG-71/763.
[73] Quoted in Oliver Marriott, *The Property Boom* (London: Hamish Hamilton, 1967), 63.

Chambers of Commerce and the National Federation of Property Owners give some indication of how widespread these trends were in reconstruction cities. The Association of Chambers of Commerce protested on behalf of its local organisations in Bath, Bristol, Coventry, Exeter, Great Yarmouth, Hull, Liverpool, London, Lowestoft, Norwich, Plymouth, Portsmouth, Southampton and Swansea. 'The small trader', the Association complained, 'is faced today with prohibitive ground rents [and] an increasing rent burden'. 'Old established traders and businesses' were being forced out by local councils offering land prices 'fixed at the highest rent it is possible to obtain'. The small traders suffered from a 'marked disadvantage in competition with the multiple firms' who were seizing the opportunities to extend their grip on city centres and to open new stores in places where they previously had no presence.[74] Such conflicts spilled out into municipal politics in a number of cities, where new parties were hastily formed to contest local elections on behalf of dispossessed and disgruntled traders.[75] The Chambers of Commerce complained to the government that 'a local authority ought not to make a profit out of town planning' although, as has been seen, this was precisely the direction in which the Ministry of Planning had been steering local authorities right across the reconstruction era.[76]

By the time Coventry set to work on the practical rebuilding of its central area in the late 1940s, such dynamics were clearly on display. The city's modern pedestrianised shopping district may have been radical in design terms, but the underlying developmental logics mirrored what was taking place in reconstruction areas up and down the country; new shopping districts built on publicly acquired land were aimed squarely at the organised sections of the retail trade, who could stand to pay the inflated rents that would provide the quickest returns on public investment. Thus, when Coventry began the development of the first five blocks of its new centre in 1948, large parcels of land with suitable dimensions and servicing for the bigger stores were leased to successful multiples to erect new buildings. In a block erected by Woolworths, for example, public powers of compulsory acquisition, and the forced removal of other premises on the site, were required to deliver the retailer the parcel of land it wanted.[77] Just as in Plymouth, and Canterbury, and Bristol, and

[74] Association of British Chambers of Commerce, 'Memorandum', April 1949. TNA-HLG-71/763.
[75] Some of these local political conflicts are documented in Hasegawa, *Replanning the Blitzed City Centre*.
[76] Association of British Chambers of Commerce, 'Memorandum', April 1949. TNA-HLG-71/763.
[77] Details of these developments given in note dated 6 November 1948. TNA-HLG-79/133.

any other city where wholesale reconstruction was required, state-sponsored redevelopment hinged upon the principle of adding value to publicly acquired land by reorganising central districts around the demands of modern retailing, before leasing this valuable urban commodity to the most profitable retail businesses. Reports from the South West region in 1949 painted a similar picture. In Exeter, Plymouth and Southampton reconstruction authorities were striking deals with numerous 'bigger multiple firms' for the leasing of land and the erection of new shop buildings. Some of these firms had been occupants of bombed-out stores, but many were new to the towns concerned.[78] The effect of this sort of redevelopment on the local business landscape and economic geography of towns was naturally dramatic. It was a mode of rebuilding that saw the largest retail businesses emerge as some of the chief beneficiaries of reconstruction planning, while many modest proprietors were expropriated and whole swathes of small businesses were expelled from redeveloped urban centres. This was a pattern which would recur repeatedly across the subsequent decades.

The Planning Ministry was certainly alive to the 'undertone of grumbling that the Councils give too much attention to the big stores', but remained entirely unsympathetic to the protests of small business groups, citing the immovable imperatives of commercial calculus. The local council, officials explained, 'naturally recommends the best rent obtainable, as would any private developer in similar circumstances'. Petitioners were informed that the multiple stores 'can offer higher rents than anyone else because their methods enable them to use [sites] more intensively' whereas small traders 'have never financed their premises properly and have deluded themselves as to the real costs of their buildings'. The government found it commercially unjustifiable that small traders should continue to occupy 'the best sites in the town [when they] could not capitalise them properly'; in any case, 'before the war the multiples were making progress at the expense of small traders generally [and] this progress is still continuing and must be reflected in the changes on reconstruction'.[79] These were intensely economistic arguments about the appropriate uses of planning powers and the legitimate objectives of public intervention. Reconstruction in this formulation would operate according to the same profit-maximising imperatives which guided large business concerns, with the state allocating land in the redeveloped city centre according to which commercial uses offered the best wealth-generating prospects. The claims of small business owners

[78] Letter from Valuation Office to Ministry of Town and Country Planning, 21 November 1949. TNA-HLG-71/763.
[79] 'Redevelopment of Central Areas', 21 November 1949. TNA-HLG-71/763.

upon their own bombed-out properties were summarily dismissed, invalidated due to their inability to reap the maximum commercial gain from the most valuable urban land. Business was business.

Conclusion

The rebuilding of Britain's blitzed urban centres was neither a utopian experiment in civic rebuilding nor a laissez-faire abandonment of bomb-damaged cities to their fate. Certainly, from the perspective of Whitehall urban reconstruction was just one among many pressing demands upon the exchequer at a time of severe national economic stress. Central government officials were thus focused upon keeping costs down while trying to wring the maximum fiscal, financial and developmental gains out of any public investment in urban rebuilding. Such an approach gelled with the broader politics of many of those serving in the central bureaucracy, who were motivated by a mix of administrative pragmatism, Taylorist developmentalism, and a modified, mid-twentieth-century mode of liberal statecraft, in which public interference in property markets and urban redevelopment could be accepted so long as it advanced an overarching agenda of efficient capitalist growth. These objectives saw the Ministry of Planning involve itself closely in the redesign of central shopping districts, and call upon new sources of expertise from the corporate retail sector, from economic geography and town planning, and from commercial property experts and estate managers, in order to do so. There was a firm faith that public planning efforts could properly be used to advance the dominance of the most organised, profitable and productive sections of the retail trade, and this was necessarily pursued at the expense of the small independent shopkeepers who continued to form the mainstay of local retailing in mid-twentieth-century urban Britain. By such means the business landscape and commercial geography of blitzed cities were transformed, as existing trends towards concentration and rationalisation in the retail sector were sharply accelerated, and central area property values began what was to become a long and sustained post-war surge. In many respects, the reconstruction-era experiments with remodelling the environment and economic geography of urban centres charted a course for much of what followed in the subsequent decades, as reconstruction gave way to a wider national programme of urban renewal and Britain's urban centres entered the age of affluence.

2   Cities in the Age of Affluence

The reconstruction of bomb-damaged cities unfolded under the firm tutelage of the Ministry of Planning, which – in Britain's centralised state structure – always retained the ability to define the political and economic parameters within which local authorities operated. The same was true of the wider planning system that was taking shape in the 1940s; local authorities' new statutory powers in the field of planning were laid down by Acts of Parliament and their exercise was overseen by the central bureaucracy. Local government in Britain operates under the constraining legal doctrine of *ultra vires*, meaning that local authorities have no power to undertake any activity that is not explicitly authorised by legislation. And yet, the planning and management of urban development is an innately local task, which must necessarily be overseen by local authorities. As a result, the cultures, traditions and agendas of local government played an important role in shaping the new regime of planning and urban redevelopment. In the mid-century moment of political reconstruction, as new planning powers were being drawn up and debated, local authorities pushed hard to secure the maximum level of institutional empowerment with which to pursue their own agendas. And these were often surprisingly expansive, stretching well beyond the familiar local planning domains of housing and public health to encompass broad programmes of economic development, modernisation and urban growth. When it came to their central areas, local authorities staked out bold developmental strategies in which shopping took centre stage and new planning powers would be bent to the task of retail sector expansion. Councils were alive to the dynamic growth of retailing – driven by full employment and rising wages in the immediate post-war years – and they sought to harness this new economic energy to secure a prosperous future for their cities and a healthy tax base for their administrations.

Such local aims, combined with the post-war surge in the retail economy, saw town centres all over Britain transformed by a wave of extravagant new shop development. Central areas were remodelled with large and elaborate new stores, which offered British shoppers the latest fashions and retail experiences at prices that only the highly organised and efficient multiple retail sector could manage. Such developments were commercially and culturally transformative for urban Britain, hiking central area property values, establishing even modest provincial towns as sites for exciting new forms of shopping, and intersecting firmly with the glamorous commercial worlds of fashion, advertising, consumption and self-curation. The nation's urban centres were thus refitted for the age of affluence, but where to strike the balance between public planning and private enterprise in this process of urban transformation remained a hotly fought political issue. Many local authorities aimed to do much more than simply oversee the retail-driven reinvention of their towns. Instead, councils hoped to participate and profit directly from this urban economic dynamism as corporate economic actors in their own right. Drawing on the rich traditions of interwar municipal enterprise, local authorities sought to acquire and redevelop key sites; to build, lease and operate new commercial facilities; to mortgage and borrow against their property holdings; and to lease or sell land to private developers when the market was favourable. Municipal entrepreneurship on this scale, however, was firmly resisted by many – not least within the Conservative Party which, when it returned to power in 1951, set about curtailing local public enterprise and dismantling labour's state-led redevelopment regime. This reorientation of the political economy of planning unleashed a remarkable boom in Britain's commercial property development sector across the 1950s, which from then on would play a decisive role in the remodelling and reinvention of the nation's urban centres.

Municipal Entrepreneurship

Until relatively recently it was a historiographical commonplace to describe urban government in the twentieth century as in a state of decline. The vibrant and distinctive urban political cultures of the great Victorian cities were, it was maintained, on the wane by the twentieth century – under threat from the steady encroachment of a vigorously expanding central state. This increasing concentration of power within the British polity culminated in the 1940s with Labour's highly centralised national welfare state, at which point urban governments supposedly became little more than local vehicles for the delivery of nationally determined and funded social welfare programmes.[1] Certainly the central

---

[1] For discussion and criticisms of this thesis see Richard H. Trainor, 'The "Decline" of British Urban Governance since 1850: A Reassessment', in Robert J. Morris & Richard H. Trainor (eds.), *Urban Governance: Britain and Beyond since 1750* (Aldershot: Ashgate, 2000), 28–46.

state's grip on public revenues and expenditure deepened across the twentieth century, and this was (and remains) a huge challenge to the independence of urban governments. Yet the story of inexorable civic decline in the twentieth century is far from a complete picture. Indeed, in many respects the first half of the twentieth century was a golden age for municipal governance, which saw energetic, enterprising and increasingly professionalised local administrations performing a remarkable range of social and economic functions. This was the high era of municipal enterprise, as urban councils not only took the lead in the provision of social services and public goods but also operated numerous commercial trading concerns within local economies.

The interwar period saw the peak of such municipal trading, with councils operating gas, water and electricity supplies; ports, airports, waterways and ferries; transport undertakings such as tram networks; and even commercial entertainment venues such as sports grounds and race courses. Revenue from these diverse ventures supplemented councils' more conventional sources of income from rents, rates (local taxation) and central government grants. The scale of these municipal trading activities was such that they were 'of an important magnitude in the national economy', in addition to reflecting a particularly vigorous culture of civic enterprise on the part of local authorities.[2] In the early 1930s local government investment in trading services represented one-twentieth of the nation's total capital investment per annum, and one in seventy of *all* registered employees in the country worked in the municipal trading sector.[3] This was by no means small fry. One in three consumers of gas in this period bought their supply direct from a trading local authority, and councils across the country in the 1930s operated showrooms, ad campaigns, mocked-up houses and kitchens, hire purchase schemes and free trial periods in order to sell gas cookers and electrical goods.[4]

Such local public enterprise was referred to then and since as 'municipal socialism', but the term can be a misleading one. In a classic urban history of 1983 P.J. Waller notes that 'if there was a distinctive ideology about it, it was rather municipal capitalism than municipal socialism'.[5] More recent accounts are in agreement; Barry Doyle writes that 'the

---

[2] Herman Finer, *Municipal Trading: A Study in Public Administration* (London: George Allen & Unwin, 1941), 18–26.

[3] Barry M. Doyle, 'The Changing Functions of Urban Government: Councillors, Officials and Pressure Groups', in Martin Daunton (ed.), *The Cambridge Urban History of Britain, Volume 3: 1840–1950* (Cambridge: Cambridge University Press, 2001), 287–314, 292–295.

[4] Finer, *Municipal Trading*, 383–388.

[5] P. J. Waller, *Town, City and Nation: England 1850–1914* (Oxford: Oxford University Press, 1983), 300.

acquisition of trading services and the aggrandisement of the local environment was invariably the product of a business view of municipal administration'.[6] Such a business view, it should be noted, was reflected in the franchise for local government, which until 1944 continued to be based on the occupation of rateable property rather than universal suffrage. This meant for example that business owners enjoyed voting rights that were independent of their residential status (a position that endured until 1969), and 'led inevitably to a great emphasis on economy by councillors who saw themselves as essentially trustees of the rate fund'.[7] Municipal trading services were run along sound commercial lines, and overseen by councillors who often continued to be drawn predominantly from business and professional backgrounds.[8] The need to gain approval from central government for any significant borrowing also meant that most municipal projects were dependent on councils being able to convince both ministers and financiers of their 'commercial trustworthiness'.[9] Interwar urban administrations were thus well accustomed to operating as major economic players in their locales, as well as viewing themselves as custodians of local business and enterprise in a more general sense. Recent studies of councils' planning and redevelopment activities in the interwar era have drawn links with these wider cultures of civic entrepreneurialism and local economic stewardship, with major projects such as Liverpool's Mersey Tunnel, or Birmingham and Manchester's municipally built airports, recast as components of councils' boosterist developmental strategies.[10]

To describe urban governance as in decline across the first half of the twentieth century is therefore something of a misnomer but the mid-century did bring a significant change. In the 1940s, with the construction of a centralised welfare state and the nationalisation of many utilities, local governments found their trading activities dramatically curtailed at the same time as they acquired a much more prescriptive set of

---

[6] Doyle, 'The Changing Functions of Urban Government', 306.

[7] Bryan Keith-Lucas & Peter G. Richards, *A History of Local Government in the Twentieth Century* (London: George Allen & Unwin, 1978), 18.

[8] Trainor, 'The "Decline" of British Urban Governance since 1850'; Barry M. Doyle, 'The Structure of Elite Power in the Early Twentieth-Century City: Norwich 1900-35', *Urban History* 24:2 (1997), 179–199.

[9] Finer, *Municipal Trading*, 89; See also Bryan Keith-Lucas & Peter G. Richards, *A History of Local Government in the Twentieth Century* (London: George Allen & Unwin, 1978), 127–135. Between the late 1890s and 1936 the borrowing of urban authorities almost doubled in real terms.

[10] Charlotte Wildman, *Urban Redevelopment and Modernity in Liverpool and Manchester, 1918–1939* (London: Bloomsbury, 2016); Colin Simmons & Viv Caruana, 'Enterprising Local Government: Policy, Prestige and Manchester Airport, 1929-82', *Journal of Transport History* 22:2 (2001), 126–146; and Tom Hulme, *After the Shock City: Urban Culture and the Making of Modern Citizenship* (London: Royal Historical Society, 2019) on the continued vitality of civic governance in the interwar period.

responsibilities for the delivery of social services, mandated and financed directly by central government. But municipal entrepreneurship did not simply disappear in the mid-century moment of national reformation. In most local authorities there were firm continuities of personnel, traditions and administrative cultures across the pre- and post-war eras. Instead, the entrepreneurial and developmental energies of local government were sublimated into those areas where councils still enjoyed substantial agency, and the sphere of planning, housing and development was chief among these. The wave of ambitious city plans that appeared in the 1940s should be seen in this light, as local authorities seized upon the energies and enthusiasms of the reconstruction era to set out elaborate visions for the (municipally managed) urban future that frequently had little to do with the restoration of war damage. The city plans of the 1940s provide an invaluable historical snapshot of the state of the art of British planning at the time but they were also political gambits on the part of urban authorities – attempts to seize the initiative in a moment of flux, to expand their powers and secure new instruments with which to pursue long-standing local agendas. The reconstruction plans of this era aimed to assert councils' continued importance as urban managers and local economic actors in their own right. Their political importance was underlined by the public exhibitions and specially produced films which councils organised to accompany and promote their endeavours.[11]

The plans for major conurbations – such as Abercrombie's 1944 *Greater London Plan*, Glasgow's 1945 Bruce Report or the 1945 *City of Manchester Plan* – could be extremely elaborate documents encompassing a remarkable range of concerns. The *City of Manchester Plan*, for example, ran to nineteen chapters across almost 300 pages. It was richly illustrated with photographs, plans and drawings and accompanied by voluminous tables of meticulously assembled statistics. In cities with strong planning traditions like Manchester the chief concern was not war damage but rather dealing with a long accumulation of urban environmental problems inherited from the era of rapid industrialisation and explosive urban growth. Housing conditions and public health were key priorities, as they were in so many other industrial conurbations, with wholesale

---

[11] For more on the politics of planning in the reconstruction era see James Greenhalgh, *Reconstructing Modernity: Space, Power and Governance in Mid-Twentieth Century British Cities* (Manchester: Manchester University Press, 2017); Frank Mort, 'Fantasies of Metropolitan Life: Planning London in the 1940s', *Journal of British Studies* 43:1 (2004), 120–151; Peter J. Larkham & Keith D. Lilley, 'Plans, Planners and City Images: Place Promotion and Civic Boosterism in British Reconstruction Planning', *Urban History* 30:2 (2003), 183–205; Charlotte Wildman, '*A City Speaks*: The Projection of Civic Identity in Manchester', *Twentieth Century British History* 23:1 (2012), 80–99.

neighbourhood-level slum clearance the proposed remedy. Local authorities were committed to the concept of 'urban dispersal' – by which their populations would be removed from crowded and decrepit inner neighbourhoods to be rehoused on spacious and airy suburban housing estates. Yet the major urban plans of this era went well beyond the traditional town planning domain of housing to set out holistic visions of the city reordered and reborn – newly equipped with efficient modern infrastructures of mobility, commerce, communication and production; with a thriving social and cultural life; and surging forward into a new era of growth and prosperity. Industrial development and employment was a key concern, but planners also hoped to relocate manufacturing away from the urban centre, shunting it off to newly planned industrial estates in concert with population dispersal.[12] For the central city, newly cleared of its dirty and disorderly industrial neighbourhoods, councils envisaged a commercial and cultural renaissance, in which jumbled districts of warehouses, factories, shops and housing would make way for a more prestigious and more prosperous city centre.

Manchester's planners were ardent about the importance of the 'central core' in securing the city's 'status as a regional metropolis'; 'it is to this patch of ground that Manchester owes its standing as the virtual capital of the North-west, as the fifth largest port in England and Wales, as a financial centre second only to London in the whole United Kingdom, and as the most important market for cotton manufactures in the world'.[13] The central area's primary function as a centre of commerce was kept firmly in mind, with an injunction that 'no sorting out should be undertaken unless it is demonstrably in the interests of the trade and business of the city centre, or of its regional importance'. The city's Royal Exchange was 'the world's largest place of assembly for all classes of traders'; its banking houses had cleared £566,000,000 of business per annum before the war; while the Ship Canal 'handled imports to the value of £45,000,000' in the year before the war. Planners were intensely keen to defend and promote these important business interests by retaining 'the financial and professional quarters' of the city centre with their offices, banks and exchanges. Yet they also saw great potential in the careful curation of new commercial districts, centred around leisure, culture, entertainment and of course, shopping. Manchester's 1945 plan suggested a vast centrally located 'amusement centre', which

---

[12] Alistair Kefford, 'Disruption, Destruction and the Creation of "the Inner Cities": the Impact of Urban Renewal on Industry, 1945-1980', *Urban History* 44:3 (2017), 492–515.

[13] Rowland Nicholas, *City of Manchester Plan 1945* (London: Jarrold & Sons Ltd., 1945), 183.

'might incorporate a cinema, a theatre, dance halls, a skating rink, a boxing stadium, restaurants, buffets and a variety of other types of entertainment'. These facilities could be integrated into a wider land- scape of commercial leisure 'which might well contain a fountain display, floodlit at nights, and trees festooned with coloured lights'. Such an offering, it was argued, 'would undoubtedly add much to the city's attractions, thereby assuring the continued prosperity of the nearby shop- ping area'.[14]

And it was the shopping area that held out the greatest promise of prestige and prosperity. Manchester's principal shopping thoroughfares – such as Deansgate, Market Street and Piccadilly – were already recog- nised as some of the nation's leading shopping attractions which fur- nished the city with its most valuable rateable property. But planners were keen to expand and improve the city's existing shopping districts by expelling other uses and experimenting with the type of retail planning techniques that were developed for reconstruction cities. Thus, the city's plan argued that 'a haphazard distribution of buildings used for com- merce, industry, shopping, administration and amusement is particularly detrimental to the shopping districts', which would be better given over to the lucrative business of shopping in their entirety. Manchester's planners understood the imperative to reorganise the central shopping areas in ways that were attuned to retailers' needs and consumer tastes. Central area road schemes and traffic planning should ensure 'excellent vehicular access for shoppers and supplies', while different types of retail develop- ment were weighed in terms of the likely consumer response and com- mercial performance; shopping arcades, for example, were dismissed because it was felt that 'the consumer still prefers the freedom of the public footpath'. The city's planners took time to consider the possible directions in which retail development might lead, speculating (fairly accurately in fact) that 'large emporiums may be housed in extensive buildings using several floors for shopping purposes and capable of satis- fying the consumer's every need', or that 'the shops of tomorrow may be built with continuous facades and canopy under which the prospective customer can walk from shop to shop in sheltered comfort'.[15]

Enterprising local authorities were thus centrally concerned with pro- moting the business of shopping, which was seen as a harbinger of prosperity, a valuable boon to the rate fund and a means to ensure 'metropolitan status'.[16] Plans for the centres of other cities followed similar developmental strategies to that of Manchester. In Sheffield the

[14] Nicholas, *City of Manchester Plan*, 199.   [15] Nicholas, *City of Manchester Plan*, 194.
[16] Nicholas, *City of Manchester Plan*, 184.

city's 1945 reconstruction plan also anticipated late-century strategies of 'culture-led regeneration' by advocating lively and attractive entertainment districts 'providing the right atmosphere [with] bright lights and neon signs' that would coax customers into town and into the shops.[17] In Birkenhead, which sits across the River Mersey from the city of Liverpool, reconstruction planners prefigured the waterfront regeneration projects of the 1980s and beyond with their proposal for a municipally run 'Crystal Palace' casino, dramatically sited (and brilliantly lit) on the riverside.[18] In an indication of how far pre-war traditions of municipal entrepreneurship continued to shape local authority thinking in the post-war era, Birkenhead's planners suggested that this casino project 'could become a very profitable civic undertaking'.[19] Again, though, it was shopping that held out the greatest prospects for local prosperity and municipal profit. Birkenhead's reconstruction plan set out detailed proposals for the creation of a remodelled and beautified shopping district that would 'express the pleasure inherent in shopping'. As in Manchester and elsewhere, the city authorities hoped to concentrate the shopping district and improve its commercial stature, tailoring the built environment, infrastructure and servicing to the 'many multiple stores [which] have recently developed here' while 'eliminat[ing] other unsuitable elements'. In practice this meant demolishing one thousand houses and displacing four thousand central area residents – a reminder that most central areas in this era still housed large residential populations. The key to Birkenhead's thinking was the commercial imperative to compete with neighbouring Liverpool as a regional shopping destination, and this would be achieved by offering the most prestigious shops and consumer amenities:

The availability of the best class of shops for clothes, furniture, cars, etc., the provision of numerous well-planned restaurants and cafes (with roof gardens . . .), the accessibility of long distance travel services and the proximity of adequate car parks, will, it is thought, ensure that the people of Wirral [the surrounding region], many of whom are now attracted to Liverpool, will in future choose Birkenhead.[20]

Shopping, then, was critical to the bold economic strategies being pursued by urban administrations in the mid-twentieth century. Councils

---

[17] Sheffield Town Planning Committee, *Sheffield Replanned* (1945), 32. See also Steven Miles & Ronan Paddison, 'The Rise and Rise of Culture-led Urban Regeneration', *Urban Studies* 42:5/6 (2005), 833–839.

[18] On waterfront regeneration see David Ley, 'Waterfront Development', in Ilse Helbrecht & Peter Dirksmeier (eds.), *New Urbanism: Life, Work and Space in the New Downtown* (Farnham, 2011), 47–60.

[19] Charles Reilly & N. J. Aslan, *Outline Plan for the County Borough of Birkenhead* (1947), 119.

[20] Reilly & Aslan, *Outline Plan for the County Borough of Birkenhead*, 81.

seized upon the reconstruction moment in order to put forward powerful developmental agendas which rested squarely upon stimulating and harnessing new models of economic growth centred around commercial consumption and leisure. Expanding and remodelling central shopping districts was fundamental to this endeavour and reflected councils' clear sense of the dynamic growth potential of the consumer economy and the importance of competitively positioning themselves as the most attractive regional shopping destination. There were also marked fiscal incentives for councils to prioritise shopping over other forms of development. The remarkable site values associated with urban retailing were attractive in and of themselves, but the fiscal bias towards shops was much more pronounced than this. Local government finance is notoriously arcane, but the upshot of various long-running political wrangles over the rating system was that many urban land users had secured exemptions or reductions in their liability for rates. Industrial and residential property in particular was heavily protected from the full burden of the rates, while shops and offices bore by far the brunt of local taxation. The implications of this for local planning authorities were clear and were set out explicitly in a town planners' training manual of 1950:

> From a rating point of view, shops are the best proposition for local authorities, and therefore the authorities in towns which are shopping centres for the surrounding district ... tend to be extremely prosperous in the local financial sense of the word ... The central conurbation, with factories concentrated, or established in a ring round the city area, with low quality class districts [sic] and areas of obsolete slums, bears a heavy financial burden which is partially, but not wholly, offset by its central shops and offices.[21]

The big retail chains understood quite clearly that they were a lucrative prospect for local authorities. Large retailers complained publicly about councils' energetic acquisitiveness in reassessing property values and applying business rates. The chair of the Lewis's group of department stores in 1956, for example, bemoaned 'the wholly disproportionate share of the rating burden' which retailers had to bear. The chairman 'strongly deprecate[d] the tendency of some local authorities almost to exploit the

[21] H. W. Singer, 'The Economics of Planning', in Association of Planning and Regional Reconstruction, *Town and Country Planning Textbook: An Indispensable Book for Town Planners, Architects, and Students* (London: The Architectural Press, 1950), 473–488, 482–483. On local taxation see Martin Daunton, *Just Taxes: The Politics of Taxation in Britain, 1914–1979* (Cambridge: Cambridge University Press, 2002), ch. 11; Allan McConnell, 'The Recurring Crisis of Local Taxation in Post-war Britain', *Contemporary British History* 11:3 (1997), 39–62. For the detail on rating adjustments: Keith-Lucas & Richards, *A History of Local Government in the Twentieth Century*, 135–141.

higher assessments to obtain a level of revenue so much greater than what appeared adequate last year'.[22]

For urban governments, promoting central area shop development was not only a route towards future prosperity for the city as a whole but also an obvious means to benefit the local balance sheet at a time when other avenues for municipal economic activity were being closed off. Indeed, as a 1954 planning study acknowledged, 'for the local authority [the city centre] may be the only area which yields more in rates than it costs to provide with public services'.[23] This study surveyed post-war development plans in thirty-three towns and cities across Britain and found that many proposed a 'tremendous expansion' of their central shopping areas. Some authorities were aiming to double the amount of retail floor space they had enjoyed in 1939. The author noted that such massive expansions of retailing were often flimsily justified by councils in social or economic terms, bearing little relation to projected population increases or regional wage levels, for example. Of course it is not possible to pinpoint precisely why councils took the planning decisions they did, and on what mix of rationales such decisions rested (the limitations of local government archiving for one thing precludes this), but given their long traditions of corporate enterprise it seems fair to conclude that rationalist town planning principles were far from the only consideration. Central government officials (whose detailed views are much more carefully preserved) were well aware of these dynamics and acknowledged as much when they noted privately that, when it came to redevelopment, local decisions were shaped by both the 'purely planning concerns' and what were euphemistically referred to as 'administrative and financial considerations'. When 'making up their minds', it was suggested, councils 'will obviously have regard to the administrative and financial considerations' and do what 'suits them best'.[24]

Municipal Property Development

The developmental ambitions of the small city of Wakefield in West Yorkshire provide an instructive case study in the type of municipal entrepreneurship that was characteristic of the era, and which settled upon the municipally managed redevelopment of central shopping areas

---

[22] 'Lewis's Investment Trust', *The Financial Times*, 27 March 1956, 12. Such complaints have not gone away, with the unequal distribution of the burden of local taxation still a major complaint for retailers in 2020.
[23] Millicent Watkins, 'Buildings in the Town Centre', *Town Planning Review* 25:2 (1954), 85–94, 85.
[24] Internal letter, 24 January 1952. TNA-HLG-71/2202.

as a favoured route to post-war prosperity. Wakefield had not suffered any bomb damage during the war and the city's plans to improve its central shopping area pre-dated the conflict. In the mid-1930s the corporation hired a leading London-based development consultancy, Goddard & Smith, to advise them on remodelling the city centre and its retail offering. By 1938, Wakefield had already secured the necessary compulsory purchase powers to redevelop its main shopping street.[25] The outbreak of war put a halt to these activities, but the new wartime enthusiasm for city planning was too good an opportunity to miss. By June 1943, an energetic local official – S. G. Wardley – had already prepared a redevelopment scheme for the entire central area. Wardley was an engineer by training, with an enthusiasm for large infrastructural projects that he had been able to pursue while working first for the leading construction contractor Robert McAlpine & Sons and later as a road-building specialist for the Corporation of Leicester in the 1930s. Like many municipal engineers of the period, he was also an enthusiast for town planning in a wider sense and he became the local planning chief for Wakefield when he was appointed to the dual roles of city engineer and surveyor and city architect in 1939.[26]

Wardley produced a shopping-driven master plan for the redevelopment of Wakefield's central district which envisaged opening up the city's narrow central streets through road-widening and the creation of more spacious and gracious environs for shopping. He proposed the demolition of significant chunks of central Wakefield, which he viewed as 'largely derelict' save for a few 'valuable shops'. In place of this older urban layout, large new shopping blocks were envisaged, with extended shop display frontages, interconnecting arcades, convenient customer carparks and of course, a new centre-wide system of service and access roads. Wider roads and larger sites would, Wardley hoped, mean that 'good shopping premises would develop to some considerable depth' and he aimed explicitly to create sites that would 'become popular for shops of a more exclusive character'.[27] Wardley presented his new scheme for Wakefield smartly, producing a glossy pamphlet with colourful plans and – in a move that impressed the jaded administrators at the Ministry of Planning – he also built a scale model of the redeveloped centre in white cardboard, for exhibition to councillors, the public and

---

[25] Goddard & Smith, 'Central Town Development', development prospectus, N.d [c. 1958?]. WYAS-LCC-817206.
[26] Simon Gunn, 'Wardley, Stanley Gordon (1901–1965), civil engineer and town planner', *Oxford Dictionary of National Biography*.
[27] S. G. Wardley, *City of Wakefield: Report on Proposed Replanning of the Central Area*, June 1943. TNA-HLG-79/799.

visiting civil servants.[28] The reconstruction chiefs at the wartime Planning Ministry – George Pepler and Lawrence Neal – applauded Wardley's 'enterprising effort' and welcomed 'a positive programme of building activity [to be undertaken] partly by the Council and partly by private enterprise'.

Wardley proceeded on the basis of strategic collaboration with important commercial interests that could further his developmental ambitions. The commercial property consultancy Goddard & Smith ('Specialist Advisors to Municipal Corporations in Shopping and Commercial Development') had been advising the city since before the war. During the war, Wardley also approached numerous national retail chains to sound them out about setting up shop in the redeveloped Wakefield and he had a number of takers by the time he presented his scheme to the Planning Ministry. Central government officials were much pleased with this, and pleased too that Wardley was keenly aware of the financial and fiscal implications of his plans. He had suggested a phased development process, in which at each stage 'an increase in rateable value due to redevelopment' could be banked and borrowed against to secure finance for further development. Indeed, the 'appreciation of site values' was the underlying philosophy of Wardley's whole scheme, and this was to be achieved through public–private urban redevelopment aimed at enhancing Wakefield's appeal as a shopping and leisure destination. Wardley's explanation of his scheme for retail- and culture-led regeneration could easily have been lifted from a late twentieth-century urban renewal prospectus:

> Since Wakefield draws a considerable population from outside its boundaries, an attractive City Centre with good shops, hotel, cafes, cinemas and theatres cannot surely fail to improve its popularity in this respect, and the capital expenditure needed should earn an adequate return with a general appreciation of the site value of the areas.[29]

Wakefield's 1940s redevelopment scheme was an exercise in municipal property development, which bore many of the hallmarks of later urban regeneration schemes intended to stimulate new economic activity, raise property values and 'bring new life' – Wardley's words – into the city by attracting prestigious retail development.

There was obviously no sense in which such a programme could be justified under war damage legislation, but when wider planning powers

---

[28] For more on 1940s planning exhibitions see Peter Larkham & Keith Lilley, 'Exhibiting the City: Planning Ideas and Public Involvement in Wartime and Early Post-War Britain', *Town Planning Review* 83:6 (2012), 647–668.

[29] S. G. Wardley, *City of Wakefield: Report on Proposed Replanning of the Central Area*, June 1943. TNA-HLG-79/799. Comments from Pepler and Neal in same file.

were granted – first by the 1944 Town & Country Planning Act and then by its more expansive successor Act in 1947 – the Corporation of Wakefield was ready to seize its opportunities. In 1955 the city became one of the earliest non-blitzed cities to complete a substantial overhaul of its central shopping area. Goddard & Smith proclaimed this endeavour 'a spectacular success' that had dramatically increased the numbers of visiting shoppers and driven up site values and retail rents.[30] The city served as an important generative site for Britain's nascent commercial development sector in this period, which – as subsequent chapters show – would go on to become such a powerful force in British urbanism across the ensuing decades. The development company Ravenseft was present in Wakefield in the immediate post-war years, putting up some of the first of Wardley's large new retail blocks on sites leased from the Corporation. The Arndale company – whose post-war shopping malls would transform the face of urban Britain – was founded in Wakefield in 1950 by two local businessmen, who earned their start in the development business dealing in the city's newly lucrative shop property. By taking the lead in central area redevelopment, bending available planning powers and working in concert with the private sector, Wakefield Corporation in the 1940s displayed precisely the 'initiatory and entrepreneurial' characteristics which later urban scholars would cast as the hallmark of post-1970s neoliberal urbanism.[31] Indeed, what is striking about Wakefield's example is that it was the new local planning powers granted in the reconstruction moment, along with the developmental agendas of mid-century urban administration, that made these new modes of public–private urbanism possible. In the process, mid-century municipalities like Wakefield fomented some of the key forces – commercial property development, multiple retailing, retail-led regeneration and the urban consumer economy – that would decisively reshape British cities across the second half of the twentieth century and ultimately come to be seen as paradigms of an altogether different political and economic era.

Wakefield's efforts were pioneering, but there were many other urban authorities pursuing similar strategies at this time. The municipal administrations of the 1940s were often intensely entrepreneurial and tended to see any extensions of their statutory powers as political and economic opportunities. Large urban authorities in particular pushed hard during the political and legislative flux of the 1940s for new powers with which to steer the future development of their cities. Local planning chiefs were

---

[30] Goddard & Smith, 'Central Town Development', development prospectus, N.d [c. 1958?], 8–9. WYAS-LCC-817206.
[31] David Harvey, 'From Managerialism to Entrepreneurialism: The Transformation in Urban Governance in Late Capitalism', *Geografiska Annaler B* 71 (1989), 4.

often in regular contact with Ministry officials, petitioning them privately and seeking to shape the content of new legislation. Manchester's planning chief, Rowland Nicholas, corresponded with George Pepler at the Planning Ministry throughout 1945 and 1946, in the build-up to the 1947 Town and Country Planning Act. Remodelling cities' shopping districts was a central element of councils' developmental ambitions, but they also wanted to secure as much control over this process as possible. In particular, councils hoped to be granted legal and financial powers with which to directly participate in, and profit from, central area redevelopment as corporate economic actors in their own right. They hoped, like Wardley in Wakefield, to establish themselves as municipal property developers by taking ownership of the most valuable central area land.

In blitzed cities such powers were a given, because the first stage of reconstruction was municipal acquisition of the district to be redeveloped. Elsewhere the situation was less clear-cut, and the progress of planning across the interwar period had repeatedly foundered on such questions; in early twentieth-century Britain, global bastion of liberal capitalism, the idea of expropriation was beyond the pale for many. In the 1940s Nicholas and other local planning chiefs sought to convince the government to grant them extensive powers of compulsory purchase, submitting detailed financial costing to illustrate how publicly acquired property might be managed, leased and redeveloped in the interests of the municipal purse. Manchester's planners sought powers to buy up city centre land wherever they saw fit, either for redevelopment by the corporation itself or for the assembly of large commercially attractive sites that they could 'dispose of . . . by lease to private developers'. The city's 1945 plan argued that the council should be able to capitalise upon 'the low rate of interest at which the corporation can borrow' in order to purchase sites in the city centre, and the council hoped to build up a portfolio of urban property to use as capital assets, borrowing against their value and redeveloping or leasing them as financial conditions were favourable. In this way, the city's planners suggested, 'the corporation could plan its long-term redevelopment programme, just as a private company does'.[32]

Other large urban authorities were equally committed to municipal property dealing. Liverpool, for example, informed the Ministry of Planning in 1943 that the corporation already owned 'a large part of the centre of the town (an estate worth about £25 million)', and had negotiated a commercial loan of £14 m from a financial house – a municipal mortgage essentially – with which it hoped to pay for its redevelopment

[32] Nicholas, *City of Manchester Plan*, 203.

projects.[33] Liverpool's council also attempted – unsuccessfully – to have the whole of the city centre designated as a development area, and thus subject in its entirety to compulsory acquisition by the authority. Bristol did the same, submitting plans for the municipalisation of a massive, city-scale area of 776 acres. Even the small coastal town of Redcar in North Yorkshire saw economic opportunity in the reconstruction moment of the mid-1940s. In 1946 Redcar's council sounded out the Ministry of Planning over its plan to buy up the town's seafront esplanade and surrounding main streets – its commercial core – in which the biggest shops and 'the highest rateable values in the town' were located. Redcar's ambition was to acquire and redevelop this entire stretch of prime urban real estate, to provide 'a new sea front, with improved building frontages and dignified elevations'.[34] Local authorities up and down the country, both large and small, were eager to dive in to the world of commercial property development and reinvent their central areas as modish shopping destinations.

The Politics of Planning

Shopping was critical to the bold economic strategies being pursued by urban administrations in the mid-twentieth century. Councils seized upon the reconstruction moment in order to put forward powerful developmental agendas which rested upon harnessing new models of economic growth centred around commercial consumption and leisure. Remodelling central shopping districts was fundamental to this endeavour and reflected councils' clear sense of the dynamic growth potential of the consumer economy and the attractive urban property values with which it was associated. Drawing on the rich entrepreneurial inheritance of the interwar era, councils did not simply hope to steer private enterprise along these developmental pathways. Rather, they aimed to participate directly in the business of urban redevelopment by applying their new planning powers to the commercial possibilities of retail development, rentiership and property dealing. How far they would be allowed to do this, however, remained deeply contentious. As has been seen in the previous chapter, in the mid-twentieth century many of the civil servants that manned the central bureaucracy of the British state remained instinctively uneasy about extending public planning powers and inflating public expenditure. There was also considerable friction between the two tiers of the state. Central government officials could be derisive in their views of

[33] 'Liverpool C.B.', internal memo, 15 November 1943. TNA-HLG-79/307.
[34] 'Meeting at Redcar', 22 January 1946. TNA-HLG-79/605.

the competence and capacities of local authorities, and the basic power-hoarding dynamics of a highly centralised bureaucracy made them reluctant to gift radical new powers to their junior partners.

There was thus considerable resistance to the municipalisation of urban redevelopment from within the state apparatus. In the wider political sphere this resistance could become vociferous. Harold Macmillan had noted the thundering of 'the extreme defenders of the rights of property' against the wartime advance of public planning powers and the continued influence of this lobby should not be underestimated.[35] The leading propertied interest group was the National Federation of Property Owners (NFPO), founded in 1888 and 'pledged to defend private ownership and private enterprise'. The NFPO's Chairman in the 1950s was Sir Eric Errington, who was also Chairman of the Conservative Party. Its registered offices were at St. Stephen's House, Westminster, a part of the Parliamentary complex controlled by the Conservative Party. The NFPO's Vice Presidents were a roll call of the largest aristocratic landowners in the realm with a good sprinkling of hard-right Tory MPs. The propertied interest was thus commanded by some of the wealthiest and most powerful figures in the country, inextricable from the upper echelons of the Tory Party, and apoplectically opposed to public sector expansionism. The NFPO served as a national umbrella group for the scores of local property owners' and ratepayers' associations that remained active and assertive in local politics in many places. Most of these local associations had been railing against municipal expansionism since the nineteenth century.[36] As the new planning system was taking shape in the mid-twentieth century, propertied interest groups stood firmly against any model of planning which involved expropriation. Indeed, they tended to oppose any extension of public planning powers on principle. Propertied interests were especially concerned about the type of planning system that a post-war Labour government might construct. The President of the Property Owners Protection Association (another staunch defender of property), Sir Robert Gower MP, warned his organisation in early 1945 that 'if we get a Labour government with a working majority after the next election, may God help the property owner'.[37] And, as the new Labour government was drawing up its planning legislation in early 1947, the NFPO issued 'a call to property owners to seek with the utmost vigour the withdrawal of the Town and

---

[35] Harold Macmillan, *War Diaries: The Mediterranean 1943–1945* (London: Macmillan, 1984), 475.
[36] Avner Offer, *Property and Politics 1870–1914: Landownership, Law, Ideology and Urban Development in England* (Cambridge: Cambridge University Press, 1981), esp. ch. 18.
[37] 'MP and Property Owners' Bogy', *The Manchester Guardian*, 14 April 1945, 3.

Country Planning Bill'.[38] There was therefore plenty of powerful push-
back within the political system against granting the government bold
new planning powers.

Labour's 1947 Town and Country Planning Act was a landmark piece
of legislation for the British state. It was one of the most complex and
consequential pieces of legislation ever passed and gave the government
an unprecedented level of control over its territory. Within the annals of
town planning history, the passage of the 1947 Act is the crucial moment
when British planning came of age and was finally established as a key
competence of the modern state. The Act, along with the comprehensive
planning system that it established, was hugely significant, but some of its
more specific provisions were something of a political anomaly and did
not sit entirely comfortably with the broadly liberal, capitalistic tenor of
British administration. The Act did not nationalise land itself (as the
defenders of property had feared) but rather the right to develop land,
so that a strong veto power was granted to local authorities to withhold
permission for private building and development projects. But the legislation was also framed around an assumption that it would be the public
sector, rather than private enterprise, which would organise and instigate
most forms of development. A tortuously complex system of 'compensation and betterment' was established, under which proprietors would be
refunded for any planning-induced losses in the value of their property
while the benefits of planning-driven value inflation would accrue to the
state. The primacy of public sector development was cemented by the
introduction of a 100 per cent 'development charge' on private redevelopment. This tax appropriated for the state the full amount of any
increase in the value of a site which redevelopment might bring, thus
removing much of the commercial incentive behind the business of
property development.

Many of the civil service chiefs who were tasked with implementing
Labour's Planning Act were deeply uneasy about what was viewed as
a clumsy and counterproductive attack on the smooth workings of the
market economy. In a 1947 lecture to the Institute of Public
Administration, Evelyn Sharp, then Deputy Secretary at the Ministry of
Town and Country Planning, gave voice to these anxieties: 'With
a hammer in one hand', she warned, 'local authorities are to have
a sickle in the other'. The choice of metaphors was telling. One of
Sharp's biggest reservations about the 1947 Act concerned 'the impact
on the private developer', who was viewed as the natural motive force
within a marketised regime of urban redevelopment. 'The administrative

[38] 'The Planning Bill', *The Manchester Guardian*, 7 February 1947, 8.

problem', Sharp argued, 'is to ensure that development is not stultified – that the owner sells, that the developer buys'. Labour's 1947 Act placed local authorities firmly in command of decisions over future land use, but Sharp's view of the appropriate balance of public and private interests was rather different. 'Better the wrong use of land than no use, and if we strangle development better for us that we had not had a Planning Act at all.'[39] Such were the views of those who actually ran the new planning machinery within central government, and there was perhaps no single figure more important to the administration of the post-war planning system than Sharp. She served as Deputy Secretary to the Planning Ministry from 1946 until 1955, when she was appointed to its most senior position as Permanent Secretary. Sharp was the first ever female Permanent Secretary in the British civil service and she held this position from 1955 until her retirement in 1966, meaning she oversaw the planning system for a full two decades after the war. In a further indication of her stature, Sharp was afforded an equal salary to that of her male counterparts when she was appointed as Deputy Secretary in 1946, long before this was required by law. She thus achieved equal pay a decade before any other woman in the civil service.[40]

Labour's new planning framework remained deeply contentious in the immediate post-war years. For Evelyn Sharp the whole thing smacked of socialism, and the Conservatives were firmly in agreement. The post-war Conservative Party remained ardently committed to the promotion of private enterprise, and the tempering of welfare state expansionism, wherever possible. Indeed, for all the talk of 'Butskellism' and a supposed consensus around the expanded social and economic role of the post-war state, the whole sphere of 'planning' – from town centre renewal to housing provision, regional policy and the New Towns programme – remained a hotly fought battleground between the defenders of private enterprise and the proponents of public sector endeavour.[41] As

---

[39] This lecture was reprinted as Evelyn Sharp, 'Town and Country Planning', *Public Administration* 26:1 (1948), 19–30.
[40] Kevin Theakston, 'Sharp, Evelyn Adelaide, Baroness Sharp (1903–1985), civil servant', *Oxford Dictionary of National Biography*.
[41] See, *inter alia*, Peter Malpass, 'The Wobbly Pillar? Housing and the British Postwar Welfare State', *Journal of Social Policy* 32:4 (2003), 589–606; Alan G. V. Simmonds, 'Conservative Governments and the New Town Housing Question in the 1950s', *Urban History* 28:1 (2001), 65–83; Peter Weiler, 'The Rise and Fall of the Conservatives' "Grand Design for Housing", 1951-64', *Contemporary British History* 14:1 (2000), 122–150; Harriet Jones, '"This is Magnificent!": 300,000 Houses a Year and the Tory Revival after 1945', *Contemporary British History* 14:1 (2000), 99–121; Peter Scott, 'The Worst of Both Worlds: British Regional Policy, 1951-64', *Business History* 38:4 (1996), 41–64; Carol E. Heim, 'The Treasury as Developer-Capitalist? British New Town Planning in the 1950s', *The Journal of Economic History* 50:4 (1990), 903–924.

soon as they regained power in 1951 the Conservative administrations that ran the country until 1964 set about radically recasting the entire framework of planning and development control. The first step was to rebrand the Ministry of Town and Country Planning as the Ministry of Housing and Local Government ('planning' itself had become a dirty word in ideological terms). Harold Macmillan served as the new Minister of Housing and Local Government from 1951 to 1954 and immediately ordered a dramatic volte-face in housing policy. The private sector would now provide one out of every two new houses (Labour had mandated a ratio of one in ten). Homeownership was vigorously promoted (and publicly subsidised) through state-backed mortgage lending, tax incentives and the sale of council housing. Macmillan lauded these changes in a speech to an amiable New Year's luncheon for the Federation of Registered House Builders at the start of 1953. The Minister commended his new policies to the leaders of the house-building industry in firmly ideological terms as an exercise in 'freeing development' and an 'experiment towards liberty'.[42] The proportion of new houses built for owner-occupation increased from 12% of total output in 1951 to 56% in 1959.[43]

The housing programme and the 1947 Planning Act were two of the key pillars of Labour's planning system. Another was the New Towns programme, and for the Conservatives this was just as dubious. Macmillan had to persuade the first Conservative Cabinet not to simply abolish the New Towns Programme in its entirety, arguing that such a move would be seen in a poor light by the public.[44] In the end, just as with mass housebuilding, the New Towns were accepted on the basis that private enterprise be pushed to carry out as much of the work as possible. Macmillan encouraged the development of privately built, owner-occupied housing in the New Towns, and thus opened up a bonanza of construction contracts for the Party's allies in the house-building industry. When it came to the development of New Towns' central districts – the commercial cores where the most lucrative development opportunities were located – the Ministry of Housing and Local Government took on a remarkable role as a commercial real estate broker in the 1950s. Property developers and City financiers could call in at the Ministry for a friendly, confidential chat and have civil service chiefs walk them

---

[42] 'Luncheon: Brief for the Minister', January 1953, TNA-HLG-117/4.
[43] Martin Boddy, *The Building Societies* (London: Macmillan, 1980), 18. See also Aled Davies, '"Right to Buy": The Development of a Conservative Housing Policy, 1945-1980', *Contemporary British History* 27:4 (2013), 421–44; Matthew Francis, '"A Crusade to Enfranchise the Many": Thatcherism and the "Property-Owning Democracy"', *Twentieth Century British History* 23:2 (2012), 275–297.
[44] Simmonds, 'Conservative Governments and the New Town Housing Question'.

through the new investment opportunities on offer in the New Towns. Following the model of blitzed reconstruction areas, the idea was that New Town Development Corporations would provide valuable, ready-to-develop plots of land on favourable long-term leases in the new town centre. Private capital could then build shops 'for letting at rack rents to shop-keepers', as the civil servants explained to one City financier.[45] The Ministry's brokerage role stretched as far as making introductions with individual Development Corporations and interceding on behalf of cash-rich, investment-seeking financial institutions such as the Church Commissioners (the financial arm of the Church of England). In 1954 the Ministry sent out a missive to the General Managers of all the New Towns explaining that 'certain of the big financial investment companies have recently taken an interest in new towns, with special reference to town centre development'. The letter reminded Development Corporation Managers that 'the Minister, as you know, is anxious to get as much private capital as possible invested in the New Towns'.[46]

After opening up two of the biggest developmental endeavours of the post-war state – the housing programme and the New Towns – to private capital, all that remained was to dismantle Labour's public sector-led planning regime. This too was done quickly in the early 1950s. The scrapping of the Development Charge tax restored full profitability to the business of property development, and the abolition of the wartime system of building licensing in 1953 removed the state from decisions about the use of materials and manpower in the construction industry.[47] The radical change of direction that took place in the whole sphere of planning, building and redevelopment in the 1950s can be easily obscured by familiar characterisations of 'post-war planning' as an ideological and chronological unity stretching from the 1940s to the 1970s, coterminous with the classic era of social democracy and the welfare state. But the significance of the change of tack was certainly recognised by contemporaries. In 1961 the American planning jurist Charles M. Haar undertook a forensic review of the legislative development of Britain's planning system since the war. Haar was clear about the 'general shift in philosophy affecting the aims of land planning' that had taken place in Britain since 1951, and which was bound up with 'the entire picture of the

[45] Notes of a meeting, 16 March 1954, TNA-HLG-90/344.
[46] Copy Letter, 28 July 1954, TNA-HLG-90/344. On the Church Commissioners, see Chris Hamnett, 'The Church's Many Missions: The Changing Structure of the Church Commissioners Land and Property Holdings, 1948-1977', *Transactions of the Institute of British Geographers* 12:4 (1987), 465–481.
[47] Stephen V. Ward, 'Public-Private Partnerships', in Barry Cullingworth (ed.), *British Planning: 50 Years of Urban and Regional Policy* (London: Athlone Press, 1999), 232–249.

relationship between Government control and private energies'. 'Initiative is now lodged with private developers', Haar wrote, and there had been a 'soft-pedalling of public enterprise' under 'a Conservative party which has discovered the market with a vengeance'. In an acknowledgement of the attitudes of figures like Evelyn Sharp, Haar noted that this reorientation of the political economy of planning had been helped along by 'the civil servant's rediscovery of private sovereignty and the market mechanism'.[48]

These technicalities of the new planning system, then, actually went to the very heart of the political economy of post-war Britain, exposing fault lines and conflicts that have often been obscured by the interlinked ideas of social democratic consensus (from historians), welfare state 'managerialism' (from geographers) and a golden age of 'compassionate town planning' (from planning and architectural scholars). The basic question in the early 1950s was whether the reformed post-war state, with its expanded social role and new developmental agendas, would retain full control over its own endeavours. Would the state pursue its major developmental projects independently of private enterprise, assuming the risks and socialising the rewards? Or would a more modest, business-friendly mode of statecraft prevail, in which the new powers and projects of the post-war polity would be made to gel with private enterprise and the market economy, boosting private sector growth, advancing corporate interests, and opening up lucrative new opportunities for the accumulation of private capital? As Haar put it in his 1961 survey of post-war planning legislation, 'this is not the first, nor the last, occasion when great social policy was secreted within the details of misunderstood technicalities'.[49]

Private Enterprise Unleashed

The political reorientation of planning that took place after 1951 was immediately felt on the ground in redeveloping cities. In Coventry, for example, a major dispute emerged between the Labour-controlled local authority and the Conservative-controlled Ministry. Coventry's council wished reconstruction to be a public enterprise, which would accrue financial benefit to the municipal purse. Thus, the first major development to be completed in Coventry's new centre was Broadgate House – a large block containing shops, offices and a restaurant which was built

[48] Charles M. Haar, 'Planning Law: Public v. Private Interest in the Land and the 1959 Act', in F. J. McCulloch et al, Land Use in an Urban Environment: A General View of Town and Country Planning (Liverpool: Liverpool University Press, 1961), 95–124.
[49] Haar, 'Planning Law', 114.

directly by the local authority as 'a new municipal venture for Coventry'.[50] The Corporation arranged a 30-year, £400,000 loan to finance the building of Broadgate House and retained ownership of the development after completion, managing the property and collecting commercial rents from its business tenants. Broadgate House was opened, appropriately enough, by Lord Silkin in 1953 (Silkin had overseen the establishment of the first New Towns as Labour's Minister of Town and Country Planning). But by 1953 the political winds had changed, and the new government was determined to prevent Coventry from carrying on the same path. The Corporation hoped to continue its 'policy of municipal development' by building the next two blocks of shops and offices in the centre as a further public enterprise. Labour councillors pointed to the booming values of commercial property in the city centre, which had been on the rise since the 1920s and were clearly set to soar in the post-war era. Central area property had been 'a wonderful money-spinner for the Corporation' in the past and the city should retain in its possession 'the wonderful, valuable, freehold land and buildings'. 'I think it behoves us', one councillor argued, 'irrespective of party, to use every endeavour to get that money into the coffers of the Corporation.'[51]

Harold Macmillan, however, was having none of it and the Ministry – firmly in control of the purse strings – simply refused to sanction the municipal borrowing that the city needed to build. The Minister, Coventry was informed, 'favoured private enterprise' and Macmillan refused to bend despite repeated pleas and delegations from the city's council.[52] The particular enterprise favoured came in the shape of Ravenseft Properties, which was waiting in the wings to take over these most lucrative chunks of Coventry's reconstruction real estate. 'Under duress', as one alderman put it, Coventry's council bowed to the inevitable and voted to approve Ravenseft's development of the sites.[53] We have seen Ravenseft at work on the retail-led reinvention of Wakefield in this era, and this remarkably energetic company managed to establish itself as an almost ubiquitous actor in the state-sponsored urban development programmes of the immediate post-war years. In the late 1940s Ravenseft's two young directors toured the blitzed cities of Britain offering their services as retail property developers, ready to rapidly re-equip cities with prosperous modern shopping districts. By 1953 Ministry

[50] 'Broadgate House Control Changes', *Coventry Evening Telegraph*, 11 December 1954, 7.
[51] 'City Council Vote Against Private Enterprise', *Coventry Evening Telegraph*, 2 December 1953, 5.
[52] 'City's Link Blocks: Private Firm Plan', *Coventry Evening Telegraph*, 30 January 1954, 1.
[53] 'Building of Link Blocks', *Coventry Evening Telegraph*, 3 February 1954, 3.

officials noted that Ravenseft 'has built in almost all the blitzed cities and is showing great interest in the new towns'.[54] The firm was well-known at the Ministry, in regular contact with Sharp and her leading officials. Such was Ravenseft's experience in the brave new world of retail property development that the public managers of some of the New Towns approached the firm directly to seek detailed advice on how to design and build their central districts. By the mid-1950s Ravenseft had won contracts to build hundreds of shops in reconstruction areas, New Towns and redeveloping town centres up and down the country. The firm could also profitably insert itself into local authority development programmes, developing a side-line specialism in building district shopping centres on new municipal housing estates. Ravenseft built a 'handsome shopping centre' for Cardiff Corporation in the mid-1950s as the centrepiece of the city's new Llanrumney estate – one of many such municipal contracts. This 'strikingly modern block' brought the latest retail experiences to the council tenants of Cardiff, with national multiples like Boots and Woolworths, 'a self-service store along American lines', and heated pavements outside the shop windows (this last feature was a 'public-spirited' gift to Ravenseft's commercial development from the South Wales Electricity Board).[55]

Ravenseft's remarkable scope of activity in this era firmly underscores how far the developmental endeavours of post-war public agencies – such as blitzed city councils, New Town Corporations, house-building local authorities, nationalised utility boards – opened up lucrative new opportunities for those commercial actors that proved adept at navigating the transformed post-war landscape. Another company that rapidly grasped the rich pickings to be had by working *within* state-sponsored development programmes was the Arndale Property Trust. This company was formed in Wardley's Wakefield in 1950 by two local businessmen, and started out with sixty-five shop properties 'in good retail trading positions in nineteen towns in the North and Midlands'.[56] Retail property values were surging after the war; one government valuation expert noted in

---

[54] Note to Evelyn Sharp, 10 April 1953, TNA-HLG-71/615. For an account of Ravenseft's early dealings see Oliver Marriott, *The Property Boom* (London: Hamish Hamilton, 1967), ch. 5. Also Catherine Flinn, *Rebuilding Britain's Blitzed Cities: Hopeful Dreams, Stark Realities* (London: Bloomsbury, 2018), ch. 6, which deals with the firm's role in the reconstruction of Hull.

[55] 'Cardiff Shopping Centre with a Difference', *Western Mail*, 28 August 1956, 8. See also James Greenhalgh, 'Consuming Communities: The Neighbourhoodgggiu Unit and the Role of Retail Spaces on British Housing Estates, 1944-1958', *Urban History* 43:1 (2016), 158–174.

[56] 'Arndale Property Trust', stock issue advertisement, *The Financial Times*, 16 November 1950, 2.

1946 that shop property values were already forty per cent higher than those of 1939 and set for major growth over the next decade.[57] Holding retail property and collecting the buoyant rents thus became a very attractive use of capital. Even more attractive, for those in the know, was the redevelopment of well-located shopping sites – if traditional shop premises in ageing high streets could be acquired, demolished and replaced with the latest modern shopping facilities, the uptick in the value of the site and the commercial rents it would generate could be dramatic. As soon as the new Conservative administration restored the initiative in urban redevelopment to the private sector, Arndale's chief property dealer – Sam Chippindale – began personally visiting local authorities all over the English North and Scotland to pitch the firm's ideas for rebuilding valuable stretches of the high street as modern canopied shopping parades. Early developments along these lines were completed in the mid-1950s at Lancaster and Accrington in Lancashire, at Sunderland in the North East and at Armley and Headingley in Leeds. Such projects represented a significant transformation of the local commercial landscape. They installed large modern shop units with more efficient access and servicing arrangements and improved facilities for advertising and alluring shop displays. As such they were aimed squarely at the successful multiple stores; 'in many cases', as Arndale's publicity explained, 'bringing a branch of F. W. Woolworth into the town concerned'.[58]

Arndale quickly followed Ravenseft into working in partnership with local authorities, moulding its business model around the new possibilities of the post-war planning regime. Like Ravenseft, the firm won its biggest early contracts by working within local authority development programmes, taking ground leases on municipally owned land to build new commercial centres for peripheral housing estates. Arndale built one of its first completely new shopping districts for the Corporation of Glasgow, providing a 'New Township Centre' with shopping parades and pedestrianised precincts for the city's new satellite town at Drumchapel.[59] The firm did similar work in Aberdeen in the 1950s, where it built a new shopping centre for the peripheral estate of Mastrick on a 'site feued from Aberdeen Corporation' (Figure 2.1). This development housed twenty or so new stores – the ubiquitous Woolworths was the main attraction – and offered 'Precinct Shopping' on the latest modern lines. The *Aberdeen Evening Express* waxed lyrical

---

[57] 'Plymouth: Shops – Ground Rents', report, 16 December 1946, TNA-HLG-79/578.
[58] Arndale Property Trust, *Arndale in Partnership with Local Authorities* (1966), RIBA Library.
[59] Arndale Property Trust, *Arndale in Partnership with Local Authorities* (1966); 'Drumchapel Township Centre', plan, available at Glasgow City Archives.

Figure 2.1 Illustration of Arndale's shopping centre at Mastrick, Aberdeen, completed in 1960. This development, incorporating the latest retail planning techniques and store designs, was built by the firm on land leased from Aberdeen Corporation, and formed the centrepiece of the city's new peripheral housing estate. Such projects showed how firms like Arndale prospered by working within the developmental programmes of the post-war state. Source: West Yorkshire Archive Service.

about the exciting new worlds of shopping on offer here in a 1960 'Mastrick Special'. The new Woolworths '"supermarket" [the term was still a novel one] with its neon illuminated sign, is ultra-modern in interior and exterior', the local paper reported, with 'an imposing façade of three shining glass display windows'. Collectively Mastrick's new shops boasted 'Burma teak, polished oak and walnut, mosaic patterns, Rubislaw granite, the liberal use of plastics, gleaming refrigerators, shining stainless steel equipment and fittings, illuminated box signs and canopies, long-polished counters and shelves, strip lighting, pleasing tile patterns in various colours, suspended ceilings, up-to-date heating and ventilating equipment, and the latest in chill-room technique'.[60] A brave new world indeed.

The activities of companies like Arndale and Ravenseft were funded by floods of investment from the British financial sector in which property holding and property-based accumulation began to loom increasingly large in the years after the war. The new parameters of the post-war economy, in which steady and sustained growth went along with constant inflation, transformed the financial calculus for large-scale investors, making traditional fixed-yield assets like government bonds less attractive. The new sphere of commercial property development, however, with its remarkable, inflation-busting rises in the value of sites and buildings came to look extremely appealing. The Church Commissioners weighed heavily into commercial property after the war, but the main players were the big financial institutions – the pension funds and insurance companies, which became 'the primary owners of British capital' in the post-war era.[61] These institutions found themselves in command of vast funds in the decades after the war, driven by high returns on investment, generous tax reliefs, and a massive growth in occupational pensions (as the affluent worker became ever more comfortable, so his pension fund and insurance pot swelled correspondingly). Although they had traditionally been wary of the speculative world of property, insurance and pension funds began to invest heavily in the 1950s, and they did so by forming new alliances with the nascent British property sector. Already in 1953, Evelyn Sharp quipped privately that Ravenseft 'is the Norwich Union in another guise'. Arndale forged profitable alliances with numerous insurance companies and pension funds across the 1950s, securing millions of pounds' worth of investment for its building projects. Another rapidly rising developer, City Centre Properties, had similar arrangements in place with Pearl

---

[60] 'These New Shops will be Eye-Catchers', *Aberdeen Evening Express*, 7 September 1960, 9.
[61] Aled Davies, 'Pension Funds and the Politics of Ownership in Britain, c. 1970-1986', *Twentieth Century British History* 30:1 (2019), 81–107, 82.

Assurance, Legal & General and the Friends' Provident Life Office by 1959. These relationships quickly came to involve more than a simple loan. Investing institutions acquired large tranches of shares, and also share options (allowing them to buy stock at a fixed price in the future, and thus profit directly from the rise in company value that their loan would unlock). They also placed their fund managers as financial directors on property companies' boards, and often acquired the freehold of new commercial properties after completion, so that they could collect the rising rents in perpetuity.

The financialisation of the post-war property business was thus rapid and thoroughgoing, with the rising property companies firmly enmeshed within Britain's sophisticated financial systems centred on the City of London (the property companies along with their supporting professions of commercial surveyors and brokers congregated in the inestimably prestigious West End districts of Mayfair and St. James, close to the centres of political and financial power in the capital). Scores of new property companies were formed in the immediate post-war years, and by the end of the 1950s property in Britain had become very big business indeed. In 1939 there were just 35 property companies quoted on the London Stock Exchange; by 1962 there were 170. The collective value of these companies' shares across that period rose from £30 m to £800 m (after correcting for inflation, this is a more than eightfold increase in value; for comparison, £800 m in 1962 would represent around £17.5 bn in 2020).[62] In 1960 *The Guardian*'s financial page reported that the value of property shares had jumped by 200% in just the previous two years, whereas the best performing industrial shares had only managed 100% growth across the same period.[63] The financial columns were awash at this time with astonished stories of the dramatic and seemingly inexorable rises in the value of property and of property companies' shares. The growth in the value of some of the leading firms was tremendous; an investment of £300 in City Centre Properties in 1948, for example, would have brought its holder £150,000 by 1960. The growth of the post-war property business clearly benefitted from Britain's long traditions in the spheres of commerce and finance. Yet it was also a uniquely post-war phenomenon, driven by new systems of wealth-holding and economic management, and aided – particularly after 1951 – by a permissive planning framework and the attractive public contracts on offer within state-sponsored development programmes. Importantly, though, the property boom was also responsive to new social demands on the ground in post-war towns and cities. This included a lucrative boom in

---

[62] Marriott, *The Property Boom*, Appendix 4.
[63] 'Notes for Investors', *The Guardian*, 29 August 1960, 8.

commercial office building and, most significantly, the remarkable expansion of the business of shopping.

Cities and the Shops Boom

The immediate post-war years are often approached through the rubric of austerity, manifested in severe constraints upon the government's financial room to manoeuvre and in the continuation of various forms of rationing and economic controls until the early 1950s.[64] Yet the narrative of austerity is not a particularly helpful one with which to understand the urban consumer economy in the period, which was positively booming. Full employment, rising real wages and the release of pent-up wartime demand meant that the retail trade in towns and cities across Britain expanded dramatically. Even the post-war Labour administration's extension of basic food rationing – often held up as a marker of continued privation – ended up serving as a fillip to consumer spending by holding down food prices and releasing disposable income for other, unrationed consumer goods. Although some controls continued into the 1950s, most forms of consumer rationing had been abandoned by 1948.[65] And while consumers were not necessarily able to spend their money exactly as they liked due to shortages and restrictions on specific goods, by 1948 the overall level of consumer spending had returned to 1938 levels.[66] Shops experienced record sales and buoyant profits in the latter half of the 1940s, and the strength of the retail trade unleashed major pressures for new shop development in Britain's urban centres along with a dramatic intensification of trading in retail property as an investment asset. Until the 1950s, however, the operation of building licensing and Labour's de-marketised planning regime acted as a brake on these commercial development pressures; the paradoxical effect of this was to further drive on property market expansion by restricting the supply of new shop buildings at a time of vigorous demand.[67] Individual cities were thus witnessing dynamic growth in the importance of shopping as a sector of the local economy and in the value of their shopping centres as physical economic assets.

---

[64] Ina Zweiniger-Bargielowska, *Austerity in Britain: Rationing, Controls and Consumption, 1939–1955* (Oxford: Oxford University Press, 2000); David Kynaston, *Austerity Britain, 1945–1951* (London: Bloomsbury, 2007).

[65] G. C. Peden, *British Economic and Social Policy: Lloyd George to Margaret Thatcher* (Oxford: Philip Allan, 1991), 142–143.

[66] Zweiniger-Bargielowska, *Austerity in Britain*, 54.

[67] On the commercial property market of the period see Peter Scott, *The Property Masters: A History of the British Commercial Property Sector* (London: E&FN Spon, 1996), 104–105.

Reports from individual retail firms indicate the rude health of the consumer economy in spite of post-war economic dislocation. In 1945 the annual report of the department store chain Debenhams painted a picture of a business in fine fettle. Despite supply shortages, rationing and other government controls, business was booming. Debenhams reported dramatic growth in profits driven by 'a substantial increase in the volume of sales of all our businesses'. The company was responsible for a number of different retail brands, including the prestigious London department store Harvey Nichols, and high turnover was driving up profits across its constituent businesses in the capital and beyond. Trade was excellent at the lower end of the social scale too, where 'the medium and lower class businesses [sic] have benefitted considerably from the high wages of munition and other workers'.[68] Overall, the Debenhams group profits had increased by 42 per cent on the previous year, to £2.5 m. The Financial Times was moved to publish an editorial on this 'remarkable advance', and the story from many other large retail groups was the same: healthy increases in profits, driven by buoyant volumes of sales.[69] The Woolworths chain, for example, also reported 'record sales and profits' in 1948.[70] In the same year the FT reported monthly increases in the overall volume of retail sales in the region of 10 per cent, and for some goods as high as 25 per cent. Again, the impact of full employment and the growing spending power of shoppers lower down the social scale were highlighted. So too was a corresponding growth of provincial shopping centres and the relative decline in the importance of central London as a national shopping attraction.[71] The waning of London's lure, it should be stressed, was strictly relative. One London department store, A.W. Gamage in Holborn, reported record levels of trade for the financial year 1946–1947. The company chairman pointed to a 'big increase in the profit for the year ... due to a most remarkable expansion of our trade with the general public'. In 1946, Gamage's had 'attracted thousands more personal shoppers to the store than at any time in [its] history'.[72]

[68] 'Debenhams, Limited: Results Exceed Expectations', The Financial Times, 23 October 1945, 2.
[69] 'Debenhams', The Financial Times, 23 October 1945, 2.
[70] 'F.W. Woolworth and Co', The Financial Times, 9 February 1948, 3.
[71] 'Retail Sales', The Financial Times, 10 July 1948, 4. On the longer history of London's West End as a national shopping destination see Erika Diane Rappaport, Shopping for Pleasure: Women in the Making of London's West End (Princeton, Princeton University Press, 2000); Rohan McWilliam, London's West End: Creating the Pleasure District, 1800–1914 (Oxford, Oxford University Press, 2020).
[72] 'A.W. Gamage Limited: Expansion of Trade', The Financial Times, 27 March 1947, 3.

The retail trade was booming in spite of the constraints of austerity, and the expansion of spending power across classes and regions was reshaping the economic and social geography of the country. Previously associated with the metropolitan middle classes and the biggest provincial cities, more luxurious forms of shopping were becoming an accessible local experience across the country by the mid-twentieth century. Such dynamism and growth in this key sector of urban economies led naturally to major pressures for redevelopment, as well-organised and well-financed retail businesses sought to expand and improve their premises to capitalise upon buoyant trade. Many retail firms in the 1940s were pursuing ambitious programmes of new store development, and soaring shop rental prices in major cities after the war indicated the strength of demand for new shop space.[73] Before the Conservative's liberalisation of building and planning, however, the only real outlet for these commercial developmental pressures was in the blitzed cities where new shop building formed a central plank of reconstruction agendas. The first stirrings of the post-war shops boom were thus felt in the reconstruction cities, and this was where the leading retailers focused their energies. The post-war expansion plans of the department store chain British Home Stores (BHS), for example, were firmly organised around the reconstruction cities. At the firm's 1951 Annual General Meeting, shareholders were assured that BHS was 'working closely with the authorities' in all the blitzed cities, with a new store under construction in Southampton set to be 'the largest unit in our chain', and another 'large new store' on the way in Exeter. By 1954, BHS had opened a new store in Sheffield, and was building in Coventry, Cardiff and Plymouth.[74]

The most spectacular example of alignment between local reconstruction efforts and the surging retail economy was in Bristol, where municipal enterprise came together with new retail planning agendas and the expansionary programmes of large retailers to radically remodel the city centre. The city of Bristol – an important port, and regional commercial and industrial centre in the South West of England – experienced substantial bombing during the war and the central shopping district around Castle Street was particularly badly damaged. Planning historians have tended to pass over Bristol's reconstruction planning as neither especially 'bold' nor based on a fervent local engagement with the ideals of the wider town planning movement. The city's reconstruction plan was not drawn

---

[73] See for example, the expansion plans outlined in 'Boots Pure Drug Co. Ltd.', *The Financial Times*, 27 July 1945, 3; 'Debenhams, Limited: Results Exceed Expectations', *The Financial Times*, 23 October 1945, 2; 'F.W. Woolworth and Co', *The Financial Times*, 9 February 1948, 3.

[74] 'British Home Stores', *The Financial Times*, 28 March 1951, 2.

up in a burst of planning idealism but was developed slowly by the city engineer on the basis of extended consultation with local business interests. The central and most important aspect of Bristol's reconstruction plan was the abandonment of the old Castle Street shopping area, and the creation in its stead of an entirely new shopping district in a different location. Such a move allowed the council to reorganise the city's previously cramped and crowded shopping district along the best modern lines with large plots for big new stores and a more efficient arrangement of traffic and service infrastructure. The leading planner Wilfred Burns described this project in 1963 as 'the most radical movement of a shopping centre proposed in the post-war years'.[75] The city's intention, as reported in the local press, was 'to provide the city with the most up-to-date shopping centre in the West Country'.[76] Bristol's plan aroused predictable hostility from smaller traders established in the old shopping area whose relatively well-organised opposition produced some political problems for the local authority. But it was of course the larger retailers at whom such a scheme was aimed and the plan received the backing of the Multiple Shops Federation in particular.[77]

Bristol's plan may not have been in thrall to planning luminaries, but the city's retail-driven, public–private developmentalism in the end served as a better guide for what was to unfold in the post-war decades. The city council recognised the economic imperative to expand and improve the central shopping area and seized the political opportunity which reconstruction powers presented. In a familiar pattern, central government resisted the full scope of Bristol's municipal ambition, delaying approval of the scheme and paring back the city's wider landholding ambitions. In the end, though, Bristol won consent to proceed with all the necessary sites in both the old and the new shopping centres designated as a Comprehensive Development Area (and thus subject to compulsory purchase) under the new Planning Act of 1947. As will be seen in subsequent chapters, the significance of this comprehensive development procedure for the practice of urban renewal across the ensuing decades cannot be overstated, but Bristol was perhaps the first case in which it was applied to the wholesale remodelling of a central shopping area. The council's entrepreneurial endeavour did not end there, however. In addition to assembling the

[75] Wilfred Burns, *New Towns for Old: The Technique of Urban Renewal* (London: Leonard Hill, 1963), 29.
[76] 'First of Bristol's New Shops', *Western Daily Press*, 24 April 1950, 1.
[77] 'Broadmead Shops', *Western Daily Press*, 18 October 1949, 1. For a detailed account of Bristol's replanning see Junichi Hasegawa, *Replanning the Blitzed City Centre* (Buckingham: Open University Press, 1992), ch. 6.

necessary plots, laying out and servicing the new shopping district, the city also set the project in motion quite practically by building and leasing the first shops directly as a public investment. Such initiatory activity was felt to be necessary to build private sector confidence in the scheme as a whole and entice further rounds of investment. Again, the similarities with later twentieth-century approaches to urban regeneration are marked.

Bristol's strategy was highly effective, and major retailers soon came on board with Woolworths and Marks and Spencer being the first to build large new stores. By the early 1950s private retail development in the new Broadmead shopping area was in full swing (Figure 2.2). The shoe chain Dolcis erected a flagship store in 1952 as 'an outstanding example of all that is best in modern store design and not surpassed elsewhere in the world'. In 1954 the Lewis's department store group committed to building a landmark store 'on a commanding site' in the new Broadmead

Figure 2.2 Image from April 1952 showing Bristol's new Broadmead shopping area nearing completion. The large modern store in the foreground was to be a new branch of Woolworths, and other stores were occupied by leading national retail chains. Bristol's reconstruction represented a major effort to overhaul the city's central shopping district. Source: Bristol Archives.

Figure 2.3 Early 1960s image of Lewis's department store in Bristol. This landmark modern store dominated the city's new Broadmead shopping district and served as a showcase for the latest ideas in large-scale store design. Source: Bristol Archives.

shopping centre (Figure 2.3). This project was set to cost £2 m and was envisaged as a masterpiece of contemporary retail design, to be built in 'Portland stone on a base of Ashburton marble … its layout and equipment will embody all [the firm's] accumulated experience of retailing, together with the most up-to-date ideas we have been able to assemble from Europe and America'.[78] By 1958, just eight years after the first construction work had commenced, around one hundred new shops had been completed with seventy-five more in progress. Bristol had successfully reinvented itself as 'the West Country's Modern Shopping Centre' and the chief shopping attraction for the wider region.[79] Development at Broadmead continued to accelerate up to the end of

[78] These details in: Upsons Limited (The Dolcis Shoe Company)', *The Financial Times*, 17 April 1953, 2; 'Lewis's Investment Trust', *The Financial Times*, 29 March 1954, 4.
[79] 'Bristol – the West Country's Modern Shopping Centre', *Wells Journal*, 5 December 1958, 7.

the decade. In 1959, BHS were putting up a £400,000 store; C&A had erected one of its glamorous modern shops; and the Cooperative Society was opening a £1.25 m department store at Broadmead. The new city centre was completed in 1961 by a major public investment in road building to service the new shopping district, with the Ministry of Transport committing £300,000 for an inner ring road as 'part of the final stages of the city's newly developed shopping area at Broadmead'. In an indication of how far the dynamics of the consumer economy had come to dictate the work of planning the post-war city, it was reported that 'if necessary, work [on the road scheme] will continue at night and during week-ends' so that it 'can be finished in time for the Christmas shopping rush'.[80]

By the end of the 1950s, Bristol had managed to re-equip itself with a prestigious new shopping district which remains central to the city's economic landscape today. This was achieved by seizing the political and economic opportunities of the reconstruction era, by re-directing local entrepreneurial energies into retail development and partnering with the biggest national retail firms. *The Financial Times* lauded Bristol's focus on 'redevelopment ... of a productive enterprise character which ... will provide a long-term major source of revenue'. 'For about the cost of a 1½d rate', the paper enthused, 'Bristol is getting a brand new city centre ... and is enhancing its importance as the industrial and commercial focus of South-West England'.[81] By 1963, Wilfred Burns was able to applaud Bristol's radical, retail-led, reorganisation of its city centre as 'undoubtedly a clear success .... Commercially this new centre seems to be thriving.' Burns reported that the council was 'spending something like £7 million on its new shopping centre, and hope for an income of £450,000 – a figure which will show a profit in the venture'.[82] In the early 1960s, Burns was applauding Bristol's endeavours precisely because the city's approach served as a prototype for what was about to unfold, as the piecemeal shop developments of the 1950s gave way to the era of comprehensive development and town centre renewal. Indeed, it was telling that the annual Town and Country Planning 'summer school' training conference was held in Bristol in 1953. This event opened with an address from Sir William Holford – distinguished architect and planner, and a key figure in reconstruction at the Ministry of Planning – who 'championed' the role of private enterprise and 'the speculative builder' in redeveloping Britain's cities. Holford lamented any separation of public

[80] 'News from the retail shops', *The Financial Times*, 5 May 1959, 9; 'Sanction for Bristol Roads', *The Financial Times*, 5 April 1961, 13.
[81] 'Bristol's New City Centre', *The Financial Times*, 17 March 1958, 10.
[82] Burns, *New Towns for Old*, 31.

planning from private enterprise, while applauding the creativity and vitality of commercial urbanism, and calling for 'new ways of linking private and public initiative'.[83] Bristol was understood to be leading the way.

Bristol's efforts at 'linking private and public initiative' may have been applauded by many planning professionals, but these new alliances between councils, multiple retailers and property developers also had a clear set of losers – namely, the small businesses that were muscled out of reconstructed city centres as a result. In some places such practices aroused not just anger but accusations of criminal wrongdoing. In Swansea in 1955 – another bomb-damaged city – a group of displaced and disgruntled small traders formed themselves into the Swansea Traders' Reconstruction Association and pooled their resources in an attempt to bid for a contract to redevelop a key shopping area in the South Wales city. The group were dismayed that 'less than one in ten of the new shops in Swansea has been built by a local trader', and that locals 'cannot even afford to pay the high rents that are being asked for shops built by the various development companies'. Swansea's council however, rejected the traders' plans and awarded the contract to the development company Bonville Investments and the architect Sir Percy Thomas – a pairing which had already undertaken a number of other developments in the city. Questions were raised about fairness and due process in the local press and by the traders themselves who concluded that, were the contract allowed to proceed, 'Swansea will become virtually dead as far as the local man is concerned'.[84]

As the 1950s wore on, an increasing proportion of the public energy which was being channelled into urban reconstruction was directed towards central area shopping developments, with reconstruction allowances for building costs often being allocated directly to major retailers like Woolworths or development companies like Ravenseft. In a 1953 government stock-taking exercise, it emerged that Bristol would allocate £9 m out of its £15 m city centre reconstruction budget to the Broadmead shopping development. The figures were even more pronounced in Plymouth, which, despite its fairly radical planning ideals of the early 1940s, a decade later was proposing to spend £12.5 m of its £16.5 m reconstruction allowance on the city's Royal Parade shopping area. The story was the same across the blitzed cities, with the lion's share of reconstruction budgets being devoted to increasingly elaborate new retail developments.[85] Bristol's example showed how such strategies

---

[83] 'The Speculative Builder Championed', *The Manchester Guardian*, 8 September 1953, 4.
[84] Details of the case and press reporting contained in TNA-BD-28/341.
[85] Letter from SW Regional Office, 'Blitz City Reconstruction', 6 January 1953. TNA-HLG-79/618. This was the case in Swansea, Birmingham, Coventry, Manchester,

could be used to stimulate and entice large-scale private investment, to remodel cities' shopping landscape, and even to adjust the economic geography of the city centre as whole. Such endeavours rested firmly upon municipal entrepreneurship, and the stewardship of the local economy, which clearly echoed the 'business view of municipal administration' which had characterised local government in the interwar era.[86]

New Sites of Consumption

The first stirrings of the post-war shops boom were thus felt in the blitzed towns and cities in the late 1940s. After 1953, with the abandonment of building licences and the scrapping of the Development Charge, the surge in the retail economy began to transform the landscape of urban Britain more generally. Retailers' expansion programmes give an indication of the scale and geographic scope of these trends. The multiple shoe retailer Dolcis, for example, was by 1953 finally able to capitalise upon its 'larger sales' and 'further expansion' by opening six new stores across the country and modernising eight more.[87] The BHS chain welcomed the return of 'a fully competitive market' and reported its best ever Christmas turnover for the winter of 1953. The company adopted a major programme of new store building across the mid-1950s, which could now look beyond the blitzed cities. 'The new stores', the firm reported, 'are much larger than those built prior to the war' and offered improved selling environments 'to display our ranges of goods to the best advantage'.[88] The Debenhams department store group in 1955 completed the redevelopment of 'eight large stores' and welcomed the fact that, 'for the first time since the outbreak of war, we shall be able to reap the benefit of trading from properly equipped premises'.[89] By the mid-1950s, large new shop developments were proceeding apace in cities all over the country, offering new types of consumer experience, and allowing well organised retailers to push forward their profit-maximising experiments with store design, marketing and the ever-more efficient seduction of shoppers.

These trends accelerated markedly across the 1950s, surging in tandem with living standards and consumer expenditures. In 1956 Woolworths built two new stores in Glasgow; the Lewis's chain of department stores

Liverpool, Portsmouth, Southampton, Exeter, Great Yarmouth, Norwich, Lowestoft, South Shields, Sheffield and Hull.
[86] Doyle, 'The Changing Functions of Urban Government', 306.
[87] 'Upsons Limited (The Dolcis Shoe Company)', *The Financial Times*, 17 April 1953, 2. The firm was also expanding its international operations in the US and Canada.
[88] 'British Home Stores: Increased Profit', *The Financial Times*, 17 March 1955, 4.
[89] 'Debenhams Limited: Results Again a Record', *The Manchester Guardian*, 15 December 1955, 10.

was rebuilding and extending its stores in Liverpool, Leicester, Manchester, Glasgow and Leeds; while Maple and Co., a high-end furnisher, opened a massive new store in Leeds in 'some very fine premises in a new building on The Headrow'. In 1957 the department store chain House of Fraser opened a large new store in Middlesbrough, with another development underway in Glasgow, while Woolworths built a large new store at Guildford, after buying up and demolishing a number of properties in the town centre. The central areas of town and cities all across Britain were being transformed by big new shops, although the most elaborate developments were taking place in the capital. Vast new stores were developed on The Strand, in conjunction with local authority road-widening and compulsory purchase schemes, including a new store for the department store chain Peter Robinson, which was set to be 'one of the most up-to-date in Europe', with 'four fashion floors connected by escalators [and] merchandise [to] include all women's fashions, accessories, beauty products, soft furnishings and household items'. Elaborate retail development was not confined only to central London but also served the sprawling suburban commuter belt. In Ilford in 1959 a department store was rebuilt to 'occupy three times the space it previously had [and to] include a restaurant and snack bar and an exhibition hall', and the multiple clothes store C&A was spending £250,000 on a new store in the town. The C&A chain was particularly active in the development of slick new stores in this era, pioneering the latest in modern retail architecture and design. The firm built a large and glamorous new store on Oxford Street in London's West End (Figure 2.4) and a similarly striking modern store in central Manchester, as well as redeveloping its large store in Newcastle. This particular project involved 'remodelling ... the shop front [with] one of the biggest plate glass windows – 25 feet long and 8 feet high – ever installed in this country'.[90]

This wave of urban retail development which took place in the 1950s did not simply reflect the replacement of damaged pre-war shops, or a backlog of repairs built up during the frugal war years. The stores being built in this period were much larger and more elaborate than those that had gone before, and drew upon the latest ideas in retail architecture along with advances in construction techniques, structural engineering and new building materials. Such facilities offered shoppers a more all-consuming

---

[90] Details of these developments in 'New Woolworths for Glasgow', *The Financial Times*, 7 August 1956, 6; 'Lewis's Investment Trust', *The Financial Times*, 27 March 1956, 12; 'Maple & Co. Ltd.', *The Financial Times*, 4 May 1956, 6; 'House of Fraser', *The Financial Times*, 5 July 1957, 8; 'Woolworth's New Store', *The Financial Times*, 23 January 1957, 9; 'New Store in The Strand', *The Financial Times*, 25 July 1956, 11; 'News from the retail shops', *The Financial Times*, 5 May 1959, 9.

Figure 2.4 Advertising image of the new C&A store on London's Oxford Street, showcasing both the latest in retail store design and also the structural engineering and building expertise required to build such stores. C&A's modern new stores in this period made maximum use of long plate glass display windows, which were important for attracting the attention of shoppers and maximising trade. Source: Advertising feature, *The Financial Times*, 10 December 1959, 15.

Figure 2.5 The men's suits department in the new Dingles department
store on Plymouth's Royal Parade, which opened in 1951, showing how
slick and sophisticated interior retail design had become at this stage.
Here the emphasis was upon targeting the smart male consumer with
dedicated clothing lines and spaces within the store. Source: Western
Evening Herald/Plymouth Live.

experience, though new arrangements of selling space, innovations in
display, advertising and branding, and the inclusion of additional amenities
like cafes (Figure 2.5). Creating stores like this was an expensive business,
requiring large investments of capital and access to the latest managerial
expertise, and only viable for the larger and more profitable sections of the
retail trade. Indeed, improvements in store design were part and parcel of
the big retail chains' wider commitment to organisational innovations. As
the chair of BHS argued in 1951, the multiple business model 'by means of
mass purchasing, market research, imaginative merchandising and scientific central management [had] become more and more able to reconcile
the problems of production with the constantly growing requirements of
the general public'.[91] The big retailers thus positioned themselves as the

[91] 'British Home Stores', *The Financial Times*, 28 March 1951, 2.

leading servants of the shopping public and essential partners to the state in the orchestration of post-war consumer democracy – the only actors capable of servicing the consumption demands of a newly affluent nation, and doing so with Taylorist efficiency.

The new stores, and the new experiences they offered, were key nodes within a burgeoning public culture of affluent consumption, in which individuals were invited to commune with a proliferation of goods, images and cultural forms. The leading stores invested heavily in print advertising. In 1957 London's prestigious stores were promoting the commercial institution of their 'January sales' in a wide range of 'national, provincial, and suburban newspapers'. In 1959 retailers spent a record £1 m on print advertising in just one quarter, making a major contribution to what was a record-breaking year for newspaper advertising revenues overall. Some of the leading chains were spending more than £500,000 per year on print advertising by this time.[92] After 1956, the coming of commercial television to Britain for the first time opened up a new medium for retail advertising, with an immediacy of communication which allowed prestigious stores to speak directly to potential customers in their own home. A 1960 TV commercial for the vast new Dingles department store – the commercial centrepiece of Plymouth's post-war reconstruction – assured the viewer that: 'You can comfortably spend the day at Dingles ... whatever your interest, there's a Dingle expert ready to receive, advise, and comfort you'. This landmark store was located on Plymouth's newly built Royal Parade (Figure 2.6) providing a theme and a pun for the commercial. 'Dingles are always on Parade, for really Royal service', a cut-glass, Windsor-esque female narrator's voice explained.[93] The royal connection was a recurrent one in retail promotions. It neatly served both retailers' ambition to cast their offerings as inestimably prestigious, as well as the post-war monarchy's efforts to ingratiate and popularise itself with a mass-consuming citizenry. As with Princess Elizabeth's opening of Coventry's new shopping centre in 1948, royal appearances were a particular coup. Maple and Co., the high-end furnishers, proudly drew attention to the 'signal and much appreciated honour' of a 'personal visit' from the Queen Mother to their exhibit at the 1956 Ideal Home Exhibition.[94] The *Daily Mail*'s long-running Ideal Home

[92] 'London stores prepare for January sales', *The Financial Times*, 27 December 1956, 9; 'Over £30m spent on press advertising', *The Financial Times*, 2 October 1959, 11. £500,000 in 1959 was equivalent to around £12m in 2019.
[93] The commercial can be viewed on the British Film Institute's online repository, under the title 'Dingles of Plymouth' (1960). For the coming of TV advertising, see Sean Nixon, *Hard Sell: Advertising, Affluence and Transatlantic Relations, c.1951–69* (Manchester: Manchester University Press, 2013).
[94] 'Maple & Co. Ltd.', *The Financial Times*, 4 May 1956, 6. On twentieth-century monarchy and its 'democratisation' strategies see Frank Mort, 'On Tour with the Prince: Monarchy,

Figure 2.6 The commercial centrepiece of Plymouth's reconstruction, the mammoth Dingles department store, which opened in 1951. Stores like this dwarfed the shops of the pre-war era, and absorbed much of the resource allocations for reconstruction in blitzed cities. Source: The Box, Plymouth.

Exhibition at London's Olympia was itself another crucial generative site for the cultures and lifestyles of affluent consumerism. Much of this promotional effort was aimed squarely at women of course, and specifically the figure of the 'mass housewife' that the advertising industry itself had done so much to construct. In the 1950s, under the influence of rising living standards, this imagined figure of the generic female consumer was increasingly taking on a more genteel, middle-class character, in a way which suited retailers' efforts to hawk ideas of luxury and prestige to a mass market.[95] Understanding how individual

Imperial Politics and Publicity in the Prince of Wales's Dominion Tours 1919-20', *Twentieth Century British History* 29:1 (2018), 25–57; Edward Owens, *The Family Firm: Monarchy, Mass Media and the British Public, 1932–53* (London: Royal Historical Society, 2019). For the Ideal Home phenomenon: Tony Chapman & Jenny Hockey (eds.), *Ideal Homes? Social Change and Domestic Life* (London: Routledge, 2002).

[95] Sean Nixon, 'Understanding Ordinary Women: Advertising, Consumer Research and Mass Consumption in Britain, 1948-67', *Journal of Cultural Economy* 2:3 (2009), 301–323; Matthew Hilton, 'The Female Consumer and the Politics of Consumption in Twentieth-Century Britain', *The Historical Journal* 45:1 (2002), 103–128. There were

consumers responded to such appeals is notoriously difficult, but the buoyant sales of the leading retail chains in this period indicates that many people were happy (and wealthy) enough to engage with new and more luxurious modes of shopping. Fashion and style were often critical to this engagement, with sales of clothing by far the most important element of the new retail economy. Carolyn Steedman's personal account of her mother's (unfulfilled) 'longing ... for the New Look' in the early 1950s remains an instructive insight into the allure of this world, even if, for plenty of people, the expense of the latest fashions kept them tantalisingly out of reach.[96] The British multiple retailers were, however, specialists in bringing high fashion (or at least a mass market version of it) to the people. Reporting on the glamorous world of haute couture from the salons of Paris and Rome in 1961, *The Financial Times*'s Woman's Editor noted the particular success of the British 'ready-to-wear and budget collections', which, with a few alterations for the demands of mass manufacturing, were able to translate high fashion into mass market products in a way which did not happen in neighbouring countries. As a result, the columnist opined with a touch of condescension, 'the French woman has no opportunity of being as well dressed as her British counterpart'.[97]

Although women may have remained the primary target, men, particularly middle-class, professional men, became an increasingly important subject of consumption in the 1950s as well. The attention devoted by Plymouth's Dingles store to its men's suits department, in Figure 2.5, gives some indication of this. So too does Frank Mort and Peter Thompson's illuminating account of the commercial strategies adopted by the Burton's menswear chain in the 1950s, which, just as with women's fashion, pioneered the retailing of ready-made, mass-produced suits while nonetheless managing to maintain an aura of prestige and exclusivity through intelligent marketing. 'The Tailor of Taste', as Mort and Thompson note, 'understood its market as a socially constituted group of men, with identifiable taste patterns and personae'.[98] Alongside adult men there was another important new subject of consumption patronising the expanded shops of post-war urban Britain. In 1959, the social researcher Mark Abrams identified the figure of *The Teenage Consumer*, in an influential market study which surveyed the

clear pre-war precursors to all this however, as shown by Judy Giles in *The Parlour and the Suburb: Domestic Identities, Class, Femininity and Modernity* (Oxford: Berg, 2004).
[96] Carolyn Steedman, *Landscape for a Good Woman* (London: Virago, 1986), 30.
[97] Our Woman's Editor, 'Following the Fashion of Paris, London and Rome', *The Financial Times*, 19 July 1961, 10.
[98] Frank Mort & Peter Thompson, 'Retailing, Commercial Culture and Masculinity in 1950s Britain: the case of Montague Burton, the "Tailor of Taste"', *History Workshop Journal* 38: 1 (1994), 106–128.

economic impact and significance of young people's spending habits. Teenagers, it was reported in 1961, were much attracted to the multiple stores like C&A and Marks and Spencer, where they could get stylish clothes relatively cheaply, and made most of their purchases (Figure 2.7). A survey of that year found that teenagers were spending on average £1 per week on clothing, which, collectively, amounted to £146 m per year or about one fifth of the total UK spending on women's wear. These were significant chunks of the retail economy, making young people another important target for the expanding domain of city centre shopping. In an indication of the wilfulness of consumers and the complexities of mass marketing, however, it was also found that teenagers 'dislike being so called ['teenagers'] and tend to resent hard selling specifically directed at their age group'. Most preferred to shop in the adults' departments.[99]

For urban governments, faced with this booming field of urban economic activity with such powerful cultural appeal, the large stores emerged as essential partners both economically and politically. The chair of BHS argued that shops like his had 'proved to be one of the greatest assets of towns in attracting the shopping public from the surrounding countryside, and most people will agree that the busiest and most important shopping centre of the neighbourhood is usually located around the large variety stores'.[100] In Leeds in the mid-1950s, the city council was being pressed by the local Chamber of Trade to offer enticements to encourage 'nationally known retailers ... to enter the City' in order to avoid 'a weakening of the City's pre-eminent position as the regional shopping centre'.[101] Urban authorities thus sought to assist and attract large retailers in order to compete with their neighbours and position themselves as pre-eminent poles of attraction within a new geographical hierarchy of affluent shopping destinations. New store openings were celebrated as civic achievements, as at Eastbourne in 1953, where the opening of a new branch of a national chain of furnishers was attended by large crowds and 'many prominent local people', including the Mayor who gave 'a happy speech of welcome' (Figure 2.8).[102]

As many councils' reconstruction plans of the 1940s had recognised, cities' status and attraction as regional shopping centres were crucial to their economic future in the post-war age. The position and prospects of

---

[99] Our Woman's Editor, 'Clothing for Teenagers', *The Financial Times*, 15 December 1961, 16.
[100] 'British Home Stores', *The Financial Times*, 28 March 1951, 2.
[101] Leeds and District Chamber of Trade, 'The Maintenance of Leeds as the Regional Shopping Centre', 19 July 1955. WYAS-LCC-816152.
[102] 'John Barker & Co. Ltd.', *The Financial Times*, 26 April 1954, 2.

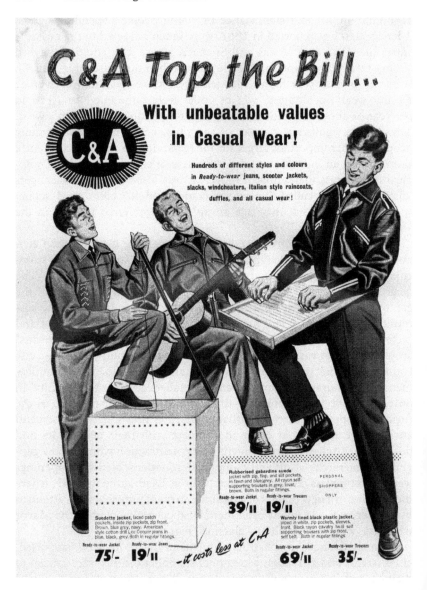

Figure 2.7 The 1957 advertisement for 'casual wear' from the C&A clothes chain. With its depiction of a fresh-faced skiffle band and offering of 'scooter jackets', 'duffles' and other youth fashion favourites, this was clearly aimed squarely at the expanding teenage market and reflected the growing importance of the teenage consumer. Source: History of Advertising Trust.

Figure 2.8 The 1951 image of crowds admiring the stylish window displays of Plymouth's Dingles department store, while awaiting the gala opening event. Store openings drew like this large crowds and garnered much interest – a sign of the prominence of prestigious shopping sites within the local context. Source: The Box, Plymouth.

individual cities within the national economy came increasingly to be tied to their performance as shopping destinations, which was in turn dependent upon councils' ability to attract major retailers. In case local administrations were in any doubt about these imperatives, the official advice from central government was that 'the Planning Authority should encourage the erection of those types of buildings which either attract other development, as in the case of branches of certain popular multiple stores, or will increase the all round [sic] attractiveness of the town, as may be done by an additional hotel, restaurant, theatre or cinema.'[103] Such models of urban economic performance also entered into academic and professional planning thought. The geographer Arthur E. Smailes, for example, whose work appeared in academic journals and town planning manuals, developed a long line of studies in 'urban hierarchy' which

---

[103] Ministry of Town and Country Planning, *The Redevelopment of Central Areas* (London: HMSO, 1947), 79.

sought to measure and rank cities' significance based upon their performance as regional shopping centres. Smailes based his classifications upon the presence of specific multiple stores, with Woolworths serving as his key index of a town's socio-economic importance.[104]

Conclusion

By the end of the 1950s, urban central districts all over the country had been transformed by elaborate new shops that showcased not just the latest fashions, but the latest in store design, multiple retail methods and new sales techniques. These were the emporia that brought affluent consumption habits to the masses, and their installation at the heart of urban life reshaped the physical, commercial and cultural landscape of the town centre. Independent, locally run stores were pushed further to the margins as the nation's town centres increasingly took on a familiar, formulaic appearance, dominated by the same nationally known and organised retail brands. In many respects this was just what urban authorities wanted; big new stores doing roaring trade and delivering top business rates to the municipal coffers. Yet the decade had also seen a dramatic shift in the underlying political economy of planning and urban development which militated against the municipal interest. Local authorities' ambitious programmes of municipally managed central area redevelopment had been pared back, leaving space for a new set of commercial actors and private interests to fill the void. The most striking feature of this period was the remarkable expansion of the commercial property business, which now emerged as not just a decisive influence on the shape and structure of cities but as a significant economic force within the country as a whole. As one prominent planning expert pointed out in 1961: 'It should ... be borne in mind that the comprehensive redevelopment of shopping centres has, since the war, become a large industry backed by the principal finance houses of the country and created in large measure by surveyors and estate agents'.[105] The dramatic growth of this dynamic new sphere of wealth creation transformed the entire landscape of post-war urbanism and planning.

---

[104] Smailes' work appeared in 'The Urban Hierarchy in England and Wales', *Geography* 29: 2 (1944), 41–51; 'The Analysis and Delimitation of Urban Fields', *Geography* 32: 4 (1947), 151–161; & (with G. Hartley) 'Shopping Centres in the Greater London Area', *Transactions and Papers* 29 (1961), 201–213. Smailes' essay 'Towns as Service Centres' appeared in the Association for Planning and Regional Reconstruction's 1950 *Town and Country Planning Textbook*.

[105] J. Seymour Harris, 'The Design of Shopping Centres', *Official Architecture and Planning* 24:6 (1961), 271–274.

In the same year that this comment was made, the Town Planning Institute organised a 'Presidents' Forum' at its annual conference, which brought together the heads of the Planning Institute, the Royal Institute of British Architects, and the Institutions of Civil Engineers, of Chartered Surveyors and of Municipal Engineers. The five men were to take questions on the state of British planning and the prospects for the future. The sense that the urban redevelopment system had become unbalanced, with the scales tipped in the private sector's favour, was clear. Questioners asked 'whether architects were the slaves of the developers', 'whether new controlling legislation was needed' and 'what should be the relationship between public authorities and private enterprise in the redevelopment of town centres'.[106] The strangely lop-sided system of urban development that had been created by the Conservatives' overhaul of Labour's planning regime was acknowledged by RIBA's president, Sir William Holford, who said that, in relation to 'the old familiar problem of compensation and betterment', 'we had dismantled the 1947 basis of planning and had not replaced it with anything else'. Local authorities were now charged with promoting the redevelopment of their towns and they possessed some bold new powers with which to pursue this. Yet councils were not empowered to finance and carry out their redevelopment schemes independently – capital investment and construction work fell to the private sector. Nor did councils enjoy an obvious means to secure a slice of the so-called planning gain – the 'betterment' or uplift in site values – that resulted from replanning and redevelopment. After the scrapping of Labour's development charges, the benefits here accrued largely to the property developers and their financial backers.

Councils were also struggling to keep pace culturally with the burgeoning worlds of affluent consumerism and commercial property development. As the President of the Town Planning Institute (and Manchester's chief planner) Rowland Nicholas noted 'it might be difficult for the local authority to assess the needs and opportunities [in central area redevelopment]; authorities almost needed commercial advisory committees'. The President of the Institution of Municipal Engineers agreed, stating that 'the local authority should go as far as was necessary to meet public needs but it might not be sufficiently in touch with those needs or possibilities to show real initiative, which must then come from the developers'. The new commercial domains of mass market retailing, consumer culture and retail property development were unfamiliar territory for local authorities and the officials that staffed them. Amid the vigorous commercialism of the age of affluence, public authorities'

[106] 'Presidents' Forum', *Official Architecture and Planning* 24: 6 (1961), 274–275.

confidence in their own ability to anticipate and manage social change faltered. Yet the participants in this 1961 discussion also looked ahead; 'public authorities must regain the initiative which had largely passed into the hands of the developers', Holford argued. Public planning must try to catch up with private redevelopment, to match its dynamism and expertise, and direct its energies along socially desirable pathways. For this, a newly bold and assertive approach to planning was required. As the 1960s progressed, this would be found in the new enthusiasms for whole-sale, 'comprehensive' central area redevelopment, for urban modernism, and a new national agenda of planned urban renewal.

3   Making the Modern Shopping City

In the early 1960s, the focus of central area redevelopment shifted away from the erection of individual large stores, or the partial remodelling of existing high streets, towards more expansive projects of urban remodelling. Taking inspiration from reconstruction cities like Bristol and Coventry, from the first wave of New Town centres that were then nearing completion, and also from continental planning efforts such as Rotterdam's Lijnbaan or the Swedish new town of Vällingby, planners in Britain began to adopt more totalising visions of the city centre remade. There was a step change in the scale, scope and ambition of urban renewal in existing city centres that was encapsulated in the new lexicon of 'comprehensive development'. To rebuild 'comprehensively' meant cutting through the quagmire of restrictive structures – physical, legal and mental – inherited from the past. Urban centres could be reimagined as gleaming beacons of (carefully managed) modernity, in which new architectures, new amenities, new infrastructures and new environments would satisfy the burgeoning demands of an age of prosperity and progress. There was a new confidence that these expansive visions could actually be realised; it would require prodigious technical expertise, sweeping expropriations and demolitions, complete environmental remodelling and careful social calibration, but it could be done. This was the era of *Boom Cities*, a moment of intense optimism and ambition carefully reconstructed in Otto Saumarez Smith's recent work, in which ideas of the urban future and the practical possibilities of planning were transformed by what David Kynaston has called an 'irresistible zeitgeist' of enthusiasm for modernity and modernisation.[1]

[1] Otto Saumarez Smith, *Boom Cities: Architect Planners and the Politics of Radical Renewal in 1960s Britain* (Oxford: Oxford University Press, 2019); David Kynaston, *Modernity Britain: A Shake of the Dice, 1959–62* (London: Bloomsbury, 2014), 278. See also Simon Gunn, 'The Rise and Fall of British Urban Modernism: Planning Bradford, circa 1945-1970', *Journal of British Studies* 49:4 (2010), 849–869; Guy Ortolano, 'Planning the Urban Future in 1960s Britain', *The Historical Journal* 54:2 (2011), 477–507.

The step change in the scale and scope of urban transformation in the 1960s was the result of a unique coalescence of social forces. Perhaps most important was a new attitude on the part of the central state – endorsed by both political parties – towards the use of public planning powers in pursuit of wholesale urban remodelling, and a corresponding willingness to countenance major reorganisations of the extant urban fabric along with all the disruptions and dispossessions that this entailed.[2] For a country with such a fervent belief in the sanctity of private property this was an important departure, and it reflected a high moment of faith in the technocratic credentials of planners and other experts as well as a more general surge of enthusiasm for ideas of 'the modern' which took hold around the turn of the 1960s. This was a moment of self-conscious modernisation, both in Britain and beyond, in which many contemporaries understood themselves to be living through an era of unprecedented scientific, social and technological advance. Such sentiments engendered confidence and ambition in the managers of post-war cities and fed directly into projects of urban transformation. As a precise and practical agenda for rebuilding cities, however, 'modernisation' was decidedly woolly and could mean all things to all people. Professional planners invested heavily in deeply technocratic visions of the city remodelled as a high-tech, high-functioning infrastructural ensemble – a mechanistic image of functional efficiency and managed social development. There was also a powerful visual aesthetics of the modern in the shape of architectural modernism, which experienced a brief heyday in culturally conservative Britain at this time and was deeply entangled with these currents of technocratic planning activity.

Many of the councillors and officials who staffed local authorities shared these new enthusiasms, but they also remained influenced by more traditional aims and imperatives of local government. For many councils the modernising moment offered a new opportunity to pursue long-standing institutional objectives. Wholesale municipal land acquisition was back on the cards, which held out the enticing prospects of large-scale development projects and radical uplifts in central area site values. Just as in the reconstruction era, councils drew heavily upon their rich traditions of competitive city boosterism and local developmentalism so that modernist urban renewal became a chance to reinvent flagging industrial cities as exciting, prosperous centres for the new economy of mass affluence. Vast new shopping complexes were installed as the centrepiece of almost all comprehensive central area schemes, overhauling the physical landscape and

[2] Saumarez Smith, 'Central Government and Town-Centre Redevelopment in Britain, 1959-1966', *The Historical Journal* 58:1 (2015), 217–244.

economic geography of the nation's town and city centres. In an era when many urban centres were facing increasingly uncertain economic prospects, the new and commercially vibrant domains of shopping, leisure and consumerism were enthusiastically embraced. Local authorities were obliged to pursue redevelopment in accordance with the legal and financial parameters laid down by central government however, and once again this meant partnering with private capital and commercial interests. The energetic British property sector was ready and waiting. The hallmark of this era was a new set of alliances between local authorities and the commercial property sector, which managed to displace large retailers as the favoured partner of the state in urban redevelopment. This saw the expanded planning ambitions and modernising agendas of the 1960s decisively shaped by the commercial strategies and financial imperatives of the development industry, and lent British urban renewal a distinctly commercial and capitalistic flavour.

Reinventing the Town Centre

The connection between the experiments with rebuilding blitzed town centres and the new wave of urban renewal which took off from around 1960 was not lost on contemporaries. The planning consultant Nathaniel Lichfield – an important figure in the development of British planning policy and expertise – noted in 1967 that:

Large-scale redevelopment in our town centres was an unhappy consequence of World War II. The list of bomb damage redevelopment schemes is a ghostly echo of Hitler's Baedeker raids. But what was more unexpected was the flood of schemes for the redevelopment of the town centres which had escaped war damage, starting as a trickle in the mid-1950's and assuming gigantic proportions only ten years later. The origins here were much more happy.[3]

Precise figures are difficult to ascertain but Lichfield was certainly not exaggerating the 'gigantic proportions' of urban redevelopment by the mid-1960s. In 1965 a new planning policy unit within government conducted its own 'census' of redevelopment schemes, identifying almost 600 projects either underway or proposed in well over 200 different towns and cities across England.[4] The most energetic English authorities – Birmingham, Bristol, Manchester and Croydon – were dealing with 20

---

[3] Nathaniel Lichfield, 'The Evaluation of Capital Investment Projects in Town Centre Redevelopment', *Public Administration* 45:2 (1967), 129–148, 129.

[4] Local authorities were asked to report on schemes of one or more acres, or which provided more than 50,000 square feet of new floor space, for which sites had already been acquired through legal agreement. These terms excluded many developments, particularly in the early stages. The resulting figures thus certainly underestimated the general phenomenon.

or more projects within their jurisdictions. Nationally by far the majority of these developments (around 80 per cent) were town centre schemes and by far the majority (around 75 per cent) related to new shopping provision. Figures for Wales were collated separately but revealed 22 town centre schemes going ahead in 15 different towns.[5] In Scotland 39 central area redevelopment schemes across the country had received legal approval by the end of 1964, with the vigorously pro-development second city of Glasgow pursuing dozens of separate schemes.[6] These were remarkable figures and they give an indication of the radical scope of urban rebuilding which was unleashed in a very short period.

This wave of redevelopment transformed Britain as significant portions of the extant urban landscape were levelled and rebuilt according to the interlinked agendas of urban renewal, modernisation and comprehensive redevelopment. It was an unusual political moment in which there was a willingness from both tiers of government and across the political spectrum to countenance the large-scale, state-backed remodelling of cities' physical fabric and infrastructure. It was a great era for urban road-building, for example, backed by grants from the Ministry of Transport. In Britain's densely built urban centres such efforts usually required substantial programmes of compulsory purchase and demolition to create space for the new arteries of the automobile age. Many local authorities were also making energetic use of the Ministry of Housing and Local Government's grants to further their public housing programmes, which were major municipal endeavours.[7] This allowed councils to pursue the agendas of slum clearance, housing improvement, public health and environmental reordering which had been a rallying cry for so many in local government and planning since the nineteenth century. Slum clearance in particular offered rich opportunities to reorganise the geography of cities by decanting inner-urban populations off to purpose-built housing estates and releasing valuable central area land for new forms of development. In many ways, then, it really was a high moment for public planning and municipal endeavour,

---

[5] See 'Census of Redevelopment Schemes', July 1966, & 'Census of Redevelopment Schemes – Wales'. TNA-HLG-136/203.

[6] T. Hart, *The Comprehensive Development Area: A Study of the Legal and Administrative Problems of Comprehensive Land Development with Special Reference to Glasgow* (Edinburgh: Oliver & Boyd, 1968), Appendix IV, Table IV, & pp. 26–35 for the situation in Glasgow. Many of Glasgow's schemes related to the city's massive housing renewal programme, but many in the city centre were focused on shopping and economic renewal.

[7] The literature on councils' housing efforts is vast. See for example John Boughton, *Municipal Dreams: The Rise and Fall of Council Housing* (London: Verso, 2018); Alison Ravetz, *Council Housing and Culture: The History of a Social Experiment* (London: Routledge, 2001); John Burnett, *A Social History of Housing, 1815–1985* (London: Methuen, 1986).

which finally began to receive the resources it needed from central government to work decisively towards improving public and environmental health, raising housing standards and improving cities' layout and infrastructure. Yet the town centre, as ever, was unique. In its dense concentration of existing built forms and social functions, its role as the commercial heart and command centre for the regional economy, and the seething, jostling mix of established uses and competing demands upon this most valuable urban space, the central area of any town or city posed singular developmental challenges.

Just as in the reconstruction era, supreme emphasis was placed upon town centres' developmental prospects and the successful husbandry of the central area economy. Here, interventionist public planning would be made to gel with commercial redevelopment by working in tandem with selected business interests to refashion urban centres for a new age of prosperity. If local authorities could deploy their bold new planning powers to take ownership of large tracts of central area land, and facilitate the comprehensive remodelling of these sites in the service of new social demands and economic opportunities, they could hope to unlock valuable new waves of private sector growth while thrusting their cities ahead into the modern age. The booming consumer economy and the exciting cultures of affluent modernity with which it was aligned became a central focus for these developmental efforts. The governments' 1965 census of urban redevelopment showed that retail developments in the town centre were by far the most common form of rebuilding; the census found 348 town centre shopping schemes going ahead in 192 different towns and cities in the mid-1960s. However, the scalar shift in redevelopment ambition at this time also saw a shift in the developmental alliances that underpinned urban transformation. Now that more expansive, comprehensive visions of the city centre remade were on the table, individual retailers increasingly fell from influence to be replaced by the surging property development sector, which could offer urban reinvention on an altogether different scale. Thus, the large-scale redevelopment projects of this era, which remodelled substantial chunks of the town centre and required widespread compulsory purchase and demolition, were most often the result of an alliance between the developmental ambitions of councils, the technocratic preoccupations of planners and the commercial objectives of retail property developers. These projects were transformative for both cities and society, as the physical environment and infrastructure of cities were remodelled around large new shopping facilities, and curious new landscapes of consumption came to dominate the nation's urban centres.

One of the earliest such enterprises unfolded in the unlikely locale of Shipley in West Yorkshire. Shipley was a modest town with around 30,000 inhabitants in the early 1960s and was traditionally dependent – like its much larger neighbour Bradford – on woollen manufactures. The town centre of Shipley was cleared and rebuilt between 1955 and 1962 by the local authority working in conjunction with an emergent local development company – the Arndale Property Trust. We have seen Arndale at work building shopping parades and precincts on new municipal housing estates in the 1950s, but Shipley offered the first opportunity to turn these techniques towards the rebuilding of an extant town centre. It was an endeavour which could only proceed in lockstep with the local authority given the reliance on widespread compulsory purchase. Three hundred houses and fifty businesses in the town centre were acquired by Shipley's council and destroyed using slum clearance powers, to be replaced by Arndale's sleek modern shopping district (Figures 3.1 and 3.2). Shipley's newly laid-out

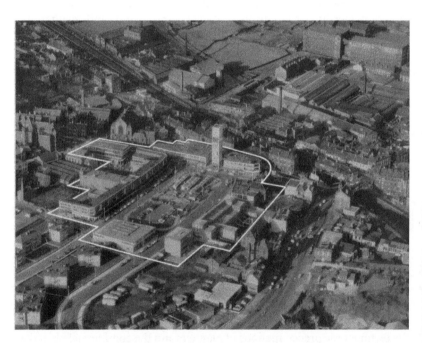

Figure 3.1 Shipley's town centre redevelopment begun in 1955 and completed by the early 1960s. The new central square, lined with new shopping complexes and parades, and with its central open space given over for car parking, can be seen outlined in white. Also evident is the wider reorganisation of the central road network which this development entailed, with major roads cutting through the town and looping into the new development. Source: RIBA Collections, courtesy P&O Heritage.

Figure 3.2 View of Shipley's new central district, showing the central car park, market and landscaped public spaces; new, modern shopping parades; and the skeleton-framed 'Clock Tower feature' standing over the new development. This was intended as the 'focal point' of a reinvented Shipley. Source: RIBA Collections, courtesy P&O Heritage.

town centre comprised a central 'market square' surrounded by canopied parades of modern shop units organised around the largest and most important retail tenants. 'Modern and imaginative architecture' housed innovative retail forms such as a stylish new market hall, accessible by escalator and offering 'market trading on modern lines'. The development brought new multiple stores like Woolworths to the town along with the self-service supermarkets, which were proliferating all over Britain at the time. Commanding the new town centre of Shipley was an unusual two-level shopping block dominated by an eighty-foot clock tower, which was conceived as the new 'focal point of Shipley'. The town's road layout, parking provision and bus routes were reorganised around the market square development so that 'the shopper (whether travelling by bus or by private car) encounters no difficulty in getting to the very doorstep of the shops and stores which retail such a vast range of commodities'.[8]

[8] All quotes from Arndale Property Trust, *Shipley Town Centre: Development by the Arndale Property Trust Limited*, development prospectus, 1965, RIBA. On supermarkets see Gareth Shaw, Louise Curth & Andrew Alexander, 'Selling Self-Service and the

Figure 3.3 Exterior of Arndale's experimental covered shopping precinct at Shipley. This development saw the company test out new retail design ideas from the United States, and apply them to 1960s West Yorkshire. All shops enjoyed dual frontage, both outwards on to the street and inwards to the pedestrianised covered space. The development thus provided both 'comfortable shopping facilities in inclement weather', and a more valuable and intensively managed form of selling space. Source: RIBA Collections, courtesy P&O Heritage.

On the southern side of Shipley's new central square an experimental 'Arndale Shopping Centre' was built (Figure 3.3). This small enclosed precinct served as a prototype for the company's later, much larger, enclosed shopping centres in Britain and was another reflection of Arndale's enthusiastic experimentation with new commercial architectures and development types. The company extolled the commercial advantages of this new structure, where 'the "shopping-under-cover" principle is fully exploited', and dual frontages – facing out to the street and inward onto the precinct – maximised the 'important advertising value' of shop window displays. The internal arrangement and

Supermarket: The Americanisation of Food Retailing in Britain, 1945-60', *Business History* 46:4 (2004), 568–582.

aesthetics of this 'attractive covered Precinct complete with ornamental pool and fountain' built upon the experiments with retail landscaping that Arndale and other developers were pursuing in their open-air pedestrian precincts at this time. The company's publicity suggested that the leisurely layout and 'unique design features' of Shipley's covered shopping precinct 'tend to give a continental impression', but the real inspiration behind these new retail forms came from the original affluent society across the Atlantic. Arndale's directors visited the United States and Canada in the mid-1950s, where they met with 'architects who specialised in covering shopping centres' and saw for themselves the new geographies of mass consumption that were emerging in North America.[9] It was the visions of affluence, mass consumption and commercial modernity that were being generated in the 'consumers' republic' of the United States that provided the bedrock of ideas and forms on which developments like that at Shipley were built.[10] The low-rise, leisured and languid landscape of the post-war pedestrian precinct came directly from American experiments in suburban commercial modernism. The new self-service stores and supermarkets which developments like Shipley invariably installed in British town centres were also American imports – their efficiency-maximising innovations in store design and retail technique were firmly promoted by the Marshall Plan-funded activities of the Anglo-American Council on Productivity.[11] Indeed, in the 1950s, retail development projects such as that at Shipley were often simply described as 'American-style shopping centres' within professional literatures and popular reportage.[12]

Shipley's redevelopment thus represented something more than simply updating the town's ageing physical fabric. It was an effort at reinvention, which was at once environmental, economic and cultural. The remodelling of Shipley's central area was designed to secure the waning manufacturing town's entry into an exciting new world of affluence, consumerism and prosperity. The attraction of big chains like Woolworths and other 'firms of National repute'[13] was critical to the

[9] 'Man who started Arndale retires', *Town & City Group News*, Summer 1977, company newsletter. Available in P&O Collection, National Maritime Museum.
[10] Lizabeth Cohen, *A Consumers' Republic: The Politics of Mass Consumption in Postwar America* (New York: Knopf, 2004).
[11] Gareth Shaw, Louise Curth & Andrew Alexander, 'Selling Self-Service and the Supermarket: The Americanisation of Food Retailing in Britain, 1945-60', *Business History* 46:4 (2004), 568–582.
[12] For example O.W. Roskill, 'The Detailed Planning of Shopping Centres', *Official Architecture and Planning* 21:9 (1958), 414–416; Robert Clyde, 'End of a High Street Nightmare', *Daily Mail*, 21 September 1959, 11.
[13] Arndale Property Trust, Shipley Town Centre: Development by the Arndale Property Trust Limited, development prospectus, 1965, RIBA.

town's image and prospects as it sought to recast itself as an important pole of attraction for the new cultures and spending habits of mass affluence. And the new architectures and retail forms tied the town to a prestigious domain of consumer abundance and commercial modernity that stretched across the Atlantic. Boosterist local reportage suggested that the new town centre had 'aroused the admiration of townsfolk and visitors alike', and that Arndale's modern precinct 'ensures the completion of the Square in a manner worthy of the great advance already made in creating a new shopping and business centre'.[14] In a further indication of the heady glamour of the cultural and commercial world into which 1960s Shipley was thrusting itself, the official opening ceremony for the new town centre was presided over by a young and spritely Bruce Forsyth. Shipley quickly emerged as a model for what might be possible in the realm of central area redevelopment. Arndale commissioned a 1966 promotional film to show off the town's transformation to interested councils and Shipley received 'over 80 deputations from Local Authorities all over the country [who] visited the town "to see for themselves"'.[15] In a 1962 parliamentary debate on 'urban central redevelopment' the Minister of Housing and Local Government, Charles Hill, drew attention to Shipley in particular as a successful example of 'partnership between local authorities and private enterprise in central area redevelopment', and something that could be emulated elsewhere.[16]

Commercial property developers were thus offering local authorities a new model of prosperity and growth, which was rooted in an exciting repertoire of cultural and architectural forms lifted from the North American heartland of affluence. Yet there were striking differences with the American experience too. Urban renewal projects like this involved overhauling the existing densely built centres of long-established settlements. Practically and legally this was a far more complex proposition than the creation of brand-new commercial centres in the wide-open spaces of America's urban peripheries. Shipley's metamorphosis required the wholesale acquisition of a large swathe of the town centre, comprised of hundreds of small, individually owned plots of land. Such projects were inconceivable without the bolstered public planning powers that local authorities were granted in the 1940s, so that the commercial endeavours of developers like Arndale and Ravenseft (who also built in Shipley) were entirely dependent upon the new public planning framework for their realisation. In Shipley the council used slum clearance powers to take ownership of the town

---

[14] 'Shipley leases its last site', *Shipley Times and Express*, 23 October 1957, 1.
[15] Arndale Property Trust, *Shipley Town Centre: Development by the Arndale Property Trust Limited*, development prospectus (1965). Available at RIBA Library, London.
[16] HC Deb. 13 April 1962, vol. 657, cc. 1724.

centre and deliver it up for commercial reinvention. This procedure had the enormous advantage of drastically reducing the costs of land acquisition, because compensation levels for slum properties were based upon the assumption that existing buildings were worthless. The use of such powers would seem to indicate that properties were in extremely poor shape, but this was not necessarily the case. Local authorities enjoyed remarkable discretion when designating 'slums' in this period, which were defined broadly and loosely, and certified by the local authority's own medical officer. Councils were not at all above bending their clearance programmes towards wider aims, and upon appeal it was not uncommon for central government inspectors to find that many properties had been unjustifiably condemned as slums (the upshot of this was increased compensation, rather than a halt to demolition). In Shipley, after a period of over-zealous slum designation after the war, there was a change of tack in what the local paper tellingly referred to as 'the town's "slum" clearance programme' in the mid-1950s, with a new recognition that previously condemned housing might 'do service for a little longer'.[17]

Slum designation thus provided a huge and somewhat dubious fillip to the finances of public–private redevelopment schemes, and illustrated how new planning powers could be turned towards developmental ends that were not necessarily quite what was intended. In Shipley aggrieved owners complained that the local authority was 'robbing people of cottages and houses in clearance areas'. One local landlord was incensed by the offer of 10 to 20 shillings each for the 127 houses he owned in the redevelopment district. This individual claimed that the council had already passed on similarly acquired houses to salvagers for £7 apiece to strip out and sell the fixtures and fittings, and would thus be turning a substantial profit on these transactions alone.[18] The redevelopment of the town raised predictable complaints from other quarters too. The Shipley Ratepayers' Association was unhappy about the scale of municipal endeavour and the new financial commitments that the council was entering into. The Association was annoyed enough to put forward its own candidates to contest every ward in the town in the local elections of 1957. The Ratepayers' body overlapped firmly with the Shipley and Baildon Traders' Association (both groups were associated with the local Conservative Club) which, as the voice of the independent shopkeeper, was also a natural opponent of the town's redevelopment. One sympathiser wrote to the local paper in 1955 to raise concerns about 'the speculative character' of 'the transformation now

[17] 'Bowing to the Inevitable', *Shipley Times and Express*, 26 October 1955, 5.
[18] 'Cricheldownery – more light on "daylight robbery"', *The Manchester Guardian*, 16 February 1955, 12.

taking place in our town'. 'The success of the project hinges on the prospect of developing Shipley as a shopping area', the correspondent wrote, but 'the need for those extra shops in the Central Area can readily be argued against'. Against the idea of 'attracting "Shoppers into Shipley"', the author pointed to the flagging performance of many shops in the town and a 'transfer of shopping potential' to other locales. 'Is there a motive behind this new era of development', the author wondered, 'that of squeezing out the "Small Man"? The Trader's Association would do well ... to resist any attempt to foster Multiple Stores and Co-op trading at the expense of the small trader'.[19] By the mid-1950s, though, this development-induced restructuring of the local retail sector was already a well-established pattern.

Shipley's case pointed the way forward for town centre renewal. It showed how public authorities and private developers could work in concert at retail-driven urban reinvention, comprehensively remodelling substantial portions – sometimes whole central districts – of Britain's towns and cities as holistically planned shopping spaces. The bolstered planning powers of post-war local authorities (along with a new willingness from central government to endorse their vigorous application) opened up radical new possibilities for wholesale redevelopment in the town centre, but the political and financial strictures that councils faced meant that such efforts could only proceed in partnership with private enterprise. There was central government grant funding for road schemes, and for housing improvement efforts, and these funding streams could certainly be applied creatively by local authorities, but the wider rebuilding of central areas always depended upon private capital and thus upon the new commercial actors like Arndale that were willing to take a punt on a town and its renewal. In Shipley, for example, Arndale paid the local authority £10,000 for the site of its experimental covered precinct to be followed by a yearly ground rent once the building was completed. Local authorities' powers of compulsory purchase delivered the land, but the rebuilding was financed and managed by the burgeoning private development sector. The basics of this relationship determined the whole course and character of British town centre renewal, which ended up as a curious hybrid – neither *dirigiste* nor laissez-faire, but rather an odd combination of both. The marketised, profit-maximising imperatives of the development industry produced a brash, capitalistic mode of redevelopment, designed to wring the maximum returns out of any patch of land. Yet the scale on which these intensely commercial modes of rebuilding were applied to the nation's urban centres was inconceivable without the sweeping deployment of

[19] 'Letters to the Editor', *Shipley Times and Express*, 26 October 1955, 5.

public planning powers, and would never have materialised if redevelopment had been left entirely to market forces.

Time and again this state-backed commercial rebuilding generated town centres that were dominated by the most expensive types of retail property, crowding out small-scale enterprise along with many other social uses for the shared spaces of the city. In Shipley, there were plenty of voices articulating alternatives to Arndale's returns-driven reinvention of the town. Like many other industrial towns in West Yorkshire, Shipley had long been a centre of non-conformism and in the 1950s the social life of the town continued to revolve around the innumerable clubs, associations and events organised by the many different congregations present in Shipley. Church groups organised youth clubs, whist drives, concerts, jumble sales, film evenings, Sunday schools, mothers' unions, brass bands, 'young wives' groups', 'men's fellowships', 'young people's day', veterans' support groups, 'farmhouse suppers', 'leisure hours' and much more besides. These religious groupings represented a rich seam of civic and associational life that was matched by secular activities such as the town's Archaeology Group and Rotary Club; the lectures organised by the Shipley Textile Society, the Round Table or the Shipley Geologists; the local Liberal, Conservative and Labour Clubs; and sporting events such as the town's 'annual hill climb' and cycling club. The redeveloped town centre made space for none of this thick slice of local life, and this did not go unnoticed. In October 1957 one Mrs Smith, chair of the Wesleyan Reform Amateur Operatic and Dramatic Society, concluded a performance of the comic opera *Iolanthe* with a public plea to Shipley's council to include groups like hers in the town's reinvention by 'providing a central hall suitable for such presentations'.[20] Other citizens were more interested in ideas like protected play streets for children or the provision of bus shelters (this was a long-running gripe in the rainy Pennine town) than they were in the latest shopping fads.[21] There were thus plenty of alternative social visions of how the built environment of a town could support the life of the local community, yet these frequently fell by the wayside in this era of public–private developmentalism.

Getting Comprehensive

The early experiments with pedestrian shopping precincts and small-town renewal schemes were important in establishing the terrain of what was

---

[20] 'Need for suitable hall in Shipley centre', *Shipley Times and Express*, 23 October 1957, 7.
[21] On the play streets movement see Krista Cowman, 'Play Streets: Women, Children and the Problem of Urban Traffic, 1930-1970', *Social History* 42:2 (2017), 233–256.

possible practically and politically in the new sphere of public–private urban renewal. They allowed commercial developers scope to experiment with new, American-inspired retail forms and to build up a store of experience and income-generating assets with which to move on to larger and more ambitious projects. The interest shown in places like Shipley – from other local authorities, from central government, MPs and planners – illustrates how such projects were part of a growing store of administrative experience too, as the political, legal and financial mechanics of public–private redevelopment were elaborated through these important examples. At the turn of the 1960s, as the finishing touches were being applied to Shipley's new town centre, the momentum that had been building across both the private development sector and the public managers of the post-war city exploded into a profusion of large-scale redevelopment proposals for towns and cities all over the country. Surveying this remarkable nation-wide surge in urban redevelopment is near impossible, bubbling up as it did in so many different places in the same moment, but the fundamental mechanism – public land supply for private redevelopment – remained the same. In the Welsh city of Newport, the developer Central & District announced 'the largest commercial development in the town's history' in January 1961. This took the form of an eighteen-storey, £600,000 shopping and office block – slick, modern, centrally sited and built on a site leased from the Corporation for a ninety-nine-year period.[22] In the nearby Welsh capital of Cardiff, the central commercial area of The Hayes was also being redeveloped with new shopping facilities on a grand scale by an alliance of the Corporation and the Capital & Counties property company. Just as in Newport, this 'fine example of co-operation between a Local Authority and a private developer' saw the city furnishing the developer with some of the most valuable land in the city on a ninety-nine-year lease, to be rebuilt with new shopping facilities in a slick modern style.[23]

In the south of England, the Kent coastal town of Margate was being redeveloped with a pedestrianised shopping precinct 'by a partnership of Margate Town Council and the Second Covent Garden Property Company'.[24] This company was another important property developer of the era, and at the start of 1961 Second Covent Garden Property had shopping developments completed or in progress at Wakefield, Southampton, Newport, Swindon, Christchurch, Walsall, Cleckheaton, Flint, Wokingham, Ilford, St. Helens, Strood and Shrewsbury.[25] Another

[22] '£600,000 Plan in Newport', *The Financial Times*, 11 January 1961, 13.
[23] 'Capital & Counties Property Company', *The Property Developer* (The Property Council: 1964), 70. Available at the British Library.
[24] 'New Town Centre', *Daily Mail*, 10 October 1963, 7.
[25] 'Second Covent Garden Property', *The Economist*, 21 January 1961, 299.

firm that was active at this time, the Shop Constructions Group, got its first public–private redevelopment work at Harlow New Town where it built a large chunk of the pedestrianised shopping centre. By the early 1960s the Shop Constructions Group had built shopping developments on sites leased from local authorities at Bristol, Birmingham, Manchester, Liverpool, Canterbury, Portsmouth, Coventry, Hastings, Brighton and Ashford.[26] In the city of Leeds, Corporation records show that by 1960 the city engineer had entered into numerous similar agreements with various development companies to provide land in the city centre on favourable long-term leases for shopping and office developments.[27] And, not content with its efforts at Shipley, the energetic Arndale company had completed more than twenty five public–private town centre developments across England and Scotland by the mid-1960s, although its activities continued to be focused mainly in the English North.[28]

In the Midlands town of Solihull, a complex legal and financial partnership between Solihull Corporation and the Norwich Union Insurance Society was responsible for a complete remodelling of the town centre in the early 1960s. Here the Corporation declared a huge, 12.5-acre swathe of Solihull town centre ripe for comprehensive redevelopment and secured compulsory purchase powers over the whole area. This vast slice of prime town centre real estate was delivered to the insurance company on a 125-year ground lease, to be redeveloped with one hundred new shops, ninety flats, a large department store, office block and the obligatory multi-storey car park and spacious new access roads. As in many other places, Solihull's reinvention was bound up with a publicly funded overhaul of the town's road network and an enthusiastic embrace of urban automobility. All the new flats would have garages, every shop would be motor accessible, and the multi-storey car park would give direct, undercover access to the new shopping area. Promotional materials enthusiastically explained that there would be 1,300 parking spaces 'within 200 yards of the central square', where 'careful landscaping, planting, turfing, choice of paving materials, layout of pools and fountains, and the careful design and positioning of street lighting and furniture' would complete the new town centre.[29] The direct involvement of

[26] 'Local Authorities and Private Enterprise', *The Property Developer* (The Property Council: 1964), 170.
[27] Letter from Town Clerk of Leeds to Town Clerk of Bury St. Edmunds, 'Town Centre Redevelopment', 13 January 1960. Available at WYAS (LCC-LLD1/2/816152).
[28] 'The Arndale Property Trust Limited', *The Property Developer* (The Property Council: 1964), 180.
[29] 'The Central Development Scheme for Solihull', *The Property Developer* (The Property Council: 1964), 171; 'Company may develop central Solihull', *The Birmingham Post*, 21 September 1962, 9.

the Norwich Union as developers in their own right in Solihull was a further indication of how deeply entangled the worlds of property and finance had become by the early 1960s. The financial set-up, which saw Solihull Corporation taking a direct equity stake in this commercial redevelopment while also overseeing it as the legal planning authority, was an indication of the depth of entanglement between the business of property and the business of municipal administration.

As the examples above make clear, this wave of large-scale redevelopment activity was by no means confined to the most important urban centres, but rather saw expensive new forms of commercial development springing up in town centres all over the country, large and small. The most elaborate projects, though, were taking shape in the nation's principal cities. Here, local authorities were working busily with developers to install mammoth new commercial complexes on an altogether different scale. A flurry of massive, centrally located and council-sponsored shopping centres opened in major cities in the decade or so from the mid-1960s to the mid-1970s, with large developments planted in Leeds, Birmingham, London's Elephant & Castle, Croydon, Liverpool, Nottingham, Portsmouth, Luton, Wandsworth, Manchester, Newcastle and Brent Cross. These new centres provided hundreds of new shops within fully enclosed US-style shopping malls, serviced by new central area road layouts and massive multi-storey parking facilities that were increasingly built to accommodate thousands of cars. Alongside shops, the new complexes included a wide range of additional commercial leisure facilities – restaurants, pubs, cafes, bowling alleys, ballrooms and nightclubs – and were often integrated with ancillary developments of hotels, office blocks, public transport hubs and in some cases housing. These were the mega, modernist, multi-functional ensembles that local authority planners hoped would solve a tricky tangle of urban problems in one fell swoop – regulating traffic flows, rationalising central area land use, boosting local economies and revitalising the city all at the same time.

One of the first such projects to be completed was Birmingham's Bull Ring Centre, which was formally opened in a ceremony presided over by Prince Philip on 29 May 1964. This complex infrastructural ensemble saw four acres of the city's traditional market district completely remodelled as 'a multi-level shopping "town" [providing] 23 acres of floor space with every modern amenity for the shopping family'; 'the most advanced shopping centre of its kind in the World', as the promotional puff pieces explained. Birmingham's new consumer paradise was to 'herald the dawn of a new era for British shoppers', with 140 new shops, the largest Woolworths in Europe, supermarkets, restaurants, coffee bars, pubs and a Mecca Banqueting Hall seating 2,000 punters. 'Once you're in', an enthusiastic British Pathé newsreel explained, 'you stay under cover all the time', while 'oil-fired central heating and air conditioning maintains a pleasant, late-spring atmosphere all year round'.[30] Birmingham Corporation put this project out to competitive tender in 1959 and selected the large construction and engineering group Laings to redevelop the site, which was provided as ever on a generous and secure long-term ground lease. The choice of Laings – which had lots of experience building motorways and large civil engineering projects in Britain and beyond – corresponded with the engineering-led vision of planning that predominated in post-war Birmingham. The Bull Ring complex was carefully organised around a motorway-scale section of Birmingham's new inner ring road (Figure 3.4); this was a major developmental priority in 'Britain's premier motor city'.[31] The technological and cultural allure of modern automobility was hardwired into the Bull Ring, with Pathé's newsreel lingering over shots of cars streaming into the complex and of the operation of the bizarre 'Pearce Autopark' system by which customers' cars were driven onto trolleys and wheeled manually into parking spaces.

The whole complex was feted for its technological novelty and ingenious engineering, with press reports highlighting the centre's forty (count them) escalators, twenty lifts and behind-the-scenes infrastructure of underground service roads, electricity sub-stations, plant rooms and boiler houses. Indeed, Laing announced that it would be appointing a 'resident chief engineer' for the shopping complex whose duties would include 'responsibility for the operation of all electrical and mechanical services' and 'the accurate reading of instruments'. In this moment of breezy technocratic enthusiasm it was even felt possible to bring the complex social domain of shopping under the purview of the omniscient engineer. Laing suggested that 'one of the most important duties' of its resident engineer would be 'the keeping of operational data and consumption records' for this shopping facility which was 'of a size and nature [that was] something new to the UK'.[32] The consumer economy was thus to be measured, managed and manipulated alongside cities' physical infrastructure and environment. Grandiose, high-tech and hyper-modern developments such as this were the stuff of dreams for

---

[30] British Pathé, 'Bull Ring Centre Opened', newsreel, 4 June 1964; 'Birmingham Bull Ring', *The Property Developer* (The Property Council: 1964), 141; 'A New Bull Ring Centre', *The Guardian*, 28 January 1963, 12; 'New Bull Ring Centre Development Birmingham', *The Financial Times*, 9 February 1960, 7; 'Laing News', *The Financial Times*, 30 January 1962, 5.
[31] Simon Gunn, 'Ring Road: Birmingham and the Collapse of the Motor City Ideal in 1970s Britain', *The Historical Journal* 61:1 (2018), 227–248.
[32] 'Engineer for Manchester [sic] Bull Ring Site', *The Financial Times*, 17 May 1962, 10.

Figure 3.4 1962 image showing Birmingham's Bull Ring complex at an advanced stage of construction. The new complex is framed by the church spire on the left and the sweep of Birmingham's new motorway-grade ring road on the right. The scale of urban re-engineering involved in this massive scheme, and the close integration with major new road-building in particular, is clearly evident. Source: Historic England Archive, John Laing Photographic Collection.

civic boosters in big, competitive urban authorities like Birmingham. The Corporation Information Department's *This is Birmingham* – a late-1960s promotional booklet – crowed that 'the modern city' was 'fast becoming transformed beyond all recognition'. The Bull Ring had been 'entirely reconstructed on a scale and to standards unrivalled in all Europe'; 'the inhabitants and visitors alike are amazed'; and 'customers . . . come from many miles around for the luxury of a day's shopping in Birmingham'.[33]

Despite their deeply commercial nature, such developments were able to intersect with the aims and aspirations of post-war town planning,

---

[33] City of Birmingham Information Department, *This is Birmingham*, city brochure, late-1960s. Author's collection.

particularly around the central issue of traffic which so exercised urban planners across the 1950s and 1960s as car-ownership exploded.[34] Until the mid-1970s urban planners imagined that they could solve the problems of congestion and ever-increasing car use through the provision of new motor infrastructures on a grand scale. Thus, from the town planning point of view, the new urban motorways and massive parking facilities which large shopping complexes entailed were just what was needed to keep the city moving. Another major appeal for planners was the new shopping complexes' segregation of different forms and flows of traffic. Physically separating pedestrians from vehicles had been a preoccupation of traffic planners since the 1940s, and this ambition was given a dramatic, modernist shot in the arm when the landmark Buchanan Report, *Traffic in Towns*, was published in 1963. Buchanan envisaged large-scale infrastructural reorganisation in cities to accommodate the motor revolution and offered alluring visual imagery of multilevel transport architectures in which pedestrians strolled along capacious walkways while fast-flowing streams of traffic whizzed by below them. In practice, urban authorities were never granted the powers or resources that would have been necessary to build such elaborate infrastructures of mobility within cities. As a result, it was the commercially orchestrated shopping complexes which brought planners closest to fulfilling their fantasies of free-flowing circulation, multimodal transport infrastructures, and the complete separation of pedestrians and vehicles.

Developers played heavily upon these aspirations in their pitches to local authorities, stressing how far their commercial endeavours were matched to public planning aims. In central Nottingham, two enormous centres opened within two years of each other in the early 1970s. The first – the fourteen-acre Victoria Centre – was built around the city's disused Victoria Station and opened in 1973. Like many such projects, this complex provided a new home for the city's traditional market, while also installing more than one hundred new shops, along with cafes, pubs, bookmakers and a bingo hall.[35] The developer behind this project – Capital & Counties – emphasised that:

The Victoria Centre has been planned to fit into the demands of the motor age . . . . Car parking for 1,750 cars – to be increased eventually to 3,000; 20 bus routes . . . give direct access to the Centre . . . and a fully covered Corporation bus station at first-floor level with 50 stands, connected directly to the shopping

[34] Simon Gunn, 'The Buchanan Report, Environment and the Problem of Traffic in 1960s Britain', *Twentieth Century British History* 22:4 (2011), 521–542.
[35] Eric Bradshaw & Tom Allan, 'England's Halfway House', *The Guardian*, 23 November 1970, 12.

Figure 3.5 Aerial photograph showing Nottingham's Broadmarsh complex, completed in 1975, and the complete overhaul of the central area transport and infrastructure this entailed. The massive multi-storey parking facility can be seen in centre, surrounded by motorway-grade roads, and housing a new city bus station. High-level walkways link the parking facility with the shopping centre itself, on the right. Source: Getty Image.

mall – all these will be part of the Centre's contribution to the free-flow of the city's traffic in the 70's.[36]

In 1975 another facility, the Broadmarsh Centre, opened at the opposite end of Nottingham's main shopping district. This complex had a similar offering – more than one hundred new shops, cafes, offices, a new bus station, and parking for over 1,600 cars in two multi-storey car parks. The Broadmarsh Centre was also served by a major new urban motorway – 'Maid Marian Way' – which cut a swathe through the city towards the shopping centre (Figure 3.5).[37] The architect responsible for this scheme told a 1970 public inquiry that 'the whole scheme was based around extremely close integration with the city's traffic planning and comprehensive objectives'. Similar appeals were made through

---

[36] Capital & Counties Ltd., 'Victoria Centre Nottingham Takes Shape' (1969), development prospectus. Available at Nottinghamshire Archives.
[37] Town & City Properties Limited, *Arndale Covered Centres* (1973), company brochure. Available at Greater Manchester County Record Office.

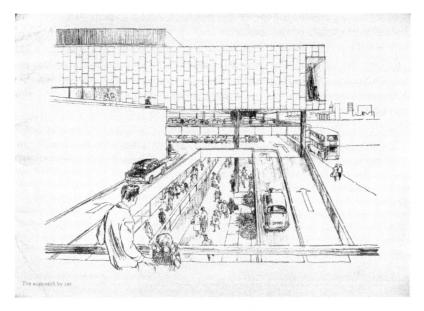

Figure 3.6 'The approach by car'. 1968 sketch of Liverpool St. John's Precinct's access and traffic systems, showing cars accessing an elevated car park via ramps over streets and pedestrian spaces below. A safely segregated pedestrian father looks on with his daughter. The commercial complexes of the renewal era offered planners their best hope of installing the elaborate, multilevel and multimodal traffic infrastructures which Buchanan had envisaged. Source: Liverpool Record Office.

alluring sketches and visualisations which appeared in developers' glossy prospectuses. These showed slick and smoothly functioning split-level traffic infrastructures, and lingered over the relaxed, leisurely and safe experience which awaited the wandering pedestrian in the new mall concourses (Figure 3.6). Most important of all, as development companies constantly underlined, the enclosed malls and internal concourses of the shopping centre achieved that 'complete segregation of pedestrians and traffic' which was the post-war transport planner's Holy Grail.[38]

These major new urban shopping complexes were thus intimately bound up with mass motorisation. Such projects intersected with planners' efforts

---

[38] Quotations in 'Inspector's Report on Public Inquiry into Broadmarsh Centre' (1970), 23. Nottinghamshire Archives [DD/1051/18].

to reorganise cities for the motor age but they were also firmly aligned with the cultural cachet of the motorcar, which served as a potent symbol of individual prestige and societal abundance. Being able to drive one's car right into the new facilities was a key selling point and promotional materials celebrated the ease, prestige and convenience of shopping by car. Without fail, press reports and promotional literatures (the two were not always easily distinguishable) trumpeted figures for the numbers of cars which could be accommodated in new multi-storey and rooftop car parks (Figure 3.7). Designers engaged in an inter-city arms race to provide the most parking and thereby attract the most 'car-shoppers' (this term entered

Figure 3.7 1966 image of the large multi-storey car park installed as part of Leeds's Merrion Centre complex, built to accommodate over 1,000 cars. An entrance to the shopping centre can also be seen, along with signs to the ten-pin bowling centre and the Merrion Hotel – an indication of the mix of facilities on offer in these new commercial complexes. The curiously shaped building in left of shot was a public house, the General Wade. Massive parking facilities like this were judged essential to the commercial viability of new centres but – in contrast to the bright and cheery depictions in artists' impressions – they often planted dreary, monolithic structures in key urban sites. Source: Leeds Libraries.

the lexicon of the traffic planner in the 1960s).[39] Once open, centres regularly hosted car shows within the spacious new concourses such as the Bull Ring's 'Triumph Week' in May 1966 when visitors could 'see the complete range of TRIUMPH cars on display' inside the mall.[40] These connections were partly about image but also importantly about business; attracting the relatively wealthy 'motorist shopper' from a wide catchment area was critical to the commercial viability of these extravagant new centres. This was readily acknowledged by both the public and the private managers of the post-war city. In the town of Stretford, within the Greater Manchester conurbation, the Arndale company was working closely with the local authority in the early 1960s to install one of its covered shopping malls at the heart of the town. This project involved the demolition of hundreds of terraced houses and the displacement of thousands of town centre residents. Yet, in reviewing the scheme, the Ministry of Housing and Local Government urged Stretford to ditch its allocations of land for rehousing 'in favour of car parking'. The council was reminded by the Ministry's planning advisors that 'the only basis upon which Stretford's trade could be expected to expand (and pay the new rents) was that car owners would be attracted'.[41] The business imperatives of this commercial retail development were to trump the needs of Stretford's displaced residents.

Despite this firm emphasis upon the wealthy and mobile 'car-shopper', mass motorisation remained far from complete in the post-war decades. Indeed, *not* owning a car remained the norm for urban households until the late 1960s and levels of car ownership were strongly shaped by social class, city and region. The biggest disparity by far lay between genders, so that while the majority of shoppers were women managing households, this group was also least likely to have access to a car.[42] It was thus also vital to establish the new shopping facilities as central nodes within urban and regional public transport systems. Integrating large new city bus stations into central area shopping complexes was common practice. The new bus station underneath Birmingham's Bull Ring centre could, it was reported, 'handle 10,000 buses a week'. London's Elephant and

---

[39] See, for example, Leeds City Council, 'Seacroft Town Centre', development prospectus, (c.1965). Available at West Yorkshire Archive Service [WYAS-LLD1/2/824956]. The term 'motorist shopper' was also used by planners, for example Manchester's Chief Planner, J.S. Millar, in *City and County Borough of Manchester: City Centre Map 1967*, 16. Available at GMCRO.

[40] 'It's a week of Triumph', *The Birmingham Post*, 12 May 1966.

[41] 'Stretford Municipal Borough: Central Area Redevelopment', notes of a meeting, 3 December 1962, 2. TNA-HLG-79/1404.

[42] Simon Gunn, 'People and the Car: the Expansion of Automobility in Urban Britain, c.1955-1970', *Social History* 38:2 (2013), 220–237, 228.

Castle complex was a 'focal point' for dozens of London bus routes with 'up to 500 buses per hour during peak periods', while in Leeds, the city's bus routes were reorganised around the new Merrion Centre at the behest of the centre's operating company. Following an agreement between the council and the Merrion's operators, passengers on Leeds Corporation buses in the mid-1960s would also have found the injunction to 'Shop at the Merrion Centre' printed on the back of their bus ticket. Rail links were also important in some cases. The Bull Ring Centre, Elephant and Castle and Liverpool's St. John's Precinct all enjoyed direct access to adjacent railway stations, while in central Manchester, the city's mammoth Arndale Centre was designed around a dedicated tube station, although in the end Manchester's long-hoped-for underground rail link failed to materialise.[43]

Beyond these preoccupations with traffic planning and new infrastructures of mobility, the very idea of 'comprehensive' urban remodelling held a powerful, atavistic appeal for the planners, architects and engineers who staffed city planning departments. In a superficial sense comprehensive development was a much-used professional buzzword and part of the legalistic terminology of planning. Yet the concept also spoke powerfully to deeper urges within the professional urban technocrat. It captured the sense that, if only a sufficiently panoramic and informed perspective were adopted, complex, multiple and interlocking social and spatial problems could be grasped, grappled with and resolved through precise expert interventions – usually by constructing similarly complex and interlocking urban infrastructural systems. The 1960s were a high moment of technocratic faith and fervour, and this was reflected in the sacrosanct, almost ritualistic way in which the language of 'comprehensive' planning was invoked at public inquiries and in professional literatures. The leading planner Wilfred Burns wrote in his 1967 plan for Newcastle (a document which he liberally peppered with biblical and literary quotations, with a predilection for the Old Testament) that 'town Planning ... has come to its prime in comprehensiveness'.[44] To proceed 'comprehensively' also meant – finally, for long-frustrated planning professionals – to adopt a bolder, more expansive approach to rebuilding, in which the long-standing British antipathy to strong positive planning and the

---

[43] These details in: British Pathé, 'Bull Ring Centre Opened', newsreel, 4 June 1964; T.W. Hearn, 'Glamour and Versatility', *The Guardian*, 9 September 1964, 21; Letter from Town Centre Securities Limited to Deputy Town Clerk of Leeds, 24 November 1966 [WYAS-LLD1/2/833178]; H.A.N. Brockman, 'St. George's Hotel Liverpool and the St. John's Precinct', *The Financial Times*, 10 April 1972, 32; 'Pic-Vic Line: Dig It?', *Manchester Evening News*, 21 May 1974, 13.

[44] Wilfred Burns, *Newcastle: A Study in Replanning at Newcastle upon Tyne* (London: Leonard Hill, 1967), 87.

expropriations this entailed might be overcome. Manchester's planning department, for example, when justifying Arndale's radical overhaul of its central shopping district in the 1960s, argued that 'the traditional shopping centre . . . is seriously in need of renewal and the poor quality of most of the existing buildings means that comprehensive redevelopment with severe "surgical" treatment, rather than improved or piecemeal development, is necessary'.[45] *Tabula rasa*, at last.

Where's Britain's Most Modern Shopping Centre?

The notion of 'comprehensive redevelopment' thus held a powerful allure for public planners, and captured a set of technocratic aspirations which could apparently be pursued in collaboration with the commercial property companies that were pushing large-scale retail development schemes. Even more than the idea of 'the comprehensive' though, it was the ubiquitous rhetoric of 'the modern' which provided a banner under which the seemingly disparate interests of professional planners, local authorities and commercial property developers could unite. The late 1950s and early 1960s were an age of gushing, often naïve enthusiasm for the rhetoric of 'the modern' and the idea of 'modernisation'.[46] Languages of modernisation, progress and of scientific and technological advance were all-pervasive. So too was an almost absurd fetishisation of technological novelty, as new machines, new buildings and infrastructures and new technical capacities were greeted breathlessly as markers of human ingenuity and achievement.[47] Underpinning all of this was the dramatic economic and industrial take-off that much of the world was experiencing in the post-war decades, which was conceptualised explicitly in terms of 'modernisation'. Britain's own economic 'take-off' in this period was more modest than that of many of its European neighbours – the easy developmental wins of industrialisation and urbanisation had been banked by Britain long before – and this issue festered into a knot of declinist angst as the 1960s wore on.[48] Yet, certainly in the earlier post-war period,

---

[45] City of Manchester Corporation & Town and City Properties Ltd., 'Manchester Market Street central area redevelopment scheme', development prospectus, c. 1966. Author's collection.

[46] See David Kynaston, *Modernity Britain: A Shake of the Dice, 1959–62* (London: Bloomsbury, 2014), 278; Becky Conekin, Frank Mort & Chris Waters (eds.), *Moments of Modernity: Reconstructing Britain 1945–1964* (London: Rivers Oram, 1999).

[47] For a scathing account of the 'reheated futurism' of this era see David Edgerton, *The Shock of the Old: Technology and Global History since 1900* (London: Profile Books, 2006).

[48] For European comparisons of economic performance see Tony Judt, *Postwar: A History of Europe since 1945* (London: Vintage, 2010), 324–330. On declinism in Britain: David Edgerton, *The Rise and Fall of the British Nation: A Twentieth-Century History* (London: Allen Lane, 2018); Jim Tomlinson, *The Politics of Decline: Understanding Post-war Britain* (Harlow: Longman, 2000).

Britons could quite reasonably feel themselves to be on an exciting upward trajectory and mass affluence – as both a structural economic reality and a powerful trope of rapid social and cultural change – was fundamental to this sense of 'becoming modern'. The new shopping complexes appealed to modernising impulses on multiple registers: as high-tech urban infrastructures, as markers of social and economic progress and, most importantly, as key sites within the exciting new commercial and cultural worlds of affluent consumerism.

Modernity and modernisation are of course extremely slippery terms, well capable of carrying a wide range of meanings for both post-war historical actors and present-day scholars. There is no intention here to engage with meta-historical questions about the essential nature of modernity, or to seek out an abstract and generalizable process of *modernisation*.[49] Rather, such terminologies were important because they featured so prominently in contemporary narrations of social change. It was because contemporaries invested so heavily in the *idea* of the modern – lending it cultural allure and rhetorical authority – that the discourse became a significant historical force in its own right. This was particularly the case when it came to urban transformation where, as Simon Gunn has noted, the post-war urban renewal programmes were guided by 'the belief in the modern as the guarantor of efficiency, progress, and human satisfaction'.[50] Indeed, what is striking about the way the rhetoric of modernisation functioned in post-war urbanism is how uncritical and unquestioning that belief often was. The language of the modern was often simply invoked, without definition or explanation, and could be applied to an almost limitless range of enterprises; these were then constructed – discursively at least – as uncontroversial, inevitable and universally desirable. The woolliness and imprecision of modernising rhetoric was precisely its value, politically and instrumentally, when it came to yoking together the disparate aims of planners, property developers and local authorities.

New shopping developments were relentlessly presented in terms of their modernity, but such language carried different inflections of

---

[49] For texts that wrestle with this question for the period, see Becky Conekin, Frank Mort & Chris Waters (eds.), *Moments of Modernity: Reconstructing Britain 1945–1964* (London: Rivers Oram, 1999); M. J. Daunton & Bernhard Rieger (eds.), *Meanings of Modernity: Britain from the Late-Victorian Era to World War II* (Oxford: Berg, 2001); David Gilbert, David Matless & Brian Short (eds.), *Geographies of British Modernity: Space and Society in the Twentieth Century* (Oxford: Blackwell, 2003); and, more generally, James C. Scott, *Seeing Like a State: How Certain Schemes to Improve the Human Condition Have Failed* (New Haven: Yale University Press, 1998).

[50] Simon Gunn, 'The Rise and Fall of British Urban Modernism: Planning Bradford, circa 1945-1970', *Journal of British Studies* 49:4 (2010), 849–869, 852.

meaning according to who was speaking. For local planning officials, the modern-ness of new shop developments was usually felt to lie not just in their satisfaction of the new demands of a mass-consuming citizenry, but also in their careful integration with a wider set of technocratic planning aims. Thus, Nottingham's City Estates Surveyor told the 1970 public inquiry into the city's Broadmarsh Shopping Centre that:

> The shopping complex being developed on the site would be one of the most modern redevelopment schemes in the country. It was now considered essential to have pleasant shopping conditions with an absence of vehicular traffic, adequate facilities for car parking and passenger service vehicles and strong pedestrian flows.[51]

Within the many boosterist journalistic accounts which circulated, it was often the modish designs and technological novelty of new shopping facilities which formed much of their modernising appeal. Journalists raved over the futuristic spaces of the shopping mall, emphasising the presence of exciting new technologies such as escalators, air conditioning and automatic sliding "air doors".[52] A *Guardian* reporter described the 'modern scheme' of Leeds's Merrion Centre, with its pedestrianised concourses and sixty-five-foot "Speed-walk" escalator, as 'almost exhilarating' (Figure 3.8).[53] The *Manchester Evening News* presented that city's proposals for its new shopping district in similar terms, describing the 'super-plan [for] covered air-conditioned pedestrian malls' as a 'futuristic picture ... of Manchester's main shopping area'.[54] Another report in the same newspaper highlighted the 'escalators and lifts connecting the various shopping levels' within this 'ultra-modern shopping and office centre'.[55] 'Ultra-modern' was one breezy superlative which cropped up repeatedly.

The architecture and imagery of Liverpool's St. John's Precinct, with its space-age 'modern observation tower', underscores how far the allure of new shopping complexes was also bound up with the self-conscious deployment of modernist design aesthetics. The St. John's Precinct was another venture from the enterprising Ravenseft company, and it marked the firm's first foray into comprehensive redevelopment in a major urban centre after it had played such a prominent role in blitzed cities and New Towns across the 1950s. The agreement for this scheme was struck with Liverpool Corporation in the high moment of renewal fervour in 1961,

[51] 'Inspector's Report on Public Inquiry into Broadmarsh Centre' (1970), 13. Nottinghamshire Archives [DD/1051/18].
[52] 'New Store in The Strand', *The Financial Times*, 25 July 1956, 11.
[53] Michael Denny, 'Leeds '84', *The Guardian*, 16 April 1964, 6.
[54] 'Super-plan may transform heart of the city', *Manchester Evening News*, 18 June 1968.
[55] 'Olde tyme touch for new-look city', *Manchester Evening News*, 19 June 1968.

Figure 3.8 1967 image of one of the sloping access ramps into Leeds
Merrion Centre, with an external escalator described as 'exhilarating' by
one journalist. New technical design features like this were an important
part of the malls' modernising, high-tech appeal, although they often
misfired. The Merrion's external escalators fared badly in the rainy West
Yorkshire climate and fell into disrepair. Source: Leeds Libraries.

and the project revolved around a complete overhaul of the city's traditional market district which linked the existing shopping area with the
civic quarter around St. George's Hall and Lime Street Station. The
reinvention of this rather down-at-heel trading district was to be 'one of
the largest comprehensive shopping developments ever created in
Britain', installing a multilevel enclosed shopping mall, a new retail
market for the Corporation, a luxury hotel with over 160 rooms, pubs
and restaurants and a large 2,000-capacity 'Ballroom Suite' built for the
Rank Organisation. Naturally the project incorporated the latest transport planning and building technologies, with 'motor traffic ... excluded
from the shopping areas'; 'automatically temperature-controlled' malls
and 'escalators [to] convey shoppers to the new high level market'.[56]
Ravenseft were explicit about their modernising intent; 'the development
was of particular interest', one director told the press, 'because of its

[56] Ravenseft Properties Limited, 'Liverpool St John's Precinct' (1968), development prospectus. Available at Liverpool City Archive.

Figure 3.9 Image showing the architectural modernism on offer at the St. John's Precinct in central Liverpool, in particular the striking observation tower complete with revolving restaurant. This project was undertaken by the firm Ravenseft Properties Limited and opened in 1969. Source: Liverpool Record Office.

modern conception'.[57] The new shopping, leisure and hotel complex was crowned by a slender, 400-foot high, observation tower – St. John's Beacon – which was designed to 'dominate Liverpool's entire central area' as 'one of its most spectacular architectural features'. This futuristic facility housed a revolving restaurant, bar and observation deck, all 'suspended on a pencil-like circular concrete shaft [and] served by high-speed lifts from the street level' (Figure 3.9). 'When illuminated after dark', the developer's publicity explained, this spectacular addition to Liverpool's landscape 'appears to float in the night sky'.[58]

In remaking the post-war city, modernising rhetoric was reinforced through alignment with architectural and aesthetic modern*ism*, which furnished a voguish repertoire of images and built forms through which 'the modern' could be conjured up and pursued. This was not necessarily a form of architectural modernism which could find much favour among

[57] 'New Heart for Liverpool', *The Guardian*, 27 May 1961, 2.
[58] Ravenseft Properties Limited, 'Liverpool St John's Precinct'.

the high-minded luminaries of the modernist movement; the commercialist parameters of British urban renewal largely precluded that. It was
rather, as Otto Saumarez Smith puts it, 'a gimcrack modernism . . . which
was the product of public-private partnership and often designed by
anonymous firms'. Or, in Simon Gunn's terms, a 'banal urban
modernism . . . diluted and vulgarized'. Amy Thomas has also written
incisively of the disdain and disregard shown for such post-war commercial building work from 'the architectural establishment'.[59] The architectural critic Ian Nairn, for example, dismissed Leeds's Merrion Centre as
a 'concrete desert' and 'a sad collection of old rope'.[60] For the true
believers in modernism's social promise, who envisaged a project of
urban reform which was at once aesthetic, environmental and social,
the modernisation of the post-war city was supposed to encompass far
more than the erection of a few shopping centres. As in Graeme
Shankland's 1965 vision for Liverpool, or Wilfred Burns's 1967 plan for
Newcastle upon Tyne, the ambition was to use modernist planning to
build a more equitable and enriching future. Burns wrote (under the
heading 'A Plan for All') that the comprehensive replanning of
Newcastle 'means looking at the problems of an area with a view to
satisfying the needs of people who are to live, work, or play in that area'.
Like Shankland, Burns's ambitions were deeply social and humane. 'The
central area', Burns stressed, should never be understood as 'just a place
for more shops, however well planned and beautifully detailed'. It was 'a
place for the parade, for stimulation, for excitement, for the religious
festivals, the teenage coffee shops and beat music, for the great symphony
concerts, and for making and exchanging money'.[61] For the radical
architect-planners who hoped to steer the course of urban renewal, the
modernisation of the post-war city was a totalising technocratic programme which, although it must include alluring new shops and commercial facilities, had its sights set upon a broader set of social and
spiritual aims.

The rhetorics and aesthetics of modernisation thus overlapped and
intersected with multiple intellectual projects and currents of change.
The modern-ness of the shopping centre could be located in its technical
sophistication as a piece of planned infrastructure; in its novel design, new
technologies and architectural aesthetics or indeed in its hoped-for position in the vanguard of a wider programme for urban social renewal.

[59] Saumarez Smith, *Boom Cities*, 2; Gunn, 'The Rise and Fall of Urban Modernism', 851;
Amy Thomas, 'Prejudice and Pragmatism: The Commercial Architect in the
Development of Postwar London', *Grey Room* 71 (2018), 88–115.
[60] Ian Nairn, 'Swimming in Style', *The Observer*, 25 February 1968, 27.
[61] Burns, *Newcastle*, 88.

Although these components of the mall's modernity likely held the most appeal for technocrats and reformist planners, they were overshadowed by a powerful set of commercial and cultural associations in which the modernity of the mall lay firmly in its character as a demotic site of affluent consumerism. Outside of the intellectualised sphere of planning policy debates, it was the capacity of new shopping developments to catapult cities and citizens into the enchantments of the consumer age which formed the cornerstone of their modernising appeal. This was a notion of social and cultural modernisation which was inextricable from mass affluence – rooted in the burgeoning commercial world of personal consumption, shopping, leisure and self-curation. To be modern in this formulation was to be young, fashionable, mobile and attuned to the new values and lifestyles of affluent consumerism. An advertisement for Leeds's Merrion Centre, which opened in 1964, captures this demotic and deeply commercial vision of affluent modernity well. The first page of this handbill flyer depicts a glamorous young woman, breathlessly enthusiastic, heavily laden shopping basket in hand, asking 'Where's Britain's Most Modern Shopping Centre?' Turning over the page reveals the demotic answer to this question: 'Bang in the Middle of Leeds'. On this page the female shopper appears again with a chicly dressed male partner. 'You're living only a few minutes away!' the ad screams, 'from the most modern Shopping Centre in Britain', with 'Everything you need!'; 'All shopping under cover'; 'No more aching feet'; 'No traffic'; 'Fine restaurants to choose from' and 'Entertainment too!'[62]

Other shopping centres were sold to the public via similar appeals to the unprecedented consumer abundance and excitement they offered, along with the voguish chic of their clientele. Nottingham's Victoria Centre, for example, offered 'a complete range of shops and stores under one roof to give the shopper freedom of choice over the widest range of goods', and would 'bring excitement and comfort to many thousands of shoppers every day'. As at Leeds's Merrion Centre, whether they were dating couples, young families or young women on shopping trips, visitors to the Victoria Centre were depicted as bright young things and always à la mode. It was the modern-ness of the new types of shopping and experience on offer in shopping centres, along with the fashionable consumer cultures with which they were aligned, which developers and operators appealed to when pitching their centres to the public. London's Elephant & Castle centre represented 'a completely new concept in modern day

---

[62] Advertisement for Merrion Centre, N.d. [c.1965]. Available at WYAS [LLD1/2/817111].

retail shopping', one booster explained, offering 'glamour and versatility'; 'the centre is planned to contain all the elements to satisfy the needs of even the most demanding shopper'.[63] Such appeals spoke directly to the post-war citizen-shopper and articulated a notion of the modern which was rooted in the burgeoning domain of affluent consumerism. Modernising a city, in this formulation, meant successfully aligning locales with the new cultures of affluence, consumption and leisure.

Peter Mandler has noted that the commercial character of town centre redevelopment across the 1950s and 1960s represented a 'different vision of modernity' to that articulated in the rationalist civic plans of the 1940s. The city of shopping centres, car parks and office blocks stood as a symbol of 'the modernity not of the expert but of the voter, the consumer, the worker'.[64] Selina Todd has gone further, casting the post-war reconstruction of the nation's town centres as a democratization of the city, in which there was a new sense that central areas should service the needs of 'ordinary working-class people'.[65] And yet, for all its demotic appeal, this populist, consumer-oriented vision of the urban modern was not defined or driven 'from below'. It was not the actual voters, consumers and workers of post-war Britain who crafted these images and environments but rather a new cadre of property entrepreneurs along with the commercial architects and retail managers they employed. For local authorities hoping to reinvent their towns as glamorous shopping destinations, the booming development industry seemed to be offering ready-made solutions. Developers were able to commandeer the rhetoric and aesthetics of the modern in order to insist upon their own vital role in satisfying the essential needs of a newly affluent, mass-consuming citizenry. Time and again development companies claimed in their public promotions and in their private overtures to local authorities that they alone possessed the requisite knowledge of the rapidly changing nature of 'modern shopping' and the new demands of the affluent citizen-shopper. It was companies like Town & City (Arndale's parent company from 1968) which, as they took care to remind councils, had their 'finger on the pulse of the market' and best understood the 'new style shopping' which the post-war citizen-shopper demanded.[66]

As well as laying claim to a privileged knowledge of the unfolding course of affluent modernity, developers were able to exploit the multiple

---

[63] T.W. Hearn, 'Glamour and Versatility', *The Guardian*, 9 September 1964, 21.

[64] Peter Mandler, 'New Towns for Old: The Fate of the Town Centre', in Becky Conekin, Frank Mort & Chris Waters (eds.), *Moments of Modernity: Reconstructing Britain 1945–1964* (London: Rivers Oram, 1999), 208–227, 209.

[65] Selina Todd, 'Phoenix Rising: Working-Class Life and Urban Reconstruction, c. 1945-1967', *Journal of British Studies* 54:3 (2015), 679–702.

[66] Town & City Properties Limited, *Arndale Covered Centres* (1973).

meanings of modernising rhetoric in support of their commercial endeavours. There was a clear technocratic and Taylorist appeal to developers' arguments about the 'outmoded' and 'inefficient' nature of existing shops and the purported technical imperatives of 'modern retailing', which went hand-in-hand with a more cultural appeal to the new norms and forms of mass affluence. At the same time, the alignment of shopping centres with notions of modernisation allowed such developments to be presented as natural, inevitable and uncontentious. The sense of inevitability which modernising rhetoric supplied was apparent within the testimony of the architect and planning consultant for Manchester's Arndale scheme, Lewis Womersley. Womersley told the 1968 public inquiry into the planning proposals that 'it is more than time that Manchester had a first-class modern shopping centre [and] this is the obvious site for it'.[67] The discourse of modernisation allowed controversial and highly sectional projects to be presented as eminently desirable, 'natural' and inherently progressive. The manager of Leeds's most elaborate new shopping development, the Merrion Centre, claimed that 'centres like ours ... are an important part of modern city shopping' in a special promotional supplement in the *Yorkshire Evening Post*. Here, again, the development was explained as 'a natural and logical extension of the [city's] existing shopping centre'.[68]

Yet there was little that could reasonably be understood as 'natural' about the creation of Leeds's biggest new shopping attraction. The Merrion Centre (Figure 3.10) included 'more than 100 shops, 120,000 square feet of office accommodation ... a bowling centre, a 1,000 seat cinema, a large Mecca ballroom, an 80 stall market hall, three night clubs, a 120 bedroom hotel and a multi-storey car park for 1,100 vehicles'.[69] This vast complex was built in a series of stages from the early 1960s to the early 1970s by the developer Town Centre Securities, which – unusually for the London-centric property business – was controlled by a prominent local businessman and civic benefactor Arnold Ziff. As in Shipley, the Merrion Centre was built on land that had been acquired and levelled by Leeds Corporation using slum clearance powers, but the site really lay outside of the central commercial core of the city, having formally been an inner-urban neighbourhood centred around Rockingham Street. Prior to its destruction by the Corporation of Leeds, the Rockingham Street district had contained a mass of small business of varying sorts along

---

[67] Womersley's statement to the inquiry was reported in Michael Morris, 'Pavement Cafes in Plan for Manchester', *The Guardian*, 20 June 1968, 20.
[68] 'Where you can go shopping in safety' & 'Stage five completes the super centre', advertising feature, *Yorkshire Evening Post*, 27 September 1973.
[69] Tom Allan, 'Millions Going North', *The Guardian*, 30 November 1972, 29.

Figure 3.10   The main frontage of Leeds's Merrion Centre, a vast urban complex built on the northern fringe of the existing commercial centre of the city. Despite its diverse mix of facilities, and the commercial fillip of being built on cheaply acquired slum clearance land, the Merrion Centre struggled consistently to perform as expected, causing serious problems for retailers, the operating company and the city council. Source: Leeds Libraries.

with a large residential population and numerous non-commercial premises such as clubs, a church and charitable alms houses. Shops, pubs and hotels mingled with printers, tailors, stonemasons, confectioners and many modest-sized engineering and manufacturing works, all interspersed within the rows of terraced housing typical of English industrial towns.[70] Using public planning powers to obliterate this mixed-use working neighbourhood and deliver it to a well-connected local businessman for redevelopment as a mammoth commercial complex is difficult to

---

[70] The Rockingham Street district was assiduously photographed by the city council in 1946, at the time of its designation as a slum clearance area. This photographic record can be seen on Leeds City Council's online image collection Leodis.net, and at Leeds Central Library. Discussion of the removal of the church and alms houses is contained within Leeds and District Chamber of Trade, 'The Maintenance of Leeds as the Regional Shopping Centre', 19 July 1955, WYAS-LCC-816152.

understand as a 'natural' process of urban redevelopment. Nor, as it turned out, was it particularly 'logical' as the unpopular Merrion Centre was dogged by dismal trading conditions and design criticisms from the moment it opened.

In an era when the state had assumed a heightened responsibility for citizens' welfare and well-being, developers' claims that their facilities would service the needs of the consuming citizen struck home powerfully. At a public inquiry into the installation of an Arndale mall in the Lancashire coastal town of Morecambe, the developer told the planning inspector that 'one of the most important aspects in the planning of new shopping centre developments is to ensure that the shopping housewife is protected so far as possible from the vagaries of the weather'.[71] Developers claimed repeatedly to be operating on behalf of the hard-pressed and windswept British housewife, arguing that the impetus for redevelopment came 'direct from the harassed housewife [who] demanded a more modern and convenient method of shopping'.[72] Nor was the development sector slow to realise the value in talking in terms of 'demand', which positioned them as essential partners if the post-war polity's promises of abundance and satisfaction for its mass-consuming citizenry were to be kept. It was, one company claimed, the 'increasing demand for easier shopping' which necessitated major retail development, and the new shopping centres were expressly designed 'to meet the inevitable ultimate increased demand'.[73] Councils were reminded wherever possible that it was developers' commercial 'know how' – their unique understanding of consumers' needs, of retail trends, of developments in the United States and elsewhere – which gave them a privileged insight into the demands and desires of the post-war citizen-shopper.[74]

Languages of consumer demand were wrapped up with claims about the welfare and comfort of the shopping housewife, and the supposedly urgent imperatives of 'the modern', to present the remodelling of cities' shopping districts as a duty incumbent upon local authorities. Arndale's chairman, Arnold Hagenbach, told his shareholders at the firm's 1964 annual general meeting that 'social betterment . . . must involve the modernisation of Town Centres all over the Country, where people can do their shopping and conduct their business under pleasant conditions of

---

[71] Lancashire County Council, 'Proof of evidence by Mr R D Longbottom', 1965, 3. TNA-HLG-79/1213.
[72] These claims come from a special promotional supplement in the *Bolton Evening News*, 29 September 1971, produced to publicise the opening of a new Arndale Shopping Centre in that year. Available at Bolton Archives History Centre, GB125.658.87.
[73] Town & City Properties Limited, *Arndale Covered Centres* (1973), 5.
[74] Arndale Property Trust, *Arndale in Partnership with Local Authorities* (1966).

safety and comfort'.[75] Similarly, Capital & Counties claimed that its Victoria Centre in Nottingham would 'make shopping convenient for the housewife and efficient for the trader'.[76] Yet there were always plenty of voices disputing these claims, and which had to be ignored and over-ridden for redevelopment to proceed. As the principal losers in the redevelopment process, it was smaller retailers who were generally the most vociferous objectors to schemes, often forming themselves into local traders' associations to organise against proposals. In Salford in 1960, an enormous £8 m redevelopment scheme was opposed by 'over 80 shop-keepers [who] have formed a traders' association [and] believe it will ruin their trade'.[77] In Morecambe opposition to redevelopment was led by the local Chamber of Trade and Ratepayers' Association. These bodies argued that traders would have to increase their turnover by 300 per cent in order to meet the costs of renting sites in Arndale's redeveloped centre, which was described as 'virtually impossible'. The joint Arndale-council scheme was 'of too grandiose a nature', and 'the rents would be so high that many local traders would be forced out of the central area and replaced by firms at present unconnected with the town'. In a direct counter to developers' claims to be servicing local shopping needs, one objector from the Chamber of Trade wrote that:

It should be realised that development companies are not interested in the provi-sion of shopping facilities in town centres other than in securing the maximum financial reward for their investments – the general effect of such development – to create that class of tenant having no direct interest in our town and thus traders who have created this shopping centre in Morecambe and given life and vitality to it and served the public over generations would be swept aside by the powerful Arndale Property Trust – seemingly with the connivance of the Local Authority and thrust out of business just because Development Companies find shops the most profitable prey in redevelopment schemes.[78]

The story was the same in Rochdale in the early 1970s, where a 'Market Hall Tenants Association' protested against a joint scheme between the council and the Laings development group. The secretary of this associa-tion wrote to the Ministry in defence of those who 'have been trading on this Market for many years' and were being sacrificed 'just to placate the large trading firms'. 'Surely', the correspondent concluded, 'we should be

[75] 'The Arndale Property Trust: Further Year of Steady Progress', *The Guardian*, 9 July 1964, 12.
[76] Capital & Counties Limited, 'Victoria Centre Nottingham' (1969), development pro-spectus. Available at Nottinghamshire Archives.
[77] 'Salford Approves Shops Plan', *The Financial Times*, 19 February 1960, 9.
[78] Letter of objection from chairman of Morecambe and Heysham Ratepayers Association, 1965. TNA-HLG-79/1213.

working for the good of the town and not the developers'.[79] Many citizens clearly agreed; a petition against the scheme signed by more than 18,000 people was presented to the 1967 public inquiry.[80] In this case even the government's own planning inspector could not agree that the redevelopment scheme was 'fully justified at this time'. The adjudicating inspector praised the town's existing 'attractive' shopping area with its 'narrow, winding and sloping streets ... and the variety and intimate character of what appear in most cases to be long-established relatively small shop and business premises'. Rochdale council, though, was unmoved, for while 'the Corporation fully appreciate[d] the effects on existing occupiers of the disturbance and increased rentals which will in most cases no doubt result', they were 'satisfied not only that the redevelopment is urgently necessary but that in the event it will prove a very sound investment for the town'.[81] This process was replicated in towns and cities up and down the country. A *Guardian* report of 1962 detailed 'complaints being made all over the country by local traders as the combination of municipal ambition and outside financial interest leads to the wholesale demolition and rebuilding of town centres'.[82] *The Financial Times* also acknowledged that 'there is little doubt that major redevelopment schemes work against the small trader'.[83]

It seems remarkable in retrospect that the public managers of post-war cities were so willing to sweep away hundreds of small businesses, and the local enterprise and employment that they represented. Yet attitudes towards small retailers were often dismissive and sometimes derisive. In Morecambe, the development proposals were blithely based upon the assumption that only a quarter of affected traders would be able to afford sites in the redeveloped centre and that 'half of those then left would find commercial premises elsewhere and the other half would go out of business altogether'.[84] In Stretford, Greater Manchester, where another Arndale shopping mall was on the way in the early 1960s, a local 'traders' protection society' tried to argue that they 'should be reaccommodated in new premises at "economic" rents until turnover justified an increase to

---

[79] See letter from Rochdale Market Hall Tenants' Association, 1 February 1972. TNA-HLG-79/1198.
[80] 'Protest over £3M Redevelopment', *The Guardian*, 13 July 1967, 3.
[81] Quotations from the Inspector's Report of Public Local Inquiry, held 11–12 July 1967. TNA-HLG-79/1198.
[82] 'Traders' Problems as Town Centres Change', *The Guardian*, 18 August 1962, 10. This report specifically documented traders' protests in Hyde (Greater Manchester), Birmingham, Bradford, Bolton and Swansea.
[83] 'Redevelopment Schemes: Is Compensation Enough?', *The Financial Times*, 14 June 1963, 15.
[84] Inspector's Report, 14 May 1965, 5. TNA-HLG-79/1213.

market value'. But there was little enthusiasm from central government for providing cut-price pitches or cheap market stalls which would eat into the profitability of the overall scheme:

I do not consider it worthwhile [one official wrote] There is no market now so traders would have to be displaced ones who cannot afford new shop rents and/or new-comers. The latter are often riff-raff and do the centre no good. The former would be just as well served in a small hall built very cheaply.[85]

The inclusion of small trader's halls 'built very cheaply' as part of new shopping developments became a familiar means of buying off at least some of this local opposition, but such facilities were generally uninviting and unsuccessful, and the rents in any case remained unaffordable for many existing traders. The modernisation of post-war cities may have been presented as an uncontroversial exercise in urban improvement, but this rather depended on one's perspective and position within the urban and economic structure.

Developmentalism against Decline

It might be thought fairly unsurprising that the vision of the modern city which was assembled and hawked by retail property developers was a deeply commercial and consumerist one. More noteworthy perhaps is the enthusiastic embrace of these models of the urban future by local authorities and their willingness to sweep away so much small-scale local economic activity in the process. Local authorities were desperate to position themselves as preeminent shopping and leisure destinations for the affluent age. In the parlance of the 1960s, this translated into claims to be the 'most modern', but the traditions of civic boosterism, municipal developmentalism and local growth promotion on which such efforts built stretched well back into the nineteenth century and beyond.[86] The voluminous municipal literatures of the post-war decades were evidence in themselves of local authorities' energetic boosterism, and included official guides, handbooks, visitor maps and pamphlets, prospectuses and commercial guides. Despite the more technocratic and social inflections which many planning professionals hoped to work into programmes of urban modernisation, when it came to marketing the modern city, local

[85] 'Stretford M.B. Central Area Redevelopment Note of a Meeting, 8th August, 1962', TNA-HLG-79/1404.
[86] Peter Shapely, 'Civic Pride and Redevelopment in the Post-war British City', *Urban History* 39:2 (2012), 310–328. On the interwar promotion of urban consumer offerings see Charlotte Wildman, *Urban Redevelopment and Modernity in Liverpool and Manchester, 1918–1939* (London: Bloomsbury, 2016).

authorities could be just as keen as their commercial partners to embrace a vision of the city remade for the affluent consumer. Birmingham's boosterist braggadocio over the Bull Ring has been seen already, and many other cities followed suit. The Corporation of Sheffield hired a public relations agency and established its own 'Publicity Department' in 1969 to lead the charge of rebranding the city as a shopping and leisure destination. The resulting 1970 *Sheffield Official Handbook* boasted that, in 'modern Sheffield', 'the central shopping facilities ... have been almost completely rebuilt in recent years'. The city could now claim 'more [department stores] than any city north of London', 'one of the most modern and spectacular [theatres] in Europe', 'two of the largest nightclubs in Europe' and 'the largest toyshop in Europe' (it is not clear who was providing accurate ranking data on the size of European toyshops – the 'biggest in Europe' claim cropped up so frequently it cannot have been correct). Sheffield's city fathers were especially proud of 'the spectacular Castle Square ... an outstanding feat of engineering [and] a fascinating underground shopping precinct'. This curious project 'served a triple purpose as vehicular roundabout, pedestrian underpass and subterranean shopping precinct' and was described by the Corporation as 'one of the main landmarks of the city centre' and 'a natural magnet for the visiting shopper'. In an indication of how far municipal entrepreneurship was being turned to the task of consumerist reinvention, Sheffield Corporation described its nearby Castle Market shopping complex as 'a daring and highly successful experiment in local government enterprise [where] from a vast array of attractive well-lit stalls, the shopper can buy anything from biscuits and shoe polish to flowers and tropical fish'. With such a wealth of consumer offerings, it was 'not surprising that Sheffield has become the natural shopping centre for a vast region'.[87]

Behind all the hyperbole and breezy superlatives, however, there were deep anxieties lurking. The authorities in many towns and cities were intensely aware of the developmental challenges posed by ongoing transformations in the country's economic and industrial structure, and the shifting geographies of wealth, employment and economic vitality which went along with them. The declining prospects of some of the traditional industrial sectors which had flourished in Britain in the nineteenth century – whose success had been the *raison d'être* for many towns and cities – were, quite understandably, viewed as an existential threat. Thus,

[87] Sheffield Corporation & Temple Publicity Services, *Sheffield Official Handbook* (1970), author's collection; Derek Brown, 'Sheffield Given a "Garden City" Look', *The Guardian*, 8 July 1970, 6.

for Bradford, previously the woollen textiles capital of Britain, narratives of retail-led reinvention were laced with doubt and desperation. The city's publicity could scarcely avoid acknowledging 'big changes' in the textile industry, and 'a certain amount of concentration', but clung to the idea that this spelt 'opportunity [which] had been grasped'. In Bradford as in so many other cities, grasping the opportunity meant massive rebuilding of its central core with major new retail and office development. 'A great deal has already been done to clear the City Centre of old and obsolete buildings and replace them by new modern attractive offices and shops.' Six million pounds had been spent, and, prospective investors were assured – with just a twinge of desperation – that 'thousands more people are now attracted to what is becoming a new regional shopping centre'.[88] Likewise, Sheffield's promotion of its 'spectacular' modern shopping facilities at the start of the 1970s was conducted against the background of rising unemployment and overdependence on the faltering local steel industry. The reinvention of cities around new forms of shopping and commercial leisure was thus a calculated developmental response to the looming threat of industrial decline in many locales. And, at a time of darkening economic prospects for many local authorities, public–private retail developments held the promise not just of 'more pleasant shopping facilities' but also 'enhanced rateable values or even a share of the profits' as a 1974 commentary in *The Times* acknowledged. Many councils, the author noted, 'were attracted by the prospect of securing the fattest ground rent'.[89]

Major cities like Sheffield could at least be sure that their sheer size would ensure them some sort of economic future. Some smaller towns in traditional industrial areas seemed already to be staring at the prospect of economic collapse and terminal decline as early as the 1950s. It was no coincidence that the mill towns of Lancashire and West Yorkshire – often heavily dependent on specific industries and even on individual works – were among the earliest and most ardent town centre developers. The Lancashire town of Blackburn pitched a massive central area redevelopment scheme to the Ministry as early as January 1952, covering 'the whole of the central shopping and market [sic], the principal business area, the main cinemas and theatres and the cathedral'.[90] In nearby Bolton, which

[88] *The City of Bradford Official Handbook* (London: Ed. J. Burrow) early 1970s. Author's collection.'.
[89] Michael Hanson, 'Local Authorities Join in Partnership Schemes', *The Times*, 23 April 1974, 12.; also Tom Allan, 'The knock it down and put up a precinct show', *The Guardian*, 22 October 1973, 19.
[90] 'Areas of Comprehensive Development', internal letter, 3 January 1952. TNA-HLG-71/2202.

had ended the nineteenth century as one of the most important centres for cotton spinning in the world, the middle decades of the twentieth century were a 'litany of industrial misery' that saw the collapse of traditional industries, consistently high unemployment and out-migration.[91] In the 1950s, Bolton became the first local authority in Britain to appoint its own 'industrial development officer' – the type of post more normally associated with late-century urban regeneration efforts – and in 1958, the town's leaders were already declaring that 'the time had come for the council to attract new industries by "selling" itself to big business interests'.[92] The 1960s saw Bolton Corporation embrace modern planning ideas and public–private town centre redevelopment, and an Arndale Shopping Centre was duly installed at the heart of the town in 1971. The new shopping centre would, the Corporation hoped, return 'industrial and commercial prosperity' to Bolton by making it 'the established regional centre for employment, shopping, and cultural and social activities [and] attracting people from surrounding districts'.[93] Redevelopment in such places was fundamentally about economic reinvention in the face of the long-term contraction of local industry, and these objectives had already acquired an existential urgency by the 1950s. Anxious aldermen in towns like Blackburn, Nelson, Rochdale and Bolton made easy pickings for developers promising brighter economic futures.

Many smaller towns in the south of England faced uncertain prospects too. Wilfred Burn's influential 1963 planning tract, *New Towns for Old*, was specifically an agenda for 'reviving' small country towns through redevelopment, informed by his time working for Surrey County Council. Burns lamented the steady leakage of population and economic activity away from 'decaying' county towns and towards the metropolis, with London's inexorable growth and economic magnetism identified as 'a problem of the very greatest importance'.[94] A government policy paper from a year earlier similarly worried about the fortunes of small country towns, struggling to compete with 'the much stronger pull of the growing regional centres', with 'the most modern and attractive shops'.[95] Such administrative concerns point to the firmly developmental objectives which governed the reorganisation of Britain's town centres in this period.

---

[91] Simon Winchester, 'Life on the dole', *The Guardian*, 21 May 1971, 13.
[92] 'Bolton apprehensive over unemployment', *The Manchester Guardian*, 6 November 1958, 14.
[93] Town & City Properties & Bolton Corporation, *The Arndale Centre Bolton* (1971), Bolton Local History Centre (henceforth BLHC).
[94] Wilfred Burns, *New Towns for Old: The Technique of Urban Renewal* (London: Leonard Hill, 1963), 5.
[95] 'Redevelopment of Shopping Centres: Small Country Towns', discussion paper, April 1962. TNA-HLG-136/88.

The large-scale retail developments which transformed cities in the 1960s and 1970s were principally acts of urban economic adaptation, as cities furiously attempted to re-fit their central areas to compete effectively under the new economic conditions of mass affluence. It was through successful positioning within an increasingly consumer-driven economy, rather than through dependence on mass manufacturing, that cities' economic future would be secured. And this was a competitive game, where failure to keep pace with rivals could spell long-term economic decline. Liverpool's 1965 *City Centre Plan* stated the position thus:

> Within the area lived in by shoppers who visit Liverpool is a wide range of smaller towns containing shops that compete vigorously to sell household goods of the durable kind. Chester, Birkenhead, Wigan, Southport, Warrington and St. Helens, and to a lesser extent Wallasey, Widnes, Ormskirk, Bootle, Crosby, Runcorn, Ellesmere Port, Prescot, Kirby and Huyton are all in this category, as are the major suburban centres of Liverpool itself. As the mobility of shoppers increases, competition between these towns will intensify, and many already have imaginative modernisation plans that will make it easier to shop in them by car.[96]

Liverpool's 1965 plan contained extensive statistical data and analysis relating to the city's performance as a shopping centre, and staked out an ambitious and expansionary programme for new retail development. 'Shops', the plan stated, 'have the highest rateable value of all land users' (in a clear indication of this essential fiscal contribution the plan highlighted the fact that shop property accounted for 38% of the central area's rateable value while occupying less than 10% of gross floor space). Liverpool's planners hoped that retail expansion would not only raise land values and tax revenues but also secure major new sources of employment. 'The proposed increase in shop space in the city centre' could, it was predicted, yield 'an increase in employment of from 19,000 full and part-time workers ... in 1961 to 20,500 by 1981'.[97] Shopping was rapidly becoming critical to cities' attempts to manage not only their revenues but their regional economic futures.

In Manchester too, the overwhelming concern for the planning authority was that the city 'retain its position as the premier shopping centre of the region'. Just as in Liverpool, neighbouring towns were eyed anxiously as rival poles of attraction, and the primary purpose of central area redevelopment was to 'compete with shopping centres like the Merseyway project at Stockport and scores of new town centres planned in Lancashire and Cheshire'.[98] Smaller towns harboured precisely the

---

[96] City Centre Planning Group, *Liverpool City Centre Plan* (1965), 25.
[97] City Centre Planning Group, *Liverpool City Centre Plan* (1965), 65, & Table B1, p.15.
[98] 'New Market St will be a shoppers' haven', *Manchester Evening News*, 19 May 1964.

same ambitions, and pursued the same shopping-based strategies. Lancaster's council in the mid-1960s was pursuing a comprehensive public–private redevelopment of its shopping district which would 'substantially increase the effective area of shopping and office space' in order to secure the position of 'Lancaster as the main commercial centre in the region'.[99] Bolton's 1964 plan rested upon a strategy to 'consolidate and extend its shops and markets' and aimed at 'shops of increased range and variety'. The imperative was 'to ensure that the creation of a modern town centre for Bolton is achieved before existing surrounding competing centres are redeveloped or new ones established'.[100]

Engineering Urban Economies

Local efforts to rejuvenate urban economies through new retail development were supported by new forms of administrative and developmental expertise. In the high moment of technocratic enthusiasm in particular there was a strong sense that comprehensive redevelopment could be used to re-engineer the entire economy of town centres, unleashing new waves of consumer-driven growth through judicious infrastructural remodelling. Much of this thinking was rooted in the same engineering-led traditions of planning that were on display in Birmingham's Bull Ring project, which placed great store upon Taylorist notions of efficiency and functionality. In a 1958 piece which appeared in the journal *Official Architecture and Planning*, the 'industrial planning consultant' O. W. Roskill expounded the detailed design principles which might be applied to produce profitable shopping centres.[101] Roskill surveyed the latest trends in the retail sector, considering the new selling and organisational techniques of multiple stores and the self-service supermarket phenomenon. 'It is important', he noted, 'for those concerned with designing shopping centres to be familiar with modern practice in shop management'. He evaluated the design specifications and commercial performance of various recently developed shopping districts in New Towns and reconstruction cities, offering advice on the precise width of pavements; the dimensions of shops; the commercial merits of various road layouts and access arrangements; along with issues of décor, aesthetics

[99] The details of this case are contained within TNA-HLG-79/1207.
[100] Graeme Shankland Associates (for County Borough of Bolton), *Bolton: Draft Town Centre Map*, 1964. Available at Bolton Archives History Centre. Shankland was also responsible for Liverpool's 1965 city centre plan, quoted above. Bolton's plan also included extensive statistical analysis of the regional consumer economy.
[101] O. W. Roskill, 'The Detailed Planning of Shopping Centres', *Official Architecture and Planning* 21:9 (1958), 414–416.

and atmosphere. Just as in the 1940s, the developmental imperatives of public planning led urban professionals into considerations of the sociology and psychology of shopping. Roskill noted that 'a shopping centre, to be popular, needs to appear alive and full of activity', and thus 'the town planner's problem is first to create congestion and then to know how to relieve it without by-passing the shopping centre or draining away its customers altogether'. These were deeply mechanistic approaches aimed at engineering new urban environments that would extract the maximum level of consumer spending, and thus achieve supreme functional efficiency as physical economic assets.

Roskill's own backstory is an interesting one, which gestures towards important lines of continuity between the urban developmental projects of the post-war decades and some of the British state's earlier political and administrative formations. Roskill was trained as an industrial chemist at Oxford and set himself up in the 1930s as 'one of the country's first management consultants' when he worked for major international firms such as Britain's ICI and Germany's Brunner Mond. His German experience and industrial expertise saw him engaged in 'various areas of economic warfare' during the Second World War, which included producing reports on 'German Aircraft Production and Capacity' as well as working to improve British military production techniques. Before the war had ended O. W. Roskill Industrial Consultants had been commissioned by the Ministry of Town and Country Planning and its Retailers' Advisory Committee to produce a 'Survey of Shopping Facilities on Housing Estates' which would guide the planning of new residential districts after the war (the determined efforts of the wartime Planning Ministry along these lines are detailed in Chapter 1). And by the early 1950s Roskill was also working for the Colonial Office on a 'Report on the Scope for Industrial Development in the Windward Islands' which formed part of Britain's efforts at holding on to its fractious Caribbean colonies – again, the modus operandi was to glean maximum developmental advantage from minimum public expenditure.[102] It was quite natural then that a figure like Roskill should also emerge as an expert voice in the domestic developmental project of remodelling the nation's urban centres in the most efficient and economic fashion. Roskill's biography is an illustration of the symbiotic relationship between large-scale

[102] Roskill's work and career gleaned from: David Roberts' Obituary, *The Independent*, 9 June 1994; Reports on 'British and German Aircraft Strength' held within the papers of Viscount Cherwell of Oxford, Nuffield College Library, Oxford University; 'Survey of Shopping Facilities on Housing Estates', correspondence, in TNA-HLG-71/762; 'Windward Islands: Printed Preliminary Report', held in Colonial Office files at TNA, CO-321/444/3.

business enterprise and the public apparatus of social administration – big business and big government expanded in tandem across the middle decades of the twentieth century. His unique career trajectory is also an indication that the developmentalism that was applied to Britain's cities in the post-war era drew upon competences and capacities associated with the mid-century 'warfare state' and with various other national and imperial projects.

Many experts whose attentions were focused more narrowly upon the domain of town planning shared Roskill's concerns with the economic efficiency and commercial functionality of different types of urban environment. Wilfred Burns, for instance, also hoped to deploy redevelopment as a means of engineering more prosperous and profitable urban economies. In his *New Towns for Old*, Burns complained that:

> A great many of our commercial areas today have solid commercial property which is uneconomic in its layout and general planning, and unsuitable for today's needs .... Victorian shopping centres were sited on the routes traversed by the pony and trap. This mixture of traffic and inefficient conditions for trading results in a great need for redevelopment.[103]

For Burns, cities' existing 'obsolete' shopping centres were simply 'inefficient and unacceptable in today's society'. The bogeyman of 'obsolescence' – another mechanistic concept which suggested that key parts of the urban economic machine were not fit for purpose – cropped up repeatedly in professional literature, public commentary, and parliamentary debates on urban issues. Burns himself was working efficiently at the production of precise technical guidance on how to engineer the new shopping centres which would excise obsolescence and replace it with 'convenience and prosperity'. His *British Shopping Centres: New Trends in Layout and Distribution*, published in 1959, sought, like O. W. Roskill, to explore best practice and identify general principles in urban retail planning.[104] Burns' book marked an early example of what became an energetic field of production in its own right, as detailed technical guides and professional literatures on engineering urban shopping centres proliferated from the 1960s.[105] Complex econometric modelling also

---

[103] Wilfred Burns, *New Towns for Old: The Technique of Urban Renewal* (London: Leonard Hill, 1963), 193.

[104] Wilfred Burns, *British Shopping Centres: New Trends in Layout and Distribution* (London: Leonard Hill, 1959).

[105] The literature within academic and professional journals rapidly became vast. For some published book-length examples see James S. Hornbeck, *Stores and Shopping Centres* (London: McGraw-Hill, 1962); Colin S. Jones, *Regional Shopping Centres: Their Location, Planning and Design* (London: Business Books, 1969); Clive Darlow (ed), *Enclosed Shopping Centres* (London: Architectural Press, 1972); David Gosling & Barry Maitland, *Design and Planning of Retail Systems* (London: Architectural Press,

25

became an important feature of cities' planning practices in the 1960s, driven by technocratic fervour and new computing technologies. Liverpool's mid-1960s city centre plan was representative of many in its extensive data collection and statistical analysis on the dynamics of the consumer economy. New representational techniques were also being developed to better understand the spatial dynamics of the urban retail economy and how best to manage it on a micro-level, on display in the mid-1960s mapping of Cardiff's central area land values (Figure 3.11).

This mix of technocratic developmentalism and economistic calculus was codified explicitly at the national level in 1962 when the government issued its key policy directive on central area redevelopment, Planning Bulletin 1, *Town Centres: Approach to Renewal*. This directive steered the course of the British urban renewal era as it unfolded across the 1960s and 1970s, setting out broad aims and guiding principles as well as offering detailed instruction on the administrative and practical mechanics of town centre renewal. In many respects it was another deeply Taylorist tract, concerned above all with town centres' functional efficiency and economic prospects. The town centre, it was stated at the outset, 'should be attractive, convenient and efficient. But today many town centres are threatened by obsolescence, decay and congestion.' The pressing contemporary concern with 'the problem of traffic' loomed particularly large, and traffic congestion was described as 'the most obvious threat to the future convenience and prosperity of every town centre'. But equally significant was the notion of obsolescence, and the way it was deployed to condemn not just decrepit or defunct urban infrastructure but anything that stood in the way of profitable redevelopment. 'Town centres today are threatened by obsolescence', the directive explained:

> The danger is both physical and functional. Not only do old buildings decay, but even sooner they become inadequate for changing needs . . . . Nowadays rebuilding of commercial buildings becomes essential, or at least an economic proposition, long before the structure itself is worn out.[106]

This statement indicates just how flexibly the seemingly technical category of 'obsolescence' was interpreted, in support of commercial redevelopment as soon as it became 'an economic proposition'. And, for all its technocratic inflections, the government's key urban renewal directive did not at all endorse remodelling Britain's town centres under the sole

1976); Ian Northen, *Shopping Centre Development* (Reading: College of Estate Management, 1984). This lucrative field of planning research and instruction has continued to burgeon up to the present day.
[106] Ministry of Housing and Local Government & Ministry of Transport, *Town Centres: Approach to Renewal* (London: HMSO, 1962), 2.

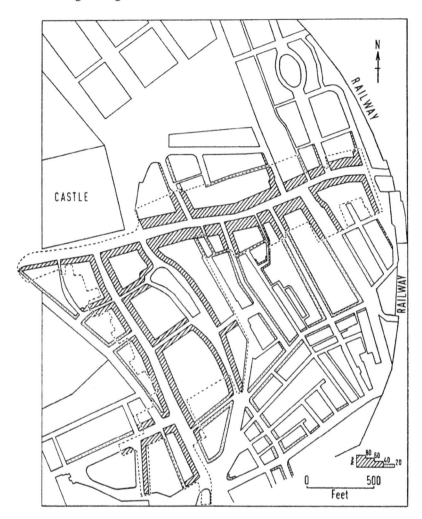

Figure 3.11 Schematic representation of the dynamics of town centre property values associated with retailing, which appeared in the *Transactions of the Institute of British Geographers* in 1966. The map shows the rateable (i.e. taxable) values of property in central Cardiff in 1961, measured in pounds per foot of shop frontage. The concentration of retail property wealth along two main axes is clear, and underlines the commercial importance of shop location and display frontages. New representational techniques like this allowed the managers of post-war cities to see how retailing interacted with property values to generate great wealth, and important revenues, in the city centre. Source: Royal Geographical Society.

purview of public planning experts. Rather, it mandated that the hybrid, public–private modes of redevelopment that had been devised and honed in blitzed cities, New Towns and redeveloping authorities like Shipley would be the linchpin of British urban renewal. The re-engineering of the nation's town centres was to be conducted in close alliance with the booming development companies and thus, was subject to the sector's commercial and financial imperatives. The powerful modernising rhetorics that supported these public–private redevelopment operations thus had an equally powerful antithesis – that of 'obsolescence' – which served to condemn existing urban environments, business practices and social habits as outmoded, inefficient and anti-modern. By laying claim to a privileged knowledge of the mechanics of the modern city, planners, local authorities and property developers were able to castigate the existing urban fabric as obsolete and out-of-step with the demands of the contemporary age, smoothing the way for compulsory purchase and demolition.

The deleterious consequences of such modes of planning for small businesses were inevitable. Indeed, local authorities could also call upon the Taylorist mantras of business efficiency and the market doctrines of competitiveness to limit the amounts of compensation payable to dispossessed small business owners. In Manchester in 1960 the City Treasurer dismissed a compensation claim from the owner of a pet food shop facing demolition and displacement with the suggestion that redevelopment had 'merely clouded the effects of competition'. In a similar case, the same official rejected a baker's compensation claim because he felt the business 'could not have been operating economically'. In support of this argument the City Treasurer cited 'a national trend for the small baker to shut down in the face of competition from bigger manufacturers'.[107] The Conservative government did legislate to improve compensation levels for dispossessed property owners in 1959, but many shopkeepers did not necessarily own the premises they traded from, and the provisions made for the disturbance of trade were much more patchy. In these cases, 'shopkeepers must rely on ex gratia payments made at the discretion of the local authority'.[108] In any case, as the *Financial Times* noted in 1963, 'the real problem of redevelopment is not fair financial compensation for purchase but how to preserve the position of the individual trader as part of renewed urban centres'. The fundamental economic logic behind commercially driven redevelopment was to raise property values, and to

---

[107] Cases recorded within the Minutes of the Health Committee, 15 March 1960, Vol. 55. Available at GMCRO.

[108] 'Redevelopment Schemes: Is Compensation Enough?', *The Financial Times*, 14 June 1963, 15.

extract as large a share as possible of the resulting higher rents for developers, investors and – where they participated – local authorities. In these circumstances many small businesses could not hope to survive in the town centre.

The plight of small businesses of all kinds – retailers, small manufacturers, small service and supply firms – became something of a rallying cry for groups opposed to the developer-dominated course of British urban renewal by the later 1960s. In 1969 the Labour government appointed a Committee of Enquiry on Small Firms, the Bolton Committee, whose 1971 report served largely to document their demise at the hands of corporate rationalisation and property-based capital accumulation. The Department of Environment told Bolton that displaced traders faced rents within redeveloped shopping centres which 'were rarely less than double', and that some traders were 'offered new premises at six or even ten times their current rent'.[109] Research by geographers at the University of Newcastle into the effect of the city's Eldon Square shopping development upon independent traders found that less than a quarter of those displaced even bothered to seek new units in the expensive new shopping centre. The same findings were replicated by studies of the effects of redevelopment in many other cities.[110] The Bolton Report did mark the beginning of a cross-party shift within central government thinking about the value of small business, which began to be talked about in terms of its innovation, enterprise and important role within local economies, although by this time the inflated land and property values of Britain's central areas had already sounded the death knell for small business in the town centre. In 1976, the pressure group 'SAVE Britain's Heritage' published a report into the 'destructive and disruptive' effects of 'insensitive redevelopment' on small businesses up and down the country, presenting detailed evidence of small business displacement all over London, as well as in major cities such as Birmingham, Leeds and Nottingham, and also many smaller towns such as Ipswich, Banbury, Andover and Yeovil.[111]

Conclusion

The 1960s verve for comprehensive redevelopment and the modernisation of cities emerged out of a complex mix of social forces and intellectual

[109] Gillian Darley & Matthew Saunders, 'A SAVE Report: Conservation and Jobs', *Built Environment Quarterly* 2:3 (1976), 211–226.
[110] P. M. Shepherd & D Thorpe, *Urban Redevelopment and Changes in Retail Structure 1961–1971* (Manchester: Retail Outlets Research Unit, 1977).
[111] Darley & Saunders, 'Conservation and Jobs'.

agendas. From the perspective of public planning, this was a high moment of confidence in the ability of experts to successfully remodel urban space and society. It was a confidence rooted in the modernising enthusiasms and technocratic fervour of the moment, and sanctioned by central government's newly permissive attitude to the large-scale, state-backed redevelopment of established town centres. Making modern shopping centres was a project that overlapped with a range of other modernising endeavours, as new and more ambitious modes of comprehensive planning sought to harness commercial development and integrate it with wider programmes of slum clearance, road-building and urban reorganisation. Much of this was driven by a mechanistic, engineering-led vision of planning which viewed both the urban environment and the urban economy as malleable, perfectible objects. For local authorities, the new planning ideas of the 1960s held out the promise of becoming fashionably modern while simultaneously addressing a set of urban problems that had worried them for some time. Waning economic vitality and industrial decline, congestion and dysfunction in the urban centre, an outworn built environment, depopulation and a loss of urban stature could all, it was hoped, be tackled through the embrace of modernist renewal. But the reinvention of the town centre was also a cultural and commercial project, in which Britain's ageing urban centres would be aligned with the exciting new worlds of shopping, affluence and consumer abundance. Urban redevelopment was underpinned by a notion of cultural modernisation that was deeply inflected with new commercial norms and forms. These were lifted from the consumer domain and mediated by the commercial development sector. In the end the model of the modern city which emerged out of the conjuncture of these cultural trends, technocratic discourses and smart commercial strategies was a far cry from what many planning professionals had in mind. It was a brash, demotic and deeply commercial urban modernity, in which reformist urbanism and civic sensibilities played second fiddle to a boisterous culture of affluence and acquisition, fomented according to the commercial priorities of retail property development.

4   The Politics of Partnership

'Partnership' between public planning authorities and private property developers was at the very heart of the British urban renewal regime. This was the central political relationship that governed urban renewal, and it was codified within planning legislation, mandated explicitly by central policy diktats and pursued energetically by individual local authorities eager to remake the image and economy of their towns. All over the country, as one contemporary commentator memorably put it, the redevelopment of town and city centres was steered by 'a quaint combination of the entrepreneur and the town clerk'.[1] Local authorities and property developers worked closely together to remodel post-war cities around the perceived imperatives of an economy reshaped by mass affluence, and their endeavours were supported by floods of investment from the British financial sector which increasingly viewed property holding and property development as a favoured use of capital. At times partnership could cross the line into illegality and become corruption, and the real extent of this is – by definition – hard to ascertain. Yet corruption was by no means a necessary feature of such relationships; instead, close and reciprocal relations between councils and developers were the highly visible, legally enshrined basis for pursuing large-scale urban redevelopment. This chapter situates the hybrid, mixed economy of planning within the wider political economy of post-war Britain, tracking the political influence and connections of the property and construction sectors as well as the attitudes and policy positions of both the Conservative and Labour Parties.

The discussion also traces how the public–private relationship worked on the ground in various towns and cities, dwelling in particular on Manchester, Liverpool and Nottingham. It details the respective aims and interests of the two parties, the legal and financial mechanics of partnership and the distinctive forms of redevelopment which this produced. The chapter also surveys some of the problems and pitfalls which this public–private mode of urban renewal presented for local authorities

---

[1] Marriott, *The Property Boom*, 234–235.

and for the places and populations they governed. For all the talk of mutuality and harmoniously aligned interests, in practice the aims of public planning authorities and private development companies often diverged. Negotiating the new legal and financial terrain of partnership could be treacherous, and smaller councils in particular often found themselves ill-equipped to manage the process according to their own best interests. Even for the big city authorities, which did not suffer from a lack of confidence or commercial expertise, the reliance on private sector initiative and investment could leave them dangerously exposed to shifting market conditions and commercial preferences over which they had little influence. The chapter shows how Manchester's council were forced into an intensely 'entrepreneurial' financial manoeuvre, which collapsed the lines between public and private enterprise, in order to save their own central area redevelopment scheme when its finances came under threat. It also traces the fate of Liverpool's ambitious mid-1960s vision for civic and social renewal, which – for all its sensitivity and sophistication on the drawing board – collapsed on contact with the commercially driven, profit-oriented and private sector-led system of British urban renewal. By the 1980s, the pitfalls of this system for less commercially favoured locales like Liverpool had become painfully clear.

The Political Economy of Partnership

In 1962, at the enthusiastic outset of the era of large-scale, state-sponsored urban renewal, the Ministry of Housing and Local Government and the Ministry of Transport issued the joint policy directive titled *Town Centres: Approach to Renewal*. This directive steered the course of urban renewal as it progressed across the 1960s and 1970s, establishing the basic political and economic principles as well as the detailed legal and financial mechanisms through which urban centres would be rebuilt. Just as in the 1940s, the view from central government was both business-like and business-friendly – focused on the economic costs and returns of redevelopment and eager to encourage private enterprise to take on as much of the work as possible. 'Renewal is an investment in the future', the directive stated, 'successful redevelopment … is a major commercial undertaking [and] calls for both skilful planning and much expertise including commercial experience. These can best be achieved by a partnership of public and private enterprise [and] it is the Ministers' policy to encourage this'. Practically and rhetorically, the idea of partnership between public planning and private development was at the heart of this document. 'Town centre redevelopment' the two ministers declared, 'is essentially a matter for co-operation between local government and private enterprise …

Renewal cannot be undertaken without public support and it cannot be carried through without private enterprise'. The directive devoted an entire chapter to 'Partnership', setting out in detail what the respective roles and responsibilities of the two parties should be, how planning powers could be used to assemble land for private development and on what terms this could be disposed of to commercial developers. An intellectual and ideological case for the private sector's role was put forward, in which the unique qualities and superior commercial knowledge of the development industry were emphasised. Successful redevelopment, it was argued, 'requires availability of capital, knowledge of the market, and the ability to exploit commercial opportunities, in which the private developer is generally better placed than the local authority'. At the same time though, the development industry was dependent upon the statutory planning powers of local authorities – most obviously powers of compulsory purchase – in order to deliver its essential raw material: urban land. Local planning powers were to be deployed to appropriate sites and assemble large plots in the best locations, in order to 'open up new opportunities for profitable redevelopment'. The conclusion was that:

The two agencies – the local authority and the private developer – thus have separate strengths and weaknesses in their ability to carry out redevelopment but these are largely complementary and point the way to successful co-operation.[2]

Whether public planning powers were best used in a way which was quite so 'complementary' to the operations of commercial property developers was not a question which troubled the relevant ministers, who in 1962 were Keith Joseph (Housing and Local Government) and Ernest Marples (Transport). Both men had close personal connections and long-standing financial interests in the spheres of property and construction. Prior to his appointment as Parliamentary Secretary to the Minister of Housing and Local Government (1959–1961), Sir Keith Joseph, Baronet, was the serving chairman and a long-time director of his family's construction firm, Bovis. Bovis had been building shops for national retailers such as Marks and Spencer since the 1920s, and in the post-1945 period the firm was building commercial offices, flats, shops and private housing. Joseph left these family business positions while in office first as Parliamentary Secretary and later as the Minister for Housing and Local Government (1962–1964), but on losing office in 1964 he took up again as deputy chairman of Bovis Holdings Limited, the property-holding arm of the group.[3] Ernest Marples had been dealing in and developing London

[2] Ministry of Housing and Local Government & Ministry of Transport, *Town Centres*.
[3] Brian Harrison (19 May 2011), 'Joseph, Keith Sinjohn, Baron Joseph (1918–1994)', Oxford Dictionary of National Biography [ODNB].

property since the 1920s. By the 1940s he had also moved into construction and civil engineering, as both a director of the building contractor Kirk and Kirk and as the founder and managing director of Marples Ridgway.[4] This second role in particular opened up Marples to long-running accusations of self-dealing and conflicts of interest as the civil engineering group was awarded numerous major road-building and construction contracts during his own tenure as Minister of Transport. Marples Ridgway built the Hammersmith and Chiswick Flyovers in London along with various chunks of the national motorway network. The firm also built a number of British power stations and dams, as well as picking up major civil engineering projects in colonies (such as the gargantuan Port Esquival facility in Jamaica, built in the 1950s to extract the island's aluminium ore) and in regions of informal economic power (road building in Ethiopia, for instance). The imperial-developmental state of the early post-war decades offered plenty of nice work if, like Marples, you knew how to get it.

The construction and development industries thus enjoyed particularly warm relations with the Conservative Party. The large building and development group John Laing & Son – which was responsible for Birmingham's Bull Ring along with innumerable other major construction and engineering projects – was firmly affiliated with the Party.[5] So too was Richard Costain Ltd, another leading construction and civil engineering firm which, like Laings, was also working extensively on large-scale building projects in Britain and across both the formal empire and the informal British economic sphere. One of Costain's directors, Sir Albert Costain, was the Conservative MP for Folkestone in Kent and served as Parliamentary Private Secretary to the Minister of Public Building and Works in the early 1960s. In this capacity Costain addressed the House of Commons in a debate on Urban Central Development in April 1962, where 'as a builder and a speculator' he railed against unnecessary 'controls' which might deter 'the speculator or investor'. Instead, Costain commended 'the happy compromise [of] a marriage between the local authorities, who, after all, have powers of compulsory purchase, the professions and the building industry, which has the experience'.[6] Somewhat ironically (given his later views on the stifling 'anti-enterprise culture' that mid-century corporatism had supposedly produced),

---

[4] D. J. Dutton (25 May 2006), 'Marples, (Alfred) Ernest, Baron Marples (1907–1978)', ODNB.
[5] Roy Coad, *Laing: The Biography of Sir John W. Laing, CBE, 1879–1978* (London: Hodder & Stoughton, 1979); 'Laing News', *The Financial Times*, 30 January 1962, 5.
[6] HC Deb, 13 April 1962, vol. 657 cc.1645–1742; cc.1738–1741; Norman Kipping (23 September 2004), 'Costain, Sir Richard Rylandes (1902–1966)', ODNB.

Joseph's firm Bovis along with these other leading construction and engineering firms had been formed into major corporate successes by wartime public building contracts. In the Second World War these firms built the industrial plant, airfields and Mulberry harbours that the warfare state demanded and emerged from the conflict transformed in size, competence and capacity. They then flourished into highly profitable corporate groupings with a global reach under the supportive political conditions, imperial (and post-imperial) commercial operations and state-sponsored development programmes of the post-war era.

The big building contractors sometimes undertook major urban development projects alone (Laings, for example, took sole responsibility for Birmingham's Bull Ring Centre), but more often they worked on contract for the new breed of dedicated property development companies which had risen so meteorically since the war. These businesses, too, enjoyed close and reciprocal links with the Conservative Party. To take a leading example, the firm Capital & Counties, which was responsible for numerous major shopping developments including Nottingham's Victoria Centre and Newcastle's Eldon Square, was led from 1967 by Sir Richard Thompson, Baronet. Thompson was a Conservative MP for Croydon (1950–1966; 1970–1974) and served as a junior minister in various departments in the 1950s and 1960s including at the Ministry of Works. When the Conservatives were out of office in 1968 Capital & Counties announced that it would contribute £15,000 to the party's re-election campaign (this is well over £250,000 in 2020 values).[7] The party's ongoing links with the reactionary aristocratic champions of private property were set out earlier in this book, and as 'the propertied interest' came increasingly to be dominated by the new post-war development companies these links remained firm. Keith Joseph contributed the foreword to a 1964 publication, *The Property Developer*, which was organised by a newly formed trade body The Property Council (chairman, Sir Ian Mactaggart, Baronet, businessman and another Conservative politician). This book showcased the activities of the booming property sector all over Britain, with contributions from many leading developers along with some of their public sector partners in local and central government. Contributions from bodies like the National Federation of Property Owners and the Association of Land and Property Owners confirmed the continued influence of propertied interest groups in this era of change. Joseph's foreword reflected on 'the role of the property developer in our modern society' and 'the scale, pace and complexity of the ceaseless changes which are taking place in our towns and cities and which are conveniently summarised by the term "urban

---

[7] 'Capital & Counties', *Daily Mail*, 5 July 1968, 11.

renewal'''. Meeting the demands of the future, Joseph suggested, would take all 'the energy and imagination' of the development sector and 'require the continuation and deepening of the now well-established partnership with local government in land assembly and construction of works'.[8]

In the year this paean to the property developer was published, Joseph would go on to lose his position as the Minister for Housing and Local Government when Labour emerged victorious from the general election of October 1964. The interlinked domains of property, planning, housing and redevelopment played a not insignificant role in this election. The Conservatives' loosely regulated, developer-driven redevelopment regime had begun generating a set of urban problems which will sound mightily familiar to contemporary ears. In the urban centres there were plenty of extravagant shops and high-spec offices being built but not enough housing. The government's concerted efforts to promote private house-building and subsidise the property-owning democracy across the 1950s also meant that most of the new housing that was being built was provided by the private sector for owner-occupation – these were, generally, more expensive properties in affluent suburbs (in London five-sixths of new private building was suburban in the mid-1960s). As part of its deregulatory agenda the Conservative government also liberalised rent control via the 1957 Rent Act. The result was huge increases in housing rents (in London, where these problems were most acute, rents doubled and in some cases trebled in the six years after the Act). For those at the lower end of urban housing markets, then, rents were being hiked dramatically while the provision of new housing was targeted firmly at more affluent groups. Municipal house-building had been tempered and pared back across the same period (local authority expenditure on housing fell from £353 m to £274 m between 1955 and 1960) and councils' house-building programmes had been steered firmly into a more constrained focus upon slum clearance rather than the mitigation of wider housing market failures.[9] These failures were most serious in the inner areas of large conurbations and in London in particular. Here, tenants were forced to pay sharply rising rents for older, outworn housing while the construction and development industries focused their attentions elsewhere. The furore over 'Rachmanism' in London – predatory landlordism in an overheated housing market – which erupted as a seedy subplot to the Profumo affair in 1963, illustrated how these inner-city housing pressures intersected with tensions over race and immigration, while also tying the dubious domain of property into what John Davis calls 'the

[8] The Property Council, *The Property Developer* (London: 1964), 'Foreword', BL.
[9] 'Wrong Emphasis in Building', *The Guardian*, 11 March 1963, 17.

Gibbonian decay enveloping the Macmillan government'.[10] The ever-disreputable Ernest Marples, incidentally, was also entangled in the sordid sexual dealings exposed by the Profumo affair, although his involvement was kept out of the public domain.

Against this backdrop, even some Conservative sympathisers voiced concern about the direction of travel in the sphere of urban redevelopment. The Conservative MP Bill Deedes secured a debate in Parliament on this issue in 1962 where he questioned the balance being struck between private interests and public needs in British urban renewal. Deedes challenged the vast sums being poured into central area shopping developments while what he described as 'the central human problem' – Britain's often decrepit inner-urban housing stock – was left to deteriorate:

> We must ... seek to restore some kind of social balance .... I cannot accept as inevitable that all urban centres shall ultimately become, virtually, commercial work-shops, gleaming false teeth surrounded by decay.... Unless we can find a formula for bringing the great mass of housing into our plans for renewal, much of our urban central redevelopment, however glossily it is presented, will be a sham and a farce.[11]

That a representative of the party of business – whose own tenets of private enterprise and profit played such a key role in shaping the political economy of urban renewal – was moved to voice such critiques is particularly striking. Labour developed many of these themes in its 1964 electoral efforts, with George Brown telling the 1963 party conference that 'the present exploitation of the land and of the people cannot be allowed to continue'. The Labour Party fought the election with a suite of policies aimed at setting urban redevelopment on a different, more equitable course. The so-called Brown Ban on London office building was enacted almost immediately after the election in November 1964. This measure aimed to cool off the capital's property markets by restricting new office development and redirecting it to other parts of the country. The Labour government also rebooted the New Towns programme, with the designation of a 'third wave' of six new town projects, as well as overseeing a renewed focus upon mass house-building, both public and private. The most ambitious initiative was certainly the new Land Commission. This was an effort at the partial nationalisation of land which resurrected old questions about 'compensation and betterment' – *cui bono*, in effect – in planning. The idea was that the new Commission would automatically and compulsorily acquire the freehold of any land that was due for redevelopment. By forcibly inserting itself into commercial land transactions in this way, the Land Commission would capture a large

---

[10] John Davis, 'Rents and Race in 1960s London: New Light on Rachmanism', *Twentieth Century British History* 12:1 (2001), 69–92.

[11] HC Deb, 13 April 1962, vol. 657 cc.1648.

share of the new value created by redevelopment and secure it for the public weal. In the end, however, this interesting initiative foundered immediately. The Commission was never given the powers it needed to be effective, in part because even some Labour ministers such as Richard Crossman were uncertain about the effects of such a strident intervention in the workings of land and property markets.[12]

As a result of these moves, the property sector's relations with the Labour Party were cagier than with its natural allies in the Conservative Party. And yet, despite the howls of anguish they provoked from the property men, Labour's moves against the development sector always had far more bark than bite and tended to peter out in muddled imple-mentation and eventual retreat. In the absence of a new mechanism for reapportioning the remarkable wealth being created by urban redevelop-ment, and in the context of the wider economic woes that engulfed Harold Wilson's governments in the second half of the 1960s, Labour struggled to decisively rebalance the urban renewal order in favour of the state. In any case, beneath the surface of policy pronouncements and rhetorical conflict, relations could be much warmer. Ewan Harrison's recent research on 'public-sector speculative development' has shown how Harold Wilson's government supported land-holding public bodies such as the General Post Office and the British Transport Commission in their forays into the murky world of speculative commercial development.[13] While at the local level, the depth of relations between Labour politicians and the property world became notorious. Harrison highlights the activities of Sir Frank Price in Birmingham (Figure 4.1), who operated simultaneously as the lead councillor for planning and redevelopment issues *and* as a property impresario and fixer with personal interests in the property business. In the 1960s Wilson's government appointed Price as chair of the Development Corporation for Telford New Town and also as the head of 'Labour Party Properties', the property development vehicle of the Labour Party. In Newcastle, meanwhile, the activities of the Labour council leader T. Dan Smith spilled out spectac-ularly into a high-profile corruption scandal in the early 1970s.[14]

---

[12] Peter Weiler, 'Labour and the Land: From Municipalization to the Land Commission, 1951-1971', *Twentieth Century British History* 19:3 (2008), 314–343. See also Phil Child, 'Landlordism, Rent Regulation and the Labour Party in mid-twentieth century Britain, 1950-64', *Twentieth Century British History* 29:1 (2018), 79–103; Michael Tichelar, *The Failure of Land Reform in Twentieth-Century England* (London, 2018).

[13] Ewan Harrison, '"Money Spinners": R. Seifert & Partners, Sir Frank Price and Public-Sector Speculative Development in the 1970s', *Architectural History* 61 (2018), 259–280.

[14] Peter Jones, 'Re-thinking Corruption in Post-1950 Urban Britain: the Poulson Affair, 1972-1976', *Urban History* 39:3 (2012), 510–528.

Figure 4.1 Opening ceremony for Birmingham's Bull Ring development, 29 May 1964. Prince Philip tours the new shopping concourses flanked by William Kirby Laing (director of the construction and development firm Laings) and Alderman Frank Price, then serving as Lord Mayor of Birmingham. Price had close connections with the property industry and sold his services as a deal broker between local authorities and developers. Ceremonies like this were highly visible indications of the centrality of local authority–developer partnerships in the remaking of post-war cities. Source: Historic England Archive, John Laing Photographic Collection.

The issue of corruption was a sensational one for contemporaries, and the satirical investigative magazine *Private Eye* did much to expose local authorities' corrupt links with the development sector. The bankruptcy proceedings and subsequent corruption trial of the architect John Poulson in 1973 in particular led to the highly public downfall of T. Dan Smith (Labour) along with the serving Home Secretary, Reginald Maudling (Conservative). And yet, despite their contemporary resonance, in retrospect the existence of individual cases of corruption is less significant than what such practices indicated about the wider political economy of post-war urbanism. The presence of corruption, sometimes on a grand scale, was merely an illustration of the depth and extent of relations between local authorities and private developers upon which the renewal of post-war cities rested. Such alliances became fundamental to the governance of British cities in the 1940s, when the local state was granted a firm veto power over all new development and became the key gatekeeper in the acquisition of urban land. The highly fragmented patterns of land ownership in Britain's long-established town centres – where innumerable small plots were held by many different owners through a variety of tenures and legal structures – made 'land assembly' – the drawing together of multiple small plots into one unified ownership, ready for redevelopment – the principal obstacle facing all attempts at positive planning.[15] The government's 1962 planning directive was clear on the importance of this issue as the starting point for partnership arrangements: 'Private developers are often prepared to undertake large-scale redevelopment schemes on lines approved or suggested by the local authority ... but are unable to assemble all the land they need by agreement'. For this, developers 'seek the local authority's assistance.'[16]

The principal mechanism for overcoming this problem was the designation of large portions of the city centre as comprehensive development areas (CDA). This status, once confirmed by the minister, empowered councils to use powers of compulsory purchase to override any opposition to redevelopment from existing property owners. Wilfred Burns' 1963 planning manual was blunt about the functioning of CDA powers, which 'act as a lubricant to the negotiations, or, in other terminology, as a threat to the reluctant seller'.[17] A 1972 *Guardian* report on the wave of public–private shopping developments sweeping the country also noted that:

One of the major problems in any redevelopment process is land assembly, and the local authorities' compulsory purchase powers facilitate assembly of key sites with an expedition and at a price that private developers can only dream about.[18]

[15] The 1940 Barlow Report gives an account of these dilemmas and of various countries' attempts to overcome them; *Report of the Royal Commission on the Distribution of the Industrial Population* (London: HMSO, 1940).
[16] *Town Centres: Approach to Renewal*, 6–7.
[17] Burns, *New Towns for Old*, 177. A detailed account of the evolution and application of these powers is given in T. Hart, *The Comprehensive Development Area* (Edinburgh: Oliver & Boyd, 1968).
[18] Tom Allan, 'The Knock It Down and Put Up a Precinct Show', *The Guardian*, 22 October 1973, 19.

Many urban authorities were not slow to appreciate the utility of such powers and began energetically designating large swathes of their central areas as soon as they were empowered to do so in the 1940s. A government paper of January 1952 was already bemoaning as a 'tiresome complication' the way in which 'the conception [of the CDA] has been adopted for administrative and financial purposes'.[19] Once CDA status had been granted, it was often not necessary for the local authority to actually go through the motions of compulsory purchase; owners understood that if they did not accept whatever they were being offered by developers, they could be forced to accept a worse price from the local authority through compulsory acquisition. In some cases, it was not even necessary to complete the CDA procedure. In Lancaster in the mid-1960s, the city council submitted plans for a substantial redevelopment of its central shopping area. Fifty new shops were to be erected by a commercial developer within modern pedestrianised precincts. This proposal would, it was argued, rid the area of 'obsolete development' and 'substantially increase the effective area of shopping and office space'. After publicising its CDA plans in 1966, and placing lists of the affected properties in the local paper, the council withdrew its CDA application three years later. The threat of the CDA designation had been enough to persuade owners to come to terms with the developer.[20]

The mid-century tussles over the shape of the planning system and the role of the state, characterised by advances and retreats on both sides and on different fronts, ended up imparting a public planning regime which was patchy and unbalanced. Local authorities were left with radically enhanced powers in some spheres – particularly around compulsory purchase, land-use zoning and the granting of planning permissions – and yet were curiously impotent in other respects. In particular, councils were almost entirely dependent upon private investment, or else on central government grants, in order to finance and carry out any actual redevelopment in the town centre. It was precisely this unevenness in the structure of planning powers and responsibilities which formed the basis for the new developmental partnerships between councils and commercial property companies. If they hoped to solve their planning problems and secure their towns' entry into the modern, affluent age, urban councils were obliged to collaborate closely with private development companies. For their part, the property entrepreneurs were somewhat duplicitous when they railed – as they did ad nauseam – against 'planning'

---

[19] Ministry of Housing and Local Government, internal note, 24 January 1952. TNA-HLG-71/2202.
[20] The details of this case are contained within TNA-HLG-79/1207.

and 'controls'. For all their talk of the superiority of free enterprise and the beneficence of market forces, what had grown up since the 1940s was a legal and practical framework for urban redevelopment which offered lucrative – and hitherto impossible – business opportunities precisely by deploying public planning powers in the developers' interest. It was the developer-friendly planning system that *created* the commercial opportunities and market conditions in which the post-war British property business thrived.

Remaking Central Manchester: Pragmatic Partnership

In the 1960s CDA powers were used extensively by councils, in partnership with developers, to take ownership of substantial portions of their central areas and install extravagant new shopping complexes at the heart of cities. In Manchester, by 1967, the city's planning officer had prepared five separate CDA proposals 'amounting to about 200 acres and representing most of the core of the Central Area'.[21] Many of these schemes never got off the ground, but the most substantial project that did go ahead was the city's remodelling of its most prestigious shopping zone around Market Street. As befits an urban authority which had long carried itself with an air of swaggering self-importance, the Corporation of Manchester in the 1960s embarked on a project to build the largest shopping centre yet seen in Britain. The council proudly reported that the new Manchester Arndale, developed in alliance with the Arndale Property Trust, would be 'a Centre which will compete with any in the world in terms of a quality shopping environment'.[22] This 'record-breaker in terms of size and cost and in the facilities and range of shopping to be provided' was to include over 200 new shops, a 100-metre tall 'Arndale Tower' office block; a large Corporation market, a bus station and a 2,000-car multi-storey car park.[23] The large new complex was planted right at the centre of the city's main shopping district (Figure 4.2), in a move that was hugely disruptive to the physical fabric and social geography of the city and displaced hundreds of residents, businesses and property owners.

The endeavour rested wholly upon close collaboration between council and developer. The Corporation trumpeted the benefits which would

---

[21] City and County Borough of Manchester, *City Centre Map 1967*, 55. Available at GMCRO.

[22] City of Manchester Corporation & Town and City Properties Ltd., 'Manchester Market Street Central Area Redevelopment Scheme', development prospectus, c. 1966. Author's collection.

[23] Town & City Properties Limited, *Arndale Covered Centres* (1973).

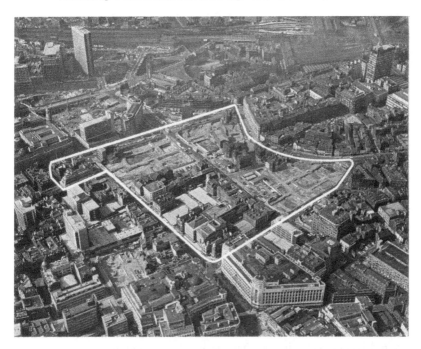

Figure 4.2 1971 aerial photograph showing the scale of destruction and remodelling involved in the creation of the Manchester Arndale Centre. This development saw fifteen acres of the city's central business district levelled and rebuilt in a partnership between Manchester Corporation and Town & City Properties. Source: P&O Heritage.

flow from its 'partnership … with Town & City (Manchester) Developments Limited'. For its part, Town & City applauded the 'positive approach to the acquisition of key sites' and was happy to be working 'in partnership with Manchester Corporation'.[24] Local authorities, the developer opined, recognise 'the value of partnership arrangements with reputable and experienced development organisations', and central government too 'saw the advantage in the welding of the powers of Local Authorities and the commercial expertise of the property company'. These were not empty boasts. Town & City was the most prolific actor in this field, having already handled around fifty such partnership schemes by the mid-1970s. The company acquired the Arndale Property Trust in 1968, taking over its nationwide programme of

---

[24] City of Manchester & Town & City Properties Ltd, 'Manchester Market Street Central Area Redevelopment Scheme'.

shopping mall development and reported that – with just one or two exceptions – all of its shopping developments had been 'provided in partnership with Local Authorities and from this co-operation between public body and private developer stems real benefits'.[25] In Manchester the depth of this collaboration was particularly striking. One reporter described planning practices in the city as having 'a great emphasis on round-table talk, on give and take between the developers and the planners'.[26] The fractious public inquiries into the Market Street scheme in the mid-1960s – at which the many objectors were able to put their case – were carefully coordinated between the two partners. The city council, for example, used its influence with the Ministry of Housing and Local Government on multiple occasions to secure postponements of the inquiry in order to allow the development company more time to buy off and whittle down the long list of objectors.[27] In the end, as one report observed, the Market Street scheme had:

... been planned as an entity after scores of meetings between planners and architects from the development group and the town hall. It is no longer just a commercial planning application submitted for approval; it is, aesthetically and socially, a submission by one partner to another.[28]

Manchester Corporation had a number of strategic rationales for engaging in this act of submission. Deep-seated fears about the region's waning industrial prowess stretched back well into the interwar period, and this threat was felt particularly keenly in a city which continued to identify itself proudly as the birthplace of the Industrial Revolution.[29] Manchester's civic leaders clearly felt the city should be in the vanguard of the age of affluence just as it had been in the industrial age. The 1967 *City Centre Plan* reveals an overriding concern with the city's economic clout and status as the 'Regional Centre'. There was also a clear recognition that the city's status as a 'centre of attraction' serving 'an extensive hinterland' depended principally upon the performance of its high-end shopping facilities. The city's offering as a shopping destination was, it was felt, 'second only to London', but the attractions of the centre were also understood to be under threat from surrounding towns with their own modernisation and redevelopment programmes. The council had conducted its own 'Shopping Study' in 1962, at a point when 'many

[25] Town & City Properties Limited, *Arndale Covered Centres* (1973), company prospectus. Available at GMCRO.
[26] George Hawthorne, *The Guardian*, 'The NEW Manchester', 29 October 1968, 5.
[27] Letter from Arndale Managing Director to Manchester Town Clerk, 17 August 1967. TNA-HLG-79/1187.
[28] George Hawthorne, *The Guardian*, 'The NEW Manchester', 29 October 1968, 5.
[29] Kefford, 'Disruption, Destruction and the Creation of "the Inner Cities"', 492–515.

major schemes to provide ambitious shopping developments were being put forward by developers'. The 'strategic pre-eminence of Market Street' as 'the heart of the regional shopping centre' had been recognised, and the council took the view that this 'traditional location could be exploited to provide a really fine shopping centre'. 'To be competitive', the planning authority felt, 'there is no doubt that Manchester's shopping centre will require not only to be convenient and efficient, but also outstandingly inviting and attractive'.[30] Local newspapers agreed whole-heartedly. The *Manchester Evening News* felt that 'the North's premier shopping thoroughfare' must 'retain its position as the premier shopping centre of the region'.[31] For the city council, transforming Market Street to provide the most up-to-date shopping facilities was about defending the city's status within the region and the country and securing its commercial future in changing economic times.

As well as trying to see off their regional rivals and secure new sources of growth, cities like Manchester were also engaged in countering another economic threat through the redevelopment of their central shopping areas. Although as an architectural form the shopping mall was an American import, the centrally located British shopping centres of the 1960s and 1970s were expressly intended to *prevent* the emergence of US-style geographies of shopping in Britain. The American model of suburban, out-of-town shopping centres – in which new poles of consumer attraction were being developed outside of existing urban centres – was viewed with extreme concern by British planners and urban authorities. Such patterns of development were associated with a dangerous hollowing out of cities, as wealth, consumer spending and economic vitality migrated away from established urban centres to the periphery and beyond. In a House of Lords debate in 1964 Lord Taylor – a member of the Development Corporation for Harlow New Town – warned of the deleterious impacts of US-style out-of-town shopping centres. 'They are very nice from the point of view of the shopper', Taylor said, being 'extremely easy to motor to'. He went on:

If you like it like that, you can have it like that; but if you have it like that, you finish our cities as we know them. Once we have things like that the economics of urban development are finis, kaput. We cannot maintain a central shopping area if we have these things.[32]

For most urban authorities, the American model was in this respect more a spectre than an ideal – fiscally horrifying and threatening ruin to central

[30] City and County Borough of Manchester, *City Centre Map 1967*, 14–16. GMCRO.
[31] 'New Market St Will Be a Shoppers' Haven', *Manchester Evening News*, 19 May 1964.
[32] HL Deb on Urban Redevelopment, 4 March 1964, vol 256, col.181.

area economies. As a result, city councils like Manchester vehemently opposed out-of-town retail development in their locales. The city's pro-active programmes of central area retail development were pursued 'against the background of a consistent policy of resisting large scale shopping developments on unrelated or fringe sites', as the city planning officer put it in 1967.[33] Developers like Town & City spoke directly to these fears when courting local authorities, warning that 'the dramatic – often disastrous – effects of the major out-town or fringe-town centres on central – or down-town – areas in American cities offer a harsh lesson to this country'. Councils could rest assured, though, that 'Town & City . . . seeks to enhance and improve the central areas of a town . . . which Local Authorities themselves seek to maintain and restore'.[34] The commercial property consultancy Goddard & Smith also took care to remind councils that 'the prosperity and future growth of every Municipality is closely linked with a successful Central Shopping and Commercial Area . . . in consequence its development must be the major concern of all progressively minded Corporations'. The solution was at hand though, as Goddard & Smith also stood ready to offer its 'unrivalled experience' and took 'pride in co-operating with Corporations who are eager to make their City or Town a model of civic enterprise'.[35] The wave of large-scale, city shopping centres which took off in the 1960s was thus a conscious local developmental effort to stimulate the retail economies of existing urban centres and to defend British cities from the threat of US-style ex-urban development. In the 1960s at least, central government remained largely in agreement with these local aims, with Ministry officials asserting that 'if [a town] went into decline as a shopping centre it would not survive as a town centre in the wider sense'.[36] Shopping was now seen as fundamental not just to cities' economic performance but to their survival.

    Against this backdrop Manchester Corporation's tight embrace of its development sector partner was certainly understandable, but it remained hugely controversial and hotly contested. Manchester's leading retailers were almost universally opposed to the redevelopment of the city's main shopping district. Market Street was the principal shopping street of one of the pre-eminent provincial cities; it was, according to one retailer, 'traditionally . . . the finest shopping street outside London', where some of the highest retail property values in the country were

[33] City and County Borough of Manchester, *City Centre Map* 1967, 16.
[34] Town & City Properties Limited, *Arndale Covered Centres* (1973).
[35] Goddard & Smith, 'Central Town Development', promotional prospectus, early 1960s. WYAS (LLD1/2/817206).
[36] 'Out-of-town Shopping Centres', discussion paper, 20 July 1962. TNA-HLG-136/88.

concentrated.[37] The retailers operating here were not the small fry or 'riff-raff' who were so easily dismissed in smaller towns. Their opposition to dispossession and redevelopment was vocal and well organised, and many retained lawyers and planning consultants to put their case effectively. Dozens of retailers lodged formal objections to the plans with the Ministry of Housing and Local Government, with many arguing that the scheme represented an unjustified imposition upon their business. The Wallis clothes chain, for example, lodged an objection to 'the distur-bance to trading facilities', which the development would entail and noted that rents in the new shopping centre would be 'beyond the means of the majority of existing traders and over-burden-some [sic] to all but a few of the minority'. The result of this, the company feared, would be that 'many traders will ... be forced out of business'. Another retailer wrote that 'the Corporation's proposals ... are unreasonable and likely to cause extreme hardship to their business'. The jewellers, H Samuel, 'considered such a grandiose scheme ... is not in accordance with good town planning principles and would result in much disruption to the Shopping Centre of Manchester', while a combined objection from Montague Burton Limited and Jackson the Tailor Limited stated that the redevelopment was 'not necessary' and 'imposes hardship upon the companies'.[38]

Given that central area shopping developments were pitched by councils and developers as essential if the demands of 'modern retailing' were to be met, it might be thought that the organised sections of the retail trade would be wholehearted in their support for comprehensive redevelopment. But this was not at all the case. Multiples, department stores and other large retailers understood that – in commercial terms – the redevelopment of shopping centres represented a fairly mercenary attempt to capture a bigger share of their profits through site rents. As a result, the most 'modern' sections of the retail trade could be just as opposed to redevelopment as the small traders. The Multiple Shops Federation – which had been the key private partner in redevelopment in the 1940s and 1950s – found its position under threat by the 1960s from the new alliances of planning authorities and property developers. In a retail planning agenda issued in 1963, the Multiple Shops Federation explained that it should:

... not be inferred ... that the Federation regards the large-scale rebuild-ing of shopping centres as in itself desirable .... An existing centre

[37] Objection letter from Prices Tailors Ltd, 17 October 1966, TNA-HLG-79/1187.
[38] See the formal objection letters from the companies: Testers, 20 October 1966; Frank Westbrook, 29 September 1966; H. Samuel Ltd, 27 October 1966; Montague Burton Ltd, 4 October 1966. All correspondence contained within TNA-HLG-79/1187.

represents the investment of a vast amount of capital; it can seldom be replaced without imposing a heavy additional burden of overhead costs for many years to come on the local ratepayers and on the traders who lease the new premises. It may fall short – perhaps far short – of the standards of convenience and efficiency that could be attained if it were to be built anew to the best possible design. But **so long as it is still doing a useful job of service to the local community, and yielding an adequate return to the traders concerned, the radical surgery of comprehensive redevelopment should not be contemplated until every possibility of making good its defects less expensively ... has been thoroughly explored.**[39]

Here then, even while paying homage to the tenets of convenience and efficiency, the principal retail trade body argued that comprehensive redevelopment was an unnecessary and expensive imposition upon its members. As earlier chapters of this book have shown, many large retailers had made substantial investments in their premises in the 1950s, refurbishing and rebuilding stores with the encouragement of local authorities. They were thus understandably aggrieved at being dispossessed by the local planning authority a decade later. In its objection to Manchester's Arndale scheme, the company Prices Tailors protested on precisely this basis. The company's premises had been 'completely rebuilt in 1953 with full planning permission', and the retailer complained that 'the proposed demolition of such a new building is wholly [sic] unrealistic'.[40]

Such conflicts were not confined to Manchester. Privately the Multiple Shops Federation had been petitioning the Ministry of Housing and Local Government in protest at the impact of comprehensive development upon its members nationwide since the early 1960s. The Federation vehemently opposed what it called the 'monopolistic redevelopment' process by which councils forcibly acquired its members' sites and handed them over to developers, who, it was argued, then 'take advantage of their virtual monopoly of first-grade trading sites' to demand 'rents [which] are unjustifiably inflated'. This was a fairly accurate characterisation of the retail property developer's business model. As the leading figure behind Arndale's shopping centre programme, Sam Chippindale, explained on his retirement: 'his motivation in starting such a development was the fact that in securing land in the right position which is then developed with the right retail ingredients one can create a position of monopoly which is unassailable'.[41] The Multiple Shops Federation argued for much stronger

[39] Multiple Shops Federation, *The Planning of Shopping Centres* (London: Fosh & Cross, 1963), 4. Emphasis in original.
[40] Objection letter from Prices Tailors Ltd, 17 October 1966. TNA-HLG-79/1187.
[41] 'Man Who Started Arndale Retires', *Town & City Group News*, Summer 1977 edition. Available in the P&O Collection at National Maritime Museum.

legal and financial 'safeguards for dispossessed occupiers' (their petitioning was partly responsible for the Conservative government's bolstering of compensation levels at the end of the 1950s). The Federation also suggested that its displaced members should be guaranteed reinstatement on good trading sites with rents fixed at low levels.[42] Ironically, it was precisely these loosely worded and unenforceable protections which had enabled the multiple stores to muscle small traders out of blitzed redevelopment areas throughout the 1940s and 1950s. Once the boot was on the other foot, the Multiple Shops Federation became an agitator for the rights of the dispossessed.

Back in Manchester, the powerful rhetorics of modernisation and obsolescence were repeatedly marshalled by both the Corporation and the developer to justify this controversial overhaul of the city's existing economic geography and business landscape. At the 1968 public inquiry, one city official argued that the existing shopping district was 'hopelessly inadequate for modern requirements'.[43] The city's planning officer, meanwhile, argued that 'action is clearly needed to deal with the evident conditions of bad layout and obsolete development'. The proposed redevelopment would, he suggested, allow for 'the development in depth of the obsolete property that lay behind the high value frontages'.[44] The critical importance of these discursive formulations was not lost on the businesses which were materially disadvantaged by redevelopment, and many of them sought to contest the meanings being attached to terms like 'modernisation' or to dispute the condemnation of their businesses as 'obsolete'. On behalf of eighteen publicans facing demolition, the Manchester and District Brewers' Society argued that:

Objector's properties are not obsolete or sub-standard nor are they in need, and certainly not in imminent need, of replacement and their designation for compulsory acquisition cannot be justified on this or any other account; they are all of them sound properties with many years of useful life before them.[45]

Dunn and Co., a multiple retailer of men's clothing, voiced similar objections. The company argued that 'our property and some others still retain an expectancy of life for many years to come'. This company also proposed an alternative, gradualist method of improving the city's shopping area,

[42] See the letter and memorandum 'Safeguards for Dispossessed Occupiers' from the Multiple Shops Federation to the Ministry of Housing and Local Government dated 28 July 1961, within TNA-HLG-141/32.
[43] Michael Morris, 'Plans for 30-Acre Shopping Precinct', *The Guardian*, 19 June 1968, 5.
[44] City and County Borough of Manchester, *City Centre Map 1967*, 58. Available at GMCRO.
[45] Objection letter from Cobbett, Wheeler & Cobbett Solicitors, 25 October 1966. TNA-HLG-79/1185.

arguing that it would be 'desirable to preserve the character of Market Street . . . and owners should be allowed to redevelop their properties . . . on a co-operative basis as and when the life of the buildings determine'.[46] The city council's notion of modernisation was explicitly contested by the shoe shop Timpson's and by Prices Tailors:

> In our opinion, the modernization of the centre of Manchester could be achieved, at much less cost, by natural development over a period of years without destroying the character of the Market Street shopping parade.[47]

Businesses understood that the meanings attached to the terms 'obsolete' and 'modern' had very concrete political and economic consequences and they sought to contest their definition accordingly. Writing about contemporary urban development, the urban political economist Rachel Weber has described the concept of obsolescence as an 'alibi for creative destruction' – and thus critical to the capitalist urban development process of demolition and rebuilding as a means of revaluing urban space and unlocking new wealth-generating capacity. Weber notes how, 'on the surface', the language of obsolescence is morally and politically neutral, 'as if the social has been removed from an entirely technical matter'.[48] Although Weber frames this functioning of the language of obsolescence as a relatively recent product of 'the marketized ideologies of neoliberalism', it is clear that the concept could be similarly instrumentalised in the post-war city. And we have seen how generously the concept of obsolescence was defined by central government, in order to justify demolition and rebuilding as soon as it became 'an economic proposition'. Such analyses offer a means of understanding how important the discursive formulations of post-war urbanism really were within political contests over the uses, values and ownership of scarce urban space and resources. Because urban change was narrated in modernising terms in the post-war period, basic material conflicts over urban space and resources were transferred into disputes over the meaning of modernisation and obsolescence, in what Weber refers

---

[46] Objection letter from Dunn & Co., 25 October 1966. TNA-HLG-79/1187.
[47] Objection letters from Prices Tailors Ltd, and from William Timpson Ltd, dated 17 and 14 of October 1966, respectively. TNA-HLG-79/1185.
[48] Rachel Weber, 'Extracting Value from the City: Neoliberalism and Urban Redevelopment', *Antipode* 34:3 (2002), 519–540. For David Harvey's account of 'creative destruction' see *The Urbanization of Capital* (Oxford, 1985), 138–139. Historians of the nineteenth-century city have also highlighted this submersion of 'the political' within 'the technical' in projects of urban improvement, for example, Patrick Joyce, *The Rule of Freedom: Liberalism and the Modern City* (London: Verso, 2003); Chris Otter, *The Victorian Eye: A Political History of Light and Vision in Britain, 1800–1910* (Chicago: University of Chicago Press, 2008).

to as 'the intense socio-political struggle' over the values attached to different uses of the urban environment.[49] Organised and well-funded retailers could at least hire lawyers and mobilise trade bodies to assist them in contesting designation and dispossession. Many of those most affected by redevelopment possessed neither the knowledge nor the capital to ensure their interests were represented adequately. This was particularly the case where central area residents were being displaced, and they often struggled to articulate their views in ways which the legal and administrative machinery of planning would acknowledge. In Manchester one resident displaced by redevelopment wished to 'object as a matter of principle' but was forced to accept that they had 'no valid objection in a legal sense'. Another simply stated that the shopping development was 'unnecessary and/or inappropriate'.[50] Small traders also struggled to negotiate the technocratic languages of planning effectively, often falling back upon relatively unsophisticated criticisms of development schemes as 'too grandiose' and 'unnecessary'.[51] As well as displacing residents and small businesses in the interests of creating efficient retailing environments, large shopping developments could also serve to destroy streets and districts which were judged undesirable in other ways. Prior to the demolition of Manchester's Market Street district, the narrow lanes and courts in the back streets of the shopping area housed a number of small clubs and music venues which formed part of Manchester's 'beat' scene. In Manchester, as in other cities in the 1960s, young people were making increasing use of venues with the nominal status of private members clubs in order to sidestep the licensing regulations and policing which more public establishments were subject to. The historian Louise Jackson has shown how such 'coffee clubs' were a source of moral panic in the 1960s.[52] In a 1965 *Times* report one journalist claimed that 'the worst of these clubs have been . . . used for drug trafficking; for the harbouring of young prostitutes, absconders and the new breed of "teenage tramps"; even for some small scale white slavery'.[53] In Manchester in the early 1960s the city police had devoted considerable resources to their attempts to infiltrate these clubs, while the council was actively seeking stronger powers from Parliament to control and close such venues.

---

[49] Weber, 'Extracting Value from the City', 523.
[50] Residents' objection letters, dated 1 March 1967 and 9 January 1967 respectively. TNA-HLG-79/1187.
[51] Letter of objection to Councillor N Bolton, 1965. TNA-HLG-79/1213.
[52] Louise Jackson, '"The Coffee Club Menace": Policing Youth, Leisure and Sexuality in Post-war Manchester', *Cultural and Social History* 5:3 (2008), 289–308, 290.
[53] 'Teenage Trouble in "Coffee Clubs"', *The Times*, 12 May 1965. Cited in Jackson.

For the city authorities, the redevelopment of the entire Market Street district provided a welcome opportunity to obliterate, rather than simply regulate, these problematic spaces. An online collection of testimonies and memories from former patrons of the clubs destroyed by the Market Street development includes images of this demolition process, accompanied by comments such as 'the sad end at Cromford Court' (site of a number of clubs), and (sardonically) 'long lost under the architectural glory that is Arndale!'[54] Details of the (now) distinguished list of bands and musicians who performed at Cromford Court have been collated and include artists such as The Rolling Stones, David Bowie, The Kinks, The Animals and Manfred Mann. While they would undoubtedly be welcomed within the entertainment economy of present-day Manchester, in the mid-1960s, and in the hard-to-regulate spaces of the city's coffee clubs, this was not the case. Yet despite the moral panic that such places provoked at the time, patrons' memories – albeit filtered through the lens of distant recollection – paint a very different picture of sociability, excitement and formative experience, which rested on a subcultural community of interest rooted in the environs of the members' club. Here in microcosm, then, is one example of the meaningful social worlds which could be violently displaced through urban renewal. Redevelopment always involved implicit political judgements about the value of particular spaces and the desirability of the practices which took place there. Decisions about which districts were 'obsolete' and 'ripe for demolition' thus comprised a process of economic and social selection – a regulation of acceptable business forms and desirable social practices which took place through the physical remaking of cities. As later chapters show, in the new urban landscapes of the shopping centre, young people's behaviour was far more rigorously policed than it had been in the secluded spaces of the beat clubs.

Major urban renewal schemes such as Manchester's thus transformed the social and economic geography of the city centre – restructuring the retail sector, radically increasing the value and wealth-generating capacity of central area land and expelling a whole range of other activities and social uses. On the one hand these were intensely capitalistic projects, which rested on the 'creative destruction' of the most valuable land in the city by commercial property developers. But the development sector could not act alone; public powers of compulsory purchase were needed to deliver the land and override local opposition and this made local authorities essential partners in these operations. In Manchester's case

---

[54] These recollections, along with images and ephemera associated with the clubs are collected on the website manchesterbeat.com.

the corporation chose to embroil itself particularly closely in the financial side of the Market Street scheme by investing £1.5 m of municipal funds in the development. Town & City, backed by the Prudential Insurance Company, was to stump up the remaining £26 m. This move was another indication of the persistence of earlier traditions of municipal enterprise in these major renewal schemes, as the Corporation sought to profit from the scheme directly as a corporate economic actor. The fact that the Corporation of Manchester acted simultaneously as both a corporate investor and the presiding public planning authority is another illustration that there could be plenty of conflicts of interest in these urban renewal projects without any semblance of criminal corruption.

Manchester's financial participation in the Market Street scheme dragged the Corporation into a crisis over the project's funding in 1971 when the Prudential unexpectedly reduced its contribution to £15 m and left a large gap in the scheme's funds which Town & City was unwilling or unable to fill. The response of Manchester Corporation was entrepreneurial in the extreme. The council enlisted the help of the merchant bankers S. G. Warburg & Co – a post-war newcomer to the City of London, which by the 1960s was well known for its aggressive and unorthodox financial operations.[55] With Warburgs' help an innovative financial arrangement was devised to save the Market Street scheme. The essence of this plan was the creation of a special-purpose company – the Manchester Mortgage Corporation Limited – which would issue stock in order to raise the required funds. Although the company operated as an independent corporate entity, its stock issue was unconditionally guaranteed by the city council and a complicated contractual system ensured that its sole function was the financing of the shopping centre. The company also, controversially, benefitted from being able to borrow at the low interest rates available to public bodies, despite its nominally 'private' status. The Manchester Mortgage Corporation's six directors were all senior councillors, while the secretary was the city's town clerk.[56]

By the later twentieth century, such municipal financial innovation and 'risk-bearing for private capital' was to become a common – and much critiqued – feature of 'the new urban entrepreneurialism'.[57] But in 1971 Manchester's experiments along these lines were novel and unorthodox.

---

[55] For Warburg's see Paul Ferris, *The City* (London: Penguin, 1965), 85–87. For the City more generally in this era, see Davies, *The City of London and Social Democracy*.
[56] The full details and discussions surrounding this scheme are contained within TNA-HLG-79/1189.
[57] Bob Jessop, 'The Narrative of Enterprise and the Enterprise of Narrative: Place Marketing and the Entrepreneurial City', in Tim Hall & Phil Hubbard (eds.), *The Entrepreneurial City: Geographies of Politics, Regime and Representation* (Chichester: Wiley, 1998), 77–102, 99. See also David Harvey, 'From Managerialism to

Indeed, the arrangement caused considerable concern at the Treasury and the Bank of England where officials were decidedly uneasy about the venture. The view here was that 'this operation was outside the scope of public expenditure'. There was concern in particular about the ambiguous status of the newly formed company as well as the Corporation's failure to obtain 'adequate security ... from the developer' in return for the cheap finance it was providing.[58] Ultimately, the Treasury and the Bank did sign off on this scheme following 'discussions with Warburgs' (which was on the Bank's Accepting House Committee of favoured merchant banks) and after accepting Manchester's arguments that the collapse of the Arndale shopping development 'could have extremely serious consequences for the City as a regional commercial centre'.[59] The Treasury recognised, though, that the case had 'implications for the wider question of methods of enabling local authorities to bring in private capital' and noted that 'the Department of the Environment are exploring generally how best to arrange partnership with the private sector in development'. Despite its reservations, in the end the Treasury acknowledged that:

The idea of a joint local authority property developer operation is one which is expected to become more popular because the scope of urban redevelopment presents problems which neither the property developers nor the City authorities involved can suitably handle on their own.[60]

This rapidly proved to be the case, with two further public–private development companies incorporated in the same year as the Manchester Mortgage Corporation, by councils in Norwich and Buckingham.[61]

The conventional wisdom within the contemporary urban disciplines remains that such developmental partnerships and financial innovations were a direct product of the transformed political economy of the post-1970s 'neoliberal' era. Indeed, the suggestion is often made that local authorities were compelled to begin operating in this fashion as part of an aggressive ideological project which was foisted upon them by central government. The usual suspects, as it were, are the 'rising tide of neoconservatism' in the 1980s and 'the ideological hegemony of the supply-side,

Entrepreneurialism: The Transformation in Urban Governance in Late Capitalism', *Geografiska Annaler B* 71 (1989), 3–17.

[58] Letter from Department of the Environment to Manchester Town Clerk, 23 February 1972. TNA-HLG-79/1189.

[59] Letter from Manchester Town Clerk to Department of the Environment, 22 October 1971. TNA-HLG-79/1189.

[60] Letter from The Treasury to Bank of England, November 1971. TNA-HLG-79/1189.

[61] These cases are mentioned briefly in Ambrose & Colenutt, *The Property Machine*, 68–69.

market-based strategies imposed by central government'.[62] In some senses the argument is not wrong but the chronology is. Local authorities did find themselves compelled to enter into new forms of political and financial partnership with private property developers in pursuit of local economic development. And this was indeed a consequence of an over-arching statutory planning framework – imposed by central government – which was market-driven in inspiration and developer-friendly in practice. But it was a framework which had evolved in a largely gradualist fashion since the mid-century, and local authorities – for a variety of motives – could be just as eager to participate as their partners in the development industry. Far from springing from nowhere, late-century urban redevelopment practices emerged out of a long store of experience with public–private collaboration in urban redevelopment; the British state had been sponsoring and subsidising commercial redevelopment projects since the 1940s. As well as revealing these important genealogies, cases like Manchester's also highlight some of the basic political dilemmas involved for local authorities. For all the talk of mutualistic partnerships, the fact remained that such public–private alliances carried with them an inherent unevenness; it was always in the developers' power to walk away should the deal start to look sour. In the case of Manchester's Market Street scheme, it was this threat of collapse – combined with the supreme economic and reputational importance which the city placed upon its retail attractions – that impelled the Corporation to cook up new financial arrangements and take on greater financial risks.

Liverpool: Civic Dreams and Commercial Realities

The political and legal parameters of post-war British urbanism forced local authorities to pursue collaboration with private commercial interests if they hoped to realise their objectives of economic and environmental renewal. Liverpool's experience provides an instructive example of how these parameters worked to produce a very particular form of town centre redevelopment in Britain – one which was sporadic, brash and often tawdry, in spite of the best endeavours of planners and local officials. Liverpool had been a hugely important port and commercial centre across the nineteenth century – a bustling entrepôt connecting Britain and the world – but by the middle decades of the twentieth century the city was in a state of physical and economic decline. The port lost much of its former

---

[62] Harvey, 'From Managerialism to Entrepreneurialism', 5; Steve Quilley, 'Entrepreneurial Turns: Municipal Socialism and After', in Jamie Peck and Kevin Ward (eds.), *City of Revolution: Restructuring Manchester* (Manchester: Manchester University Press, 2002), 76–94, 77.

stature and importance, and the mass employment it had provided in the city waned substantially. In the 1960s Liverpool's population was falling, unemployment was twice the national average and the city's economy was characterised by low wages, low demand and a low-skilled workforce. Such conditions resulted in a distinct lack of private investment for redevelopment of the city centre and its often shabby, largely nineteenth-century physical fabric. By the mid-1960s Liverpool's planners felt that 'about two-thirds of the city centre is in need of renewal'.[63] The surge of enthusiasm for comprehensive urban development was thus seized upon eagerly by Liverpool's city fathers, who were aided from 1962 by the appointment of two forward-thinking planners of the moment – Walter Bor and Graeme Shankland, acting as City Planning Officer and hired Planning Consultant, respectively.

In his recent account of Shankland's endeavours at Liverpool, Otto Saumarez Smith describes this duo's 1965 *Liverpool City Centre Plan* as 'the most visionary and ambitious of any British city centre plan in that decade'.[64] It certainly was a remarkable work of comprehensive planning, rooted in extensive statistical and geographical surveys and analysis, and offering a vision of the city reborn as a thriving civic, cultural and commercial centre. Liverpool's plan was highly responsive to the Buchanan report, *Traffic in Towns*, both in its aspiration to construct new car infrastructures on a grand scale and in its sensitivity towards the environmental quality of those spaces which would be safely separated from the car. In Liverpool's new, largely pedestrianised central core, shopping was to be balanced with serenity. Shankland imagined 'a zone of vivid contrasts with busy shopping streets only a step away from modern restful equivalents of Lincoln's Inn Fields . . . water and fountains will have a great role to play in the traffic-free area, not only because they are fascinating to look at but also because their sound can add to and blend with the background clatter of footsteps'.[65] This sensitive, humanistic approach, and the effort to balance commercial revitalisation with a more rounded care for civic and cultural life, ran through many aspects of the city's plan. Most obviously, the plan envisioned a redeveloped 'Civic Centre' around the historic St. George's Hall where the city's main cultural amenities were located. This area was to be reborn as 'a centre for the city's civic, legal and social life' where the citizens of Liverpool could benefit from such facilities as swimming baths, a youth centre and a further education

---

[63] City Centre Planning Group, *Liverpool City Centre Plan* (1965).
[64] Otto Saumarez Smith (14 February 2019), 'Shankland, Colin Graham Lindsay (1917–1984), Architect and Urban Planner', *Oxford Dictionary of National Biography*. Though the substantive treatment is in Saumarez Smith, *Boom Cities*.
[65] John O'Callaghan, 'Zone of Contrasts in City Centre', *The Guardian*, 15 December 1965, 5.

college.[66] Given the city's problems with its low-skilled workforce, this emphasis upon education for both young and old was particularly sensible. The amount of floor space devoted to education in the central area was to be increased by a third, and jobs in education increased by a half. The leader of the council meanwhile announced in 1965 that spending on the arts was to be increased by a quarter.[67]

Thus, while 'the general aim [was] to ensure that Liverpool remains the main commercial, shopping and entertainment centre of Merseyside', the city's renewal planning contained a sensitive mix of economic, social and civic objectives which had been carefully tailored to meet its specific needs and challenges. There was a proposal to repopulate the city centre through the major development of 'a new central residential community' at Paradise Street, whose residents would be well served with a full array of civic and commercial amenities.[68] There were also intelligent plans for repurposing and regeneration down on the city's decaying docks, most notably via a late-1960s proposal for the redevelopment of Albert Docks with commercial offices, new shopping and leisure attractions such as the proposed Maritime Museum.[69] The problem for all of this sensitive and forward-thinking planning, however, lay in the basic political economy of urban renewal in Britain; the reliance on private interests and investment to carry out redevelopment left councils' redevelopment programmes at the mercy of commercial actors and market incentives over which they had relatively little influence. Thus, the Albert Docks scheme fell apart as successive development companies – which included Harry Hyams' Oldham Estates and Charles Clore's City & Central Investments – pulled out. The innovative Paradise Street neighbourhood, intended to repopulate the city centre, could only proceed as 'a joint municipal-private enterprise', and this too failed to get off the ground as negotiations with indifferent developers went nowhere.[70] This was despite the fact that the city council owned most of the land in question and had already cleared it at public expense, meaning that even the most lukewarm developer would certainly have been offered an attractive, heavily subsidised commercial opportunity.

In the commercially optimistic moment of the early 1960s Liverpool's council had been buoyed by its negotiations with numerous development companies over various projects 'which together would transform the

[66] 'Liverpool's Dreams Put On Paper', *The Guardian*, 26 March 1963, 16.
[67] John O'Callaghan, 'Zone of Contrasts in City Centre', *The Guardian*, 15 December 1965, 5.
[68] 'Liverpool's Dreams Put On Paper', *The Guardian*, 26 March 1963, 16.
[69] Set out in Liverpool City Council, *Waterfront Development: Planning Brief* (1967). Available at Liverpool City Archives.
[70] Michael Hanson, 'Offices Just Waiting to Be Built', *The Guardian*, 24 June 1974, 21.

centre of the city at a cost of some £45 millions'. The Leeds-based developer Arnold Ziff's Town Centre Securities pitched a major 'two-level shopping precinct' for the city with all the voguish add-ons of pubs, restaurants and multi-storey car parks. There was much enthusiasm for the way these projects would gel seamlessly with the city's 'comprehensive' planning objectives and modernising intent. Ziff's shopping centre was to provide a 'pedestrian shopping arcade [which] would be linked by a tunnel and escalator to Central station while, at the other end, a bridge over a main road would provide access to the new markets', as one journalist explained. This would mean 'that pedestrians could move under cover and free from traffic through a considerable part of the city centre'.[71] This project also failed to materialise. In the end, of the four major developments proposed in Bor and Shankland's 1965 plan, only one was ever built. This was Ravenseft's St. John's Precinct – a shopping centre, hotel and leisure complex designed as an ultra-modern replacement to the city's traditional market district (see Figure 3.9, previous chapter).

Ravenseft's scheme was also agreed with the council amidst the intense optimism of the early 1960s renewal fervour. The scheme was approved by the city in 1962, with a leading alderman applauding its 'astonishing architectural ingenuity'. Boosterist reportage explained that Ravenseft's architect had placed 'great emphasis ... on visual contrasts and stimulus', with the scheme to incorporate 'pedestrian ways at different levels, several ornamental pools, and a 50ft high mural in the central concourse'. The new commercial complex was crowned by a slender, 400-foot high, observation tower, St. John's Beacon, complete with a revolving restaurant. This would, the architect explained, 'sparkle like a Christmas tree' when illuminated at night. Once again, the tenets of comprehensive planning were invoked, especially around the idea of pedestrianisation. When the Ravenseft scheme was approved, Shankland explained that 'apart from Venice', the plans for the city centre 'would provide the biggest pedestrian shopping precinct in Europe, possibly in the world'.[72] Ravenseft was an accomplished operator within the complex public–private political economy of post-war British planning. In Liverpool, the firm adroitly positioned its St. John's Precinct at the heart of the city's renewal programme, confidently talking the languages which planners and councillors longed to hear:

The St. John's Precinct ... is integrated with, and forms the cornerstone of the extensive redevelopment of the City of Liverpool, designed by Graeme Shankland

[71] 'Plan for City Shopping District', The Guardian, 26 September 1961, 16.
[72] 'Plan to Rebuild Liverpool City Centre Approved', The Guardian, 21 September 1962, 24.

and Associates, the City's Planning Consultants. It gives this metropolis and great seaport modern traffic-free shopping facilities unequalled in Europe, bringing together under one roof a new Retail Market for the Corporation of Liverpool, Shopping Arcades, a 162 bedroom luxury Hotel, a Ballroom Suite, Licensed Premises and a Covered Car Park.[73]

The firm was even happy to describe the shopping centre's mall concourse as 'a water garden' in an obvious sop to Shankland's vision for pleasant and playful pedestrian areas and gestures towards Venetian parallels.

Whether or not the St. John's Precinct should properly have been understood as 'the cornerstone' of Liverpool's ambitious city-wide programme of physical, economic and cultural renewal became largely immaterial once it was clear that it was the only element of the plan which would come to fruition. The shopping centre opened for business in 1969, with little positive effect for the city either economically or environmentally (Figure 4.3). Architecturally uninspiring, with cheap finishes and materials which aged badly, the *Financial Times*'s

Figure 4.3 Ravenseft's St. Johns Shopping Precinct in central Liverpool, pictured in 1975. For all its sleek modernist design on the drawing board, the development was not warmly received upon completion. Nor was the shopping centre a commercial success: here shop units are notably being advertised to let six years after opening. Source: Getty Images.

[73] Ravenseft Properties Limited, *Liverpool St John's Precinct* (1968), development prospectus. Available at Liverpool City Archive.

correspondent described the complex as 'a disappointing result'.[74] By 1972 a *Guardian* report was telling of the 'shopping blight' which was plaguing Liverpool as the city's central shopping areas 'virtually collapsed' with major knock-on effects for land values in the centre. Population, prosperity and investment continued to drain inexorably away from the city while the problems of dereliction, unemployment and a decaying inner-area housing stock were beginning to look increasingly insurmountable. 'Few like to remember', the *Guardian*'s correspondent now opined, 'that cities have died in the past – the Mediterranean is full of them – and there can come a point when a place no longer serves quite such important a role and has to shrink, if not disappear'.[75] This pessimistic rumination came a decade before Margaret Thatcher's first government also wondered privately whether 'managed decline' might not be the most practicable future for Liverpool.[76] Even at the height of a frenetic commercial property boom which took hold nationally in 1973, development activity in Liverpool 'hardly kept pace with the overall rate of decay', as the county planning officer explained, and rents for commercial office space in the city remained at pathetically low, 'sacrificial' levels.[77] Meanwhile, the futuristic revolving restaurant at the top of St. John's Beacon closed just eight years after opening. The tower sat unused and abandoned for the next fifteen years.[78]

With few capacities to substantively address Liverpool's ongoing battering by the fickle fortunes of market forces, the city authorities were left to plough the same old barren furrow. In 1972 the planning department 'pioneered a positive approach to planning' by publishing 'a plan of the city centre giving full details of development opportunities' in another failed bid to entice developers and investors.[79] As the sole product of Liverpool's ambitious mid-1960s renewal programme, then, the St. John's Precinct also stood as a monument to the limitations – the meanness and shabby commercialism – of Britain's urban renewal regime. This significance was not lost on contemporaries. In a public

[74] H. A. N. Brockman, 'Merseyside's Latest Landmark', *Financial Times*, 10 April 1972, 32.
[75] Judy Hillman, 'The Deep End of the Pool', *The Guardian*, 15 September 1972, 12. For more on Liverpool's economic and environmental woes in this era see Aaron Andrews, 'Dereliction, Decay and the Problem of De-industrialization in Britain, c. 1968-1977', *Urban History* 47:2 (2020), 236–256.
[76] Simon Parker, 'The Leaving of Liverpool: Managed Decline and the Enduring Legacy of Thatcherism's Urban Policy', available as an essay on the *LSE British Politics and Policy* online repository, accessed 21 May 2020.
[77] Michael Hanson, 'Offices Just Waiting to Be Built', *The Guardian*, 24 June 1974, 21.
[78] 'St John's Beacon Liverpool', 2019 visitor brochure. After extensive rebuilding the tower now houses a local radio station and a re-opened observation deck.
[79] Michael Hanson, 'Offices Just Waiting to Be Built', *The Guardian*, 24 June 1974, 21.

talk given in 1963, a lecturer in economic history at the University of Leeds, Dr Eric Sigsworth, complained that 'Britain was concentrating too much money and effort on building "superfluities"' and 'pleasure dromes', 'instead of getting rid of its slums'. This attack on the political and economic priorities which governed the course of redevelopment in post-war Britain was prompted, Sigsworth explained, by his revulsion at a full-page ad in the *Guardian* for the St. John's Precinct and its towering Beacon. As well as giving visitors an 'uninterrupted view of the coastline and the surrounding countryside', Sigsworth railed, '[the Beacon] will also give them the finest view of the ripest, rottenest, filthiest, and most extensive slums in the country'.[80] Sigsworth was a historian but also a contemporary social investigator, surveying inner-city districts and conducting detailed analyses of housing policies. As a knowledgeable expert and familiar critic of post-war slum clearance and housing policies, Sigsworth regarded Britain's often dilapidated urban housing stock as a social, economic and human problem of the first importance, which demanded far more attention and resources from the state. He noted that local authority expenditure on housing had fallen substantially in the second half of the 1950s while public expenditure on other forms of building had risen dramatically. He also noted that the boom in central area commercial property development had seen private expenditure on shop and office development rise dramatically from £350 m to £568 m across the same period. 'In these circumstances', Sigsworth explained, 'his heart scarcely warmed to the [St John's] precinct and he wondered whether this was what society really wanted, or whether it wanted more houses'.[81]

The Perils of Partnership

In their separate ways, the two cases of Liverpool and Manchester point to some of the obvious problems with Britain's hybrid public–private redevelopment regime. Liverpool's darkening economic prospects ultimately meant that the city struggled to drum up the necessary interest and investment from private capital to finance its renewal. Meanwhile, the one redevelopment that went ahead – the St. John's Shopping Precinct – proved woefully inadequate as a means of arresting the city's wider

---

[80] 'Wrong Emphasis in Building', *The Guardian*, 11 March 1963, 17.
[81] All these details in 'Wrong Emphasis in Building', *The Guardian*, 11 March 1963, 17. For Sigsworth's work on contemporary housing issues see R. Wilkinson & E. M. Sigsworth, 'A Survey of Slum Clearance Areas in Leeds', *Bulletin of Economic Research* 15:1 (1963), 25–51; E. M. Sigsworth & R. K. Wilkinson, 'Rebuilding or Renovation?', *Urban Studies* 4:2 (1967), 109–121.

economic decline. In Manchester, a more full-throated central area remodelling was rammed through the public planning system but only after the
city itself was forced to step in and shore up the scheme's finances with
dubious borrowing and further public subsidies. This was a pattern
repeated elsewhere, as those cities that felt themselves most in need of
commercial reinvention were forced into submissive positions to entice
footloose developers. S. G. Wardley, who had overseen first Wakefield's
and then Bradford's redevelopment as city engineer and chief planner,
explained how this worked in the mid-1960s. Like Liverpool, Bradford
faced severe structural economic woes in the post-war decades tied to the
decline of its traditional textile industries. When Wardley arrived in
Bradford in 1946, he found the city centre 'had assumed a grim atmosphere of obsolescence with vacant sites and outmoded buildings'.
Wardley wrote of the need 'to engender confidence in the investor' and
of 'the resistance of the economic psychology which has been built up and
which must be overcome if investment in new development is to be
encouraged'. 'It is one thing to produce a Town Plan', he went on, 'but
another to attract the resources to effect its implementation'.[82] In
Bradford this had entailed a long series of abortive negotiations with
various commercial interests as successive projects fell apart when developers and investors walked away.

Ultimately, it was only through extensive concessions and generous
financial incentives that the city was able to realise any positive redevelopment. The main development in Bradford was the Forster Square
shopping and office complex, for which 'the Council assumed prodigious
financial obligations' over and above the provision of the required land.
The city took on all the costs of servicing the redevelopment site, re-laying
sewers, water, gas and electricity lines as well as reorganising the city
centre road network. At every step of the process the developer was
granted additional financial enticements such as options to build on
other sites in the city, generous ground rents from the Corporation and
the various 'escape clauses' that entitled them to abandon projects without penalty if they lost confidence in the scheme. Wardley, for his part,
was pleased with the results (although he readily admitted to 'looking at
life through rosy spectacles'). Bradford's persistence in courting and
coaxing private developers did result in substantial redevelopment in
the city, but the asymmetry of the relationship was striking. And, in any
case, the city's shiny new shopping complexes once again proved inadequate to stem the tide of long-term industrial decline. By the early 1970s

---

[82] S. G. Wardley, 'Partnership', in The Property Council, *The Property Developer* (London:
1964), 37–39.

the city's comprehensive urban renewal programme had collapsed in a storm of criticism, with Wardley's planning accused of giving 'too high a priority to redevelopment of the City Centre' at the expense of new industrial development and job creation. Local industries were in a state of utter collapse, in a process which had cost the city tens of thousands of jobs since the war. In 1972 the city's unemployment rate stood at over 7 per cent and was rising almost 2 per cent per annum; the government placed Bradford in 'Intermediate Area' status (an emergency designation for special economic assistance) in the same year.[83]

Some more of the perils of partnership were on display in Stretford, Greater Manchester, in the 1960s. Here the borough council was working closely with the Arndale Property Trust to redevelop the town centre with one of Arndale's modern shopping complexes. In this case Stretford's council, rather unwisely, allowed an Arndale employee to draw up the central area CDA plans, 'since the shopping precinct was going to form the basis of the Comprehensive Development Area'. The outsourcing of public planning work to the developer which would profit directly from it led Stretford's scheme to become steadily more elaborate and expensive. In particular, the project shifted from being a relatively modest open-air pedestrian precinct to a full-blown, enclosed and air-conditioned shopping mall, with three covered concourses, along with rooftop multi-storey parking for around 1,000 cars. This radical expansion of the scheme was made at the suggestion of the developer's architect, who impressed Stretford's civic officials with talk of 'a covered "mall" which idea [sic] was becoming popular in other parts of the country following a fashion adopted in the United States'. Stretford's Deputy Town Clerk was pleased to report to the Ministry that: 'Mr. Gray [Arndale's star architect] tells me that the scheme is based on one or two he has himself dealt with in Canada and the United States.'[84] In 1963 the idea of bringing a little bit of Southdale, Minneapolis (site of the first US mall) to Stretford, Manchester was no doubt an exciting one for local officials.[85]

Stretford's case points to some of the obvious dangers which local authorities faced in attempting to navigate the potentially treacherous terrain of collaborative redevelopment. The new political and financial relationships of urban renewal were essentially ad hoc and experimental. There was no fixed model of contractual relations between council and developer, and everything depended upon negotiation. Contracts and terms varied significantly in different locales. Developers often stood to

---

[83] Gunn, 'The Rise and Fall of British Urban Modernism', 849–869.
[84] These details of Stretford's redevelopment are contained within TNA-HLG-79/1404.
[85] See M. Jeffrey Hardwick, *Mall Maker: Victor Gruen, Architect of an American Dream* (Philadelphia, University of Pennsylvania Press, 2010).

benefit from this lack of coordination and standardisation, and they thus 'strongly recommend[ed] the negotiated deal as opposed to tenders or private auctions',[86] while, for their part, the more cautious Town Clerks wrote to their counterparts at other councils enquiring about their experiences with different developers and the terms arrived at. Larger urban authorities, with long experience in the profitable management of their own estates, were relatively savvy and not so easily pressured into signing contracts on unfavourable terms (unless, like Bradford, they were desperate). Smaller urban authorities, however, did not necessarily enjoy the same confidence and expertise. Indeed, officials at the Ministry of Town and Country Planning had realised as early as the 1940s that many councils suffered from a 'quite appalling' lack of expertise in property valuation and estates management given their new powers over the assembly and disposal of urban land.[87] Even by the mid-1960s, officials at the Ministry of Housing and Local Government continued to worry that many councils did not hire outside planning consultants to advise them when embarking upon major redevelopment schemes.[88]

Stretford's case illustrated what could go wrong when councils failed to play their hand astutely in dealing with developers. In this instance, the development company had been busily buying up properties in the redevelopment area prior to the CDA submission (as was common practice). The council then failed to apply for purchase and CDA powers over any of the properties already owned by the developer (whose architects, it will be remembered, drew up the CDA map on the council's behalf). This move effectively sealed the developer's control of the whole project. Officials at the Ministry of Housing and Local Government were quicker than Stretford's city fathers to realise that this would mean that 'the scheme could not proceed without Messrs. Arndale's full support and cooperation' and 'would place the council completely at the company's mercy'.[89] Partnership in post-war urbanism was ubiquitous, but each arrangement was negotiated and constructed on its own terms and much depended upon the confidence and experience of local officials. The devil really was in the detail.

Despite the dangers involved in cutting deals with commercial developers, some councils no doubt felt they had played their hand relatively

[86] Arndale Property Trust, *Arndale in Partnership with Local Authorities* (1966), company prospectus. Available at RIBA Library, London.
[87] Ministry of Town and Country Planning, internal note, 7 June 1949. TNA-HLG-71/523.
[88] This concern was evident in the Ministry's 1965 'census' of redevelopment schemes. See TNA-HLG-136/203.
[89] Stretford Municipal Borough Central Area Redevelopment', 10 January 1963, 1. TNA-HLG-79/1404.

well in this era. Small towns might have suffered from a lack of expertise and the limited prospects of their own modest economies. And cities with severe structural woes like Liverpool and Bradford quickly found that retail development was hopelessly inadequate to rescue them from long-term decline and post-industrial malaise. But in places where the prospects were less bleak, local authorities' financial manoeuvres were likely viewed as reasonably sound investments. In the relatively prosperous post-war Midlands, the city of Nottingham saw two major mall developments opened in the first half of the 1970s. Nottingham Corporation was involved in both of these schemes, although it harnessed itself particularly tightly to the fortunes of the second complex, the Broadmarsh Centre, which opened in 1975. In this case, the Corporation already owned much of the land needed for the new shopping complex as a result of pre-war slum clearance activity in the district, and the city struck a partnership deal with the developer (first Arndale and later Town & City) in 1964. This agreement saw the city deliver the land – worth around £3.5 m – to the developer on a 150-year lease for a basic ground rent. The real incentive, though, from the municipal point of view, was that the Corporation was to take a share of the Broadmarsh Centre's operating profits once it was up and running.[90] In the roaring optimism of the early 1960s this surely seemed like an enticing prospect, and indeed the city did fairly well out of its stake in the Broadmarsh complex. At the time of the centre's opening, and in spite of the much higher costs of building and borrowing by the mid-1970s, *The Financial Times* reported that 'the development has proved if anything more profitable to the partners than was originally expected'.[91] Although the faltering prospects of the national economy at this time raised questions about how long this success would last, in the end Nottingham's shopping complexes remained successful well into the 1990s, when the city enjoyed a reputation as one of the best performing retail centres in the country. As frequently happened in such cases, the council's financial stake in the Broadmarsh development had been eroded over time, bartered away over the years to cover the extremely high costs of running and renovating such centres. Nonetheless, at the close of the century, council planners continued to judge that the Broadmarsh scheme had been a successful developmental endeavour for the city of Nottingham.[92]

---

[90] This arrangement set out in City Estates Surveyor and Valuer's Proof of Evidence, 'Broad Marsh Redevelopment Area', November 1969. Available at Nottinghamshire Archives (DD/TS/6/4/17).
[91] John Trafford, 'Shopping Centres: Hiatus for Stocktaking', *The Financial Times*, 2 April 1975, 28.
[92] Virginia Marsh & Dan Bilefsky, 'Australian Developer in £400m Nottingham Retail Plan', *The Financial Times*, 23 February 2000, 6. Also, author's interview with former Nottingham City Council planner, May 2019.

In Manchester, too, by the 1990s the city council no doubt judged that the controversies and compromises that were necessary to realise the city's Arndale Centre had been a price worth paying. The Market Street redevelopment transformed the structure of retailing in the city, producing a marked concentration of the shopping economy within the new complex and a corresponding decline of adjacent shopping streets and districts. In the economically challenging 1980s there were major concerns about these trends as well as a recognition that the scale of the scheme had been excessive and resulted in an over-supply of high-end retail space. A 1980 planning report acknowledged that 'the shock waves associated with [the Market Street redevelopment] are likely to continue to be felt in the City Centre for some considerable time' and now deemed it 'unwise to proceed with any substantial additions to the existing stock of shops in the City Centre'.[93] But by the more prosperous mid-1990s, the Manchester Arndale was generating £20 m a year in rents and was one of the busiest shopping areas in the country in terms of sales. The complex did its job in terms of defending the central area retail economy from the rise of out-of-town competition, which arrived in Greater Manchester in the shape of the edge-of-conurbation Trafford Centre which opened in 1998.[94] The price, though, in both Manchester and Nottingham, was a consolidation of the cities' retailing in these expensive new complexes, where only the most profitable retail businesses could afford to operate, and where large shares of the wealth generated by shopping were extracted out of local economies and onto the balance sheets of the large institutional investors who owned these facilities. Whether these modes of redevelopment had benefitted cities and citizens in a broader social sense remained, as subsequent chapters show, highly questionable.

Conclusion

The high era of British urban renewal saw urban centres transformed by new developmental partnerships between local authorities and commercial property developers. While these projects built firmly upon earlier experiments with reconstruction and renewal, they were enacted on a scale that was altogether new. The widespread use of CDAs and compulsory purchase in existing centres allowed councils to take control of central area property, but in order to realise redevelopment local

---

[93] Manchester City Council, *Manchester City Centre Local Plan* (1980), 21.
[94] Gwndaf Williams, *The Enterprising City Centre: Manchester's Development Challenge* (London: Spon Press, 2003), 172; Nigel Stocks, 'The Greater Manchester Shopping Enquiry: A Case Study of Strategic Retail Planning', *Land Development Studies* 6:1 (1989), 57–83.

authorities were required to work in partnership with developers and other private interests. One notable dynamic of this era was the way the development sector managed to supersede individual retailers as the favoured partner in urban renewal; councils looked to redevelop comprehensively rather than piecemeal, and developers offered the wholesale replacement of existing shopping districts with entirely new commercial complexes. This created the unusual situation in which the dominant retail trade body, along with many of its constituent members, lined up alongside small traders and central area residents in opposition to urban renewal. Major retailers understood well that these acts of urban economic engineering were designed to inflate land values and capture everlarger shares of their profits in site rents, and they contested projects of urban renewal and modernisation accordingly. Meanwhile, many other less profitable and less privileged patterns of land use were expelled altogether from the town centre by mammoth redevelopment projects. Local authorities were impelled by statute and by necessity to pursue redevelopment in this fashion and many councils clearly felt that partnering with the commercial property sector was a developmental imperative to stave off post-industrial decline. However, as the cases of Liverpool and Bradford show clearly, as a remedy for post-industrial decline such modes of redevelopment proved decidedly inadequate. Other cities like Manchester and Nottingham fared better, but there was always a dangerous asymmetry in these public–private alliances, which frequently left local authorities politically and financially exposed. Whether these experiments were judged successful or not developmental terms, they nonetheless transformed the social and economic landscape of Britain's urban centres, and Chapter 5 turns to examine the character of these curious new urban spaces more closely.

5   Landscapes of Leisure

The major city centre renewal schemes of the post-war decades swept away diverse, mixed use, urban districts and replaced them with new landscapes of affluence, in which urban space and experience was tightly organised around the profit-maximising imperatives of efficient retailing. Central areas came to be dominated by large, holistically planned commercial complexes, with grandiose shopping malls at their heart. The new consumer landscapes possessed strange, almost surreal, environmental qualities, which combined an emphasis upon spectacle, novelty and display with an atmosphere of comfort, safety and leisured lethargy. The careful arrangement of spaces and sensory stimuli within shopping environments, the insipid piped-in 'Muzak' and precise control over temperature and climatic conditions, were designed to induce a state of passive enjoyment and suggestibility in the shopping citizen. The internal layouts of malls promoted gentle but continuous 'circulation', channelling customers past alluring displays and on to the next spending opportunity. There is an important body of scholarship which deals with the environmental and experiential qualities of these new consuming spaces, which proliferated in cities across the advanced capitalist world in the later twentieth century. Cultural theorists have interpreted the shopping mall as an archetypal 'non-place' of postmodernity – a 'hyperreal' consuming environment in which the spaces and experience of shopping are themselves commodified, and sign, symbol and image replace substance, solidity and meaning.[1] Politically and socially, the postmodern shopping

---

[1] The term 'non-place', and its association with 'post-modern' consuming environments, has been adopted from Augé, *Non-Places* [orig. French edition, 1992]. 'Hyperreality' is a term coined by theorist of postmodernity Jean Baudrillard in *Simulacra and Simulation* [orig. French edition, 1981]. For accounts which treat shopping malls in these terms see Jameson, *Postmodernism, or, the Cultural Logic of Late Capitalism*; Harvey, *The Condition of Postmodernity*; Clarke, *The Consumer Society and the Postmodern City*; John Goss, 'Modernity and Postmodernity in the Retail Landscape', in Kay Anderson & Fay Gale (eds.), *Cultural Geographies* (Australia: Longman, 1999), 199–220; Mark Gottdiener (ed.), *New Forms of Consumption: Consumers, Culture and Commodification* (Oxford: Rowman & Littlefield, 2000). And for clear and useful discussion of urban studies'

mall is frequently held to represent the triumph of rampant consumer capitalism, and its neoliberal underpinnings, over urban space, civic values and the public domain.[2]

These theoretical models and cultural critiques carry some force and provide a useful means of thinking through the significance of new sites of consumption. Yet the post-war British shopping centre does not fit entirely neatly within these postmodern terms of enquiry. The urban shopping centres of the 1960s and 1970s emerged out of a very specific conjuncture – a moment in which the technocratic and welfarist aims of public officials came together, somewhat uneasily, with the forces of consumer capitalism and commercial property development around ideas of affluence, leisure and a new entitlement of the masses to enjoy themselves. The public planning apparatus of the post-war state was instrumental in the production of the elaborate commercial complexes which came to dominate the city centre, and this – in theory at least – lent British shopping centres a distinctive ideological flavour. Paradoxically (and, in the end, somewhat optimistically), some planners strove to cast these 'temples of frenetic consumption' as a new and invigorating type of civic space, reformulated for the age of mass affluence, in which a mix of municipal and commercial facilities reflected the wider mingling of the categories of social democratic citizenship and the affluent consumer, of welfare statehood with consumer capitalism.[3] New urban shopping spaces, with their municipal libraries, sports halls and communal events, were intended as facilities for a new type of subject – the post-war mass-consuming citizen – whose access to leisure and pleasure had now to be serviced alongside their entitlements to welfare, healthcare and education. Indeed, for some of the more patrician planners, carefully crafting the new landscapes of leisure with a specific 'civic' inflection was an important public duty lest the citizen succumb to the more deleterious social and moral temptations of their newfound affluence.

engagement with such ideas see Sharon Zukin, 'The Postmodern Debate over Urban Form', *Theory, Culture and Society* 5: 2–3 (1988), 431–446.

[2] William Severini Kowinski, *The Malling of America: An Inside Look at the Great Consumer Paradise* (New York: William Morrow, 1985); Sharon Zukin, *Landscapes of Power: From Detroit to Disneyworld* (Berkeley: University of California Press, 1991) & *The Cultures of Cities* (Oxford: Blackwell, 1995); Hannigan, *Fantasy City*. The much smaller literature on British shopping spaces has taken its cue from this scholarship, see Michelle Lowe, 'From Victor Gruen to Merry Hill: Reflections on Regional Shopping Centres and Urban development in the US and UK', in Peter Jackson, Michelle Lowe, Daniel Miller & Frank Mort (eds.), *Commercial Cultures: Economies, Practices, Spaces* (Oxford: Berg, 2000), 245–260; Miles, *Spaces for Consumption*.

[3] The phrase is Guy Debord's, from *The Society of the Spectacle* (London: Rebel Press, 2004) [orig. French edition, 1967], 174.

Planning for Pleasure

The shopping complexes of the 1960s and 1970s offered consumers a new type of shopping experience in a new kind of environment, in which the shopping trip was decisively recast as an enjoyable leisure activity in its own right rather than a mundane domestic chore. Languages of pleasure, leisure, relaxation and comfort ran consistently through the presentation of these facilities, which stressed how far the new centres had transformed the very nature of shopping. In a 1964 report on London's Elephant and Castle centre, the author welcomed this 'completely new concept in modern day retail shopping' with these thoughts:

The fact, so long taken for granted, that shopping is a tedious, and in congested town centres all too often dangerous, business has been faced and, it is hoped, overcome with the new centre. Shopping can now be done in leisure and indeed even with pleasure.[4]

Shopping centre developers stressed the transformative impact which having centres fully enclosed would have upon the shopping experience, particularly with regard to the British weather. The Arndale Property Trust bemoaned the 'high winds, rain, snow and fog, an abundance of which is unfortunately part of our every-day life'. 'What can be done', the developer wondered rhetorically, 'about making shopping a delight and a pleasure instead of an obligation and a chore often spoiled by bad weather?'[5] Capital & Counties, the developer behind Nottingham's Victoria Centre, also talked of 'Making Shopping a Pleasure' and noted that 'full enclosure ... will offer much more than protection from the elements':

The enclosed mall will provide controlled lighting, shrubs, fountains, seating and other special features which contribute towards the creation of an exciting environment where shoppers can meet under conditions which are more attractive, more convenient, far safer and cleaner than are possible in the high street.[6]

Much was made of the safety, comfort and convenience that 'one-stop shopping' in an enclosed centre would offer 'the British shopper'. The ritualised invocation of this figure was itself a clear sign of the central place which commercial consumption had come to occupy in post-war public life, as businesses, governments and political parties jostled to present

---

[4] T. W. Hearn, 'Glamour and Versatility', *The Guardian*, 9 September 1964, 21.
[5] Arndale Property Trust, *Arndale in Partnership with Local Authorities* (1966), company prospectus. Available at RIBA Library, London.
[6] Capital & Counties, *Victoria Centre Nottingham* (1970), development prospectus. Available at Nottinghamshire Archives.

themselves as the foremost advocates of 'the consumer' and their famous 'interest'. Although appeals to 'the consumer' were becoming less heavily gendered in this era, when speaking of 'the British shopper' there was rarely any ambiguity about the gender of this favoured subject.[7] 'The British shopper', one journalist wrote, 'is a determined woman with an eagle eye for a bargain. She is amenable to change so long as it is not too complicated, avid for comfort, and sick to death of getting wet in the High Street'.[8] The offerings of the new shopping centres for the British house-wife were repeatedly stressed. 'The comprehensive facilities' of the Elephant and Castle centre, claimed its architect:

... will help to satisfy the varied needs of the housewife. She can shop with her children without worry, meet her friends at the cafes, purchase her daily, weekly, or monthly needs, all under one roof. Owing to the complete control of the environment both from weather and traffic point of view, the customer is able to relax and to enjoy the social as well as practical side of shopping.[9]

Town and City Properties noted that, 'because they are safe ... Centres are attractive to mothers with young children and the Company has made special provision for the entertainment and amusement of youngsters'. Arndale shopping centres all incorporated specially designed 'high quality play features' for kids, while at Birmingham's Bull Ring there were rides, play features and a crèche – 'plenty to keep the children amused and out of trouble'.[10] The banishing of vehicular traffic from the pedestrianised shopping landscapes was held out as a particular boon to mothers: 'You don't have to worry about the traffic – there isn't any traffic! So safe for children!' as one ad emphasised.[11]

It was clear that shopping – especially as it related to the practical business of running a household and provisioning a family – remained largely a feminine domain, but much was made of the new centres' attractions for

---

[7] On gendering the consumer in this period see Ina Zweiniger-Bargielowska, *Women in Twentieth-Century Britain: Social, Cultural and Political Change* (London: Routledge, 2001); Hilton, 'The Female Consumer and the Politics of Consumption in Twentieth-Century Britain', 103–128; Caitríona Beaumont, *Housewives and Citizens: Domesticity and the Women's Movement in England, 1928–64* (Manchester: Manchester University Press, 2013); Peter Gurney, 'Redefining "the Woman with the Basket": The Women's Co-operative Guild and the Politics of Consumption in Britain during World War Two', *Gender & History* 32:1 (2020), 189–207.
[8] Tom Allan, 'The Shopping Scene', *The Guardian*, 11 November 1971, 21.
[9] Paul Boissevain, 'Fulcrum of an Ordered World', *The Guardian*, 9 September 1964, 19.
[10] Town & City Properties Limited, *Arndale Covered Centres* (1973), company prospectus [Available at GMCRO]; British Pathé, 'Bull Ring Centre Opened', newsreel, 4 June 1964; 'New Bull Ring Centre Development Birmingham', *The Financial Times*, 9 February 1960, 7.
[11] 'Where's Britain's Most Modern Shopping Centre?', promotional pamphlet, mid-1960s. Available at West Yorkshire Archive Service [LCC-817111].

men too. Here it was the recasting of shopping as a leisure activity and the incorporation of additional facilities like pubs and restaurants which were key. Arndale claimed that its centres promoted 'family shopping':

> Husbands are no longer reluctant to accompany their wives on shopping expeditions and both husband and wife can be certain that their children can enjoy safety and comfort in the traffic-free, climatically controlled environment. Shopping can be rediscovered as a pleasure – and families can relax in the comfort of an Arndale Covered Centre.[12]

The idea of shopping as a family leisure activity was a powerful and a powerful and oft-repeated one. It relied not only on the idea of shopping for fun, rather than out of necessity, but also upon the internal arrangements and décor of the centres themselves. Architectural experimentation with 'distinctive decorative features', 'colourful lighting' and 'bright, colourful elevations', was explicitly intended to create 'gaiety', 'to add to the shoppers' pleasure' and 'emphasise the fun in shopping'. The eclectic mix of additional leisure facilities centres meant a trip to the shopping centre could also mean visiting cafés, pubs, restaurants, nightclubs, bingo halls, bowling alleys or a 'Golf-O-Tron' game. In Leeds, customers were reminded that: 'The Merrion Centre gives you a lot more than shopping. There's bingo, bowling, dancing, a cinema – even nightclubs! No doubt about it – this is the place you can really enjoy your shopping.'[13]

Such facilities need to be understood in the context of the rapidly expanding domain of leisure and the attempts to plan and provide for this on a hitherto unprecedented scale. Indeed, 'Planning for Increasing Leisure', became an important preoccupation for planners from the 1960s, and studies of 'The Demand for Recreation' advanced in parallel with the growing affluence and extended leisure time of the general population.[14] City plans of the period began to talk explicitly about accommodating 'leisure needs', as in Newcastle's 1967 plan, which made space for an entire chapter on 'The Leisure Plan', 'now that we have all come to understand better what increased affluence and greater leisure might mean'. This dealt with sports facilities, swimming pools, parks and open spaces, professional football, theatre, concerts, horse racing, fairs, cinemas, arts festivals and dancing and had as its centrepiece 'an outstanding scheme for leisure' centred upon remaking the 1,000-acre Town Moor as 'a great family

---

[12] Town & City Properties Limited, *Arndale Covered Centres* (1973).
[13] Where's Britain's Most Modern Shopping Centre?', promotional pamphlet, mid-1960s.
[14] See, for example, R. I. Maxwell, 'Planning for Increasing Leisure: Problems of Town and Country', *Royal Society of Health Journal* 82 (1962), 319–323; Patrick Lavery, 'The Demand for Recreation: A Review of Studies', *Town Planning Review* 46:2 (1975), 185–200. And, for further discussion, Ortolano, 'Planning the Urban Future in 1960s Britain', 477–507.

recreation centre'.[15] Mid-1960s plans for other cities began to address similar concerns, and the proliferation of promotional city guides of the era came to include discussion of cities' leisure offerings – for both residents and visitors – as standard.[16] By the 1970s, a new type of planned facility dedicated to fun and recreation – 'the leisure centre' – had emerged. The proliferation of such centres across the country was a clear symbol of the new public responsibility to service popular pleasure.[17]

Holidays, both domestic and international, were another booming sphere of the post-war leisure economy and it is notable that, in searching for similes with which to convey the mall shopping experience to the uninitiated British shopper, promoters turned repeatedly to the language and imagery of the holiday resort. With their languid layouts, colourful décor and amusing novelties the new urban landscapes of mass affluence resembled the resort and the holiday camp more than they did the traditional British high street. Aviaries, curiously, were a regular feature within post-war shopping centres and 'deservedly popular features with an enthusiastic shopping public' according to one developer.[18] Fountains and pools (often with live fish in them) were ubiquitous, for 'there is ... nothing more beautiful than cascading or tumbling water', one company director explained (Figure 5.1).[19] At Nottingham's Victoria Centre spectacle and novelty in the retail landscape were taken even further. Here, the mall's centrepiece was 'a dream-like water clock by [the sculptor] Roland Emmet [which] every half hour ... provides a musical and gyratory spectacle rarely watched by less than 200 people'.[20] At times the link with resort environments was made explicitly, as in Leeds city council's promotion of its Seacroft shopping facility:

Shopping at Seacroft Centre will be in a relaxed "resort" atmosphere with the noise and harassment of traffic safely out of the way. This will be a particular pleasure to old people and mothers of young children ... Paved courts will be laid out with seats, trees and flowers – an agreeable place to linger.[21]

[15] Burns, *Newcastle*, Chapter 5 'The Leisure Plan'.
[16] See, for example, City Centre Planning Group, *Liverpool City Centre Plan* (1965); City of Birmingham Information Department, *This is Birmingham*, city brochure, late-1960s; Sheffield Corporation & Temple Publicity Services, *Sheffield Official Handbook* (1970); *The City of Bradford Official Handbook* (London: Ed. J. Burrow), early 1970s; *Newcastle Upon Tyne: Official Industrial and Commercial Guide* ((London: Ed. J. Burrow), mid-1970s.
[17] Otto Saumarez Smith, 'The Lost World of the British Leisure Centre Boom', *History Workshop Journal* 88 (2019), 180–203.
[18] Town & City Properties Limited, *Arndale Covered Centres* (1973).
[19] Sam Chippindale, 'Building Design', in A. W. Davidson & J. E. Leonard (eds.), *The Property Development Process* (Centre for Advanced Land Use Studies, 1976), 129–137, 136.
[20] A. S. Bowley, 'The Police and the Planners', *The Police Journal* 46 (1973), 308–314.
[21] Leeds City Council, 'Seacroft Town Centre', development prospectus, (c.1965). West Yorkshire Archive Service [LLC-824956]

Figure 5.1 1964 image of one of the decorative spaces within Birmingham's Bull Ring complex, showing the predilection for pools, fountains, greenery and flower arrangements. Experimentation with the creation of new types of decorative, leisurely spaces was a key element of post-war shopping centre design, and often drew upon forms and motifs lifted from holiday camps and resorts. The early results, as can be seen here, were not always entirely convincing. Source: Historic England Archive, John Laing Photographic Collection.

Elsewhere the parallels between mall shopping and holidaying were drawn more obliquely, as with the frequent references to shopping spaces incorporating 'features which tend to give a Continental impression' (this was in Shipley, West Yorkshire); or the 'open planned continental-type restaurants set amid attractive garden displays' and 'giant internal piazza ... in contrasting shades of Italian quartzite' (in this case, in Birmingham).[22] The post-war exoticism of 'the continent' no longer resonates in quite the same way, but in an era when more and more

[22] Arndale Property Trust, *Shipley Town Centre: Development by the Arndale Property Trust Limited* (1965), development prospectus [RIBA, London]; 'New Bull Ring Centre Development Birmingham', *The Financial Times*, 9 February 1960, 7.

families were abandoning the traditional British seaside resort, and dipping their toes in the Mediterranean rather than the Irish Sea for the first time, the 'continental' imagery certainly carried cultural cachet.[23] Others reached for the idea of the exhibition in order to explain the new environments and their experiential qualities. Planners in Manchester hoped that 'the City's central shopping area could be transformed to take on something of the quality of a well set out and continuously changing permanent exhibition'.[24] Central government planning advisors also felt that shopping centres should aim for an 'exhibition-like atmosphere in an exceedingly gay and entertaining setting'.[25] In making such comparisons, planners – whether knowingly or not – were hinting at the longer genealogies of these post-war retail spaces. The emphasis upon spectacle, variety and display; on entertainment and the presentation of amusing novelties to enrapt observers had a lineage which stretched back through *fin de-siècle* shopping arcades and department stores, to the grand exhibition spaces, galleries and promenades of the mid-nineteenth century and earlier.[26] The architectural lexicons of 'the mall' and (in the romance languages) 'the *galleria*' made clear the connections between these later shopping environments and the elite exhibition spaces of earlier eras. The modern shopping mall was a mid-twentieth century incarnation of these spaces of entertainment, curiosity and spectacle, repackaged and massified for the age of consumer democracy (Figure 5.2).

The post-war retail landscape was thus constructed out of a more complex cultural and architectural repertoire than might be thought. Yet despite the frequent references to a glamorous but nebulous thing called 'the Continent', in practice the most important influence was undoubtedly the United States. The first enclosed shopping centre in the United States – Victor Gruen's Southdale Centre in Minneapolis –

---

[23] On British resorts and holiday habits, see John K. Walton, *The British Seaside: Holidays and Resorts in the Twentieth Century* (Manchester: Manchester University Press, 2000); Sina Fabian, 'Flights to the Sun: Package Tours and the Europeanisation of British Holiday Culture in the 1970s and 1980s', *Contemporary British History* (2021). On ideas of 'the continent' in 1960s Britain, see Mathias Haeussler, 'The Popular Press and Ideas of Europe: The Daily Mirror, the Daily Express, and Britain's First Application to Join the EEC, 1961-63', *Twentieth Century British History* 25:1 (2014), 108–131.

[24] J. S. Millar, *City and County Borough of Manchester: City Centre Map 1967*, 59 [GMCRO, Manchester].

[25] Letter from Ministry of Housing and Local Government to Manchester Chief Planning Officer, 2 August 1966 [TNA-HLG-HLG 79/1188]

[26] On the longer development of spectacular consuming spaces see Hetherington, *Capitalism's Eye*; Rudi Laermans, 'Learning to Consume: Early Department Stores and the Shaping of the Modern Consumer Culture (1860–1914)', *Theory, Culture and Society* 10:4 (1993), 79–102.

Figure 5.2 Artist's impression of the interior of the Doncaster Arndale Centre, illustrating the surreal character of these new retail landscapes with their emphasis upon spectacle, novelty and display. Lavish and intricate décor, exhibition, variety and an assault of brand advertising dominate an environment which would later come to be dubbed 'hyperreal' by postmodern theorists. Source: RIBA Collections, courtesy P&O Heritage.

had opened in October 1956, ten years ahead of the first British centres. *Time* magazine described Southdale as a 'pleasure-dome-with-parking', and many of the entertaining novelties and sumptuous design features of Gruen's mall – which included 'sculpture, glass mosaics, fountains, exotic birds, and tropical plants' – cropped up repeatedly in British designs.[27] The American connection was a very real one: Arndale's directors were regular visitors to the United States from the 1950s, and the company employed architects with experience working in the United States and Canada on many of its British schemes.[28] Ravenseft began working on commercial schemes in Canada in the mid-1950s, while the British developer (and aristocratic landholder) Grosvenor Estates built shopping centres of its own in Canada, on the US mainland and in Hawaii, and flew its British architects out to learn from these developments. The 'overall quality and taste of the terrazzo-floored malls and marble-faced walls' at Grosvenor's Runcorn Shopping City reportedly represented the fruits of this transatlantic experience.[29]

Despite these strong American influences, it was not possible to simply import the American consumer experience 'off the shelf'. This was as true for mall design as it was for the pitching of advertisements. One example was the overzealous enthusiasm for installing bowling alleys and golf ranges in shopping centres – both American imports. At one point in the early 1960s, the bowling alley in particular seemed to British developers to be an essential facility that no shopping centre could do without. American manufacturers were keen to hawk the necessary machinery and equipment for bowling alleys to new markets, and British developers signed agreements with firms to fit out alleys as part of their retail developments. The bowling bubble rapidly burst however, once it became clear that British punters were less keen on the game. Alleys quickly dropped out of the designs for new shopping complexes, and many existing facilities closed after only a few years of disappointing trading. The bowling alley at Leeds's Seacroft Centre closed down less than two years after opening, having already been stripped out and converted into a social club in an attempt to recoup losses. Nationally, the alley's operating company went into liquidation in 1967 and closed down its other facilities at Morecambe, Rotherham, Leigh and Crawley just a few years after opening.[30]

[27] M. Jeffrey Hardwick, *Mall Maker: Victor Gruen, Architect of an American Dream* (Philadelphia: University of Pennsylvania Press, 2003), 143–148.

[28] 'Man Who Started Arndale Retires', *Town & City Group News*, Summer 1977, company newsletter. Available in P&O Collection, National Maritime Museum.

[29] Kate Hutchin, 'Courageous £10m Shopping City Confounds Critics', *The Times*, 4 May 1972, 2.

[30] 'Boom and Bust', *The Economist*, 30 May 1964, 1024; 'Bowling Chain Go Into Liquidation', *The Times*, 11 August 1967, 21.

Elsewhere shopping centre designers recognised the need to tailor facilities to suit local tastes, although this was not necessarily done with a great degree of sophistication. An obvious case in point was the increasing nods towards towns' history in retail design. New mall concourses were often named after the pre-existing streets they had replaced, and, curiously, sometimes after specific entertainment venues – such as theatres – that had been destroyed in the redevelopment. Sometimes individual historic buildings deemed to be of particular value were spared demolition and incorporated into redeveloped shopping areas, as happened with Manchester's Market Place development and Nottingham's Victoria Centre. The developer Town and City boasted that 'murals in both sculpture and other art forms are a feature of many Centres and these often depict events which are part of the town's history'. A mural at Poole, for example, 'express[ed] the town's affinity with the sea and things nautical', while another at Middleton 'depict[ed] part of the town's long and fascinating history'. At Jarrow, in the once-Scandinavian North East of England, Arndale installed a large bronze statue of two stylised Vikings at the intersection of the new 'Viking Precinct' and 'Bede Precinct' (a nod to the town's Venerable eighth-century Saint). And in its Nelson shopping mall, Arndale installed a bust of Lord Nelson and a decorative 'floor compass' as part of a 'naval theme'.[31] Although the Lancashire town of Nelson reportedly took its name from a historic pub named after the admiral, it is not clear how much the new shopping centre's 'naval' theme would really have resonated with the inhabitants of a Pennine mill town forty miles from the coast. Nonetheless, such experiments represented attempts to lend unfamiliar new facilities a sense of place by making reference to the history of specific locales. As such, they clearly foreshadowed later, more sophisticated, efforts at commercially repackaging local 'heritage' in the service of cultural and economic regeneration.[32]

Managing Mass Affluence

The effects of mass affluence, combined with the expanded planning responsibilities of the post-war polity, brought the state ineluctably into the management of mass leisure. Post-war efforts to plan for an increasingly leisured populace wavered between unabashed enthusiasm for the newfound abundance of the post-war era and a more anxious, paternalistic concern with how

[31] These details in Town & City Properties Limited, *Arndale Covered Centres* (1973).
[32] For these more recent developments see Rebecca Madgin, *Heritage, Culture and Conservation: Managing the Urban Renaissance* (Saarbrucken: VDM Verlag, 2009).

the newly leisured masses might spend their time and money. Such concerns were hardly new of course – 'the problem of leisure' had been a moral quandary for the hand-wringing middle classes since at least the Victorian era – but the mass affluence of the post-war decades brought a new urgency to such anxieties, given the relatively rapid elevation of so many to a hitherto unfamiliar state of leisure.[33] Nor was the idea of 'shopping for pleasure' a new one. As a higher-class urban pastime this stretched back through the mid-nineteenth century department store to the rich traditions of early modern consuming cultures. Popular access to such leisured experiences of shopping, meanwhile, had been steadily widening since at least the turn of the twentieth century and broadened decisively with the economic expansion and wage growth of the interwar years.[34] What was novel in the post-war era was the more thoroughgoing massification of such leisured lifestyles, as the broader social reach of mass affluence now left only a minority excluded from participation in the leisure economy through lack of means.

Some of the issues around planning for mass leisure in the post-war era have begun to be explored by a school of architectural historians at work on the continent, whose studies of French youth clubs, Belgian holiday camps and Scandinavian shopping centres usefully remind us not only that 'mass leisure was a new-fangled category that needed to be established and defined', but also that this was by no means a uniquely British story.[35] Across Western Europe, the social democracies of the post-war era were at least as focused upon servicing the leisure and consumption needs of their massed majorities as they were on providing welfare and poverty relief for the worst off in society; indeed, these two projects were inextricably intertwined. Across the Atlantic, the post-war 'Consumer's Republic' of the United States was 'built around the promises of mass consumption'.[36] Nor were these new projects of social provision confined

---

[33] For the longer trajectory of such anxieties see Peter Bailey, '"A Mingled Mass of Perfectly Legitimate Pleasures": The Victorian Middle Class and the Problem of Leisure', *Victorian Studies* 21:1 (1977), 7–28, along with Bailey's subsequent work in this field.

[34] For these longer histories see Erika Diane Rappaport, *Shopping for Pleasure: Women in the Making of London's West End* (Princeton: Princeton University Press, 2000); Crossick & Jaumain, *Cathedrals of Consumption*; Peter Borsay, *The English Urban Renaissance: Culture and Society in the Provincial Town 1660–1770* (Oxford: Clarendon Press, 1989). On British consumer culture in the twentieth century, see Benson, *The Rise of Consumer Society in Britain, 1880–1980* ; Scott, *The Market Makers*.

[35] Tom Avermaete, 'A Thousand Youth Clubs: Architecture, Mass Leisure and the Rejuvenation of Post-war France', *Journal of Architecture* 18:5 (2013), 632–646, 632, along with the rest of this special issue. Also Janina Gosseye & Tom Avermaete (eds.), *Shopping Towns Europe: Commercial Collectivity and the Architecture of the Shopping Centre, 1945–1975* (London: Bloomsbury, 2017); Kenny Cupers, *The Social Project: Housing Postwar France* (Minneapolis: University of Minnesota Press, 2014).

[36] Lizabeth Cohen, *A Consumer's Republic: The Politics of Mass Consumption in Postwar America* (New York: Knopf, 2003), 7.

only to the Western consumer democracies. The Cold War competition between East and West often focused upon which political and economic system could secure the choicest comforts for the greatest number, and the urban managers of Eastern Bloc states were also engaged in planning for new leisure needs, albeit with a different ideological inflection.[37]

The efforts of British planners to service the affluent society displayed the same tension between accommodating new social freedoms and retaining some degree of cultural control, as their counterparts on the continent and elsewhere. Wilfred Burns argued in his 1963 agenda for urban renewal that, 'we have to realise that we are at the beginning of an age of what we hope will be increasing prosperity, with . . . greater freedom and leisure for everyone'. Burns' anxious ruminations on the significance and the dangers of this 'greater freedom' are worth quoting at length:

An image of society in the future is ... difficult to forecast. On the one hand educational advances and progress must surely mean new values in society. On the other hand society as a whole is tending to be depersonalized – a collective society in a mass environment, with mass transport and mass entertainment, and where one job is like another and one housing area like another; the individual drives one of the multitude of cars and then sits in front of his television set. Can these two opposing streams be married so that increasing leisure can be made to give, through education, a new opportunity for active pleasure and participation, for something personal and unique? Perhaps our ... city centres should be planned to give as many opportunities as possible for this development: the personal and human in the midst of technological achievement and conformity.[38]

Burns' fears around mass culture, 'conformity' and the erosion of individual personhood and identity are clear, and they came to rest upon a distinction between 'active' and 'passive' leisure which echoed the long-established moral category of 'rational', improving recreation. Other leading figures in British planning thought similarly, and it was almost always the changing lifestyles of 'the lower brackets' upon which their anxieties were focused.[39]

Such concerns were part and parcel of a wider cultural context of anxiety around the political and moral consequences of affluence, both

---

[37] For the global Cold War context see Victoria de Grazia, *Irresistible Empire: America's Advance through Twentieth-Century Europe* (Cambridge, MA: Belknap, 2006); Ruth Oldenziel & Karin Zachmann (eds.), *Cold War Kitchen: Americanization, Technology, and European Users* (Cambridge: MIT Press, 2009). On Eastern Bloc leisure planning see 'Architecture for Leisure in Post-War Europe, 1945-1989', *Journal of Architecture* 18:5 (2013).

[38] Burns, *New Towns for Old*, 195–196.

[39] This phrase appears in the 1961 Parker Morris report into housing standards and the social impacts of mass affluence, see Alistair Kefford, 'Housing the Citizen-Consumer in Post-war Britain: The Parker Morris Report, Affluence and the Even Briefer Life of Social Democracy', *Twentieth Century British History* 29:2 (2018), 225–258.

for the individual and for society as a whole. The television was a particular focus of these fears, understood to have a deadening, stupefying effect upon viewers' critical faculties and civic engagement. So too was advertising, whose seductive techniques attracted much critical comment, particularly after the appearance of the American Vance Packard's insider exposé, *The Hidden Persuaders*. Packard's book detailed the industry's sophisticated engagement with psychoanalysis and 'motivation research' and provoked much concern when it was first published in 1957. Penguin quickly reprinted the book as a cheap paperback edition in 1960, and it was reissued repeatedly across the 1960s and 1970s.[40] Also hugely influential was the American left-liberal economist John Kenneth Galbraith's *The Affluent Society*, which provided the epithet for the age and attracted reams of commentary in Britain after it was published in 1958. Galbraith proffered stark warnings about 'the problems of an affluent world'; attacking the cyclical logics of a political economy geared towards ever-expanding production, to meet ever-expanding 'demand', which was itself being orchestrated by producer interests. Such a system, in Galbraith's view, was illogical and dangerous from a political, moral and environmental standpoint alike. J. B. Priestley's neologism 'Admass' entered the popular consciousness and the *Oxford English Dictionary* in the later 1950s and was used to decry much the same system of consumer temptation and the mass media management of demand.[41]

Wilfred Burns' anxious account of the dehumanising tendencies of mass culture clearly echoed such concerns. Both of the main political parties were wrestling with their collective consciences over these questions as well. The anxieties surrounding mass affluence were particularly acute for Labour and the British left, but they were also present within some strands of Conservative thinking. The senior Conservative and sometime leadership candidate Reginald Maudling penned a think piece for the *Daily Mail* in 1962 in which he fretted over 'the boredom of modern life in comfortable suburbia' and lamented 'the listless follies ascribed to modern youth'. There was, Maudling suggested, a 'growing sense that material affluence in itself is not enough', and people were 'feeling in their hearts the

---

[40] See Lawrence Black, '"Sheep May Safely Gaze": Socialists, Television and the People in Britain, 1949-64', in Lawrence Black (ed.), *Consensus or Coercion? The State, The People and Social Cohesion in Post-war Britain* (Cheltenham: New Clarion, 2001), 28–48; Nixon, *Hard Sell*; Vance Packard, *The Hidden Persuaders* (Harmondsworth: Penguin, 1960).

[41] John Kenneth Galbraith, *The Affluent Society* (London: Hamish Hamilton, 1958). The OED entry for 'Admass' gives a precise timeline for the word's entry into common usage. For evidence of the influence of this idea, along with Packard's book, see Terence Morris, 'Motive Research', letter to the editor, *The Times*, 17 April 1959, 15. Morris was an LSE Sociologist.

lack of a sense of purpose of this freedom and affluence'.[42] Through some particularly tone-deaf editorial work, Maudling's column was sandwiched between an ad for du Maurier's 'exceptional cigarettes' and an assurance that 'Butlin's in June and July will be just fabulous'. In any case, Maudling's qualms over the excesses of materialism may have been rather more philosophical than practical; the personal financial gains he made through his dubious engagements with various British property companies led to his political downfall ten years later.

The Labour Party in this era was in danger of tearing itself apart over its agonised response to the coming of the affluent society, whose cultures of individualism and acquisitiveness were felt by many to be entirely antithetical to the Party's collectivist ideals and socialist mission. This perspective was articulated most clearly by Richard Crossman's 1960 Fabian Tract, *Labour in the Affluent Society*, which decried compromise with 'the British version of the Affluent Society which has emerged under successive Tory Governments since 1951' and argued that Labour 'must remain a Socialist challenge to the established order'.[43] Crossman's *cri de coeur* was a counter to 'the revisionists' within the Party, most obviously Tony Crosland, who sought an accommodation with the values and ideals of the affluent age. Crosland's 1956 work, *The Future of Socialism*, questioned 'why high consumption and brotherly love should be thought incompatible'; 'why should not the brothers be affluent, and the love conducted under conditions of reasonable comfort?', Crosland mused.[44] Despite these modernising agendas, though, many on the left remained deeply uneasy about the social, cultural and electoral implications of mass affluence.[45]

More radically, Frankfurt School theorists such as Theodor Adorno and Herbert Marcuse were busy denouncing the very foundations of the productivist political economy of mass affluence, along with its moral and political consequences. Marcuse's *One Dimensional Man* – first published in 1964 in Britain and again widely read and reprinted – deplored what he saw as the decline of 'independence of thought [and] autonomy', amid the 'comfortable, smooth, reasonable, democratic unfreedom [which] prevails in advanced industrial civilization'.[46] In 1963 the social

---

[42] Reginald Maudling, 'We'll Be All Washed Up Unless ...', *The Daily Mail*, 21 June 1962, 8.

[43] Richard Crossman, *Labour in the Affluent Society* (London: The Fabian Society, 1960), 1 and 5.

[44] Anthony Crosland, *The Future of Socialism* (London: Jonathan Cape, 1956), 246.

[45] See Lawrence Black's work on this: *The Political Culture of the Left in Affluent Britain, 1951–64: Old Labour, New Britain?* (Basingstoke: Palgrave, 2003); *Redefining British Politics*.

[46] Herbert Marcuse, *One Dimensional Man: Studies in the Ideology of Advanced Industrial Society* (London: Routledge & Kegan Paul, 1964), 1.

Civic Spaces of Consumption

researcher and theorist of welfare statehood Richard Titmuss updated his 'Essays on "the Welfare State"' with a new chapter excoriating 'The Irresponsible Society'. Taking his cues from Galbraith, Titmuss lambasted what he saw as the stark contrast between private opulence and public squalor in a 'more affluent and seemingly arrogant society'. He bemoaned the celebration of 'cupidity and acquisitiveness' and gave ominous warnings of the political consequences of the new 'concentrations of economic and financial power' within 'the managerial capitalist system'.[47] Galbraith then reprised and expanded these ideas himself, delivering the 1966 Reith Lectures for the BBC on the subject of *The New Industrial State*, and publishing a book of the same title a year later. This too was churned out for the more thoughtful segments of the masses as a cheap Pelican paperback by the publisher Penguin and was repeatedly reprinted for British readers. Galbraith's 'revolutionary bestseller' denounced consumer freedom and market competition as convenient fictions within a political economy dominated by large and sophisticated corporate bureaucracies. Such myths, he argued, masked a more sinister reality in which a managerial 'technostructure' shaped society and the economy in its own interests.[48]

Civic Spaces of Consumption

Against this intellectual backdrop, it might be thought remarkable that public planners ever countenanced the widespread reconstruction of city centres as seductive consumer playgrounds. As has been seen in earlier chapters, planning outcomes on the ground in cities were firmly shaped by the hybrid political economy of British urban renewal, which relied on melding the powers of local authorities with the commercial projects of property developers. Many local authorities also took a fairly hard-nosed attitude towards urban renewal, viewing large-scale retail developments as one of the few promising options on the table in their pursuit of prosperity and growth. Where they did seek to pursue alternative, less commercially driven models of urban and social development, local authorities were routinely frustrated by the inadequate powers and insufficient resources afforded them by the central state. Yet it is also important to understand

---

[47] Richard M. Titmuss, *Essays on 'The Welfare State'* (London: Unwin University Books, 1963), 215–243.
[48] John Kenneth Galbraith, *The New Industrial State* (Harmondsworth: Penguin, 1975) [first edition 1969]. For more on Pelican and the market for 'serious non-fiction' in the United States and the United Kingdom, see Peter Mandler, 'Good Reading for the Million: The "Paperback Revolution" and the Co-Production of Academic Knowledge in Mid Twentieth-Century Britain and America', *Past & Present* 244:1 (2019), 235–269.

how the anxious strand of planning thought which Wilfred Burns articulated was reconciled to the consumerist remodelling of the city. Many planners hoped to imbue new shopping developments with a distinctive 'civic' character and were thus able to imagine them as bulwarks against the worst social and moral consequences of mass affluence.[49]

Concerned planners were at pains to emphasise that new shopping centres were not merely commercial spaces but should also be seen as a new type of civic space, which would fulfil a wide range of social functions and revitalise urban communities. Picking up on the ideas of the Austrian-born urbanist and US mall designer Victor Gruen, British planners sought to draw a line of historical continuity between the ancient Greek agora, the Roman forum, the medieval marketplace and the twentieth-century shopping centre. In this formulation, the shopping centre, like its illustrious forebears down the millennia, would be the bustling, beating heart of the urban civitas. The planner-architect Hugh Wilson's account is representative:

From early times the market place has been the centre of city life, where people could meet and exchange gossip. The Greek Agora and the mediaeval market place were examples of the integration of commercial activity with other town centre functions. With the vast expansion of cities, the old centres play a less important part in social life and therefore the new shopping centre, apart from performing a commercial function, must act as a place of public gathering where social and cultural activities can be enjoyed.[50]

The promoters of individual centres spoke in similar terms. The Elephant and Castle's architect suggested that 'a well used [sic] shopping centre can provide a social fulcrum for the area'. Developers were happy to go along with this of course, with Town and City presenting its shopping centres as 'a focal point of the town's social and economic life' and affirming 'the company's view that towns must have a focal point comprising attractive shopping, leisure facilities and public services ... which forms the commercial heart of the community'.[51] Councils, for their part, were often insistent that new shopping facilities be classified as *civic* amenities. In a promotional visitor map produced by Leeds's Central Information Bureau, the Merrion Shopping Centre was clearly included within the category of 'Civic Buildings' alongside the city's train station, infirmary, technical college and town hall.[52]

[49] A point also emphasised in Saumarez Smith, *Boom Cities*.
[50] Wilson, 'Civic Design and the Shopping Centre', 271–274.
[51] Paul Boissevain, 'Fulcrum of an Ordered World', *The Guardian*, 9 September 1964, 19; Town & City Properties Limited, *Arndale Covered Centres* (1973).
[52] Leeds Central Information Bureau, *Leeds*, city map and guide (1971). Author's collection.

Key to this civic character was the much-vaunted incorporation of new municipal facilities within shopping centres. 'In many Centres', Town and City noted, 'libraries, civic theatres, clinics and other public and cultural facilities are provided as an integral part of the overall design'. For the Arndale Property Trust, 'this new conception ... provides an entirely different atmosphere and the centre becomes part of the community life and its contribution to the civic facilities can be outstanding'. This was not entirely hyperbole. Poole's shopping centre, opened in 1969, incorporated a new central library and a municipal sports hall. Morecambe's shopping centre included a newly laid-out 'Town Square' and a new public library. And Luton's mammoth town centre complex also incorporated a public library and a faux-traditional 'village atmosphere' pub with frontage onto a new patch of public open space. Almost all centres were linked with newly built municipal bus stations, and many also included municipally operated markets and car parks. Development companies were pleased to trumpet the fact that 'partnership with Local Authorities can bring forward the provision of much-needed civic and leisure facilities', though the careful choice of language here is telling.[53] It was local authorities that invariably paid for these facilities, despite the fact that many of them – car parks, public toilets and bus stations in particular – were essential for the new centres' commercial success. Public–private development partnerships thus included negotiated agreements whereby councils paid developers to build municipal facilities like market halls, libraries and car parks for them. These arrangements were liable to descend into acrimonious disputes when – as frequently happened – the civic facilities that councils were contractually obliged to pay for were delayed, defective or poorly built.[54] Overall, the commitment to such civic provision was less than wholehearted, with municipal facilities often being quietly dropped from schemes once construction was underway and costs inevitably rising; 'few of the grandiose and public spirited plans for sports halls, cinemas, and restaurants have been translated into concrete', one journalist observed.[55]

In addition to the mix of civic and commercial facilities on offer in new centres, the civic character of the new urban spaces being created was repeatedly stressed, as was the range of social and community activities

---

[53] These details in Town & City Properties Limited, *Arndale Covered Centres* (1973).
[54] This is particularly well documented in Manchester, Bolton & Newcastle: Minutes of the Economic Planning Group (a council committee) for 31 May 1977 and 22 June 1977 [available at GMCRO]; 'Report of the Council Solicitor and Chief Estates Surveyor', 29 February 1988 [GB125.658.84, Bolton Local History Centre]; Minutes of Eldon Square Development Subcommittee, 31 October 1977 [available at Tyne & Wear Archives].
[55] David Ward, 'Sales Pitch', *The Guardian*, 16 October 1978, 8.

which could take place in the new mall concourses. The mall concourse – an indoor, heated, carefully arranged space between individual shops – was the central environmental innovation of the post-war shopping centre. It introduced an unfamiliar type of urban space into the heart of towns and cities all over the country, and once again councils and developers were at pains to stress its civic character. Promoters spoke often about concourses being 'meeting places', as with this description of the Elephant and Castle: 'Lined with shops on either side, and with pavement cafes, displays, decorative plants, and pools, the concourse is designed to serve as a social focus and meeting place.' The range of public events and entertainments which could take place in such spaces was frequently emphasised. The 'very large concourse areas' at the Elephant and Castle, its architect explained, 'can be used for a variety of social activities, seasonal trade shows, exhibitions, dancing, carol singing, lectures and meetings'.[56] Promotional materials often foregrounded images of such events taking place in new shopping centres; carol concerts and fashion parades were the most common. Town and City Properties also stressed the 'tremendous scope for exhibitions, displays, fashion shows, etc. during day time and also after hours when the shops are closed'.[57]

Councils were intensely keen on these ideas and strongly encouraged civic and charitable events within malls. In 1966 Leeds's Merrion Centre hosted a municipal exhibition to promote 'National Library Week', for example, while in 1967 a student art exhibition was held in the centre with members of the shopping public judging artwork and awarding prizes. Manchester's malls hosted numerous events and exhibitions on behalf of the city, such as a 1971 exhibition promoting the Port of Manchester, or in conjunction with local charities, such as a 1979 art exhibition organised by the learning disability charity Mencap.[58] The commitment of local authorities all over the country to holding events such as these within shopping malls was a clear sign of their serious civic intent for such spaces. So too was the placement of temporary, 'pop-up' council services within shopping centres. In 1974 Leeds City Council opened a 'planning shop' in the Merrion Centre so that visitors could take a break from shopping to find out if their houses were scheduled for demolition. The desire to make council services consumer-friendly was clear in the words of a city official who hoped that the facility would have 'a very informal atmosphere more

---

[56] T. W. Hearn, 'Glamour and Versatility', *The Guardian*, 9 September 1964, 21; Paul Boissevain, 'Fulcrum of an Ordered World', *The Guardian*, 9 September 1964, 19.
[57] Town & City Properties Limited, *Arndale Covered Centres* (1973).
[58] Michael Parkin, 'Art Selection Panel Lets Them All In', *The Guardian*, 6 March 1967, 3. Images and ephemera relating to various events and exhibitions within Manchester's shopping spaces can be viewed at GMCRO.

akin to a shop' and speculated that 'an old lady whose house is going to
come down would be quite happy to come into a place opposite
a supermarket to ask about compensation'.[59] In the mid-1970s this was
what passed for customer-focused public services. Leeds city council also
had wider plans for a one-stop 'advice supermarket' in the mall – again,
the impact of the consumer domain upon the rhetoric and provisions of
public governance is clear. In a similar example of bringing public services
to the shopping centre, the *Daily Mail* in 1983 reported on 'the mobile tax
team' from the Inland Revenue which had set up shop in Chatham's
Pentagon Centre and would soon be visiting shopping centres in
Manchester, Middlesbrough and Bradford.[60]

Holding public events and exhibitions, and securing public access to
centres 'after hours', were especially important for councils because they
went to the heart of the question of whether the new shopping environments could really be imagined as *public* space, on a par with the conventional streets and squares of the city. Legally of course, they simply were
not; the internal spaces of shopping centres were privately owned by
commercial operating companies. But councils pushed hard when hammering out development agreements to secure out-of-hours access and
legal rights of way through malls. Many authorities sought to link up mall
concourses with the larger, citywide network of streets and public spaces,
promoting access and circulation by planning pedestrian walkways through
the centres, and insisting upon access points and connecting footbridges to
link the malls with the city centre as a whole. Most of this was dramatically
scaled back by developers after the deals were signed. Once centres were
open and trading, there was always an easy business case to be made that
round-the-clock public access was unsafe and commercially unviable. Few
of the proposed footbridges and twenty-four-hour access points, which for
optimistic town planners would have secured the 'public' character of the
shopping mall, ever materialised. 'Most centres pull down the vandal-proof
shutters at 6 pm and do not raise them again till 9 am', as one reporter
noted, 'so depriving citizens of a large chunk of their town or city for the
greater part of each day'.[61] At the Manchester Arndale, the only deck
access out of the shopping centre that was ever actually built led directly
into a neighbouring retail development, and this was only erected after the
Arndale's operators had become the owners of both sites.[62] There was an

[59] Michael Parkin, 'Bureaucracy Puts On an Acceptable Face', *The Guardian*,
23 April 1974, 7.
[60] Stephen Trevor, 'The Flying Taxman Comes to the Rescue', *Daily Mail*, 13 July
1983, 22.
[61] David Ward, 'Sales Pitch', *The Guardian*, 16 October 1978, 8.
[62] Michael Hanson, 'Britain's Largest Shopping Centre', *The Times*, 8 April 1976, 6.

obvious conflict between planners' aspirations for unfettered pedestrian circulation and the commercial intentions of retail operators to keep customers on site and spending money. Such intent was explicitly acknowledged by one leading retail property developer, who stated that 'the best entrances [to malls] are those which attract shoppers into the centre yet, whilst being readily recognisable, need a conscious effort to locate when the shopper is ready to leave'.[63]

Newcastle's Eldon Square complex provides the clearest example of how bold civic intentions for the new urban landscapes of affluence were frequently frustrated and neutered in the process of partnering with commercial forces. Indeed, there was perhaps nowhere bolder in its civic intent than Newcastle – a staunchly leftist authority whose 1960s planning had been led by the cerebral, Reithian figure of Wilfred Burns. By the 1970s, Burns had departed the city to work for central government, but the developments he set in train were coming to fruition. Pre-eminent among them was the Eldon Square shopping centre – a vast sprawling complex which was (controversially) overlaid upon the city's elegant Georgian Grainger Town.[64] The city council had partnered with one of the leading property developers, Capital & Counties, to build this complex, and the incongruity of this pairing was well illustrated by the carefully drawn up guest lists for Eldon Square's grand opening ceremony in 1977. The city council was determined to invite an exhaustive panoply of regional dignitaries, including the local heads of publicly owned utilities and corporations, trade union and business leaders, women's groups and a plethora of civic and charitable organisations – an expansive cross-section of post-war corporatism and associational life. The 'friends of Capital & Counties', on the other hand, were their business associates in the world of high finance – the pension funds of Shell and BP which funded the company, along with an august roll call of representatives from all the major City banks. The only additions to this parade of financial titans were the Crown Agents (an archaic imperial financial institution with whom Capital & Counties was embarked on some dubious overseas operations); the British Property Federation (the development industry's extremely well-connected trade body, represented by two knights of the realm); and the Milton Keynes Development Corporation, which was being courted by Capital & Counties.[65] Here

---

[63] Quoted in David Ward, 'Sales Pitch', *The Guardian*, 16 October 1978, 8.
[64] For the background to this scheme, see John Pendlebury, 'Alas Smith and Burns? Conservation in Newcastle upon Tyne City Centre, 1959-1968', *Planning Perspectives* 16:2 (2001), 115–141.
[65] Guest lists in Minutes of Eldon Square Development Subcommittee, 9 February 1976 [Tyne & Wear Archives]. For Milton Keynes Development Corporation and its careful negotiation of the terrains of social democracy and market liberalism, see Ortolano, *Thatcher's Progress*.

then, lined up against one another, were the representatives of two competing visions of both the shopping centre and post-war Britain as a whole – the one corporatist, civic and social democratic, the other intensely commercial and capitalistic, even mercantilist.

The key civic offering of Eldon Square was a large council-run 'Recreation Centre', which occupied the entire upper floor of the complex (Figure 5.3). Here, citizens could apply themselves in the squash courts or on the indoor bowling green, sign up for the judo or fencing club or simply relax in the licensed bar and entertainment centre. The Eldon Square development, however, was plagued with difficulties and setbacks. Construction got underway during the recession of the early

Figure 5.3 1986 image of the interior of Newcastle's Eldon Square complex, showing the access point from the shopping mall to the council recreation centre. The inclusion of such municipal facilities reflected councils' wish to provide civic and social amenities alongside shopping, as did their ambition to retain mall concourses as public rights of way. Also clear from this image is the complete experiential transformation of the former city centre streets that such projects entailed. Source: Newcastle Libraries.

1970s, and was beleaguered by spiralling costs, the three-day week and by endless wildcat strikes and walkouts by Newcastle's militant construction workers. The finances of the developer, the council and the project began to creak, and costs were cut wherever possible. Also creaking and straining was the building itself as it took shape, as the real costs of constructing these elaborate, multifunctional ensembles using untested techniques and materials began to show itself. There were manifold problems with materials, finishes and the servicing of the building. Retailers were aggrieved because the air conditioning system did not work; electrical systems and plant rooms failed to operate properly; bus stations, service roads and multi-storey parking were built defectively and condemned to remedial works by safety engineers and fire officers; even the commemorative 'Jubilee Clock', installed to celebrate Eldon Square's opening by the Queen in the twenty-fifth year of her reign, kept stopping with the frequent power outages and could not be restarted. At the council's Recreation Centre, cost-cutting pared back many of the finishes and attractions; special events and TV filmings had to be abandoned due to terrible acoustic design; and the sports centre's showers rained water through the floors and into the shop units below.[66]

Faced with all these operational difficulties and 'the need to make drastic economies', as the council put it, anything deemed non-essential was abandoned. The hoped-for footbridges that would tie the shopping malls into the wider pedestrian networks of the city were scrapped. Long delays in construction and spiralling costs changed the financial prospects of the scheme as a whole. The council complained that delays and faults were extending 'the period during which the council is receiving no return at all on its investment either by way of rent or rates'. While for the developer, living on borrowed money, delays meant substantially larger interest payments and ultimately less 'equity available for distribution'. The profit shares and financial arrangements agreed between council, developer and investor were based on calculations which no longer held true. Straitened financial circumstances meant a narrowing of what was deemed possible and commercially viable and strengthened the case against any aspect of design or use which would not directly benefit economic performance. Sustained problems with 'vandalism and rowdyism' in the complex forced the council to accept the closure of the malls outside of shop trading hours. The city also 'accepted with great reluctance the need to close the Centre completely on a Sunday'. These measures not only drastically reduced custom for the council-run entertainment centre, putting its finances further in peril, they

[66] These details in Minutes of Eldon Square Development Subcommittee, October 1974–December 1978 [Tyne & Wear Archives].

also shattered the key civic ambition of free, round-the-clock public access to mall spaces. Dismayed, council officers became embroiled in a dispute with the centre's operators, over whether the malls could be 'kept open as City streets (as originally intended) for special events not necessarily of a commercial nature'.[67] This was the nub of the issue; did these new urban spaces have any claim to serve public purposes outside of – or even in conflict with – the commercial imperatives of their private owners. The Eldon Square Centre remained closed.

Shut up shopping centres, phantom footbridges and shoddily built sports halls begin to illustrate some of the limitations and naiveté of these attempts to revitalise the urban civitas in close alliance with commercial actors. There were some basic unresolved tensions between the civic ambitions of public planners and the profit-maximising imperatives of their private sector partners which local authorities were either blind to or wilfully ignored. Nonetheless, councils' strenuous efforts to cast urban shopping centres as spaces of civic and social renewal show how, rhetorically and ideologically, public planning and private development were able to come together to install transformative new leisure facilities at the centre of Britain's cities. Despite these ambitious public intentions, in practice the attempt to harness new types of consumer experience with an expansive model of active citizenship was inherently unstable, particularly as it relied so heavily upon the commercial property sector for its delivery. For the real owners of new urban shopping complexes, 'success' was judged solely in terms of facilities' performance as a financial asset and a piece of efficient retailing infrastructure, and where these commercial imperatives clashed with more civic-minded objectives, it was generally the business case which won out.

The Society of the Spectacle

While many public planners may have felt themselves to be engaged in the production of a new and energising type of civic space, for their business partners a different set of imperatives took precedence. Developers, retailers and shopping centre operators were, quite naturally, concerned much more narrowly with centres' profitable performance as a commercial trading concern. Even councils' attempts to construct shopping centres as new social and community hubs were accepted by their business partners largely on the basis that they corresponded with the commercial need to attract custom to their experimental new

[67] Minutes of Eldon Square Development Subcommittee, 15 May 1978 [Tyne & Wear Archives].

facilities. For these commercial actors, the promotion of new shopping facilities as 'fulcrums' of local community life was based, not on a commitment to revitalising local communities, but rather upon extracting the maximum expenditure from them. A 1970 article by an architect specialising in shopping centre design states the case clearly:

> Let us make no mistake about it, the primary object of a shopping unit is profit, and without an acceptable profit any shop is a failure. But to succeed it must attract the customer, and to do this the whole centre must attract and please the public.[68]

It was this imperative to 'attract and please the public' which, for owners and operators, drove ostentatious opening ceremonies and underpinned their enthusiasm for hosting events and attractions within their centres. Indeed, while councils saw the staging of public events in malls as part of their innate civic character, operators understood such practices to be an essential part of a wider marketing strategy, which was explicitly designed to entice reticent British shoppers into a new and unfamiliar shopping landscape.

Despite developers' claims, there was in fact no clear and unambiguous public demand for the new shopping facilities which sprang up so rapidly in cities across Britain. Indeed, many centres experienced protracted difficulties attracting trade, as shoppers displayed a marked reluctance to abandon long-established shopping habits and patronise the new centres. In this context, developers and operators were well aware that, in order to get off the ground, new centres required vigorous and sustained programmes of marketing and publicity. A year before the Bull Ring Centre's opening, the developer Laing was already publicly promising to commit £40,000 to 'finance the promotional campaign'. This sum (around £800,000 in present-day values) was 'designed to attract over 3¼m. shoppers within easy reach of the Bull Ring' and covered only the first year of trading – more funds would be needed after this point.[69] The fact that such sums were being put up by the developer reflected the clear need to convince both shoppers and retailers to patronise the new centre. Another report a year later noted that the Bull Ring's grand royal opening was only 'the beginning of promotional activities to focus attention on the attractions of this specially designed traffic-free centre ... A Summer Show is to be staged featuring aspects of country life and including floral displays, fashion parades, car and boat shows. Plans are also in hand for a toy fair for the Christmas season as well as further promotions during 1965' (Figure 5.4).[70]

[68] Nadine Beddington, 'Shopping Environment: Efficiency and Fun', *Official Architecture and Planning* 33: 1 (1970), 41–44. Beddington subsequently published a number of books on shopping centre design.
[69] 'Laing to Help Promote Bull Ring Scheme', *The Financial Times*, 22 January 1963, 6.
[70] 'Birmingham's £5M. Centre for Shopping', *The Financial Times*, 24 January 1964, 8.

Figure 5.4 1964 promotional event for Brooke Bond's 'PG Tips' tea brand, held within the central concourse of Birmingham's Bull Ring centre. Large crowds gather to see two chimpanzees dressed in branded clothing and given miniature props to play with. The event also offered the public the chance to win prizes and obtain other promotional products. Inane spectacles like this contained something of the vaudevillian about them, and in retrospect look fairly depressing, but they were judged important in drumming up interest in new shopping centres and were part of a process in which marketing and promotional strategies were steadily refined. Source: Historic England Archive, John Laing Photographic Collection.

These promotional endeavours were replicated all over the country. In Nottingham, the developers of the Victoria Centre, Capital & Counties, pursued an especially energetic programme of publicity. 'New shopping centres don't sell themselves', a company brochure explained, 'they have to be marketed, like any other piece of merchandise'. Capital & Counties had letting agents working locally and nationally to identify and entice prospective retail tenants and developed an expansive set of strategies to promote the new centre to potential customers. The development company was giving monthly presentations to numerous local interest groups and associations, from the Nottinghamshire Law Society to the City Business Club, local Conservative Associations and the Nottingham Ladies Circle (women's groups were a particular target). The company also targeted children, sending out promotional posters to schools in the region in the hope they might adorn classroom walls. The Victoria Centre hosted a plethora of promotional exhibitions and events, from car shows to beauty contests, and offered its space to advertising from credit card companies, television, radio and newspapers and many other commercial concerns. 'The Centre is being merchandised as a unified project', Capital & Counties explained, with a Centre Manager 'to arrange promotions and exhibitions, such as fashion shows, specifically designed to attract people to the Centre, thus increasing the number of potential shoppers'.[71]

Likewise Town & City Properties stressed that each one of its Arndale Centres, 'in addition to being a development of the highest quality, is also a well planned [sic] merchandising project'. Like Capital & Counties, the company had:

... appointed a Promotions Manager to co-ordinate and encourage promotional activity within the Centres in the form of trade exhibitions, displays, social functions and special events which in turn improve trading and increase the value of each Centre as a focal point for community activity.[72]

Fashion shows and beauty contests in particular seem to have been part of operators' efforts to entice more men into their centres, as they were 'invariably appealing for shoppers of both sexes'. Town & City ran crass 'Miss Arndale' contests in its many malls nationwide, in which local girls stripped down to swimsuits in an attempt to win £100. Celebrity appearances were another common feature. Bruce Forsyth was the presiding guest of honour at the opening ceremony for Arndale's Shipley development in the mid-1960s. The comedians Eric Morecambe and Ernie Wise appeared at the opening of the Morecambe Arndale Centre in 1972 (Eric's stage name reflected his birth in the Lancashire coastal town), while in October 1971, large crowds flocked to the Stretford Arndale to

---

[71] Capital & Counties, *Victoria Centre Takes Shape* (1969), promotional pamphlet; Capital & Counties *Nottingham Victoria Centre* (1970), development prospectus. Both available at Nottinghamshire Archives.
[72] Town & City Properties Limited, *Arndale Covered Centres* (1973).

hear Muhammed Ali stand in Tesco's and declare: 'I am the greatest . . . and so is Ovaltine.' In June 1976, the Stretford Arndale played host to 'an exhibition of exciting photographs of famous TV stars', titled 'These TV Times'. Organised by Kodak and the *TV Times* magazine, this exhibition promised 'Stars, Stars all the way', with photographs of 'all the TV favourites' from shows like *Coronation Street* and *Upstairs Downstairs*, as well as 'top international stars' like Barbra Streisand, Rock Hudson and Omar Sharif.[73]

Such activities illustrate that the new shopping centres were not simply destinations to pick up the latest fashions in the most prestigious shops – important though these retail offerings were. Malls were also key nodes in a burgeoning domain of commercial mass culture, in which shopping, advertising, television and celebrity all played a part (Figure 5.5). Indeed, these spheres intersected and overlapped with each other, lending credence to their respective claims to cultural significance through this cross-referencing. Shopping centres were generative spaces not just for the booming retail economy, and the proliferating cultures of consumption and self-curation which sustained it, but also for a more expansive web of commercially defined cultural forms which was rapidly unfurling itself across British public life. For the uninitiated, the mall, just like the television, was an important vector – a point of contact and entry into a dynamic commercial–cultural domain. Just as they ruthlessly commercialised the public spaces and experience of the city, the shopping centres of this era were also part of a more thorough-going commercialisation of post-war public life and culture, in which traditional sources of cultural authority in the public sphere were increasingly drowned out and superseded by new commercial agents and forces.

We should not, however, imagine that the post-war public were all green unwitting dupes, or that they were necessarily all that impressed by these cultural offerings (the hostility which such projects provoked from some sections of the public is dealt with in Chapter 6). Nor was it the case that the British public had no previous experience of commercial mass culture; there was already wide engagement with the sophisticated consumer cultures of the interwar period. Yet the post-war citizenry was being offered something novel – a more advanced and assertive commercial culture and a structural economic backdrop which dramatically expanded many people's opportunities to engage with it. The mall experience too was an unfamiliar one; there was a clear

---

[73] 'These TV Times', press release and poster, June 1976 [GMCRO]; *Town & City Group News*, company newsletter [P&O Collection, National Maritime Museum].

Figure 5.5 1965 promotional display of televisions within the Bull Ring's central concourse, illustrating the connection between the new malls and wider cultures of mass leisure and entertainment. Despite local authorities' wider social aims, these curated spaces of consumption served primarily as sites for the propagation of new sales and advertising techniques. Source: Historic England Archive, John Laing Photographic Collection.

sense that the public had to be properly courted, and their shopping habits changed, in order to ensure commercial success. Indeed, the marketing men felt that this was particularly the case when it came to 'the British public [which was] more conservative and less flexible in its habits that than of America'. It was this that was at the heart of shopping centre operators' expensive programmes of publicity, as was confirmed by a London-based public relations professional in the *Estates Gazette* in 1965:

The centre is "sold" to the public over a wide area as a merchandising unit under the shopping centre's umbrella, with a series of constant events, "something doing" 12 months in the year, from cooking competitions to local art exhibitions, from children's pet shows to square dancing, from bands and concerts to "do-it-yourself" displays, linked up with collective advertising and home-delivered flyer distribution . . . North American experience . . . has shown that promotion must be on a continuing basis, and that year in and year out, month in month out, promotion (which includes advertising) is essential. Particularly must this be true in Britain, where shopping habits have to be changed.[74]

This candid account makes clear how commercially important the orchestration of a new public culture of mall shopping was held to be by industry experts, in what was ominously described as the 'process of consumer re-education'.

Engineering Spectacle

Alongside these extensive programmes of promotional events, the very landscape of the new shopping spaces – their physical layout, design and atmosphere – was conditioned by the profit-maximising imperatives of efficient retailing. It was the lively, visually stimulating spectacle of mall shopping spaces which was central to their attractions as a novel shopping experience and thus to their commercial performance (Figure 5.6). In Birmingham's Bull Ring, shoppers were met with 'an iridescent "wall of light" high above the floor of the Centre Court present[ing] an ever-changing kaleidoscope of colourful patterns'.[75] In Arndale's shopping centres, 'sculptures, fountains, murals and generous planting combine to create an ideal shopping environment', and the company's lead director on retail design was clear about the purpose of all this:

I personally place a great deal of importance on the internal finishes of a covered shopping centre . . . one cannot necessarily pinpoint one particular item or a special kind of material: it is the combination of everything that goes to creating the total concept – the right environment which in itself is the basis for maximum intake of people and therefore for maximum turnovers.[76]

This commercial mobilisation of spectacle and novelty was central to postmodern theorists' later critiques of such environments as distracting, semantically empty 'pseudo-places'. Indeed, as early as 1967, the French Situationist Guy Debord had denounced 'the society of the spectacle' in its entirety. Debord castigated what he saw as a system of social and cultural organisation in which passively consumed 'spectacle' was elevated as the

[74] H. Newman, 'How to Promote a Shopping Centre'. This article was published in the *Estates Gazette* on 10 July 1965, but was subsequently circulated by the author to local authorities to advertise his services.
[75] 'Birmingham Bull Ring', *The Property Developer* (The Property Council: 1964), 141.
[76] Chippindale, 'Building Design', 129–137, 134–135.

Figure 5.6 1976 image of the newly opened Eldon Square centre in Newcastle. The spectacular and surreal character of these new urban spaces became an integral part of the overall shopping experience, and something that retail designers placed great store on as part of their attraction. The mushroom-like structure in centre housed a circular cafe. Source: Newcastle Libraries.

highest end in itself, merely to serve the productivist interests of the prevailing economic order – bread and circuses for the twentieth century. Much of Debord's critique was in the abstract, but he did point in particular to the 'giant shopping centres', or 'distribution factories' as he also called them, as the most concrete manifestation of 'spectaclism'. These 'temples of frenetic consumption' were, Debord claimed, 'the most visible aspect of the general process of decomposition that has brought the city to the point of *consuming itself*.[77]

This was heady stuff, and a radical attack on the cultural and political dynamics of mass affluence, although – as the developers and PR men acknowledged – Debord was not so wide of the mark in his account of the orchestration of consumerist spectacle. More surprising was the acquiescence of the public managers of the post-war city in these attempts to captivate and seduce the shopping citizen, and thereby relieve them of their faculties and their money. One professional planning journal enthusiastically reported that the shopping centre at Harlow New Town had been laid out to channel citizens through 'short cuts' where they would be confronted with lively displays designed to 'encourage what Americans term "impulse buying"'.[78] More explicit commentary was provided by a central government planning expert, advising Manchester Corporation on the detailed designs for their city centre Arndale mall. The council were instructed that, in order to maximise commercial performance, the 'new centre must achieve an intensely busy exhibition-like atmosphere in an exceedingly gay and entertaining setting where pedestrian flows are almost compelled to circulate and re-circulate along display frontages'. It was necessary to induce an 'almost involuntary circulation of shoppers around attractive display frontages'; 'intensity and brilliance' in the retail landscape would secure the captivated pedestrian flows which 'seem to be important sources of retail trade'.[79]

These are remarkable aims for a public planner and civil servant to endorse, although – as was seen in Chapter 1 – the government planning apparatus had long been concerned with micro-engineering the most efficient, expenditure-extracting urban shopping environments. In the reconstruction era, the government's ideas on engineering efficient selling spaces had been considerably more advanced than those of the retail industry. By the 1960s, the sector had caught up, and retailers were developing increasingly sophisticated methods of managing and manipulating the shopping subject in space. One industry expert, affiliated with the British Institute of Management, noted at the end of the decade that 'the 1960s were the years of the development of merchandising, promotions, point-of-sale aids – all the scientific panoply of strident modern marketing'. And it was, he continued, the dynamic and expansionary multiple stores that were 'the whizzkids of the retail scene'.[80] In 1963, the Multiple Shops Federation

[77] Debord, *Society of the Spectacle*, 174.
[78] 'Harlow Shopping Centre', *Official Architecture and Planning* 30: 8 (1967), 1108–1109.
[79] Letter from Ministry of Housing and Local Government to Manchester Chief Planning Officer, 2 August 1966 [TNA-HLG-HLG 79/1188].
[80] E. MacFadyen, 'Retailers at the Crossroads', *Building with Steel* 10 (May, 1972), 2.

produced a detailed prospectus on *The Planning of Shopping Centres*, which argued that 'the layout and design of a shopping centre must be such that its atmosphere is conducive to pleasurable shopping . . . Shopping (and window-shopping) should be fun'. For the Federation, this commitment to jollity and spectacle was entirely utilitarian and aimed solely at 'maximum efficiency'. No architectural design scheme, the Federation argued, 'should ever take precedence over [a shopping centre's] functional efficiency as an apparatus for the sale and purchase of consumer goods';

> It is . . . essential to the functional efficiency of a shopping centre that it should be at all times attractive, and there is everything to be said for the embellishment of its walkways with such amenities as fountains, seats, trees, sculpture and gardens, provided these are not allowed to obstruct the shopper's access to, or view of, the shops across the way.[81]

This principle of completely unhindered access and open lines of sight was key; so too were ideas about using the mall environment to hold the shopper's interest and coax them on to the next spending opportunity. The Multiple Shops Federation prescribed relatively narrow mall concourses lined with continuous displays, 'so that the shopper's eye no sooner turns from one window display than it is caught by another alongside it or across the way'. Internal walkways were to be arranged so that, 'the stream of pedestrian traffic, drawn by the sight of more shops ahead, flows naturally from one shop building to another, never encountering needless setbacks'; nothing at all that 'might allow a shopper's interest to flag, or discourage him from exploring further'. The distribution of specific shops within centres was also crucial, and developers became adept at arranging stores of varying types and sizes, and with different pulling power, in order to maximise footfall and trade throughout the development. Such principles were confirmed by one of the directors of Capital & Counties, R. I. Northen, who went on to produce a number of commercial manuals for the design and development of shopping centres. 'The shoppers have to be guided directly into the different parts (of the centre) without realising that they have been given no choice of route', Northen wrote. It was also important to use physical layouts and sensory stimuli to manage the speed and direct the attention of perambulating shoppers; 'having achieved a concentrated pedestrian flow, it is no good allowing the shoppers to be swept along with the tide: the run must be slowed down to encourage them to look into the shops they are passing'.[82]

[81] Multiple Shops Federation, *The Planning of Shopping Centres* (1963), author's collection.
[82] See R. I. Northen & Michael Haskoll, *Shopping Centres: A Developer's Guide to Planning and Design* (Reading: Centre for Advanced Land Use Studies, 1977); Northen, *Shopping Centre Development*.

The spectacle of the new shopping landscape – even where it was intended to induce fun and enjoyment – was thus firmly shaped by the imperatives of efficient wealth creation. The public endorsement of these retail planning ideas is a further indication of the prominence of commercial logics within British urban renewal. For local authorities, which had invested so much financially and reputationally in these schemes, acquiescence in the seduction of citizens became a necessity. Such strictures meant that the very fabric of everyday life in the post-war city was engineered ever more tightly around the smooth generation of profit. Yet this was not a straightforward task. Seductive consumer landscapes had first to be imagined, designed and realised, and they were not necessarily all that efficient and effective in their seduction from the outset. Indeed, there is plenty of evidence to suggest that the siren calls of the new shopping landscape often failed to strike the right notes with the public. Instead, there was a process of trial and error in retail planning as different designs and techniques were tested, applied and refined.

These dynamics are well illustrated by the commentary of one architect specialising in shopping centres, which was published in 1970 under the title 'Efficiency and Fun'. Here, the author made the case explicitly that 'flamboyance and excitement' in the retail landscape had to be provided as a matter of commercial necessity – the logics of efficient accumulation demanded it. Yet she also drew upon a recent *Which?* survey of shoppers to argue that many centres were failing in this imperative to engineer fun. The consumer affairs magazine had suggested that many new shopping environments suffered from a 'puritan attitude', and the article's author argued that 'aesthetic over-control ... and inefficient understanding of the retailers' and shoppers' needs ... frequently distil out of a scheme just those very attributes that should provide the stimulus and attraction'. For the author:

Shopping is the heart of the town, an escape from the humdrum. It presupposes bright lights – cafés, bars, restaurants, cinemas; it must offer an atmosphere of gaiety, variety, perhaps vulgarity and certainly *joie de vivre*.[83]

Shopping, in short, needed spectacle, but there were plenty of missteps on the road to developing slick and effective landscapes of pleasure. Indeed, architectural and design ideas seem to have misfired fairly regularly in their efforts to woo the shopping public. In a dramatic departure from the gushing reportage of the mid-1960s, from the end of the decade criticism of centres' appearance became almost de rigueur. Portsmouth's Tricorn Centre was voted one of the 'ugliest buildings in Britain' in 1967; while

---

[83] Beddington, 'Shopping Environment', 41–44.

the mockery of the Manchester Arndale Centre's tiled external façade as 'the longest lavatory wall in Europe' became a serious reputational problem for the new centre even before it opened.[84]

Internally, too, design ideas often missed their mark. An early preoccupation with elaborate decorative lighting installations had been at the expense of windows and natural light. As a result, centres were often felt to be dark, dingy and depressing – a far cry from the gay and luminescent landscapes sketched by artists like Peter Sainsbury (see Figure 5.1). In Runcorn Shopping City, the commercial megastructure at the heart of the North West New Town, the problem of 'shop-girl syndrome' was identified, 'where they are apparently probing the disorientation prompted by the deprivation of natural light, air, and normality'; 'everyone in here gets colds', one young female shop assistant complained, 'it's so warm and then we have to go outside'. One 'harassed mother' in the same centre complained about 'the sweet and undemanding pop echoing all about her from unseen speakers'; 'This canned music', she moaned, 'it's giving me a headache'.[85] In the mid-1980s, the manager of the Manchester Arndale Centre publicly acknowledged 'complaints ... about the claustrophobic effects of the centre' and pointed to an ongoing 'major facelift' for the centre in which 'parts of the roof are to be replaced with glass domes, to let in the daylight'.[86] The fact that £2 m was being spent on overhauling the design and décor of this centre just six years after opening is a clear indication of the limitations of retail design expertise. Similar vast sums, running into the millions of pounds, were spent refitting and illuminating first-wave malls all over the country in the 1980s and 1990s. The Brent Cross shopping centre in suburban north London opened one year before the Manchester Arndale, in March 1976. Here too, a major study commissioned by the Greater London Council found a third of respondents complaining about 'the design and atmosphere of the centre', which was felt to be 'too crowded, closed in, hot and stuffy'.[87] By the 1980s, a burgeoning professional literature on shopping centre design was littered with such cautionary tales, pointing out common design flaws and recommending perpetual programmes and rolling

[84] Harvey Elliott, 'Is this Britain's Ugliest Building?', *Daily Mail*, 23 October 1967, 9; Stephen Gardiner, 'Strength and Order: Architecture', *The Observer*, 2 November 1975; Ian Nairn, 'Swimming in Style', *The Observer*, 25 February 1968, 27; Winn Walsh, 'Bringing Back the Shoppers', *Manchester Evening News*, 1 July 1976, 9.
[85] Reported in David Ward, 'Sales Pitch', *The Guardian*, 16 October 1978, 8.
[86] Bernard Spilsbury, 'A Facelift for the Arndale Super-loo?', *Manchester Evening News*, 1 November 1984, 5.
[87] Peter Downey, 'The Impact of Brent Cross' (1980), report commissioned by GLC with funding from the Department of the Environment. Available at University of Leicester Library.

budgets for internal remodelling and redesign. The growth of such literatures, along with a new breed of retail design consultants who produced
them, was itself part of the increasingly organised retail sector's mechanisms for learning from its own mistakes in order to better engineer 'the
ideal shopping environment'.[88]

Spectacle on Sauchiehall Street

From the later 1960s, ideas about the organisation of selling space that
had been pioneered within enclosed shopping centres came increasingly
to be turned outwards and applied to cities' central shopping districts as
a whole. The open-air streets and spaces of the town centre were reimagined as interconnected landscapes of consumption in which – just as in
enclosed malls – the environment and experience of consumption could
be managed and manipulated in order to promote trade. Widespread
pedestrianisation of central shopping areas took place from the 1970s,
but such efforts extended further than this to the beautification of the
town centre, to transport and infrastructural reorganisation and also
attempts to induce the kind of environmental and experiential spectacle
that was being achieved within enclosed shopping spaces. Such ideas
could be seen in gestation within the city centre plans produced by large
urban authorities such as Liverpool and Manchester in the mid-1960s. In
1969, they were articulated clearly within a set of proposals to overhaul
the landscape and economic performance of one of Glasgow's principal
commercial streets – Sauchiehall Street. Glasgow was one of the most
energetic and interventionist urban authorities in the country, with
a firmly leftist political complexion. For all but nine of the fifty-five
years between 1945 and 2000 the council was Labour controlled, and
the city's traditions of public enterprise and municipal socialism stretched
back deep into the nineteenth century. Glasgow had long led the way in
the realm of urban renewal, forming the country's first Improvement
Trust in 1866, which raised municipal funds to clear slums and put up
public housing.[89] In the post-1945 era the city was equally energetic.
Glasgow had one of the largest public housing programmes in the country, with 43 per cent of the city's housing in public hands by 1965.[90] This

---

[88] For example, Northen & Haskoll, *Shopping Centres*; Nadine Beddington, *Design for Shopping Centres* (London: Butterworth, 1982); N. Keith Scott, *Shopping Centre Design* (London: Van Nostrand Reinhold, 1989).

[89] C. M. Allan, 'The Genesis of British Urban Redevelopment with Special Reference to Glasgow', *Economic History Review* 18:3 (1965), 598–613.

[90] Michael Pacione, 'Housing Policies in Glasgow since 1880', *Geographical Review* 69:4 (1979), 395–412. See also the important new work on Glasgow housing programmes in

was pursued through a combination of vigorous slum clearance in the central area and the construction of large 'overspill' housing areas in more peripheral locations. The city was unusually ardent in its embrace of urban modernism – both as a governing ethos and an environmental aesthetic – putting up a string of high-rise housing schemes and throwing itself into an expansive programme of urban motorway building. In the mid-1960s the city council was pursuing twenty-nine separate (and sizeable) CDA schemes, which represented around a third of the total for Scotland as a whole.[91]

All of this public enterprise and endeavour did not, however, correspond to an evacuation of commercial concerns and projects from the city's renewal; rather, the decanting of housing and population away from the centre was intended to free up space in the city's core for a rejuvenation and expansion of its commercial functions. The vast, 114-acre Anderston Cross redevelopment area, for example, which sat on the edge of the existing city centre, was used to extend the commercial centre of the city westwards and saw a shabby, mixed-use, residential and light industrial district replaced by high-end office development and a new shopping plaza. The city also hoped to rejuvenate one of its principal shopping thoroughfares, Sauchiehall Street, which ran from just north of Anderston Cross eastwards into the heart of the city. In the early twentieth century, Sauchiehall Street was a glamorous district of department stores, luxury hotels, clubs and theatres, but by the early 1960s it was a place of faded grandeur. The area had declined in status and prosperity, theatres and hotels had closed, and its vitality was not helped by the swathes of clearance going on around it with all the social and economic disruption this entailed. The *Financial Times* in 1971 lamented the fact that 'shops ... have been closing at an alarming rate' and suggested that 'drastic measures are required to put Sauchiehall Street back on its pedestal'.[92] The proposed solution to these problems rested upon applying the environmental and commercial principles of the shopping mall to the public city street; through pedestrianisation, decorative landscaping, orchestrated spectacle and holistic management of the environment as a totalising selling space, the seductive landscapes and efficient retail conditions of the mall were to be recreated in the open streets of the city. These proposals were worked up in 1969 by an association of retailers, the Sauchiehall Street Association, in conjunction with the city

Lynn Abrams, Ade Kearns, Barry Hazley & Valerie Wright, *Glasgow: High-Rise Homes, Estates and Communities in the Post-War Period* (London: Routledge, 2020).
[91] Hart, *The Comprehensive Development Area.*
[92] A. J. Thomson, 'Massive Redevelopment Programme Under Way', *The Financial Times*, 8 November 1971, 14.

council. Together they produced an alluring prospectus to showcase the future of Sauchiehall Street, which drew its ideas, imagery and language directly from the retail planning agendas which accompanied mall shopping developments. Pedestrianisation was the linchpin of these plans, and its benefits were presented in identical terms to those deployed by mall designers. 'Pedestrianised shopping streets', it was claimed, are 'a joy to shop in'; they 'form sanctuaries where the public may shop or relax at will . . . free from the dangers and discomforts of fast flowing traffic'. In such leisured urban landscapes, 'the pace is that of the person [and] careful attention to landscaping is taken to refresh the eye and the senses with an interesting and exciting sequence of experiences'. The Sauchiehall Street agenda laid out careful plans for the curation of the shopping experience and the orchestration of spectacle. Relieving the street of vehicular traffic would free the space for new architectural arrangements and decorative treatments. 'Street surfaces rich in colour and texture [would] intrigue the eye'; a bespoke set of street furniture was proposed, in which seats, lights, bollards and plant boxes would conform to a house style; trees, posters and colourful umbrellas would add 'variety and interest'; while the introduction of pavement cafes, kiosks, overhead canopies and free-standing displays would drag the selling space firmly out of the shop door and into the street. 'The kiosk', it was explained, 'is an extension of the shop into the street, or could be the fringe of a café with gay umbrellas spread under the trees. Its very casual nature gives another dimension to the mood of the place'.[93] The ideas and principles behind these attempts to engineer spectacle, to invoke 'greater informality' and to create a languid, leisured, resort-like atmosphere mirrored precisely the environmental and architectural experiments which were being conducted within enclosed shopping centres.

The promoters of Sauchiehall Street aimed to emulate the mall in other ways too. Recasting the space as 'the Sauchiehall Street Precinct', they argued: 'To be successful, the precinct must be more than an arbitrary collection of stores and shops. [It] has to develop a corporate image.' A Precinct Management Group was proposed, which would coordinate both the environmental improvements and 'the promotion of the Precinct through press and other media'. Just as in the mall, 'regular promotions . . . and seasonal events are envisaged'; 'a wide range of activities . . . makes the street more attractive and leads to an increase in trading'. This of course was the bottom line – public and private investment in the creation of 'a unique shopping area' was 'essential if this important shopping street is to

[93] Sauchiehall Street Association, 'Sauchiehall Street', planning prospectus, 1969. Available at Glasgow City Archives.

maintain its prominence', and would, it was hoped, 'lead to an increase in trade'. In the end, these elaborate plans were only ever partially implemented. The eastern end of Sauchiehall Street, running into the city centre, was pedestrianised in the mid-1970s, but the greater investment that would have been needed to carry through the wider environmental reorganisation was not forthcoming (as was often the case with such proposals, it was never clear which parties would actually stump up the funds for this; the implicit hope from businesses was that local authorities would pay). Venerable department stores on flagship pitches in Sauchiehall Street continued to close, with sites subsequently lying idle and undeveloped for lack of demand. As the 1970s wore on, few could continue to believe that Glasgow's prosperity was going to be substantially boosted by some playful paving arrangements. 'Instead of too much money chasing too few goods', one reporter noted in 1973, 'there are too many shops chasing too few people'. And while Glasgow Corporation was 'still hopeful of the effect of changes in the [city's] infrastructure,' she continued, 'at last it is beginning to be aware that the real need is for a sound economic base'.[94]

Glasgow's plans for Sauchiehall Street were far from unique among British cities, nor within the city of Glasgow itself. The city's most successful shopping thoroughfares – Argyle Street, Buchanan Street and Renfield Street – were already pedestrianised, and the Sauchiehall Street plans rested upon linking with, and extending, this existing network. The Corporation's ambition was to create a series of 'communicating pedestrian shopping streets' within the city's commercial heart, bounded by the new inner motorway ring. In this way, just as with the enclosed shopping mall, pedestrianisation and motorisation proceeded in tandem; the guiding principle was to provide speedy vehicular access – via large new roads feeding mammoth car parks – to a newly pedestrianised and carefully curated shopping zone. Such experiments with citywide networks of pedestrianised and beautified urban spaces marked a scalar shift, in which attention turned from individual shopping centres and streets to the orchestration of the city centre as a whole. Planners and public officials sought to recast entire central districts as spaces of leisure, consumption, novelty and display in which the pedestrian could circulate freely and shop at will. Through such means the central urban environment in its entirety was recast as a consumer amenity and a consumable good. In Liverpool, the city's planners wrote explicitly of 'The city as Entertainment':

The whole central shopping and entertainment area should have the character of a "bright lights" district, that it is fun to visit for its own sake – a kaleidoscope of colour, sound and activity . . . illuminated signs and displays will be encouraged . . .

[94] Judy Hillman, 'The City Centres' Hollow Ring', *The Guardian*, 10 May 1973, 16.

the main shopping precinct should be dotted about with light-hearted cafes, kiosks and small exhibitions ... [to] foster ... a changing and stimulating environment.[95]

In Manchester too, the central district was to be remade according to the commercial and aesthetic imperatives of the consumer economy. The city's chief planner wrote in 1967 that, 'to be competitive, there is no doubt that Manchester's shopping centre will require to be not only convenient and efficient, but also outstandingly inviting and attractive'. This was to be achieved by coordinating individual shopping developments and stringing them together into a network of beautified pedestrian ways and curated spaces, with 'the whole system designed to provide safe and civilised conditions for shoppers' as the city planner explained.[96] Through such means, 'the City's central shopping area could be transformed to take on something of the quality of a well set out and continuously changing permanent exhibition'.[97] Although such experiments were often presented in terms of the enjoyable sensory experience of individuals, there was a clear recognition among the post-war managers of the city that they were also vital to cities' successful positioning within an increasingly consumer-driven economy. Manchester's officials were typically explicit about these hard-nosed economic imperatives:

Landscaping and open space, good civic design and fine buildings, freedom to walk about in safety, all that is meant by the word "amenity" are becoming increasingly recognised as essential ingredients to the success and survival of a metropolitan centre and are by no means just "frills" to be added to the most economic and functional solutions.[98]

The management of traffic and mobility was critical to the remaking of the central area as a consumer amenity, and this entailed not only the elevation of the pedestrian but also discriminating between different types of visitor and different forms of mobility. These dynamics were clearly evident in the way that the city of Leeds managed its central area. Like Glasgow, Leeds threw itself into urban motorway building with gusto in the 1960s, aiming to reinvent itself as 'the motorway city of the seventies'. The city was one of the case studies for the Buchanan Report and considered itself to be at the forefront of integrated transport and land use planning. In 1969, in conjunction with the Ministry of Transport and

[95] City Centre Planning Group, *Liverpool City Centre Plan* (1965), 67–68.
[96] J. S. Millar, *City and County Borough of Manchester: City Centre Map 1967*, 32. GMCRO
[97] J. S. Millar, City and County Borough of Manchester: City Centre Map 1967, 59. GMCRO
[98] J. S. Millar, City and County Borough of Manchester: City Centre Map 1967, 39. GMCRO

the Ministry of Housing and Local Government, the report *Planning &
Transport – the Leeds Approach* was produced to showcase the city's
achievements.[99] The Leeds Approach revolved around the construction
of a comprehensive network of urban motorways and saw a swathe of
inner urban Leeds sacrificed to the central ring road in particular. As
a result, transport planning in the city was loudly cheered by the principal
roads lobby group, the British Road Federation.[100] Leeds's car-centred
reorganisation has generally been interpreted as yet another example of
how 'the priorities of private motorization prevailed over other transport
priorities' in the era of post-war renewal, but this was not the whole of the
story.[101] While it was predicated on major expansions of the city's road
network, the Leeds approach did not envisage access for all motorists.
Instead, the city's planners sought to distinguish between different types
of motorist by identifying 'essential' and 'non-essential' journeys, and it
was 'the motorised shopper' who was favoured above all others.

The *Leeds Approach* was clear that commuters wishing to drive to work
in the city should be prevented from doing so and directed to use
improved bus routes instead, whereas 'the use of the private car for
shopping and business journeys will be encouraged'.[102] The clear privileging of the automobility of shoppers was emphasised in the British Road
Federation's *Look at Leeds* pamphlet, which reported that 'shoppers who
need their cars close at hand to carry their purchases [were] being given
top priority'.[103] The control of parking facilities was the primary mechanism for achieving this, with a new network of easily accessible shoppers'
car parks scattered liberally around the major city centre roadways, while
long-stay commuter parking was relegated from the central area. These
shopping-centred transport policies were replicated in many cities.
Manchester's 1967 Joint Report on Car Parking aimed 'at providing the
greatest possible accessibility and convenience for the short-term parker'
(who was invariably a shopper). Like Leeds, the city used charging
structures to discriminate against other visitors while prioritising 'parking
facilities for the motorist shopper ... on whom the prosperity of the City
depends'.[104] Celebration of such measures within the populist sphere of
local press reportage illustrated how far the model of the shopping city – in

---

[99] HMSO, Planning & Transport – the Leeds Approach (London, 1969).
[100] The British Road Federation produced the pamphlet, *Look at Leeds*, to celebrate the city
council's approach to transport planning, available at WYAS – LC/Planning/4095.
[101] Gunn, 'The Buchanan Report', 538.
[102] HMSO, *Planning & Transport – the Leeds Approach*, p. 17.
[103] British Road Federation, *Look at Leeds*, pamphlet, n.d. [c.1971?]. WYAS – LC/
Planning/4095
[104] J. S. Millar, *City and County Borough of Manchester: City Centre Map* 1967, 35.
GMCRO

which urban mobility, infrastructure and experience would revolve around the demands of shopping – had come to be uncritically accepted in many quarters. The *Manchester Evening News* applauded the city's 'new cheap parking deal for shoppers' and in 1977 welcomed the 'good news ... for the city's top retailers' that thousands of shopper parking spaces in the city's Arndale complex would be 'open in time for Christmas shopping'.[105]

Back in Leeds, the promotion of shoppers' automobility also went hand in hand with far-reaching plans for the pedestrianisation of its central area, aimed squarely at boosting the retail economy. By 1970, one and a half miles of shopping streets had already been given over to the consuming pedestrian, with plans to double the size of this area by 1978. The city's new 'pedestrian precinct' was formally opened by the first secretary of the newly created Department of the Environment, Peter Walker, in November 1970.[106] Although pedestrianisation was framed by the Secretary of State and the city council in terms of 'environmental improvement', it was clear that the intention was also to enhance the quality of the centre as a shopping space.[107] The Conservative leader of the city council explained in a letter to *The Times* that the objective behind pedestrianisation was 'to improve the environment of the central area as an attractive place for shoppers'.[108] Retailers were sometimes hesitant about the desirability of pedestrianisation, and there were predictable grumbles from some sections of the public, but in most cases the impact on trading turned out to be beneficial. The view of pedestrianisation as an important stimulus to city shopping, and a key asset for inter-urban competition and place promotion, was confirmed in press reporting. In Leeds, one reporter wrote that, by 1972, 'a half mile square of traffic-free streets has been turned into the most attractive and lucrative shopping centre in Britain, with more pedestrianisation coming soon'. 'It is the shopping area of Leeds', he continued, 'which distinguishes the city from the rest of Britain, demonstrates the civic will and energy, and gives visual proof to the property men who believe that the city has a healthy future'.[109] In all these cases, cities' environmental and infrastructural improvements were aimed squarely at bolstering the image and performance of the shopping city.

[105] 'Shoppers Snap Up City Parking Deal', *Manchester Evening News*, 30 June 1977. GMCRO – M507/Box 1
[106] BRF, *Look at Leeds*, pamphlet, n.d. [c.1971?]. WYAS – LC/Planning/4095; and 'Leeds Traffic Plan', letter from the leader of Leeds City Council, Frank Marshall, to *The Times*, 14 November 1970, 13.
[107] HMSO, *Planning & Transport – the Leeds Approach*, 23.
[108] 'Leeds Traffic Plan', letter from Frank Marshall to *The Times*, 14 November 1970, 13.
[109] Michael Wand, 'Where the Motorway Leads', *The Guardian*, 3 August 1972, 17.

Conclusion

There is much force in both the radical Marxian and the 'postmodern' critiques of the new landscapes of consumption which were developed in the post-war decades. Such places were indeed designed as seductive spectacles, carefully engineered to dazzle, amuse and entertain. They were intended to stimulate new wants and demands, to draw in an often-hesitant public and to relieve them of as much of their money as possible. One critical reporter concluded that 'it might be fairer if all enclosed centres carried prominent warning notices, advising customers that developers and traders are seldom entirely altruistic and that the price of warmth and comfort is loss of freedom'.[110] Post-war retail developments installed curious, at times surreal, new landscapes of consumption at the heart of British urban life, which were certainly somewhat detached from the familiar spaces and experiences of the mid-century city. The new retail landscapes quite purposely extracted signifiers – a place name, a historical figure or event – from the local context and repackaged them as part of a more systematically commodified urban experience. It seems plausible that, just as many cultural theorists have suggested, such signs and symbols – bastardised and recycled for commercial purposes – lost much of their cultural resonance along the way. Yet it is important to understand the historicity and genealogies of such developments. The large commercial complexes dealt with in this chapter – while they possessed some curious new qualities – were not quite the ethereal pseudo-places of postmodern theorising. Newcastle's Eldon Square or Runcorn Shopping City are definitively *places* and they emerged – like scores of similar complexes all over the country – out of a very specific conjuncture in post-war Britain. Their spectacle and 'hyperreality', far from being instantly mesmerising, was often a flop when first unveiled and only became effective after extensive adjustments and recalibrations.

Post-war British shopping centres, with their nods towards civic renewal and placement within the wider realm of mass leisure, were emblematic products of Britain's consumer-oriented social democracy, in which the provisions of technocratic welfarism were to be harmoniously combined with the new commercial offerings of mass affluence, and delivered in partnership with the private sector. The public–private co-production of such facilities lent them a distinctive flavour and allowed idealistic planners to imagine them as sites of participatory citizenship and active leisure. Ultimately, though, this attempted alliance proved to be fairly unstable and outsourcing the delivery of these new facilities for the

---

[110] David Ward, 'Sales Pitch', *The Guardian*, 16 October 1978, 8.

citizen-shopper introduced a number of tensions and unresolved conflicts. The various commercial actors involved had little interest – either intellectually or financially – in promoting the kind of affluent civics which many planners had in mind, and the divergent interests of the public and private partners revealed themselves in conflicts over the detailed design and running of new shopping centres. Over time, the already-tenuous 'civic' character of new centres diminished while the seductive techniques of retail planning and consumer psychology became ever more sophisticated. For local authorities, a mix of pragmatism, economism and the straitened financial circumstances of the 1970s led to their acquiescence in a brash, commercial and profit-driven vision of the city remade. For the public, the forms of participation on offer within the redeveloped city centre did not seem to be especially 'civic' at all. On the contrary, they were invited to engage with a burgeoning commercial domain of shopping, advertising, entertainment and leisure as it gathered ever more purchase within post-war public life and culture. These commercially driven transformations of urban space and public culture did not go unchallenged, however; as Chapter 6 shows, there was plenty of dissent and discontent with the offerings of the consumer age.

6 Demand and Discontent in the Shopping City

The retail-led redevelopment of Britain's town and city centres was predicated on a set of assumptions about the coming of mass affluence, the expansion of the consumer economy and the changing nature of consumer demand. Planners and developers observed prodigious increases in consumer spending in the early post-war period, along with rapid changes in the business of retailing, and sought to build new urban facilities which would respond to, and capitalise upon, these trends. This chapter begins by surveying some of the structural transformations in the British economy which mass affluence unleashed, showing how rising disposable incomes and a remarkable expansion of consumer credit fuelled the expansion and transformation of the retail sector. It looks at how councils and developers interpreted these trends, and shows how statistical projections of future demand became a key intellectual underpinning of large-scale shopping-centred urban redevelopment projects. The chapter also unpicks some of the many problems which this approach created, highlighting the surprising paucity of detailed knowledge about the actual preferences of consumers, and a reliance instead upon aggregated projections of surging consumer demand which frequently turned out to be wildly over-optimistic. I also assess the responses of consumers to new shopping facilities once they were open and trading, showing how often new shopping facilities struggled to attract the anticipated levels of consumer expenditure and enthusiasm. As with other spheres of consumer provision like advertising, the promoters of post-war shopping centres quickly found that consumers were a far more diverse and discerning bunch than they had imagined, and this posed real problems for the commercial viability of many developments. Indeed, the embarrassing failures of many shopping developments prompted both the state and the private sector to adopt a much more serious approach to investigating, and providing for, consumer demand.

The chapter also uses some of the travails of new urban shopping developments to probe some broader questions about the nature of Britain's post-war affluent society. By the later 1960s, it was already clear that projections of inexorably expanding prosperity were misjudged, and the

installation of expensive new shopping facilities at the heart of British urban
life began to look somewhat odd, particularly in regions that were struggling economically. I also highlight the rising currents of anxiety and
protest against the commercially driven course of urban transformation
which became increasingly pronounced at this time. Like individual consumers, these voices were diverse, motivated by a range of grievances and
taking aim at multiple targets. The focus here is on the increasingly vocal
challenge to the retail-led transformation of the city, and the commercial
forces which were steering it. Citizens, activists and academics began to
critique the encroachment of the retail economy over ever more of the city's
shared spaces, and took aim at the new urban norms and forms which this
produced. In particular a controversy in 1968 over the uses of shared urban
space in Birmingham produced a storm of protest from groups and individuals seeking to defend 'the right to the city' against the depredations of
commercial efficiency. The chapter concludes by considering the political
and behavioural implications of the widespread installation of enclosed,
privately owned shopping spaces across the urban centres of post-war
Britain, highlighting the new commercially determined regimes of policing
such spaces entailed, and the extent of mistrust and misbehaviour which
this provoked.

Projecting Demand

Along with the rhetoric of modernisation, the notion of consumer demand
was critical in making the case for the retail-led remodelling of Britain's city
centres. For councils and their development industry partners, it was the
vigorous and expanding demand for 'modern shopping' from an affluent,
mass-consuming citizenry which formed the principal justification for their
large-scale retail developments. There was much truth in this of course. In
the post-war decades, Britain became a society characterised by mass affluence. Real wages grew at a substantially faster rate during the 'Golden Age'
of 1951–1973 than at any other time in the modern era, at the same time as
working hours decreased and holidays increased.[1] Workers' average weekly
earnings more than doubled between 1950 and 1961, while retail prices rose
only by around 50 per cent. This radical wage-based growth in spending
power did not even capture the full extent of consumers' expanded buying
capacity because of the dramatic upsurge in hire purchase. One

---

[1] See Nicholas Crafts, 'The British Economy', in Francesca Carnevali & Julie-Marie
Strange (eds.), *20th Century Britain: Economic, Cultural and Social Change* (London:
Routledge, 2007), 7–25. Crafts gives the figures for real wage growth in this period in
Table 2.5 (3.16 per cent p.a.), which are more than double that of other periods. Due to
the method of calculation this figure is, as Crafts acknowledges, an underestimate.

contemporary analyst suggested that 'the growth of the hire-purchase debt has been one of the outstanding features of the post-War economy'; this rose from £442 m in mid-1957, to £1,386 m at the end of 1965 (after allowing for inflation, this is a real terms increase of over 150 per cent in just eight years).[2] All of this amounted to an unprecedented expansion in consumer spending, and the vast majority of increased incomes was spent rather than saved. Food continued to form by far the biggest individual component of consumer spending, but there was rapid and sustained growth in spending on cars, clothing, motorbikes, televisions, household goods and furnishings, records and stereos, along with holidays and leisure activities, and the more traditional British staples of alcohol and tobacco.[3] Retailing boomed, with annual turnover rising from £5 bn in 1950 to £14 bn by 1970. Employment in the 'distributive trades' – which encompassed retailing alongside all its supporting sectors such as transport, warehousing, advertising, financial and legal services, management and administration – expanded by more than 50 per cent between 1950 and 1964, from 2.3 million to 3.5 million, and accounted for around a fifth of the workforce.[4]

Rising disposable incomes and the extension of affluence thus transformed the economy and society of post-war Britain. There was an extraordinary expansion in the business and the cultures of shopping, buoyed by vigorous demand from a wealthier and widening customer base, and widespread access to credit. The nature of shopping itself was changing dramatically too. Bigger incomes saw a shift towards more luxurious items of consumption, and a heightened emphasis upon shopping as a leisure activity in its own right, rather than a more prosaic job of household provisioning. At the same time, rising standards and expectations meant that items which might previously have been thought luxuries

[2] Pauline Gregg, *The Welfare State: An Economic and Social History of Great Britain from 1945 to the Present Day* (London: Harrap, c. 1968 [undated]), 236–240. These figures were extracted from the Ministry of Labour's *Statistics on Incomes, Prices, Employment and Production* (1962). On HP see Peter M. Scott & James T. Walker, 'The Impact of "Stop-Go" Demand Management Policy on Britain's Consumer Durables Industries, 1952-65', *Economic History Review* 70:4 (2017), 1321–1345, for an account of central government's 'rationing' of lower-income groups' access to consumer credit in the interests of financial retrenchment, the City and the international position of sterling.

[3] See Gregg, *The Welfare State*, for detailed figures on consumers' spending habits. Also Sue Bowden & Avner Offer, 'Household Appliances and the Use of Time: The United States and Britain since the 1920s', *Economic History Review* 47:4 (1994), 725–748, which shows how rapid the uptake of new household consumer goods was in the decade from 1953 to 1963.

[4] Figures from Gregg, *The Welfare State*, based on the Annual Abstracts of Statistics; Robert Millward, 'The Rise of the Service Economy', in Roderick Floud & Paul Johnson (eds.), *The Cambridge Economic History of Modern Britain: Structural Change and Growth, 1939–2000* (Cambridge: Cambridge University Press, 2004), 238–266.

came to be viewed increasingly as ordinary purchases, and 'the line between utility and prestige-buying [became] somewhat thin'.[5] More luxurious forms of shopping experienced rapid expansion and in the process became normalised as an unremarkable aspect of everyday life and leisure for an ever-widening section of post-war society.

New models of selling, and new types of shopping environments, were critical to this 'retail revolution'. Shopping became a far more sophisticated industry, where innovations in store design, marketing, logistics, organisation and management could produce substantial rises in efficiency and profitability. Supermarkets and other forms of self-service store experienced exponential growth (Figure 6.1); starting from a base of virtually

Figure 6.1 1964 image of the interior of a new Fine Fare supermarket within Birmingham's Bull Ring shopping centre. The self-service supermarket was an American innovation and its adoption in Britain promoted by the Anglo-American Council in Productivity. The British food retail sector became highly efficient in the two decades after the war, and was dominated by a handful of nationally organised chains. Source: Historic England Archive, John Laing Photographic Collection.

[5] Gregg, *The Welfare State*, 238.

none in 1950, there were around 28,000 self-service stores in Britain by the early 1970s.[6] The dynamic and expansionary multiple stores were 'the whizz-kids of the retail scene', as one industry expert put it in 1972.[7] Their share of the total retail trade increased from 28.3% in 1961 to 36.8% in 1970, and in some individual sectors this figure was much higher (already in 1959 the multiples had captured 60% of footwear sales and 43% of menswear sales). Even these commanding figures did not do justice to the dynamism and dominance of the multiples, whose new selling and organisational techniques allowed them to generate on average three times as much turnover per store as their competitors.[8] This meant that, while retail turnover in the country as a whole was expanding rapidly, the number of actual shops was decreasing as the trade became dominated by fewer, more efficient stores. The post-war state, in its anxious pursuit of growth, productivity and efficiency, firmly supported these transformations in the retail trade. In 1964 the National Economic Development Council applauded the advances of multiple retailers and called on them to continue 'to expand research, to improve the layout of shops and to increase the use of mechanical and electronic aids'. The government's Resale Prices Act of the same year also advanced the interests of large retailers by abolishing the long-standing practice of 'resale price maintenance', whereby manufacturers had been able to fix the prices at which their own goods retailed in the stores. This too was intended by the government to 'increase efficiency in distribution'.[9] As an economic sector and as a realm of social experience, shopping saw prodigious growth, but control over this critical domain of post-war life was being concentrated more than ever in the hands of large, nationally organised retail businesses, which were proactive in applying organisational innovations in the interests of expansion and efficiency. The nation of shopkeepers, which the retail studies of the late 1940s had found to be surprisingly still intact at the end of the Second World War, was being steadily dismantled. It was giving way to a nation of shoppers, serviced by an increasingly efficient and well-organised corporate retail sector.

There was thus clear enthusiasm and rising demand not just for shopping per se, but for new forms of shopping, in new environments, offering

---

[6] E. MacFadyen, 'Retailers at the Crossroads', *Building with Steel* 10 (May, 1972), 2–6. See also Gareth Shaw, Louise Curth & Andrew Alexander, 'Selling Self-Service and the Supermarket: The Americanisation of Food Retailing in Britain, 1945-60', *Business History* 46:4 (2004), 568–582.

[7] E. MacFadyen, 'Retailers at the Crossroads', *Building with Steel* 10 (May, 1972), 2.

[8] 'The Battle of the Stores', *The Financial Times*, 27 June 1959, 4.

[9] National Economic Development Council, *The Growth of the Economy*, Part III, 17: 'Distribution'; J. F. Pickering, *Resale Price Maintenance in Practice* (London: George Allen & Unwin, 1966).

new types of consumer experience. Given the obvious evidence of this, local authorities could be forgiven for concluding – as Leeds Corporation did in the mid-1960s – that 'the constantly increasing and insistent demand is for shops selling every sort of commodity'.[10] Councils all over the country sought to use their redevelopment schemes to get ahead of this curve, refitting central areas in an effort to ensure that they were best placed to capitalise upon dramatic growth in the retail economy. Optimistic projections of unhindered expansion into the 1980s were widespread, as in Liverpool's 1965 city centre plan which attempted to model regional demand using figures from the National Economic Development Council, and proposed enormous expansions of selling space in the central area. The plan confidently predicted that:

It is certain that the higher incomes in real terms and the tendency of a more affluent society to increase its spending on durable goods more than on convenience goods ... will result in more money being spent in Liverpool.[11]

City planners also hoped to gear local retail economies towards the more prestigious and valuable end of the retail trade, reinforcing the trends towards luxury shopping and the dominance of the larger stores. In Liverpool it was felt that:

The quality of shops is important because it affects the buyer's choice and the appearance and atmosphere of a shopping centre ... rising national prosperity will increase the demand for goods and services of a higher standard.[12]

Bolton's 1964 city plan – which, like Liverpool's, was produced by the planner-architect Graeme Shankland – took a similar line. The town must, it was felt, encourage the development of 'shops of increased range and variety'. Redevelopment would allow Bolton 'to increase its share of hinterland trade'; larger shops and new layouts would make 'increased turnover possible'; and the town's 'potential retail trade' was projected to expand by around 100 per cent by the mid-1980s.[13] In Manchester, too, similar ideas and models of demand formed the principal rationale for major central area redevelopments. In justifying the city's enormous central area shopping redevelopment, the city planning officer claimed that 'there is an undoubted demand for some additional and well located shopping space'.[14] As in Liverpool and elsewhere, Manchester's

[10] Leeds City Council, 'Seacroft Town Centre', promotional brochure, n.d.[c.1965?]. WYAS – LLD1/2/824956.
[11] City Centre Planning Group, *Liverpool City Centre Plan* (1965), 26.
[12] City Centre Planning Group, *Liverpool City Centre Plan* (1965), 65.
[13] Graeme Shankland Associates, *Bolton Draft Town Centre Map* (1964), 68, 75, 84. Available at Bolton Archives History Centre.
[14] City and County Borough of Manchester, *City Centre Map 1967*, 15. GMCRO.

planners imagined that it was the expensively housed and higher-end modes of shopping that were in demand, rather than the more modest and 'obsolete' forms of retailing that cities were eliminating from their central areas.

Languages of demand became an essential element of the legal arguments for redevelopment which were presented jointly by councils and development companies at public planning inquiries. Here, demand was couched in increasingly scientised terms and enumerated precisely in square feet of shopping space. In Lancaster, a new shopping precinct was expected to increase the city's central area shopping floorspace from 65,700 square feet to 93,000 square feet. 'The justification for this', argued the council, 'lies in the growing affluence of society and the increase in population not only within the boundaries of Lancaster but also within the catchment area which focusses on Lancaster as the main commercial centre in the region'.[15] Development companies quickly became adept at marshalling the scientised languages of demand in support of their projects. In Morecambe, the Arndale company assured a fractious public inquiry that:

[The company had] given careful consideration to the assessment of the future potential retail trading levels in Morecambe ... and we have shown in our plans the optimum size of development necessary to cope efficiently with the future potential in this area.[16]

Arndale also prepared a supporting document, 'Economic Analysis for Development Planning', to bolster its case in Morecambe. Commissioning expert planners to produce 'scientific' reports which explained why the proposed development was necessary became a familiar strategy, and a sub-industry of commercial planning consultancy grew out of such practices. At Manchester, Arndale hired Nathaniel Lichfield 'to prepare a report on retail shopping floorspace needs in central Manchester to support their case at a planning inquiry'. Lichfield was a leading planning expert in Britain; he had pioneered the application of cost-benefit analysis to planning, worked on a number of New Towns and in the mid-1960s was Professor of the Economics of Environmental Planning at University College London. He founded the consultancy Nathaniel Lichfield and Associates in 1962 (the firm remains one of the country's pre-eminent development consultants). Lichfield appeared as an expert witness for Arndale at the public inquiry held in 1968 in Manchester, where he was able to provide detailed statistics on

---

[15] Lancashire County Council, 'Lancaster St. Nicholas Street Area: Written Analysis', 1966, 5. TNA-HLG-79/1207.
[16] Proof of evidence of Arndale Developments Ltd to public inquiry, 1965, 6. TNA-HLG-79/1213.

the workings of the city's retail economy, and predict that, by 1981, 'shops in central Manchester should be able to attract spending power equal to an increase of between 96 and 130 per cent over the 1961 total'.[17] Such practices reflected the need to speak to government decision-makers in the precise and positivist languages of scientific expertise and appealed to the technocratic identities of those responsible for administering the public planning machinery. As verifiable projections of social needs, consumer tastes and future spending patterns, however, they were fairly spurious exercises. The certainty of consultants' claims misrepresented the extent to which the identification and enumeration of consumer demand was a decidedly experimental science and very much in its infancy in this period. For all their supposed local sensitivities and tailoring, all the 1960s retail planning projections made essentially the same prediction – that retail expenditure would double by the 1980s – regardless of the specific locale in question, or the countervailing tendencies towards urban depopulation and declining employment which were already obvious in many places. Such projections were based on tracing forward the trends from a particularly buoyant moment at the turn of the 1960s (the 1961 Census of Distribution), and glossed over some inconvenient truths both locally and nationally (such as the nationwide stagnation of retail sales during an economic downturn in 1962/3).[18] 'Retailing', as one historian of the trade puts it, 'is a barometer rather than an engine of change'.[19] The sector, which rests upon levels of disposable income and individuals' willingness to part with it, is self-evidently highly susceptible to fluctuations in the wider economy in ways which were insufficiently acknowledged in the over-confident 1960s. In any case, where consultants failed to provide the desired prediction, they could simply be ignored. In Nottingham, when the council hoped to justify building a second large shopping centre in the city (from which it was to profit directly), the analysis commissioned threw up 'three alternative projections of the future demand'. Only 'the most optimistic one showed that there was a demand in the fairly near future' for a second mall in the city; naturally, this was the scenario favoured.[20]

As the sociologists Peter Miller and Nikolas Rose have suggested, the development of new forms of consumer knowledge 'does not merely

[17] Letter from Nathaniel Lichfield and Associates, 15 August 1967, public inquiry documents, TNA-HLG-79/1187; 'Attracting Spending Power', *The Guardian*, 3 July 1968, 3.
[18] National Economic Development Council, *The Growth of the Economy*, 125.
[19] Winstanley, 'Concentration and Competition in the Retail Sector', 236–262, 237.
[20] As recorded in a letter from Harlow & Shelton Estate Agents to Nottingham Trustee Savings Bank, 24 May 1968, Nottinghamshire Archives [DD/HA/1/4/8/297].

uncover pre-existing desires or anxieties: it forces them into existence ...
it renders them thinkable by new techniques of calculation, classification
and inscription'.²¹ Developers, councils and planning consultants were
inventing rather than identifying future patterns of shopping demand and
the more circumspect technocrats readily acknowledged this. Wilfred
Burns, for example, noted in his 1959 study of *British Shopping Centres*
that 'we still have not worked out even a quasi-scientific basis for estimat-
ing shopping requirements'.²² With regard to the Manchester central area
development, the largest shopping scheme in the country, experts at the
Ministry of Housing and Local Government also remained unconvinced
despite the predictions of the hired consultants. The Ministry's planning
advisors declared themselves 'seriously concerned about the enormous
build up in shopping space that such a development would entail' and
viewed the development as a 'dangerously large extension' which was
likely to compete with, and take business from, surrounding shopping
streets and districts (this, in the end, was precisely what happened).²³
Like Wilfred Burns, the Ministry's advisors also questioned the expertise
upon which calculations of 'demand' were based, with one official concluding that 'we do not know of a forecasting method we could trust to
guarantee the success of a scheme as large as this'.²⁴ Similar reservations
were expressed with regard to schemes elsewhere. In Rochdale, both the
Ministry's planning inspector and its technical staff opposed local plans
for town centre redevelopment as 'a risky scheme', which raised 'the risk
of over shopping' and had the potential to 'become a white elephant and
a burden on the ratepayers'.²⁵ In Wigan in the mid-1960s the Ministry
rejected another town centre redevelopment plan 'on the ground that the
increase in retail shopping was unjustified'.²⁶

Locally, too, there were fundamental disagreements about the nature
and extent of demand. Although property developers and planning consultants attempted to assert a privileged knowledge of the consumer
economy and its future trajectory, there were many local actors who
disputed and discredited their claims. Local retailers in Morecambe, for

²¹ Peter Miller & Nikolas Rose, 'Mobilizing the Consumer: Assembling the Subject of
Consumption', *Theory Culture Society* 14:1 (1997), 1–36, 31.
²² Quoted in 'Shopping and Town Centre Redevelopment', *Official Architecture and
Planning* 30: 8 (1967), 1106–1107.
²³ See MHLG, 'Manchester: Market Street C.D.A.', internal note, 10 March 1967, TNA-
HLG-79/1184; & MHLG, 'Manchester – Market Street C.D.A. Technical Report',
June 1967, 2, TNA-HLG-79/1188.
²⁴ MHLG, letter to City Planning Officer, Manchester, 2 August 1966. TNA-HLG-79/
1188.
²⁵ 'Rochdale C.B. Central Area Shopping', memorandum, 23 March 1972. TNA-HLG-
79/1198.
²⁶ 'Attracting Shoppers to the New Town Centres', *The Guardian*, 15 November 1965, 16.

example, where Arndale claimed that its new shopping mall represented 'the optimum size of development [for] the future potential of the area', pointed out that the seaside town's trade was entirely seasonal. This meant that even major stores like Woolworths and Marks and Spencer closed down completely during the winter, while many smaller shops remained closed for three quarters of the year. These facts, coupled with the town's ageing population and preponderance of empty shops, 'stressed the lack of demand', rather than any demonstrable need for an expensive covered shopping mall.[27] In Manchester, too, retailers and businesses affected by redevelopment disputed the constructions of demand upon which it was based and staked out alternative claims to knowledge of the consumer's needs. Eighteen publicans and restaurateurs argued that 'the need for a comprehensive plan for this central area of Manchester is incapable of proof' and suggested that the development would 'result in grave injury being done to ... the welfare of the public whose essential requirements will not be met'.[28] Numerous other retailers objected that the scheme was 'excessive and too far reaching', 'overambitious', 'not called for' and 'not justified by the state of the national economy'.[29] Similar questions about planning expertise and consumers' needs were raised by the Secretary of the Scottish Federation of Meat Traders' Associations (a butchers' trade body), who wrote in protest to the government: 'After all who knows the public better – the Researchers who send me questionnaires, or the practical men whose successful business demonstrates their knowledge and their success!'[30] Although appeals to consumer demand and the essential needs of 'the shopper' were central to the way major redevelopment schemes were justified, even among the experts there was precious little agreement about what this actually meant.

Demand and Ambivalence

Disputes and uncertainties over the demand for new shopping facilities reflected the fact that 'demand', like 'modernisation', was an ill-defined rhetorical construct, rather than a precise programme for providing specific urban infrastructures. In practice it was not at all clear that buoyant

---

[27] Inspector's Report of public local inquiry, 14 May 1965, 12. TNA-HLG-79/1213.
[28] Objection letter from Cobbett, Wheeler & Cobbett Solicitors, 25 October 1966. TNA-HLG-79/1185.
[29] See the objections from the companies Alexandre Ltd, 27 October 1966; William Timpson Ltd, 14 October 1966; Testers, 20 October 1966. All within TNA-HLG-79/1187.
[30] Letter from Scottish Federation of Meat Traders' Associations to National Economic Development Office, 9 September 1968. TNA-FG-2/830.

consumer spending in the economy could be translated into a confident claim that shoppers en masse demanded wholesale redevelopment and the installation of new urban shopping complexes. Rather surprisingly, given the rapidly advancing state of market research in this period, little effort was made to consult shoppers themselves before planning decisions were taken.[31] Once new shopping complexes were open and trading, however, it was possible to get a clearer indication of the shopping public's response to them. Here the picture was decidedly ambivalent and did not at all support the idea that the new facilities had satisfied a voracious pre-existing demand. A precise understanding of the new centres' trading performance is difficult to ascertain, partly because there was much variation between centres and between regions and partly because – with centres' prospects so dependent on image and confidence – there were many Panglossian accounts in circulation.[32] Yet there is plenty of evidence from a wide array of sources that most centres struggled to attract sufficient numbers of shoppers and also often failed to persuade retailers to take on leases for the expensive new sites. Indeed, a public narrative quickly emerged of new shopping developments as 'white elephants which bear testimony to over-optimism and bad judgement', in the words of a *Guardian* property correspondent. 'The shops in these developments remain unlet', the writer continued, 'and local pride is shaken by the failure to attract tenants'.[33]

Many of the flagship developments of the period experienced significant, and sometimes severe, commercial difficulties, especially in their early stages of trading. On the day of its 'gala opening' in March 1965, only forty out of 100 new stores in London's Elephant and Castle centre were let. Over a year later, more than a third of the shops were still empty; the centre's operating company was now getting into serious financial difficulty and offering 'rent holidays', loans and other incentives in a desperate attempt to entice retailers.[34] Similar reports of poor trading and slack uptake of new shopping units plagued developments all over the country, as commentators acknowledged that 'many shopping schemes have not produced the expected returns'.[35] Birmingham's Bull Ring and

---

[31] See Brückweh, *The Voice of the Citizen Consumer*.
[32] See, for example, *The Guardian* property correspondent Tom Allan's boosterist reporting; 'The View Through the Builders' Dust', *The Guardian*, 13 October 1971, 19'; 'Taking the Ache out of Shopping', *The Guardian*, 27 January 1972, 19.
[33] Richard Mallinson, 'No More White Elephants?', *The Guardian*, 28 November 1968, 13.
[34] 'Traders Snub the Elephant', *The Daily Mail*, 26 March 1965, 13; 'Rent Incentives for Tenants of Elephant and Castle Centre', *The Financial Times*, 21 October 1965, 15; Elizabeth Gundrey, 'Consumer's Column', *The Guardian*, 4 April 1966, 6.
[35] Richard Mallinson, 'Lively Demand for Offices in Manchester', *The Guardian*, 19 June 1969, 14.

Manchester's Arndale Centre (opened in 1964 and 1976, respectively) both experienced difficulties attracting custom, while an earlier development in Manchester city centre – the Piccadilly Plaza – had failed to let half of its shopping units a year after completion. Here, the architecturally innovative 'first floor piazza' was described as 'a scene of concrete emptiness' where only three out of thirty units were occupied.[36] New developments in major cities were at least guaranteed some trade. In smaller towns and suburbs, which did not enjoy the natural attractions of major urban centres, more modest retail developments sometimes failed to ever reach the critical mass needed to get off the ground commercially. Small centres at Altrincham, Cheshire; Seacroft, in suburban Leeds; and Perry Barr, north of Birmingham, suffered this fate, with 'many shops . . . empty since the centres were built'.[37]

In his 1967 book on the property development sector, *The Times*'s property correspondent Oliver Marriott diagnosed the problem of 'White Elephantiasis', citing dozens of cases in towns and cities across the country where 'the problems flowing from over-optimism' had led to over-provision, unlet shops and financial difficulties.[38] In Leeds, the city's landmark Merrion Centre ran into sustained difficulties after it opened in 1964. Two years after opening, many units in the centre remained unlet, one major retailer had already closed its store and the remaining business tenants were petitioning for rent reductions to compensate 'for their disappointing trading experience [and] substantial losses'. Merrion tenants claimed that 'there was a distinct chance that 90% of the shops in the Centre would be vacated within the next six months'.[39] While such difficulties should have remained a commercial problem for the operating company, the public–private nature of shopping schemes meant that poor trading became a public problem. Councils which had staked their town's image as 'modern, go-getting shopping centres' on these developments, and often sunk substantial amounts of municipal funds into schemes, could ill afford to see them go under.[40] This placed them in an extremely difficult position when the breezy promises of roaring commercial success failed to materialise. In Leeds, the Merrion Centre's operating company used tenants' complaints about poor trading to pressure the council into accepting reduced ground rents and taking on more of the running costs

[36] 'Attracting Shoppers to the New Town Centres', *The Guardian*, 15 November 1965, 16.
[37] Rosalind Morris, 'Super Shops Do Not Attract Housewives', *The Guardian*, 16 October 1969, 15.
[38] Marriott, *The Property Boom*, ch. 15.
[39] Letter from Town Centre Securities to Town Clerk, 24 November 1966. WYAS – LLD1/2/833178.
[40] The phrase is Bolton Metropolitan Borough Council's. Land Sub-Committee Report 1988. Available at Bolton Local History Centre.

of the facility.[41] As corporate economic actors – the proprietors of the land on which new centres were built – councils should have resisted these demands in order to defend their rental income and projected returns. But as public authorities, with a duty to promote the overall success and image of their redeveloped town centres, it was difficult to avoid making concessions. Such dilemmas exposed some of the risks inherent in councils' attempts to simultaneously perform the sometimes-contradictory roles of public authority and property entrepreneur.

On the basis of new shopping centres' commercial performance, then, there is little evidence to support the view that such facilities offered precisely tailored satisfaction to an insatiable consumer demand. Indeed, once they were given some sort of voice, consumers often expressed their dissatisfaction, rather than enthusiasm, with these facilities. *The Guardian*'s 'Consumer's Column' made some of these complaints clear in 1966. 'Planners everywhere seem wedded to the now fashionable shopping centre concept', the columnist noted, 'even though some look like being rather costly follies'. The case of Cambridge was cited, where, in the absence of any sort of consultation from the city council, a local consumer group had organised its own survey of 200 of its members in order to gauge opinion on a proposed shopping development. The housewives of Cambridge complained, not that they did not have enough high-end, luxury shopping, but that basic necessities were unavailable in the city, forcing them to travel elsewhere or use mail order services. A quarter of respondents simply wanted more ironmongers in the city. Similar complaints were made about the type of shops being provided in new shopping centres all over the country, where 'there may be several radio shops, say, while not a fishmonger exists for miles around'. The columnist extolled the virtues of 'those useful all-purpose corner shops ... or the small shopping parades, neither of which impose prohibitive rentals but do provide a maximum of convenience to local shoppers'. In Cambridge, the council acknowledged that these more prosaic demands from actual consumers ultimately mattered little to the process of redevelopment, which was driven by other priorities. The city planning officer was forced to admit that 'shopper's needs are unlikely to determine what shops are provided: so high are the rents going to be that small, specialist shops will not have the turnover to afford them'.[42]

Despite the prevalent planning narrative that the shopping public demanded to be rid of 'obsolete' forms of shopping, in actuality many

---

[41] See the 1966 correspondence between Town Centre Securities and Leeds Corporation within WYAS – LLD1/2/833178.

[42] All details from: Elizabeth Gundrey, 'Consumer's Column', *The Guardian*, 4 April 1966, 6; Richard Mallinson, 'No More White Elephants?', *The Guardian*, 28 November 1968, 13.

shoppers were slow to abandon long-established habits and routines. They tended instead to put great store upon 'convenience', which largely meant how easily they could get to a shop, and many also continued to rely upon cheaper, more prosaic forms of shopping. There was often a marked reluctance from shoppers to engage with new shopping environments and a surprising longevity to the popularity of the 'obsolete' types of shopping space and experience which were being marginalised through redevelopment. In Birmingham, where the Bull Ring's centuries-old market was retained as part of the new shopping complex, it was initially the market, rather than the gaudy new shopping mall, which prospered. 'The shoppers were used to coming to the market', reported one commentator, 'and they happily used the new covered market, on the ground floor of the new centre . . .. Although lifts, escalators, and stairs were provided to the shops above, at first many people using the market ignored the shops'.[43] This story was replicated elsewhere. On the outskirts of Leeds, where the corporation built a council-owned shopping complex at the centre of its new satellite town of Seacroft, it was the Seacroft Centre's market alone which managed to draw the crowds (Figure 6.2). The shopping centre's overall trading performance was dismal – at great financial and reputational cost to the council – and the success of its market was acknowledged by city officials to be 'the most beneficial publicity that Seacroft Centre has ever had'.[44] The continued importance and popularity of markets has been further underlined in historian Sarah Mass's recent work on Glasgow, Bradford and Chesterfield. In Glasgow in particular Mass notes that localised deprivation 'invited low-profit, informal retail economy' of the type offered by markets, and that planners were often confronted 'by a shopping community whose boundaries and motivations did not fall within the behavioural norms of the imagined "mobile consumer" in retail and infrastructure planning'.[45]

The continued popularity of markets was one indication of the persistence of long-established shopping habits, even at a time of significant change within the overall shopping landscape. Such continuities of shopping habits underline the quotidian nature of shopping, which was bound up with the rhythms and routines of everyday life and often resistant to

---

[43] Rosalind Morris, 'Super Shops Do Not Attract Housewives', *The Guardian*, 16 October 1969, 15.
[44] See the comments and reports attached to the minutes of a meeting of the Housing and Property Management Committee, 30 July 1968. WYAS-LCC-824956. Emphasis in original.
[45] Sarah Mass, 'Cost-Benefit Break Down: Unplannable Spaces in 1970s Glasgow', *Urban History* (2018), 3; Sarah Mass, 'Commercial Heritage as Democratic Action: Historicizing the "Save the Market" Campaigns in Bradford and Chesterfield, 1969-76', *Twentieth Century British History* 29:3 (2018), 459–484.

Figure 6.2 1967 image of Leeds Corporation's Seacroft shopping precinct, on the outskirts of the city. The precinct is seen here two years after a prestigious royal opening event in October 1965, and notably underused. Poor trading at the Seacroft Centre caused persistent political and financial problems for Leeds Corporation, and the entire complex was eventually demolished in 1999. Source: Leeds Libraries.

change. The findings of a 1968 Gallup opinion poll suggested that 'the evidence is that shopping centres, with their supermarkets and stereo-typed shop sizes, may not give shoppers all they want. A third of British housewives [according to the poll] still go shopping every day and prefer to make many small purchases rather than a large one. Only one in six housewives goes shopping by car'.[46] A 1976 survey of 6,000 households in an inner area of Manchester also found that 'wives have demanded the return of the old corner shop' and that 'large precincts are out with young families'.[47] Even in New Towns, where the transfer of populations to new locales might have done more to dislodge established shopping habits, markets remained important and well patronised. A 1967 study of Harlow's shopping scene placed great emphasis on the 'commercial

---

[46] Rosalind Morris, 'Super Shops Do Not Attract Housewives', *The Guardian*, 16 October 1969, 15.
[47] 'Snub on Street of Dreams', *Manchester Evening News*, 24 January 1976.

success' of the town's new market, and pointed out that, before it had
been installed, many of the New Town's residents trailed all the way back
to the markets of East London every Saturday.[48]
The dissonance between the imagined shopper of development
promotions – wealthy, leisured, mobile and enrapt by novelty – and
the everyday reality of shopping for many women managing households was clear. The continued importance of local, daily shopping,
and of inexpensive retail settings like markets, was an indication that
not all shoppers were willing or able to throw themselves into the
expensive modes of shopping which councils and developers sought
to promote. The poorer, less mobile households that continued to be
concentrated in many inner urban areas, for example, were less likely
to find satisfaction among the higher-end offerings of shopping malls.
Sometimes shoppers simply outmanoeuvred the corporate retail strategies which underpinned new developments. In Bradford, the Forster
Square shopping development suffered because 'Bradford housewives
are patronising the supermarkets [in Forster Square] for their cheap
offers but are tending to return to the local traders ... for their normal
grocery orders'. This practice, the local Chamber of Trade acknowledged, was 'threatening the economic basis of supermarket trading,
which is to attract the housewife by cheap offers in the belief that
money will then be spent on profit-making items once she is in the
shop'.[49] The *Guardian* cited this approvingly as an example of 'the
canniness of shoppers in the North of England', and it was undoubtedly the case that there was a highly uneven geography of affluence
across the country. The *Board of Trade Journal* in 1965 highlighted
marked regional disparities in levels of consumer expenditure, with
London and the South-East 'lead[ing] Britain in consumer retail
spending'; while a 1962 study in the *Town Planning Review* compared
all the major urban centres in the United Kingdom and found dramatically differing levels of retail turnover per head in different locales.
Less wealthy regions predictably trailed far behind.[50]
Britain's calamitous regional divides were growing steadily across the
post-war decades, and this was clearly expressed in the divergent performance of local retail economies. Growing regional divides were another
indication of the engrained liberalism of the polity – reluctant to stand
firmly against what were seen as the 'natural' ebbs and flows of market

[48] 'Harlow Shopping Centre', 1108–1109.
[49] 'Traders' Problems as Town Centres Change', *The Guardian*, 18 August 1962, 10.
[50] 'Where the Cash Is', *The Daily Mail*, 30 April 1965, 6; H. R. Parker, 'Suburban Shopping
Facilities in Liverpool', *Town Planning Review* 33:3 (1962), 197–223. The study surveyed
all urban centres with a population over 250,000.

forces – and they were little helped by the Board of Trade's less-than-wholehearted commitment to its own regional development policies.[51] Such regional disparities, along with the lack of enthusiasm for expensive new facilities from many shoppers, point to some of the limits of affluence in post-war Britain. Despite the unprecedented economic expansion of the post-war decades, and the extension of popular access to more affluent lifestyles and living standards, it was certainly not the case that all households entered into a leisured state of luxury and plenty. Social scientists in Britain came increasingly to recognise these facts from the mid-1960s, and this drove their so-called rediscovery of poverty as confidence in both the provisions of the welfare state and the prospects for the affluent society waned in tandem. The over-confident projections of *embourgeoisement* and affluence for all which caused so much excitement in the early 1960s were quickly discredited and disavowed once the faltering of Western capitalism's golden age and the persistence of social disadvantage came more clearly into view. In Britain, the disillusionment was more marked than elsewhere. The country had grown and prospered much less dramatically than many of its European neighbours during the post-war boom – there was no *trente glorieuses, miracolo economico* or *Wirtschaftswunder* here, given Britain's much earlier urbanisation and industrialisation – and ideas about economic performance and national prospects were tinged with the self-doubt and pessimism of a waning imperial power.

For the largest of the post-war shopping centres, like Newcastle's Eldon Square or Manchester's Arndale Centre, which opened in the tail end of the urban renewal boom in the mid-1970s, the sense that affluence was faltering, and perhaps fleeting, infected the schemes with a climate of uncertainty before they were even completed. Both centres had to be built under the unpropitious conditions of the three-day week in early 1974, and both experienced difficulties and delays due to fraught labour relations on site. Eldon Square in particular was plagued by toxic conflicts with workers and unions, with construction regularly brought to a halt by walkouts and the site picketed aggressively on multiple occasions. Disputes and delays in a context of spiralling inflation dramatically increased the costs of such projects – the bill for the Manchester Arndale Centre rose from £30 m to £100 m across the mid-1970s – and this made their commercial success ever more questionable.

[51] On regional policy and regional problems see Scott, 'The Worst of Both Worlds', 41–64; Rosevear, 'Balancing Business and the Regions', 77–99; Martin, 'The Political Economy of Britain's North-South Divide', 389–418; and, more generally, Scott, *Triumph of the South: A Regional Economic History of Early Twentieth Century Britain* (Aldershot: Ashgate, 2007); Baker and Billinge, *Geographies of England*.

Questions also began to be asked about the notions of affluence and regional demand upon which such developments rested. By the time Newcastle's Eldon Square was finally opened in 1976, one reporter noted that while the development 'certainly exudes confidence and prosperity ... it contrasts oddly with this week's council report that one in five of the city's households are on or below the poverty line'.[52] Similar concerns were expressed in Manchester, where the tone of coverage in the local press shifted markedly in the 1970s. In 1968 the *Manchester Evening News* was still confident that the Arndale development would be 'a paradise for shoppers'; by the time the complex was gearing up to open in 1976 the paper was running anxious think-pieces highlighting Manchester's faltering economic prospects and questioning whether 'the new development [would] do its job and attract shoppers back into the city'.[53] The wind had also been taken out of the city authorities' sails, with Manchester's chief planner already striking a much more cautious note in 1975 and signalling a 'rethink in big city development' to the *Evening News*.[54]

The limits of consumer demand were also underlined forcefully when it became clear that, rather than catering for ever-expanding consumer appetites, redeveloped shopping centres were actually engaged in fierce competition with each other to attract finite regional shopping expenditures. 'Over-shopping' in an individual city or region was rapidly identified as a major problem and a key cause of the widespread phenomenon of empty shops in redeveloped centres. The planner Max Lock complained as early as 1962 about councils' 'slap-happy over-provision of shopping floor space [which] can only sanction the robbing of Peter's established trade to pay the apparently insatiable Paul'.[55] *The Guardian* also warned that 'as more and more towns in a small area ... redevelop their centres and build expensive shopping districts ... it is likely that one town's catchment area of shoppers may begin to overlap with that of another'. The paper called for planning decisions to be 'supplemented by rigorous and professional economic surveys of shopping potential, retailers' desires, and population increase to ensure that expensive council schemes are commercially viable'.[56] Central government – which had always been rather more circumspect than many councils about some towns'

[52] John Ardill, '"Giant" Is Ready to Do Business', *The Guardian*, 5 March 1976, 6.
[53] 'A Paradise for Shoppers Planned', *MEN*, 19 June 1968; Winn Walsh, 'Bringing Back the Shoppers', *MEN*, 1 July 1976.
[54] Bernard Spilsbury, 'Victoriana? It's Here to Stay..', *MEN*, 11 December 1975.
[55] Lock's review of Planning Bulletin 1, which appeared in the *Journal of the Town Planning Institute* in 1962, quoted in the file TNA-HLG-136/89.
[56] 'Attracting Shoppers to the New Town Centres', *The Guardian*, 15 November 1965, 16.

prospects for inexorable commercial expansion – agreed with this diag-
nosis. In 1963 the government set up a Working Party on Shopping
Centres in direct response to the 'good deal of anxiety being expressed
in the Press and elsewhere about the possibility of gross over-provision of
shopping facilities ... and the risk of damaging competition between
neighbouring centres'.[57]

The group's initial findings did little to allay these fears. It was discovered that many town centres had increased their total retail floor space
by 'as much as 50%, and in one case 200%'. Given the major improvements in the efficiency of selling space, 'such increases postulate[d]
a prodigious increase in turnover'. The working party concluded that:

> There is little to suggest that many local authorities ... know how to check the
> viability of such proposals, or even how to assess their implications. Nor are they
> able to judge the value of consultants' reports: some authorities are being blinded
> with pseudo science, judging by some of the reports we have seen.[58]

It was the growing recognition of these problems which prompted the
development of more rigorous and objective approaches to planning the
geographies of mass consumption and a more serious engagement with
the nature of consumer demand. The government's working party, in
recognition of the paucity of its own knowledge, generated further
research which sought to develop more accurate techniques of modelling
shoppers' needs and retailing potential. The state turned increasingly to
universities to supply this, commissioning studies on 'the economics and
planning of covered shopping centres' from Strathclyde University's
Department of Urban and Regional Planning, for example, or on 'shopping gravity models' from the University of Manchester's Centre for
Urban and Regional Research.[59] Academics and planning professionals
also worked independently to produce new, more reliable models for the
'The Assessment of Shopping Potential and the Demand for Shops', in
which they stressed the importance of shopping centres' overlapping and
competing spheres of attraction.[60]

---

[57] Working Party on Shopping Centres, 'Interim Report', February 1964, 2. TNA-HLG-
136/89.
[58] Working Party on Shopping Centres, 'Interim Report', February 1964, 2. TNA-HLG-
136/89.
[59] 'Covered Shopping Centres: Research into Implications', Report for the Department of
the Environment. AT 80/65; Economics Centre for Urban and Regional Research,
University of Manchester, 'Ministry of Transport Shopping Attractiveness Study',
19 July 1972. TNA – Ministry of Transport [MT] – 189/1/1.
[60] J. Parry Lewis & A. L. Traill, 'The Assessment of Shopping Potential and the Demand for
Shops', *Town Planning Review* 38:4 (1968), 317–326; M. E. Thomas & W. L. Waide,
'Shopping Centres and Community Investment', *Official Architecture and Planning* 30:8
(1967), 1094–1100; R. L. Davies, 'Store Location and Store Assessment Research: the

Such studies proliferated within the professional and academic literatures and quickly developed a sociological and psychological bent once it
was recognised how far 'efficiency' and 'performance' in retailing
depended upon the subjective wants and whims of myriad individual
consumers. One 1967 study titled 'Planning for the Customer', was
essentially an anthropology of a small suburban shopping centre, based
on participant observation and in-depth interviews with shoppers and
shopkeepers. A 1974 study concerned 'The Spatial Information Fields of
Urban Consumers' and sought – rather ambitiously – to translate the
'cognitive images' which shoppers held of specific shopping facilities into
algebraic equations.[61] The worst of these studies probably did little to
advance the state of retail geography beyond the 'pseudoscience' being
peddled by hired planning consultants, but they did serve to highlight the
complexity and intense diversity of shopping habits. Indeed, the more
experts tried to grasp at 'demand' as a unitary and quantifiable social
phenomenon, the quicker it dissipated along innumerable different chan-
nels, categories and sub-types. Retail planners and geographers adopted
commercial advertising's method of dealing with this intense heterogeneity, by 'segmenting' both shoppers and shopping into various typologies;
'"Daily" shopping versus "occasional" shopping', for example, or the
less-than-earth-shattering observations that 'milk bars [and] music
shops generally appeal to the younger generation', while 'gentlemen's
hairdressers are essentially a male preserve'.[62] Although it was becoming
more sophisticated and reliable, and gaining increased acceptance within
the academy, retail geography still had some way to go.

Dissent and Discontent

While many shoppers remained hesitant about patronising the gaudy new
facilities of the shopping-centred city, and others were simply not wealthy
enough to enjoy the experience, among some sections of the public such
developments aroused intense opposition and hostility. Often this came
from the left – from the type of individuals who might have been reading
cheap paperback editions of Marcuse's *One Dimensional Man* or

Integration of Some New and Traditional Techniques', *Transactions of the Institute of
British Geographers* 2:2 (1977), 141–157. Similar examples abound in these and other
journals.
[61] These two studies appear as: Patricia M. Green, 'Survey of a Local Shopping Centre:
Planning for the Customer', *Official Architecture and Planning* 30:8 (1967), 1101–1104;
Geoffrey C. Smith, 'The Spatial Information Fields of Urban Consumers', *Transactions
of the Institute of British Geographers* 1:2 (1976), 175–189.
[62] These revelations appear in Parker, 'Suburban Shopping Facilities in Liverpool',
197–223.

Galbraith's *New Industrial State* – and displayed the same anxieties about the unspoken moral and political content of the affluent society that troubled many in the Labour Party. At the opening of the Elephant & Castle shopping centre in Southwark in 1965, the 'thousands of housewives' in attendance were joined by what the *Daily Mail* described as 'a crowd of Communists who distributed leaflets and tried to interrupt'.[63] The detailed views of protestors on occasions like this usually remain a mystery, but the legal process of the public planning inquiry which accompanied large and contentious developments did offer a chance for dissenting views to be aired and recorded. In Cambridge in 1960, 'a stormy 15-day inquiry' was held into a joint council–developer scheme to install a £5 m shopping centre in the centre of the city. In this case, opposition to the development was led by the University, whose representatives were well equipped to cut through the 'clouds of statistics' with which the scheme had been justified. In a clear clash of cultures, the university's advocates rejected the proposal 'on grounds of commercialisation', while the local authority retorted that 'if necessary the university would have to find "quiet cloisters and places for reflection" elsewhere'.[64] This was one of the rare occasions when the government planning inspector sided with the objectors, ruling that the proposal was 'basically unsound' and refusing planning permission. The success of opposition in this case appears to have rested upon the university's ability to offer sophisticated refutations of the planning and business case for redevelopment, and presumably also its unique status and influence within an unusual urban setting, but the unease over 'commercialisation' pointed to wider anxieties around the social currents which such building projects were held to represent.

The principal constituency of objectors at public planning inquiries remained the displaced traders and dispossessed property owners who were the most materially disadvantaged by redevelopment. From the later 1960s, though, they were increasingly joined by citizens and local interest groups who raised a more abstracted set of political and moral objections to the commercial remodelling of the city. The politics of such groups were variable and often difficult to pin down. Where they were identifiably leftist, they were not generally reducible to the formal party politics of the British left, but tended to stem from local associational forms of political activity which might include membership of a Constituency Labour Party, a trade union or other local political grouping. In many cases, broadly leftist moral critiques of consumer capitalism and anxieties

---

[63] 'New Elephant', *Daily Mail*, 27 March 1965, 1.
[64] 'Cambridge Plan is Turned Down', *The Daily Mail*, 31 August 1960, 7.

over corporate influence were blended with more conservative, preservationist arguments about the life of the city and its historic fabric. Indeed, dissenters were often more localist than leftist – concerned with place, environment and its experience, and aggrieved by what they saw as the imposition of a brashly commercial, profit-driven and developer-led model of urban transformation on their locale.

The 1970 public inquiry into Nottingham's Broadmarsh redevelopment provides an instructive example of these dynamics, as well as the depth of hostility which redevelopment aroused from certain groups. The Broadmarsh was an ancient thoroughfare leading into the historic centre of Nottingham from the south. The area had been mostly acquired by Nottingham Corporation before the Second World War using slum clearance powers, and by the later 1960s the council had entered into a partnership with the developer Town & City Properties to erect a large enclosed Arndale shopping centre on the site, complete with over 100 stores, new office space, a bus station and two multi-storey car parks. Planning permission for this scheme had already been granted after an earlier public inquiry for which objectors were unprepared, but a second inquiry in December 1970 – which specifically concerned the stopping up and enclosure of Broadmarsh as a public right of way – offered them another chance to air their grievances. Opposition appears to have been led by a small but determined group of women, five of whom gave evidence in person at the inquiry, backed up by a wider grouping of supporters who submitted a few dozen written letters of objection. These characters were firmly of the preservationist persuasion, with almost all citing 'the ancient history of the city' and deploring the damage being done by 'the Corporation vandals [who] destroyed all old Nottingham'. Many questioned the demand for a second large shopping centre in the city and called instead for the provision of alternative civic facilities such as a theatre or concert hall. 'The whole scheme' claimed one objector, 'was quite unnecessary for the city's needs'. 'Why another large shopping area which nobody wanted', another asked, 'when such a large number of shops were still standing empty and unused . . .. Was it progress to thrust upon the city a large scheme that most citizens did not want and felt that the city could not afford?'[65]

Many objectors criticised the commercial character and priorities of redevelopment in the city, complaining that the 'provision for shops and offices was excessive', or that 'the Corporation's planners have only one idea in mind – shops and offices – and more and more shops and offices

[65] All these comments recorded in the Planning Inspector's Report, 1970. Available at Nottinghamshire Archives.

266   Demand and Discontent in the Shopping City

which were and would remain empty'. There was mistrust around the relationship between the council and the development company and much annoyance at the participation of a public body in what was understood to be a commercial, profit-driven project. One objector raged against 'wholesale and widespread devastation carried out by the Corporation in pursuit of financial gain'. 'Broad Marsh could be left as an open pedestrian way', she continued, 'but that would be uneconomic in the eyes of the developers so the citizen must be engulfed in a complex of shops with an eye to larger profits'. The terms of the corporation's partnership agreement were well understood by the protestors; the council 'hoped to share the commercial profit equally with the developers after 1975 so the tills must be made to click and an open road might provide a form of escape which was unthinkable in these avaricious men', one speaker complained. The protestors also understood the underlying commercial imperatives that drove urban design in such spaces, which aimed at channelling pedestrian flows and maximising retail turnover. 'As a citizen', one woman stated, 'she claimed the right to walk the streets of her city and not be driven like a rat into proposed pedestrian ways'. The vehemence of opposition led some to deploy languages of sexual violence and other corporeal taboos. The city was being 'horribly disfigured' one objector argued; another quoted the purported words of a council member (presumably an opposition councillor) that, 'this scheme is an illegitimate birth'. Such metaphors prefigured what would become the principal tract of the preservationists nationally when it was published in 1975 – Colin Amery and Dan Cruickshank's *The Rape of Britain*. The use of such terms reads somewhat distastefully today, and reflects the rather different linguistic (in)sensitivities of the post-war decades, but they were a sign of the visceral reaction which demolition and redevelopment could elicit from some quarters. Despite the force of these complaints, in Nottingham the objectors' protests fell upon deaf ears. The Corporation dismissed all the criticisms as 'uninformed and unjustified', and the government's planning inspector was entirely unmoved, declaring he had 'no hesitation' in recommending approval.[66]

The preservationists in Nottingham and elsewhere were part of a growing body of opinion which took shape in reaction to the large-scale urban redevelopment of the renewal era, but which remained diffuse, aimed at multiple targets and articulated by a range of actors, with differing motivations. Local civic societies (Nottingham's was formed in 1962) and conservationist pressure groups such as SAVE

---

[66] Comments in the Planning Inspector's Report, 1970. Available at Nottinghamshire Archives.

Britain's Heritage (formed in 1975 'to defend the civilizing fabric of the past') represented a strand of anti-development sentiment that was concerned above all with the loss of historic buildings and the heritage value of the urban built environment.[67] A slightly different form of environmental sensitivity came to the fore in protests against urban road building and the demolition, increased traffic and air pollution brought by urban motorway schemes in particular. In 1973 the Greater London Council bowed to popular pressure and abandoned its expansive programme of urban motorway construction, and this presaged the wider 'collapse of the motor city ideal' which occurred in the mid-1970s.[68] There was also a growing backlash against the property development industry which had grown and prospered so explosively under the favourable conditions of the post-war planning regime. 'More millionaires have been thrown up by the property business in Britain since the war than by any other industry', *The Economist* reported in 1972, and the exposure of widespread corruption in the sector at this time, along with lurid reports of the personal wealth, avariciousness and spending habits of individual developers fuelled public anger.[69] The developer Harry Hyams in particular emerged as an archetypal 'Mephistophelian' property magnate following a long-running controversy over his Centre Point office tower in central London, which remained empty for around a decade after its completion in 1966. In 1974 the vacant building was briefly occupied by housing protesters who put up signs in the windows reading: 'We're just wild about Harry, and Harry's wild about us.'[70]

Within the academy – in departments of geography, sociology and urban studies – increasing numbers of scholars were beginning to turn away from the dominant positivist, practice-oriented traditions of British urban scholarship and instead develop radical, systemic critiques of the capitalist urban development process. The geographer David Harvey's 1973 book, *Social Justice and the City*, was an early English-language example of the new Marxian urban political economy which was taking hold in France at this time. In 1976 the British sociologist Christopher Pickvance's collection, *Urban Sociology: Critical Essays*, introduced English readers to works in translation by Manuel Castells and other

[67] Darley & Saunders, 'A SAVE Report', 211–226; see also Mass, 'Commercial Heritage as Democratic Action'.
[68] Simon Jenkins, 'The Politics of London Motorways', *The Political Quarterly* 44:3 (1973), 257–270; Gunn, 'Ring Road', 227–248.
[69] 'Property: The Philosopher's Stone', *The Economist*, 18 March 1972, 135.
[70] Laurence Marks, Anthony Bambridge & Iain Murray, 'Everyone's Wild about Harry', *The Observer*, 2 July 1972, 9.

'neo-Marxist' urban theorists working in French.[71] Such ideas generally filtered into British scholarship by taking on a more empirical, less theoretically driven bent, and they found receptive audiences among a younger generation of urban scholars but also within a wider milieu of activists and researchers involved in housing campaigns, social policy work and community development projects.[72] The most prominent example was Peter Ambrose and Bob Colenutt's *The Property Machine*, which appeared as a Penguin Special in 1975. Ambrose was a lecturer in Community Studies at the University of Sussex and affiliated with the Open University. Colenutt was an urban geographer, then working as a researcher for the North Southwark Community Development Group. *The Property Machine* dissected Britain's developer-led, heavily financialized and profit-driven urban redevelopment regime from the perspective of the authors' concerns with distributional justice, the supply and cost of housing and their work with community development projects in London and elsewhere. It was a coruscating critique of the whole post-war course of planning and redevelopment in Britain. 'Our aim', the authors stated, 'is to relate redevelopment to the general debate about wealth inequality by asking *who gains and who loses* from this process'. 'The property system', they concluded, 'benefits almost exclusively the wealthiest sections of our society'.[73]

Ambrose and Colenutt spoke directly to the popular anti-developer sentiments which were being articulated at protests and public inquiries, but maintained that 'the defects of the system as a whole are more important than the individual cases of corruption and collusion evident within it'. This brought the planning system itself, and those who operated it, directly into the frame, and while Ambrose and Colenutt were clear that it was the unusually marketised and money-grubbing thrust of British urban redevelopment that was their principal target, others fixed upon 'the planners' themselves – those faceless, authoritarian bureaucrats – as the root of the problem.[74] Such arguments chimed with a strong current of anti-intellectualism and anti-statism within British culture and could easily find favour on the right, where many remained unconvinced about the entire post-war project of welfare state expansion (often still described in terms of 'socialism' at this time) of which 'planning' was understood to be a key pillar. *The Daily Mail*, which was still running

---

[71] For discussion of these works and their reception, see John Walton, 'Urban Sociology: Critical Essays. By C. G. Pickvance', *American Journal of Sociology* 83:3 (1977), 799–803.
[72] Martin Loney, 'The British Community Development Projects: Questioning the State', *Community Development Journal* 16:1 (1981), 55–66.
[73] Ambrose & Colenutt, *The Property Machine*, 13.
[74] For example, Davies, *The Evangelistic Bureaucrat*.

under the banner 'For Queen and Commonwealth', ran a front-page commentary in 1968 lambasting the 'so-called experts', 'the planners' and 'the bureaucrats'. 'They can be beaten', the paper affirmed; 'All over Britain people are tired of bowing to the whim of authority'.[75] It was these rightist and libertarian strands of anti-planning thought which were picked up and mobilised so effectively by the New Right in Britain in the later 1970s as they developed their own critique of the supposedly out-of-control statism of the post-war decades.

The Right to the Shopping City

Citizens' opposition to urban shopping developments was thus bound up with a much broader set of concerns and grievances which surrounded the whole course of urban, and state, transformation across the post-war decades, but which was multivalent, often inchoate and at times contradictory. From the later 1960s, the urban renewal order, along with many other facets of social policy and administration, came under attack from multiple directions in a process which ultimately spelt the end of the era of high modernism and a loss of confidence in the state's ability to deliver on the promises of the earlier post-war period.[76] Yet there was also something distinctive about opposition to the shopping-centred transformation of the city, which sat outside the rise and fall of meliorist modernism; this process had never been a straightforward product of public planning endeavour, but rather reflected a harnessing of new state powers to the commercial projects of retail expansion and property-based accumulation. As such, its course did not follow that of modernist mass housing schemes or urban motorway building, and its impact and long-term significance was recognisably different. Urban retail developments aroused special complaints, which revolved around the seemingly inexorable encroachment of consumer capitalism and its commercial cultural forms into the various spheres and spaces of post-war social life. There was an immediacy and tangibility to this process in the urban setting, as the shared spaces of the city were appropriated, commodified and remodelled in the interests of retail and property capital. For the individual citizen, their experience of the city and its codes of conduct, conditions of access and enjoyment – what would come to be called 'the right to the city' – became tightly defined by the profit-making imperatives of retail businesses and their commercial landlords.

[75] 'Comment', *The Daily Mail*, 10 September 1968, 1.
[76] Philip Harling, *The Modern British State* (Cambridge: Polity, 2001), ch. 5, 'The Welfare State and Its Discontents'; Aaron Andrews, 'Multiple Deprivation, the Inner City, and the Fracturing of the Welfare State: Glasgow, c.1968-78', *Twentieth Century British History* 29:4 (2018), 605–624.

This process, and the broad-based opposition it aroused, is well illustrated by a controversy which erupted over Birmingham's redeveloped Bull Ring area in 1968. The Bull Ring was the site of the first covered shopping centre which opened in Britain, in 1964, as part of a large complex of redevelopment carried out by the Corporation in conjunction with the construction and engineering contractor Laings. The area had a long and colourful history. As the Corporation's 1960s brochure *This is Birmingham* explained, the Bull Ring was 'the oldest inhabited area in the city, settled probably in Anglo-Saxon times [and] has been a market centre since the 12th century'.[77] A Corporation Market Hall had been installed in 1834, which was destroyed by bombing in 1940, and this, along with the district's centuries-old role as the commercial heart of the city, made it an obvious choice for the Laing shopping development in the 1960s. The Bull Ring was not just a commercial hub though; it was also a bustling and at times tumultuous centre of social, religious and political life in the city. Citizens enjoyed a right to assembly there, which stretched back at least to the mid-seventeenth century. A church had stood on the site since the thirteenth century, and there was a long tradition of open-air preaching and religious activity. In 1744 Charles Wesley promulgated the new doctrine of Methodism here (he was rewarded with 'dirt and stones' and 'several blows from the mob').[78] Birmingham's Methodist congregations continued to regard the site as their symbolic centre and preached weekly open-air sermons here throughout the twentieth century. In 1839, the Bull Ring Riots shot the district to the centre of national political life when two Chartist riots took place in two weeks, resulting in extensive property damage as buildings were burned, windows smashed and goods looted from the commercial district.[79] The Corporation gestured towards this unique history in its promotional account of the redevelopment:

Many Birmingham people have vivid memories of the Bull Ring as it was before the present redevelopments, just as it had been for many many years on market days. There were stalls gay with flowers, farm produce and bright fabrics; kerbside vendors offering toys, balloons and novelties; cheapjacks, showmen, preachers, politicians, quacks and their medicines, and everywhere the lively crowd enjoying the busy scene well after dark by the light of the naphtha flares.[80]

---

[77] City of Birmingham Information Department, *This is Birmingham*, city brochure, late-1960s. Author's collection.

[78] Recorded in Wesley's diary; John R. Tyson (ed.), *Charles Wesley: A Reader* (Oxford: Oxford University Press, 1989), 251.

[79] Michael Weaver, 'The Birmingham Bull Ring Riots of 1839: Variations on a Theme of Class Conflict', *Social Science Quarterly* 78:1 (1997), 137–148.

[80] City of Birmingham Information Department, *This is Birmingham*.

The open-air market remained integral to the redeveloped Bull Ring – indeed, it was initially more popular than the covered mall – but a Corporation proposal in the late 1960s to introduce new byelaws to better regulate the market area aroused a storm of protest. The Laing redevelopment had not banished religious and political activity from the district altogether. The Victorian parish church, St Martin in the Bull Ring, was left untouched, although engulfed, by the 1960s development (see Figure 6.3), and open-air preaching and political activity was to be confined to a small reserved area around the church, adjacent to the market. But the new council byelaws were about regimenting the market, and ensuring that all aspects of its physical space and arrangement, along with the behaviour of individuals within it, served its overriding

Figure 6.3 1964 image of the redeveloped Bull Ring area, showing the relationship between the new shopping centre, the redeveloped market and the long-established church of St. Martin in the Bull Ring. At issue in 1968 was the acceptable use of this shared space and whether the commercial needs of the retail market could take precedence over citizens' rights to assembly, public speaking and protest. Source: Historic England Archive, John Laing Photographic Collection.

commercial function. To this end the Corporation sought to introduce a strict set of behavioural regulations, enforceable by a steep fine of £5 (over £110 in 2019 values), which would grant the council expansive powers to determine whether any person, object or action within the market was impeding the conduct of business. These included detailed and rigid rules about how and where to store boxes, for example, or vehicle access to stalls, who could use the toilets, or ring a bell or make a loud noise. The regulation which ultimately provoked the most ire from citizens was the suggestion that: 'No person shall wilfully loiter or stand in such a manner or in such a position as to cause obstruction or passage in the market or in the immediate approaches thereto.'[81] This, it seemed to many, granted the council carte blanche to penalise and prohibit almost any activity that was judged commercially undesirable in the spaces around the market.

The resulting hail of protest revealed something much greater than a mere back and forth over some obscure council regulations. It exposed a rich seam of local associational life which stood outside of the burgeoning cultures of affluent consumption, and a strand of public opinion which was profoundly opposed to the encroachment of commercialism upon these alternative social domains. The Ministry of Housing and Local Government was surprised to find itself in receipt of an avalanche of objection letters from a plethora of organisations, campaign groups and individuals. The Birmingham Borough Labour Party wrote to complain that 'this hits directly at the traditional right of Birmingham citizens and organisations to hold meeting, demonstrations, exhibitions etc. in the Bull Ring'. A lecturer at the University of Birmingham also protested that there could be no 'justification for a law which would restrict the traditional . . . rights of ordinary citizens to organise meetings or proclaim their views in Birmingham in the hallowed place set apart for that purpose'. The Birmingham Trades Council complained, as did many individual trade unions, along with the local sections of the Communist Party, the CND, the Council for Peace in Vietnam and the National Council for Civil Liberties. The Young Socialists of Selly Oak wrote to 'strongly protest at the proposed curtailment of the liberties of the citizens of Birmingham' and warned that this 'proposal was a pernicious one, which is likely to be disobeyed'.

Methodist, Anglican and Catholic associations registered their opposition. The Methodists felt it 'essential that there should be opportunities within our great cities for freedom of speech in the open air' and argued

---

[81] City of Birmingham, 'Bull Ring Open Air Market', proposed byelaws, 1 March 1968. TNA-HLG-120/999.

that 'the recent disturbances in cities all over the world emphasise[d] more than ever the necessity for this opportunity of expression' (this was 1968). The Catholic Evidence Guild, which held meetings at the site, also worried about 'the rights of public assembly and free speech' and argued that 'traditionally the public market place is the appropriate place ... for the exercise of these civic liberties'. Residents' associations, student bodies and women's groups also wrote in protest, as did many individual citizens. These included a young woman who saw the proposals as 'a direct attack on the liberty of the individual and the right of free speech [in a] centre for ... the free demonstration and interchange of ideas'; or a local solicitor who complained (as did many others) that 'assurances were given that when the Bull Ring was redesigned the traditional rights of holding, speaking at, and attending meetings would not be injured'. The new byelaw, he noted, 'clearly gives priority to commercial users of the Bull Ring as against those exercising freedom of speech'. One 'Citizen of the City' worried that the new rules 'will restrict the already restricted freedom of speech in the city of Birmingham'; while another, perhaps channelling Marcuse, wrote to register 'my protest as an individual and self-thinking human being', adding as an aside, 'yes there are a few of us remaining'. In an indication of the local colour and character which was under threat at the Bull Ring, the most esoteric interpretation of the moral and juridical basis of market byelaws simply read:

THE FREEDOM OF SPEACH [sic] IN THE BULL RING BIRMINGHAM.
WHO SO EVER SHALL REMOVE THIS FREEDOM SHALL BE DOUBLE CURSED.
FOR THEY CURSE THEMSELVES.
ALL THE LAWS HANG UPON THE PROPHETS.
I AM ELIJAH THE PROPHET

The list of complaints and complainants went on and on, and the noise generated began to cause political discomfort. A local councillor felt compelled to make representations to the Ministry in response to this 'threat to democracy'; so too did a local Labour MP, Christopher Price, who submitted a detailed memorandum on the historic liberties of the Bull Ring. The issue made its way into the national press, by which point both the Ministry and the Corporation were beginning to feel decidedly embarrassed by the affair. In the increasingly febrile atmosphere, calls for a public inquiry into the matter were unwelcome and firmly resisted. The Ministry in particular had one eye on the rather more dramatic urban protests unfolding on the continent and elsewhere in the summer of 1968. Officials worried privately that 'the matter is controversial [and] any enquiry would undoubtedly be a stormy one particularly at the moment when demonstrating is fashionable'. Ultimately the Corporation of Birmingham capitulated, abandoning all of its proposed byelaws for the Bull Ring market towards the end of 1968.[82]

In one sense then, the Bull Ring episode reveals the limits of commercial encroachment upon the urban public realm. A point of obstruction was reached, at which enough voices were raised in opposition to force a change of course, and a set of rights had to be acknowledged which could not easily be swept aside in the interests of commercial efficiency. Yet we should not be misled by this. The Bull Ring affair was simply a flare-up in a long-running process – a moment of reaction against the general direction of travel. It was not the first time, and certainly not the last, that the public managers of the post-war city had sought to extinguish rights and impinge upon freedoms in the interests of the smooth running of the retail economy. A few years earlier in Coventry, for example, local trade unions were protesting against a police ban on the use of loudspeakers at meetings in the reconstruction city's carefully curated new shopping precincts.[83] While in Cardiff in 1983, 'a fierce political battle' erupted when the city council banned CND and other 'quasi-political organisations' from campaigning in the shopping centre. The Conservative council leader explained that he was aiming to stop shoppers being 'pestered by pressure groups' (religious speakers, by contrast, were permitted, in 'a corner set aside for preachers').[84] Such conflicts revealed a clear clash between citizens' political use of central urban space and the commercial ends and imperatives to which it was increasingly being turned. These would only intensify as retail environments expanded to encompass ever more central urban space in the nation's town and city centres.

Policing the Shopping City

The crucial distinction between the case of the Bull Ring market and that of so many other redeveloped shopping environments was the legal status of the land involved. Birmingham's market area remained legally public space, owned and managed by the Corporation, which, as an elected public body, was susceptible to political pressure. This was not the case in the scores of enclosed shopping centres which were being developed with such frequency all over urban Britain at this time, which collectively

[82] All of these complaints, along with the council and Ministry responses, are collected in TNA-HLG-120/999.
[83] 'Protest', *The Daily Mail*, 22 May 1961, 7.
[84] Paul Brown, 'Councils Row over Shopping Centre CND Ban', *The Guardian*, 27 June 1983, 4.

saw large swathes of centrally located public space transferred into private ownership and subjected to new, commercially defined regimes of policing. Once again, the ambiguous public–private character of such places caused problems. In Runcorn Shopping City, the enclosed megastructural complex serving as a town centre for the North West New Town, Cheshire Constabulary were concerned that, while 'it was desirable for the police to maintain a presence in such an important centre of public resort . . . some disquiet was felt about the question of patrolling on private property'.[85] Police forces all over the country had to remind local authorities that, while shopping malls may have been conceived as hybrid public–private facilities, there was nothing ambiguous about their legal status and policing activities were necessarily constrained and complicated by operating on private property. Inside Birmingham's Bull Ring, where the privately owned shopping centre was plagued by 'hooliganism', 'disorderly conduct' and 'unsavoury incidents', the police had to remind traders that 'because the centre is private property [they] cannot interfere unless invited to do so'.[86] Agreements were often struck so that police officers could enter and patrol shopping malls 'by invitation' from their private owners, but there were still many problems around police powers, insurance and permissible conduct.

The new urban landscapes of affluence thus posed 'an unusual policing problem', as the Chief Constable of Nottinghamshire Constabulary A. S. Bowley pointed out, and yet they also required particularly intensive police attention. Nottingham's Victoria Centre, Bowley noted, 'generates an average of 50 to 60 incidents requiring attention by the police each week', with many more at busy periods, despite the fact that police officers did not patrol the mall. Bowley offered a 'typical breakdown for a week', which included multiple cases of violent assault and robbery; dozens of thefts and burglaries; vehicle thefts; bomb hoaxes; drunken misbehaviour and violence; malicious damage to the facility and to customers' cars; as well as disputes between security staff and the public; 'football supporters causing trouble'; 'children playing in [a] railway tunnel' and a 'boy interfering with [a] fire hydrant'. 'Juvenile crime' was a particular problem in this centre as it was in many others all over the country, with Bowley reporting on the special problems caused by the 'delinquent groups' and 'juvenile shoplifting teams which proliferate in the Centre'. Specially trained officers, including female officers, were assigned to deal with youth crime. The chief constable was particularly

[85] Chief Inspector B. H. Gibson, 'Policing New Towns', *The Police Journal* 44 (1971), 340–345.
[86] 'Traders to Use Dog Patrols', *The Birmingham Post*, 11 May 1970, 1.

struck by 'the dominance of the shoplifter' in the new shopping centre, noting that the Victoria Centre had become 'a focal point' for this in Nottingham, with numbers dropping everywhere else in the city. The police arrested 517 shoplifters in the first five months of 1973, and vigorous procedures of police liaison, private store detectives, staff training and information sharing had to be instituted to try to maintain control of this problem. In the end, though, Bowley concluded that 'it is perhaps fortunate that the overall volume of thefts from shops remains a very dark figure'.[87]

In a further blow to the idea that such facilities would be taken to heart by the public as enriching sites of civic renewal, new shopping malls in fact emerged as sites of frequent public disorder and prime targets for criminal activity. Often these problems were surprisingly severe and new shopping facilities required far more intensive policing than had been expected. In Newcastle 'vandalism and rowdyism' in the Eldon Square complex was serious enough to cause major safety and security problems, forcing the centre to close on numerous occasions and to abandon altogether the ideal of round-the-clock public access. In Birmingham's Bull Ring, traders took the shopping centre operator to court because of losses related to 'hooliganism and shoplifting'.[88] In Luton, misbehaviour in the town's new Arndale Centre was so severe that the local police force decided to set up a dedicated substation in the centre, manned by fifteen officers, in order 'to control rowdies and vandals'. 'The air-conditioned centre', it was reported, 'has attracted school truants and teenage gangs ... shoppers have complained of abuse and rowdyism and fights have broken out on Saturday nights'.[89] In Leeds's Merrion Centre, too, the police regularly had to intervene in incidents of violent disorder, often involving young people, while problems of vandalism and low-level misbehaviour were a constant.[90] One intriguing solution to this in the Merrion Centre was to employ a full time 'town crier', whose job was 'shout out, every hour, snippets of local and national news and such shopping information as the price of Typhoo Tea at Tesco'. The crier was instructed to hand out sweets to children, but only if they were accompanied by parents; there were to be no sweets for 'snotty-nosed little hooligans', the General Manager explained; 'we don't want to encourage gangs of kids in the centre'.[91] The status of young

---

[87] Chief Superintendent Bowley, 'The Police and the Planners', 308–314.
[88] 'Traders to Use Dog Patrols', *The Birmingham Post*, 11 May 1970, 1.
[89] 'Police Post at Shops', *Daily Mail*, 18 September 1975, 16.
[90] 'Court Clears Four PCs', *The Guardian*, 19 April 1972, 8; Leeds City Council, 'Merrion Centre', Health Department memo, 19 December 1968. WYAS – LLD1/2/833178.
[91] Michael Parkin, 'All the News That's Fit to Shout', *The Guardian*, 27 September 1966, 4.

people in shopping centres was an ambiguous one. As the manager of a facility in Bolton explained:

Their presence represents firstly, potential customers and, secondly, a potential threat to security. The change from the former to the latter usually occurs when the individuals coalesce into a recognisable group, whether by their all wearing football scarves, adopting a particular mode of dress or moving though the Market Hall in unison. Then the task is to remove the source of anxiety as quickly as possible by persuasion or force of law if necessary.[92]

In this facility, too, young people were held to be largely responsible for the 'epidemics of shoplifting' as well as the constant problems with 'vandalism and hooliganism'.

Unruly and aggressive behaviour from wayward teenagers thus presented a major problem for those seeking to manage the experience and environment of the new landscapes of affluence. Yet new shopping centres also had to be designed and secured against more serious and organised criminality. Such facilities represented a large investment of capital, which owners expected to be protected round-the-clock, and the presence of large inventories of expensive and easily portable goods made centres a prime target for burglary. From the outset centres were designed with such concerns in mind, incorporating sophisticated alarm systems with direct lines to local police stations and private security firms. The Victoria Centre contained 100 different alarms interlinked into one system, while as early as the 1960s the 'comprehensive alarm system' in Blackburn's shopping centre contained advanced 'contact triggers' on doors supplemented by 'infrared rays'. New defensive architectures – what one policeman called 'the problem of locks, bolts, and bars' – became integral parts of retail design, with architects consulting with private security firms and police forces when drawing up plans.[93] The widespread deployment of heavy metal grilles, used to secure individual shop units, to subdivide internal concourses and to defend malls from the surrounding public streets, was commonplace, introducing a fortress-like feel to such places out-of-hours. Shopping centres were also some of the earliest sites for the introduction of closed-circuit surveillance systems in Britain, and heavy expenditures on such advanced technologies of policing quickly became an accepted running cost for operators. The use of private security personnel equipped with dogs and radios, and coordinated by dedicated control centres, also exploded. Such was the demand

---

[92] Bolton Metropolitan Borough, *Report on the Market Place to the Land Subcommittee* (1988). Available at Bolton Local History Centre.
[93] These details in Sergeant J. Clark, 'Security and the Development of a Town Centre', *The Police Journal* 41 (1968), 23–26; Bowley, 'The Police and the Planners'.

for this service that the development company Town & City decided to diversify into private security in the later 1970s, establishing its own force of uniformed 'Sterling Guards' which recruited ex-military men to patrol the new shopping environments of urban Britain.[94]

One of the major attractions of using private security personnel was that they could do far more than public police forces to shape the experience and manage the environment of shopping. Indeed, there was a revealing linguistic shift as 'policing' dropped out of usage in favour of 'security' – a term which encompassed a far more insidious level of social control. The private owners of new shopping facilities were able to introduce entirely reworked behavioural codes and conditions of access into the shared urban spaces of post-war Britain, which were rigorously enforced by private security personnel. Now, any individuals or behaviours which were deemed to threaten the smooth workings of the retail economy, to annoy or distract shoppers or to unsettle the sanitised landscape of pleasure, could be quickly and ruthlessly expelled. In the contemporary city, such privatisation of urban public space attracts reams of criticism, with many urban theorists denouncing this 'curtailment of the public sphere' as part of 'the neoliberalisation of public space'.[95] Once again, important post-war precursors raise questions about some of these characterisations and chronologies, but the essential critique remains a powerful one; the privatisation of urban space clearly involved significant curtailments of citizens' rights and freedoms. The process was not quite so simple as replacing 'democratic' public space with 'undemocratic' private space, however, given that the public spaces of the city had long been inscribed with codes of access and participation which could be experienced variably according to distinctions of class, gender and race, for example. Perhaps more significant was the way in which new shopping spaces redefined 'the right to the city' according to each individual's status as a consuming subject. Teenagers, as has been seen, could be welcomed as potential customers or expelled as troublemakers depending on the context. It was the commercial imperatives of the retail economy which served as the determining factor in these judgements about access and permissible conduct. Indeed, an awful lot of regulatory effort was expended upon maintaining a certain experiential state within

---

[94] 'Guards Make Dynamic Start', *Town & City Group News*, Spring 1978. Available in the P&O Collection, National Maritime Museum.
[95] Setha M. Low & Neil Smith (eds.), *The Politics of Public Space* (London: Routledge, 2006), 12. Also: Brenner, Marcuse & Mayer, *Cities for People, not for Profit*; Ash Amin, 'Collective Culture and Urban Public Space', *City* 12:1 (2008), 5–24; Mitchell, *The Right to the City*.

shopping centres and in the minds of shoppers. As one retail manager explained:

Security can be defined as a sense of safety, freedom from care, anxiety or apprehension .... We are therefore, concerned with people, whether the public generally, shoppers, shop staff, management or the landlord .... Security is intelligent anticipation [and] a state of benevolent vigilance towards the public, tenants, staff and contractors by a way of well thought out and constantly reassessed routines and resources.[96]

Just how 'benevolent' such vigilance was is open to question; in this case the manager concerned advocated intense scrutiny of every activity and every person in his centre, including the shop traders themselves and even his own staff of cleaners, guards and other operatives. 'Security' in this case proceeded from the premise that nothing must be allowed to puncture the carefully curated atmosphere of languorous leisure which encouraged docile subjects to keep on shopping, and yet at the same time, everybody should be viewed as a potential threat to this curious experiential bubble. The suspicion and paranoia that was built into the fabric of such facilities, and which ran right through their increasingly organised managerial procedures, was remarkable and stands starkly at odds with the visions of civic revitalisation which had been used to justify such projects. This cannot have gone unnoticed by the public, who often voiced their discontent and disgruntlement at the way they were managed in the retail environment. Criminals meanwhile, along with the 'rowdies' who caused so many problems in shopping centres, clearly viewed such places as fair game and much more deserving of their attentions than many other sites in the city. The lucrative new landscapes of consumption were certainly not run in the interests of the urban civitas, as was very obvious to all concerned. This cannot but have affected the way they were viewed, used and abused by individual citizens.

Conclusion

Once the enthusiasms which surrounded the coming of the affluent society and the verve for comprehensive urban renewal cooled in the later 1960s, a more complex and conflicted picture came into view. The bold projections of inexorable consumer expansion upon which so many redevelopment schemes had been based rapidly turned out to be over-optimistic, as consumers proved more discerning and, in many places, less prosperous than had been imagined. The commercial difficulties

---

[96] Bolton Metropolitan Borough, *Report on the Market Place to the Land Subcommittee* (1988). Available at Bolton Local History Centre.

which many new shopping developments faced after opening were testament to some of the limits of affluence in post-war Britain, as well as the limits of both public and private sector experts' abilities to predict and plan for consumer wants and preferences. Instead, a picture of intense (and intensifying) diversity emerged which shattered simplistic models of 'demand' and also of 'the consumer' as a unitary subject. As one of the academic studies commissioned by the Department of the Environment concluded in 1974, 'there is insufficient knowledge currently available about the shopping centre customer' and 'considerable complexity inherent in present consumer behaviour'. All that could really be surmised was that as 'shopping behaviour [is] a product of individual family and economic circumstances there is a variety of types of consumer and types of consumer attitude and behaviour'.[97] Such heterogeneity was only expected to increase as the complex cultural domain of commercial consumption was further elaborated. All of this made planning for the imagined affluent subject a decidedly difficult project and certainly not one which could be easily achieved with the rather blunt technical and intellectual tools that were proffered by retail planners and commercial property developers. Experts and professionals across both the public and the private sectors did much to talk up the sophistication of their new planning techniques and social knowledge but, even at the time, it was obvious to many that there was considerable intellectual overreach going on.

If the designers and developers of new retail landscapes failed to convince many shoppers, they failed utterly to persuade the growing chorus of voices that were increasingly being raised in protest against this type of redevelopment and its impact upon the shared spaces of the city. The 1970s in particular saw powerful critiques of the British urban renewal regime being developed in the academy, as well as among activists and concerned members of the public, many of whom sought to promote an alternative, less capitalistic vision of the form and function of cities. Overall though, such dissenting voices proved fairly ineffective when it came to influencing the general direction of travel in urban redevelopment, which continued to see increasing portions of the city brought under the direct control of commercial landlords, and subjected to ever-more intensive regimes of private policing and control. The surprising extent of disorder and criminality which plagued such places was an indication of both the intensity of surveillance and regulation, along with the failure of public planners' efforts to cast these facilities as participatory sites of social

[97] Alistair MacLeary, 'Regional Shopping Centres', report commissioned by the Department of the Environment, January 1974, 256–7, TNA-AT-80/65.

renewal and active citizenship. Indeed, in many places, such as Birmingham and Bolton, public authorities could be just as active as private landlords in advancing this project of 'retailising space', in which not only the urban landscape but also the conditions of access and codes of conduct within them were reworked around the commercial imperatives of the shopping experience.[98] The financial and developmental logics which drove this thoroughgoing commodification and reworking of urban space in the end proved to be much more powerful in shaping the course of central area redevelopment than any countervailing currents of protest or reformist urbanism. Chapter 7 of this book examines how these forces played out at the close of the twentieth century, once the post-war project of planned urban renewal had been abandoned in favour of a new urban policy agenda of 'regeneration' in which shopping continued to take centre stage.

[98] Mattias Kärrholm, *Retailising Space: Architecture, Retail and the Territorialisation of Public Space* (London: Routledge, 2012).

7   Triumph of the Shopping City

By the closing decades of the twentieth century, the era of urban modernism and comprehensive redevelopment may have passed, but the forces that militated towards large-scale retail development and the shopping-centred remodelling of cities had only grown stronger. Indeed, the techniques of environmental and experiential management that were honed within enclosed shopping centres came to be applied to central areas in their entirety, which were reconceived as consumer 'amenities' to be carefully managed in the interests of the retail economy. A new field of professional competence in 'town centre management', which blurred the lines between public administration and commercial enterprise, was indicative of a wider shift whereby local authorities became directly responsible for the economic 'health' of their town centres, which by this time was conceived almost exclusively in terms of shopping. At the same time, the development of enclosed and privately owned shopping spaces continued apace, occupying ever more of Britain's shared urban spaces and spreading in particular to many smaller towns which had escaped the first round of malling in the 1960s and 1970s. These changes were unfolding against a backdrop of far-reaching structural economic shifts, in which the final collapse of industrial Britain was taking place, and all doubts were removed that the future for local economies lay with services and shopping. Personal consumption emerged as a linchpin of the national economy, as well as a cultural and political emblem of the times in an age which celebrated aspiration and individualism. This chapter traces these urban, social and economic transformations as they played out in various towns and cities in the later twentieth century. It also stresses how partial and problematic the triumph of the shopping city was. The consumer-driven economy was never so solid and secure as its boosters would have it; prosperity remained patchy and urban centres were forced into ever-fiercer competition for their own slice of the economic action. A newly permissive approach to out-of-town retail development dramatically intensified these pressures, and the emergence of an urgent new public policy agenda of 'urban regeneration' was itself a reflection of the inadequacies of British planning and urban management.

Leaving the City Behind

While urban governments were doing all they could to remodel their central areas around the needs of shoppers and retailers, the privileging of the consumer economy in matters of planning, infrastructure and development would ultimately come to present them with some intractable problems. This was because, despite the best efforts of city planners, the logics of retailing efficiency and consumer convenience led inexorably away from the traditional urban centres, to the development of new, ex-urban geographies of shopping – in edge-of-town 'hypermarkets' and 'retail parks' on the city fringes and in behemothic out-of-town 'regional centres' serving millions of motorised shoppers. Until the 1970s, one of the principal stands which the British planning system had taken against commercial development pressures had been its resistance to retail development on any large scale outside of existing urban centres. The whole thrust of policy in the era of urban renewal and comprehensive town centre redevelopment was to retain new commercial development within the bounds of established city centres. This was relatively unusual internationally; it stood in marked contrast to the rampant suburban mall development of the United States, and also to the pattern in many European states, where historic centres were generally left intact while new retail and warehousing districts were allowed to proliferate on the urban periphery. In Britain, as the urbanist Peter Hall concluded in 1974, 'instead of new suburban shopping centres built for the car, we have had drastic surgery of the existing city centres'.[1] This was a somewhat incongruous outcome, given the strong patterns of suburbanisation in Britain and the planned decentralisation of population; it came about through a combination of the planning machinery's commitment to defending central area economies and land values, and rural-preservationist resistance to commercial development in the hallowed British countryside.

Despite these planning commitments, the pressure from retailers and developers to set up shop beyond the city limits was always there. Already by 1971, Lancashire County Council had received around forty applications for out-of-town retail, permitting just six to go ahead in some modified form, while a plum site on the new M5 motorway north of Bristol was being squabbled over by five different companies with hopes

[1] Peter Hall, 'The Containment of Urban England', *The Geographical Journal* 140:3 (1974), 386–408, 404.

for a regional-scale shopping centre. The French hypermarket developer Carrefour was making overtures to councils in many parts of the country in this period, seeking approval for its large edge-of-town superstores, and the leading British supermarket chains had similar ambitions.[2] The remarkable gains in turnover and efficiency in the UK retail sector had been made by scaling up wherever possible; nationally organised chains operated out of large new stores, retailing high volumes of goods and exploiting economies of scale, bulk purchasing power and logistical innovations wherever possible. There were some basic physical limits to how far this model could be pushed within densely developed urban centres, however liberally local authorities were willing to apply their compulsory purchase powers. Space in the city centre was necessarily limited and expensive, and the prodigious increase in car ownership meant that, infrastructurally, it was simply not possible to accommodate ever-increasing numbers of 'car shoppers'. The geography and scale of the retail economy had outgrown the traditional town centre. In these circumstances, as one retail industry expert wrote in 1972, 'the battle of the 1970s will be fought over location'.[3]

Controls were relaxed gradually at first and on an ad hoc basis. New Towns and designated growth regions were seen as appropriate places for large new edge-of-town superstores. Carrefour were permitted to build at Telford in the West Midlands in the early 1970s, and Sainsbury's allowed to build a large superstore in the Greater Peterborough expansion area.[4] Superstores were also seen as 'a potential life-saver for overcrowded historic centres'; in places like Chester, Norwich and York – whose ancient urban fabric had spared them from the 'drastic surgery' which was visited on less venerable cities in the urban renewal era – large discount food stores on the urban periphery were viewed as a means to protect historic centres.[5] In the end though, the arguments around consumer cost-savings and convenience proved irresistible all over the country. The development of edge-of-town superstores was aimed squarely at the motorised housewife, provisioning the household with a large load of shopping once a week, with no desire to drive into a city centre and to pay for the privilege. 'The benefits to the large mass of consumers are pretty obvious', one journalist explained, 'hypermarkets can sell goods at

---

[2] Judy Hillman, 'SHOP! Could the Nation of Shopkeepers Turn Into a Countryside of Hypermarkets?', *The Guardian*, 29 October 1971, 14; Michael Little, 'Hypermarkets', *Building with Steel* 10 (May, 1972), 11. The Bristol site eventually became the Cribbs Causeway regional shopping centre.
[3] E. MacFadyen, 'Retailers at the Crossroads', *Building with Steel* 10 (May, 1972), 2.
[4] Michael Little, 'Hypermarkets', *Building with Steel* 10 (May, 1972), 11.
[5] Judy Hillman, 'SHOP! Could the Nation of Shopkeepers Turn Into a Countryside of Hypermarkets?', *The Guardian*, 29 October 1971, 14.

considerable discount, so that families shopping once a week can make worthwhile savings'.[6] Once the principle of free parking and cheap, bulk-buying on the edge of town was accepted, it did not take long for this to move beyond food shopping. The superstores themselves branched out ever-further into non-food retailing, and before long a new breed of 'retail parks' had emerged – collections of warehouse-like DIY, furniture and electrical stores gathered around car parks on outer ring roads. The first of these opened in 1982, and by 1989 such retail parks accounted for half of all the new shopping space opened that year.[7]

The most important development of the 1980s, however, was undoubtedly the relaxation of controls on major, out-of-town 'regional shopping centres'. As with many policy reforms in the Thatcher era, although this was presented as a straightforward liberalisation – a return to laissez-faire and free enterprise – the reality was much more confused and contradictory. Policy began to change without any clear statement of intent or guiding legislation; instead there was a quiet withdrawal from some aspects of retail planning. The 1981 Census of Distribution – the mammoth survey of retailing across the nation which had taken place decennially since 1951 – was simply scrapped, causing chaos for public inquiries and the planning projections which they relied upon. Yet central state initiative was the fundamental factor in the development of the first out-of-town centres, which were built within the flagship Thatcherite Enterprise Zones, in Merry Hill west of Birmingham, and Gateshead in the North East (Enterprise Zones elsewhere housed other forms of out-of-town retailing, as at Swansea in Wales and Rotherham in South Yorkshire). The Enterprise Zones offered businesses and developers relaxed planning controls, tax concessions and a ten-year exemption from paying local rates, so that while ministers may have claimed they were relinquishing control and implementing a 'commercially neutral planning policy', this was not really the case at all.[8]

What the government did do in the 1980s, albeit with much equivocation, was signal to developers that their proposals for large out-of-town centres would be looked on much more favourably than in the past, while at the same time attacking the sources of knowledge and sub-national structures of governance through which effective, coordinated planning of the geography of consumption might take place. The Department of

[6] Judy Hillman, 'SHOP! Could the Nation of Shopkeepers Turn Into a Countryside of Hypermarkets?', *The Guardian*, 29 October 1971, 14.
[7] Patrick Haverson, 'Add Leisure – and You've Got a Day Out', *Financial Times*, 27 October 1989, 38.
[8] Paul Cheeseright, 'Out-of-Town: Avoiding an Empty Heart', *Financial Times*, 10 June 1987, 51. See also Sam Wetherell, 'Freedom Planned: Enterprise Zones and Urban Non-Planning in Post-war Britain', *Twentieth Century British History* 27:2 (2016), 266–289.

Environment eventually got round to codifying its thinking in 1988, by issuing formal Planning Policy Guidance on Major Retail Development (PPG6). This directive stated unequivocally that 'Government will not identify locations for retail development' and that it was 'not the function of planning to inhibit competition or preserve existing commercial interests'. It then proceeded to equivocate by adding that 'in exceptional circumstances' the effect of new retail development upon 'the vitality and viability of town centres' could be a consideration. This directive served to cement, rather than banish, confusion, causing the leading retail geographer R. L. Davies to conclude that while 'some would say that the dawn of an era of non-planning has arrived ... in reality the system is in disarray.'[9] The most important practical effect of the government's chaotic approach to planning was to make major development proposals intensely difficult to adjudicate, and essentially undecidable at local government level, thus more or less guaranteeing that all such applications would be 'called in' and determined by the minister. For all the rhetoric of liberalisation and entrepreneurial freedoms, the Thatcherite planning system retained precisely the same stringent veto power over all forms of development that the state had granted itself in the 1940s; it simply ensured that central government, rather than local authorities, would be best able to make the really significant decisions.[10]

The first full-blown out-of-town shopping centre in the United Kingdom was the MetroCentre, which opened in 1986 in the Tyneside Enterprise Zone a few miles outside of Gateshead, south of the river from Newcastle. The development company behind this scheme was Cameron Hall Developments, with the Church Commissioners lined up as buyers to own and operate the new centre (the financial arm of the Church of England had been investing in state-sponsored property development since it weighed in to New Town centres in the early 1950s). The MetroCentre was the biggest shopping complex in the country, and Europe's biggest out-of-town mall, and the scheme took full advantage of the tax reliefs and advantages on offer in the Enterprise Zone. The Financial Times described it as 'an attempt to create the amenities of a town centre on a marshy ash dump of an old power station'.[11] The entire complex was gargantuan (see Figure 7.1). The first two phases,

---

[9] Ross Davies & Elizabeth Howard, 'Issues in Retail Planning within the United Kingdom', Built Environment 14:1 (1988), 7–21.

[10] Otto Saumarez Smith identifies a similar disconnect between Thatcherite rhetoric and practice in relation to the inner cities, in 'Action for Cities: the Thatcher Government and Inner-City Policy', Urban History 47: 2 (2020), 274–291.

[11] Paul Cheeseright, 'Changing the Shopping Pattern in Gateshead', Financial Times, 24 April 1987, 18.

Figure 7.1 1996 aerial view of the MetroCentre complex outside Gateshead, showing the vast new scale of these ex-urban megamalls and their integration with regional motorway networks. Major out-of-town retail developments like this dwarfed what had gone before, transforming both regional and national economic geographies. Source: Newcastle Libraries.

opened in 1986, amounted to one million square feet of retail space. A third phase, opened the next year, added another 500,000 square feet, a bus station, ever more car parking, a ten-screen cinema, a funfair and a bowling centre. It was regarded, as one academic appraisal stated, 'as an innovative, glamorous development ... with large amounts of surface car parking, a spacious layout, leisure activities associated with the shopping, and late evening opening, of a kind which had not previously been seen in the UK'.[12] The developer John Hall was keen to argue that the project, in this Enterprise Zone in a struggling region, would have a major regenerative effect on the North East. Hall claimed that his development had 'cleared the dole queues on the south bank of the Tyne', and he won 'plaudits [from] the Prime Minister ... as a North East economic messiah'.[13] Newcastle City Council were naturally opposed to the MetroCentre development, having just spent decades bringing the Eldon Square complex to fruition; so too were Newcastle's retailers, who objected to the low-tax, rate-free competition over the river. The obvious and unresolved question which this scheme raised, as one journalist put it, was 'whether the country can ... permit developers and retailers to establish major shopping centres out of town and at the same time regenerate decaying city centres'.[14]

The MetroCentre did not just compete economically with established urban centres, it was also pitched very explicitly as an alternative – indeed, superior – form of 'town centre' in its own right. The scale of the place encouraged such comparisons. By the end of the 1980s, the MetroCentre housed 360 shops and employed around 5,000 people. The managerial staff alone numbered almost 200, and the centre employed its own fireman, chaplain and private police force. The centre regularly attracted 200,000 visitors a week, with this figure rising to well over half a million in busy periods. In 1988 alone, 'up to 19 m people [had] wandered through [the MetroCentre's] three tiled and palmy miles of shops, restaurants, cinemas, bowling alleys and the Metroland funpark'. Annual turnover was somewhere around £350 m in these years. The MetroCentre's manager did not shy away from the fact that the centre offered a heavily sanitised and rigorously policed analogue of an actual town centre – jokingly referring to it as 'Toytown'. The MetroCentre was designed to meet 'the public's suppressed demand for a clean, safe, town centre with

[12] E. B. Howard & R. L. Davies, *The Impact of Regional, Out-of-Town Retail Centres: The Case of the Metro Centre* (Oxford: Pergamon Press, 1993), 96.
[13] Paul Cheeseright, 'John Hall: Latest Apostle of the North East', *Financial Times*, 24 April 1987, 18.
[14] Paul Cheeseright, 'Changing the Shopping Pattern in Gateshead', *Financial Times*, 24 April 1987, 18.

free parking and quality shops', its manager claimed, and he was particularly proud of the centre's 'social success'; 'people dress up to come here',
he stated, and they had created 'an orderly society within the confines of
the development'. This was achieved through 'gently shaping the social
environment', drawing on the full panoply of retail design and centre
management techniques, and enforced by a private army of security
guards who kept the centre 'free of social nuisance'. As private property,
it was the MetroCentre's landlords (the Church Commissioners,
a registered charity) who decreed what was, and was not, permissible
behaviour within the terrazzo-tiled malls. This, as one journalist noted,
left the centre's manager 'free to mould their town centre, untrammelled
by the jigsaw complexities of zone and byelaw rules and the union, local
authority and political pressures which define the planning of real [town]
centres'. This, then, was not just an economic alternative to the established town centre, but a microcosm of an alternative urban polis, with
reworked codes of access, conduct and participation, and a transformed
structure of governance and political oversight. 'It is political', the
MetroCentre's manager concluded, 'but we don't see it as politics. I call
it social engineering'.[15]

It was precisely these troubling social and political dynamics that
motivated a growing chorus of criticism of such facilities in the 1980s
and 1990s. Within the academy, geographers and sociologists in particular took their cues from a burgeoning field of critical scholarship in the
United States, which decried the 'Disneyfication' of the social landscape
and denounced the duplicitous 'magic of the mall'. 'The designers of the
retail built environment', the American geographer Jon Goss wrote in
1993, 'exploit the power of place and an intuitive understanding of the
structuration of space to facilitate consumption and thus the realization of
profits'.[16] In practice, of course, this had been the *raison d'être* of
organised selling space since the mid-nineteenth century (as had been
perceptively dissected by Émile Zola in his 1883 novel of the Parisian
department store, *Au Bonheur des Dames*), but the megamalls of the late
twentieth century ratcheted up these techniques to an unprecedented
degree. Their ex-urban locations made the new regional centres stand
very obviously in contrast, and competition, with the traditional city

---

[15] These details from: Mark Nicholson, 'Running His Own High Street', *Financial Times*,
27 October 1989, 40; Paul Cheeseright, 'Changing the Shopping Pattern in Gateshead',
Financial Times, 24 April 1987, 18.

[16] Jon Goss, 'The "Magic of the Mall": An Analysis of Form, Function, and Meaning in the
Contemporary Retail Built Environment', *Annals of the Association of American
Geographers* 83:1 (1993), 18–47. For 'Disneyfication', see Zukin, *Landscapes of Power*.
For a similar British treatment see Hannigan, *Fantasy City*.

centre, and for their critics they came to represent the triumph of consumer capitalism and the profit motive over urban public space and the
collective civic realm – indeed, over the city itself.

Much of the shopping public remained untroubled by such academic
concerns, and while the regional centres often failed to perform quite as
spectacularly as hoped, they were undoubtedly commercial successes. By
the 1990s there were four regional centres open and trading in Britain (the
MetroCentre and Merry Hill were joined in 1990 by Lakeside on
London's orbital motorway in Essex, and Meadowhall on the M1 outside
Sheffield). In 1995 these four centres were the most successful trading
locations in the United Kingdom, when judged on the basis of net
profitability and turnover per square metre; the MetroCentre, the largest,
topped the list on both of these measures. For some, these were national
tourist attractions (Meadowhall received coachloads of shoppers from as
far away as Penzance, in Cornwall) but, just as expected, the regional
centres catered overwhelmingly to wealthier, car-borne shoppers, leaving
poorer and less mobile households out in the cold.[17] Controlling these
most valuable piles of commercial real estate became a major attraction
for investing institutions. When the Church Commissioners found themselves in financial difficulty in 1995 and offered the MetroCentre for sale,
they were 'knocked down in the rush' of offers to purchase their 'biggest
and most profitable commercial asset'. Dozens of bids were received,
some from British property companies and financial institutions, many
from international investing funds, and the Church sold in the end to
Capital Shopping Centres, for £325 m, in what was thought to be the
largest single property transaction ever completed in the United
Kingdom.[18]

The MetroCentre's new owner, Capital Shopping Centres, was the
product of a typically tortuous tale of corporate takeovers, mergers and
restructuring, which in itself illustrated how tightly the geographies of
development and the fabric of everyday life in late-century Britain had
become bound up with financial systems of investment and accumulation
which operated on an increasingly global scale. Capital Shopping Centres
was a subsidiary holding company of Liberty International – originally
a South African insurance company, listed in Johannesburg since the
1950s, which had internationalised its business in the 1980s. Liberty

---

[17] These details in: Simon London, 'Shopping Centres in the Lead', *Financial Times*,
9 July 1996, 8; 'Taking a Malling', *The Economist*, 12 September 1998, 34; Howard &
Davies, *The Impact of Regional, Out-of-Town Retail Centres*.
[18] Ruth Gledhill & Paul Wilkinson, 'Church Sells Giant Shopping Centre to Ease Cash
Crisis', *The Times*, 8 February 1995, 4; Carl Mortished, 'MetroCentre Sale Nets Church
£75m', *The Times*, 7 July 1995, 24.

acquired a controlling share in the British property company Capital &
Counties in 1985, gaining access to both the firm's extensive property
portfolio and its listing on the London Stock Exchange. A new company,
Capital Shopping Centres, was splintered off from the rest of this portfolio in 1994, so that it could focus exclusively upon operating the most
valuable retail property assets. These were principally nine major shopping centres, including Nottingham's Victoria Centre and Newcastle's
Eldon Square, the mammoth new Lakeside regional centre, and, following its purchase in 1995, the Gateshead MetroCentre. Liberty
International now became one of the most important forces in property
and redevelopment in the United Kingdom; by the early 2000s it was the
third-largest property company in the country, with a portfolio of shopping centres judged to be worth £1.7 bn, which attracted more than
180 m visits from shoppers each year. The company continued to aggressively expand its retail property holdings in the United Kingdom across
the early years of the twenty-first century, buying up dozens of shopping
centres all over the country, including a remarkable 2011 purchase of
Manchester's out-of-town Trafford Centre at a valuation of £1.6 bn. By
the time it rebranded itself as 'Intu' in 2013, the company's holdings
stretched across all four nations of the British Isles, and ran the full gamut
from 1970s public–private developments (such as Eldon Square, the
Manchester Arndale and Nottingham's Broadmarsh), to the privately
developed city malls and edge-of-town retail parks of the 1980s and
1990s, to the new breed of regional megamalls (the company ended up
in possession of about half of all of these in the country). This dynamic
and expansionary financial actor also managed to pick the commercial
fruits of Britain's most energetic New Town project, acquiring Milton
Keynes's central shopping complex in 2013, as well as operating
a number of major malls across Spain.[19]

   The creation from the 1980s of these eye-wateringly expensive regional
malls thus delivered a sharp boost to a process which had been rumbling
along in Britain across the post-war decades, aided by the developer- and
investor-friendly planning system. This was the transformation of the
urban retail landscape into a lucrative tradable commodity and its enlistment into wider financial systems of wealth holding and accumulation.
The large shopping centres which the state and the development sector

---

[19] These details within: Jenny Davey, 'Liberty Chief Has Sights Set on Crown', *The Times*,
10 March 2003, 25; Pauline Springett, 'Shops in £800m Visit to Market', *The Guardian*,
4 February 1994, 12; 'Capital Shopping Centres PLC', *The Sunday Times*,
6 March 1994, 4; Intu Properties Plc, 'Acquisition of Midsummer Place, Milton
Keynes', press release, 27 February 2013; James Thompson, 'Trafford Centre Set for
£1.6 bn Sale to CSC Group', *The Independent*, 25 November 2010.

had conspired to install up and down the country became 'trophy properties' in the portfolios of investing institutions, and the value of the biggest
British malls as financial assets was such that they were subsumed into
a global investment market for the most lucrative chunks of commercial
real estate.[20] These markets reached a frenzied pitch in the early 2000s.
The year 2004 in particular was a record-breaking year, when around 150
UK shopping centres worth over £6.5 bn were traded between international investors in a 'spending orgy'; 'the market is incredibly strong' as
one financier explained at the time.[21] Such trends necessarily transformed judgements of 'value' by shifting the calculus upon which this
was based. The value of an individual retail property came to be determined less by its function within a regional shopping economy, and more
by its potential performance as a large investment asset, within an over-
arching financial system which operated with its own internal logics and
dynamics and at an entirely different scale. The value of a shop, in short,
became increasingly detached from the actual business of shopping. At
the time of writing, this system of financialised retail property is in a state
of collapse, with calamitous consequences for the urban centres and local
economies which it has so comprehensively reshaped. The retail property
hegemon Intu in particular, whose position had appeared unassailable
less than a decade ago, is in a state of financial free fall. The conclusion of
this book returns to address the contemporary collapse of this system and
the shopping city ideal which had underpinned it since the mid-twentieth
century. At the end of the twentieth century, though, the question which
vexed planners and politicians was not the viability of the urban retail
system as a whole, but rather the impact of the new out-of-town megamalls upon the established urban centres of late-century Britain.

Malling the City

For the urbanists who worried about the effect of the new out-of-town
complexes on 'the vitality and viability' of existing city centres, the consequences – while certainly significant – were not quite as dire as had been
feared. This was principally because central government did not usher in
an unplanned, out-of-town free-for-all, but rather maintained strict controls on the numbers of regional centres. Although developers in the later
1980s were pushing around sixty separate out-of-town schemes, the vast
majority of these were not permitted, and by 2000 there were only ten

---

[20] Jenny Davey, 'Liberty Chief Has Sights Set on Crown', *The Times*, 10 March 2003, 25.
[21] Jim Pickard, 'Sales of Shopping Centres Heading for Record High of £6.5bn', *Financial Times*, 1 November 2004, 2.

regional centres in Britain. The impact of those regional centres which were built was certainly felt by nearby cities; retail trade in the centre of Sheffield dropped by 30 per cent following the opening of the Meadowhall Centre. In the north east, the centre of Newcastle managed to hold its own against the Gateshead MetroCentre (largely because the two centres served different hinterlands) but the bigger problem – both in the north east and elsewhere – was a calamitous drop in trade for less prominent urban centres. The MetroCentre precipitated a collapse of shopping trade in Gateshead itself, and there were marked declines in places like Durham, Sunderland and South Shields. It was these smaller, second-order towns, which were often already struggling to maintain a prosperous shopping centre, that paid the real price of out-of-town developments. In Greater Manchester, the opening in 1998 of the out-of-town Trafford Centre threatened Manchester city centre with a loss of trade in the order of 10 per cent or so; but it was the surrounding sub-centres like Stockport, Altrincham, Wigan and Bolton, which were facing calamitous declines of 20–30 per cent of their former trade.[22]

Anxieties began to be expressed about the long-term future of such places, and a discourse took shape of 'dying' town centres in left-behind locales, characterised by unattractive and underused high streets, filled with charity shops, budget retailers and steadily growing numbers of empty shops. In 1995, a House of Commons debate on retail planning policies saw many MPs voice their concerns about these trends. The MP for Blackpool North, Harold Elletson, noted that 'more than a quarter of the nation's shopping space [was now] out of town', with such sites accounting for one in every three retail sales. Elletson warned of the danger of creating a 'wasteland in our towns and cities', and called for 'new initiatives to ensure that our towns and cities are vital, vibrant and vigorous and places that we will be able to leave as our inheritance to our grandchildren'. Others viewed the problems in similarly existential terms; 'above all we need to ensure that town centres stay alive', as the MP for Bromsgrove in the Midlands put it. MPs of all parties criticised the government's chaotic approach to planning, exemplified by the lack of 'clear and consistent planning guidance', and exacerbated by central government attacks on the planning capacities and revenues of local authorities. The abolition in 1986 of an entire tier of conurbation-scale local government, in the shape of the Greater London Council and the six metropolitan counties which had served England's biggest urban agglomerations since 1974, had done nothing to advance the cause of coordinated sub-national planning. Yet even during its short lifespan, this

---

[22] 'Taking a Malling', *The Economist*, 12 September 1998, 34.

patchy, city region structure was not enough to overcome Britain's woeful lack of a coherent system for managing its own development on a regional scale. In the absence of an effective administrative geography, individual local authorities were largely left to fend for themselves, and it was thus no surprise that poorer and less attractive towns consistently fell behind in this competitive game, whether it was out-of-town malls or major city centres they were up against.

For the big cities, weathering the storm of out-of-town competition meant pushing ever harder to reinvent city centres in their entirety as glamorous and glitzy consumer amenities. The closing years of the twentieth century saw a new surge of city centre redevelopment and refurbishment, and a marked intensification of the type of holistic environmental management of central areas which councils like Glasgow and Manchester had been experimenting with since the 1960s. *The Economist* noted in 1998 that 'people will desert traditional shopping streets in favour of the rain- and car-free walkways of malls if city centres have no obvious counter-attractions'. 'The lesson that town centres have learned', the piece continued, 'is that they have to ape the management techniques of the malls, with local councils and traders collaborating to provide what people want'.[23] This was an expensive and complex business. In Sheffield, for example, the council had to corral 700 different city centre traders, and spend £300 m on city centre improvements, in order to defend its economic base from the out-of-town competition. Pedestrianisation projects, and environmental improvement schemes, proliferated in cities all over the country, aimed squarely at improving the city centre shopping experience and boosting central area trade. Local authorities were compelled to dramatically intensify their efforts at rearranging the form and function of the city as far as possible around the demands of the retail economy and the convenience of shoppers. By the end of the 1980s, councils had 'definitely put more pep into town centres by improving the infrastructure and parking facilities, and adding environmentally-pleasing pedestrian malls and food courts', as one commercial surveyor noted.[24]

Such imperatives prompted the emergence of 'town centre management' as a new field of professional competence, with its own scholarly literatures and recognised practitioners. This new field of expertise blurred the boundaries of academic, administrative and commercial forms of knowledge, and saw councils enjoined by retail managers and university business schools to reconceive of their town centre as 'the

---

[23] 'Taking a Malling', *The Economist*, 12 September 1998, 34.
[24] Anne Sacks, 'Town Centres: Shoppers Call the Tune', *Financial Times*, 27 October 1989, 38.

shopping destination product', which must be managed and marketed according to a clear set of commercial strictures.[25] Town centre management encompassed not just the physical beautifications which aped the holistic retail environment of the mall, but also many of the policing and public order innovations – experimentation with CCTV and various other new security technologies was commonplace. Councils now became directly responsible for the general economic health of the town centre, understood in terms of its competitive performance as a shopping destination. 'Town centre managers', as one advocate put it, 'are there as a result of competition, largely from out-of-town shopping centres because it is now universally recognised that competition can be met only by improving and constantly managing town centres'.[26] The MPs debating the future of failing town centres in 1995 saw the appointment of designated town centre managers as just the panacea that was needed, and over eighty councils had already done so by this time. Some of these positions were jointly funded by the public and private sectors, with contributions gathered from local Chambers of Commerce, or leading retailers in the town, thus formalising the public–private administration of the city.

Administrative changes such as this were part of a wider shift in the responsibilities of local government; increasingly reconceived as 'governance' rather than government, councils now became responsible for marshalling and coordinating a seemingly endless parade of 'stakeholders' – businesses, landlords, residents, development agencies, quangos and amenity groups – towards the goal of local prosperity. Successfully orchestrating commercial growth and vitality in this manner would have been a tall order by any measure; given the limited powers and resources of local government in late-century Britain it was faintly absurd, and certainly unlikely to be an economic silver bullet for struggling locales. In effect these were calls for ever-greater public assistance and subsidy for local retail economies, the success of which was now established as a public responsibility placed upon local authorities. For all the talk of partnership and teamwork, one local government officer in the North East noted that 'the private sector always seems to be a willing participant until the subject of financial contributions is mentioned'.[27] This individual, who was the chief engineer at South Tyneside Metropolitan Borough Council, laid out a litany of environmental,

[25] See, for example, Gary Warnaby, 'Marketing UK Cities as Shopping Destinations: Problems and Prospects', *Journal of Retailing and Consumer Services* 5:1 (1998), 55–58.
[26] D. R. Pigg, 'Securing the Future of Town Centres', *Municipal Engineer* 93:4 (1992), 193–198, 197.
[27] Pigg, 'Securing the Future of Town Centres', 193.

infrastructural and administrative experiments being pursued in the numerous town centres under his jurisdiction which were 'being given a new lease of life with shopping malls and pedestrianized zones'. The majority of these measures were focused on security, surveillance and policing, and crimes against retail property (such as 'a surge in ram-raiding') continued to be a major problem in many places. But the aim of 'improved amenity' also encompassed a wide range of shopper-focused environmental and experiential measures: 'the emphasis is on increased attractiveness ... to help people to relax'. Such moves entailed a transformation in the traditional professional role of a municipal engineer, who now had to corral his stakeholders and seduce his shoppers at the same time as keeping the city safe and sanitary. 'The challenge for the municipal engineers', the Tyneside official explained, 'is to bridge the gap between the private and public sector', and to acquire 'a greater understanding of customer perceptions which are rarely focused on pure engineering issues'. This new 'social dimension of the work of municipal engineers' was only expected to intensify.

In addition to an acceleration of shopping-centred urban governance, the later years of the twentieth century also witnessed a dramatic upsurge in new mall building and retail redevelopment in the nation's town and city centres. Again, this was a response to the out-of-town competition, as any shopping facilities which began to feel a little passé could be quickly written off. 'The concrete masses of early shopping centres are considered cold, unsympathetic and outmoded by today's sophisticated shopper', one retail expert noted in 1989, and the shopping centres which had been erected at such great expense in the 1960s and 1970s were impelled to embark upon lavish programmes of refurbishment. In Birmingham, £250 m was spent overhauling the Bull Ring complex in this period, while the Arndale company, recognising that 'the image factor is all important for success in retailing', announced 'ambitious revitalisation plans ... for all its centres, bringing them firmly into the 1990s'.[28] Britain emerged as a recognised world leader in retail design and architecture in this period – a development which was tied to related commercial strengths in advertising and PR and built directly upon the long store of post-war experience in retail property development. Specialist architects and designers developed a fairly generic 'postmodern' style, with quirky external facades, and busy, varied interiors. Tacky, faux-classical features such as columns and statuary became a commonplace; designed to conjure up opulence and splendour, when taken to its extreme this 'retailers'

---

[28] Wendy Smith, 'Civilising the Concrete Jungle', *Financial Times*, 27 October 1989, 39; 'Arndale Shopping Centres Limited', *The Times*, 7 July 1987, 42.

rococo' saw some centres created as self-parodying temples of consumption (Figure 7.2). There was also a heightened emphasis upon restoring,
or else mimicking, traditional architectural features. Exposed iron structures housing lift shafts and supporting glass roofs harked back to the
grandiose department stores and Victorian market halls of the previous
century, and the idea of the market hall in particular was repeatedly
repackaged for the late twentieth-century consumer. Monolithic modernism was out, postmodern pastiche was in, and Victoriana – suitably
glammed up for the age of aspiration – was back in style.

From the mid-1980s, then, new malls came to be built again in many
places, after a period of slump and hiatus in retail property development
since the mid-1970s. Many smaller towns, which had missed out on the
first wave of mall development in the 1960s and 1970s now received their
own glamorous covered centres. In the late 1980s, the Arndale company
was bringing its brand of shopping spectacle to unspectacular places like
Halifax, Christchurch, Accrington and Paisley for the first time. In the big
cities, too, the development of new malls along with major extensions to
existing centres proceeded at pace. The year 1988 was a record-breaking
year for retail development, with more new shopping centres opened that
at any time previously. By 1993, there were around 800 shopping centres
in Britain, ranging from the modest to the megalithic. Like town centre
management, shopping centre management became steadily more for-
malised and professional; the British Council of Shopping Centres, established in 1982, began to offer a Diploma in Shopping Centre
Management.[29] This organisation followed the model of a parent organisation in the United States, and, through research and publications,
conferences and seminars, award schemes and a quarterly journal, the
Council promoted both the interests of its members and an industry-wide
growth in the sophistication and efficacy of the sales-driven management
of urban space. The proliferation of these curated retail environments in
British towns and cities, combined with the growing technical sophistication of managerial practices, meant that the seductive spectacle of shopping loomed ever larger in the organisation of collective urban space and
experience. As one prominent American theorist of 'the cultural logic of
late capitalism' complained, in 'the postmodern city ... the former
streets ... become so many aisles in a department store'.[30]

---

[29] Tony Taylor, 'The British Council of Shopping Centres', *Planning Practice and Research*
8:3 (1993), 43–44.
[30] Jameson, *Postmodernism, or, the Cultural Logic of Late Capitalism*, 98. Similar critiques
were being advanced by the sociologist Sharon Zukin, and the geographer David Harvey,
in this moment.

Figure 7.2 The interior of the Trafford Centre, a regional shopping centre on Manchester's orbital motorway. The complex is shown here a few days before the opening on 10 September 1998. Architecturally, the extreme self-parody of a postmodern temple of consumption is clearly on display. The Trafford Centre facility was sold to Liberty/ Intu in 2011 at a value of £1.6 bn, in the United Kingdom's largest ever property transaction. Source: Getty Images.

Retailing as Regeneration

By the closing years of the twentieth century, British urbanism had cohered around a new rhetoric of 'urban regeneration'. The rise of this policy agenda along with the new wave of urban initiatives it encompassed is well-trodden terrain within urban scholarship.[31] The regeneration agenda was simultaneously a response to long-term structural processes (the decline of traditional industries and manufacturing centres); medium-term urban management problems (the perceived failings of post-war urban renewal and planning approaches) and the immediate political and economic pressures of the 1980s (urban unemployment, dereliction and social unrest in 'the inner cities'). Regeneration was aimed at physical renewal and economic revitalisation in Britain's extant urban centres; post-war programmes of urban dispersal were abandoned, and there was a firm focus on rejuvenating central cores and redeveloping post-industrial 'brownfield' sites. The initiative in urban policy came to rest more firmly with central government (often working through newly formed development agencies and targeted funding streams), and supreme emphasis was placed upon encouraging new inward investment and private sector growth. In practice, as has been seen throughout this book, much of this was rather less novel than is often assumed; locally, many urban authorities had been pursuing similar aims via similar methods for many decades. Just like these authorities before them, the new centrally mandated agents of urban regeneration found that physical renewal could be achieved easily enough by partnering with the energetic and well-funded private development industry, but that the aim of a more thoroughgoing and holistic revitalisation of local economies was rather more elusive. Such was the prevalence of physical redevelopment within these programmes that a powerful critique of this model of 'property-led urban regeneration' rapidly emerged, which saw the benefits to local populations as largely cosmetic, and the benefits for the redevelopment industry as very great indeed.[32]

---

[31] See, for example, Brian T. Robson, *Those Inner Cities: Reconciling the Economic and Social Aims of Urban Policy* (Oxford: Clarendon, 1988); Paul Lawless, *Britain's Inner Cities: Problems and Policies* (London: Paul Chapman, 1989); Susanne MacGregor & Ben Pimlott (eds.), *Tackling the Inner Cities: the 1980s reviewed, prospects for the 1990s* (Oxford: Clarendon, 1990); Nick Oatley, *Cities, Economic Competition and Urban Policy* (London: Paul Chapman, 1998); Alan Cochrane, *Understanding Urban Policy* (Oxford: Blackwell, 2007); Andrew Tallon, *Urban Regeneration in the UK* (London: Routledge, 2009); Phil Jones & James Evans, *Urban Regeneration in the UK* (Los Angeles: SAGE, 2013).

[32] See, for example, Patsy Healey, Simin Davoudi, Mo O'Toole, Solmaz Tavsanoglu & David Usher (eds.), *Rebuilding the City: Property-led Urban Regeneration* (London: E&FN Spon, 1992); Susan S. Fainstein, *The City Builders: Property, Politics & Planning in London and New York* (Oxford: Blackwell, 1994).

Also familiar to the practitioners of post-war urban renewal was the strong focus upon retailing within urban regeneration agendas, which continued to be viewed as a key marker of prosperity and as a potential source of new jobs to plug some of the many gaps in local employment. Once again, the agendas of urban improvement and retail growth were brought together to install a new wave of extravagant, state-sponsored shopping facilities at the heart of Britain's cities. In central Glasgow, for example, the Scottish Development Agency was instrumental in the rein-vention of the former St. Enoch railway station as the St. Enoch Centre – a large shopping and leisure complex on Argyll Street, in the heart of the city's main shopping district. The nineteenth-century St. Enoch station had ceased operating in 1966, and in 1977 the Development Agency bought the site, cleared it and prepared it for redevelopment at public expense. The Agency managed to entice around £60 m of investment from the Church Commissioners and the retail and property company Sears Holdings to redevelop this valuable site in 'the city's prime shopping pitch', with further financial contributions from Strathclyde Regional Council. The St. Enoch Centre opened for business in 1989, comprising a large covered shopping and leisure complex under one of the biggest glass roofs in Europe, with an ice rink, a hotel and a multi-storey car park (Figure 7.3). It was heralded as a symbol of Glasgow's mid-1980s 'metamorphosis', as the city sought to cast aside its gloomy inheritance of deprivation and decline and reinvent itself as a vibrant and prosperous centre for shopping and services. In 'the revamped, credit-card Glasgow', as one booster had it, 'the soot and smog are being cleared', and new developments like the St. Enoch Centre were 'marks of a singular recovery in morale and spirit of the city and its inhabitants'.[33] The St. Enoch centre was formally opened, appropriately enough, by Mrs Thatcher in early 1990. The Prime Minister unveiled the obligatory commemorative plaque, before borrowing £30 from the Scottish Secretary Malcolm Rifkind to purchase a (blue) bottle of perfume.[34]

As the commentaries on Glasgow's St. Enoch Centre make clear, such developments were inextricable from broader currents of economic and cultural change which were washing over Britain in the 1980s. After the

[33] George Parker-Jervis, 'A New Image for Glasgow', *The Observer*, 5 June 1988, 63. For more on Glasgow's problems with 'multiple deprivation' in the 1970s, see Andrews, 'Multiple Deprivation, the Inner City, and the Fracturing of the Welfare State', 605–624.
[34] These details in: Jasper Becker, 'Thatcher Perceives no Protests in Scottish Purple Passage', *The Guardian*, 10 March 1990, 24; Colin Amery, 'The Best of British', *Financial Times*, 14 January 1991, 15; William Cochrane, 'Sears to Fund Part of St Enoch', *Financial Times*, 21 June 1985, 37; 'Battle for the Shops', *Financial Times*, 8 June 1984, 16. For the Scottish Development Agency, and its turn to property-led regeneration, see Urlan Wannop, 'The Evolution and Roles of the Scottish Development Agency', *Town Planning Review* 55:3 (1984), 313–321.

Figure 7.3 Image of Glasgow's mammoth St. Enoch Centre, opened in 1989 as part of a Scottish Development Agency regeneration initiative. The enormous glass roof was one of the largest in Europe, and housed a plethora of consumer and commercial leisure attractions inside. Source: Metrocentric.

fiscal travails of the 1970s and the recession of the early 1980s, the country entered a period of consumer-driven expansion in which retailing boomed once again. The three years from 1985 to 1988 in particular were, as one business analyst noted, the 'most rapid years of retail spending growth that we've ever had'.[35] Commentators began to talk of a 'retail revolution', overseen by a sector which was 'restless and growth hungry' and had been promoted 'to the premier league of British industry'.[36] Trends in the sector which had been brewing for some time – towards large-scale multiple retailing, concentration, innovations in marketing and the swift adoption of new technologies and organisational forms – all came to fruition in what has been called the 'golden age' of British retailing.[37] The success of the

---

[35] 'The Property Market', *Financial Times*, 17 March 1989, 18.
[36] See, for example, 'Retailing: Financial Times Survey', *Financial Times*, 10 June 1987; Carl Gardner & Julie Sheppard, *Consuming Passion: The Rise of Retail Culture* (London: Unwin Hyman, 1989).
[37] Carlo Morelli, 'Increasing Value? Modern British Retailing in the Late Twentieth Century', in Richard Coopey & Peter Lyth (eds.), *Business in Britain in the Twentieth Century: Decline and Renaissance?* (Oxford: Oxford University Press, 2009), 271–295.

retail sector took on a cultural and political resonance, as part of what Frank Mort has described as the 'self-confident display of commercial optimism' of the later 1980s, in which the Thatcherite agendas of entrepreneurship and flexible, dynamic capitalism seemed at last to be bearing fruit. Retailing appeared, as Mort notes, as 'a test-bed for the economics of the future', and individual retail bosses were celebrated as titans of (post-Fordist) industry.[38] Just as important, politically and culturally, was the proliferation of what some at the time called 'retail culture' – a nexus of commercial images, cultural identifications, aspirational agendas and symbolic practices which could exercise a powerful hold over individuals and intersected decisively with the politics of the age. The elaboration of this dynamic and participatory cultural system ensured that the expansion of shopping held a social significance that went far beyond its immediate economic metrics. In a 1989 commentary on the retail-led transformation of town centres, the *Financial Times* maintained that: 'In the next decade, the consumer will be king ... and Mrs Thatcher's enterprise culture may finally have arrived.'[39]

The 1980s consumer boom provided the context and the incentive for the new wave of urban shopping development and retail refurbishments which took off from the mid-1980s. Retailers sought to expand rapidly, and there was a 'race for space' which saw shop rental levels soar by anywhere between 50 and 150 per cent in many cities across the second half of the 1980s.[40] These were precisely the conditions to entice commercial property developers and the institutional investors who backed them, and they explained why 1988 was such a record-breaking year for new shopping centre openings. And yet, like post-war affluence before it, this picture of consumer-fuelled urban growth remained highly variegated throughout the country; shop rents may have surged by almost 200 per cent in Oxford, and by similar amounts in Manchester and Nottingham, but in less favoured locales like Liverpool and Birmingham there were only modest rises of 30 per cent or so. The picture facing many smaller towns – often overshadowed by their larger and more prosperous neighbours – could be much bleaker. Consumer spending and demand, and the urban investment which came along with it, was intensely uneven in its distribution both between and within regions, producing a clear set of winners and losers in the race for retail-fuelled

---

[38] Frank Mort, *Cultures of Consumption: Masculinities and Social Space in Late Twentieth-Century Britain* (London: Routledge, 1996), 2–4.

[39] Anne Sacks, 'Town Centres: Shoppers Call the Tune', *Financial Times*, 27 October 1989, 38.

[40] Paul Cheeseright, 'Long Term Enterprises', *Financial Times*, 27 October 1989, 38. Also, Healey & Baker, *Retail Report 1985* (Oxford: Nuffield Press, 1985).

redevelopment. In struggling towns, programmes of urban regeneration came to revolve around attempts to conjure up prosperity, mimicking the commercial success of other locales by using state subsidies to induce developers to install the elaborate shopping complexes that were springing up with less enticement elsewhere. If the image and the environment of prosperity could be created, it was hoped, the reality would materialise in its wake. As a strategy for local economic development – and indeed as a piece of logic – this was somewhat curious, and relied upon a leap of faith concerning the local economic and employment benefits of such projects. Nonetheless, this became a hallmark of late-century urban regeneration, and it is useful to close by considering how one such endeavour played out in a specific locale: Bolton, a former mill town and sub-regional centre in the orbit of Manchester.

Bolton: The Failure of Retail as Regeneration

In the nineteenth century, Bolton had been a fast-spinning flywheel in the South Lancashire urban-industrial engine which drove Britain's manufacturing economy. An archetypal Lancashire mill town, Bolton remained a global centre for the production of cotton well into the twentieth century, with a town centre dominated by a hulking neoclassical town hall, completed in 1873, which stood as a typically brash symbol of civic grandeur paid for by industrial prowess. The decades after 1945, though, were a familiar 'litany of industrial misery' for Bolton, as traditional industries contracted, textile and engineering works closed, and unemployment ran consistently higher than the national average.[41] By the early 1970s (before the 1973 oil price shock) the town had already shed tens of thousands of manufacturing jobs since the war and unemployment stood at 8 per cent.[42] Faced with this declining industrial and employment base, Bolton's leaders alighted on urban renewal, and the economic promise of redeveloping the town centre, as a solution. Graeme Shankland's 1964 plan for the town was typical of the urban renewal era, laying out a holistic vision of environmental and economic rejuvenation in which an expansion of shopping would fuel the rebirth of the town centre. The concrete outcome of this vision was also a typical one; the council partnered with Town & City Properties to install a Bolton Arndale Centre in the heart of the town, which was opened amid much civic fanfare in September 1971. The new shopping centre was built directly opposite the nineteenth-century town hall, so that the two

---

[41] Simon Winchester, 'Life on the Dole', *The Guardian*, 21 May 1971, 13.
[42] 'Bolton Appeals on Jobs', *The Guardian*, 28 January 1972, 16.

buildings faced each other across the central civic space of the town, Victoria Square. Just like its Victorian predecessor, this twentieth-century symbol of civic prowess was to be 'worthy of a progressive town like Bolton'. It would, the council hoped, cement the town's 'forward-looking reputation' and furnish Bolton with a 'town centre ready for the next century'.[43]

As the 1970s wore on, however, the regenerative potential of this development proved to be rather less than hoped. Firm closures continued, with corresponding rises in unemployment, and the town's population dwindled at an ever-accelerating pace. The projections of permanence 'for the next century' were quickly forgotten and by the 1980s the council was embarked upon a new mission to transform the town centre. A Town Centre Redevelopment Group was formed, and a commercial consultancy was commissioned to advise the authority on the shopping potential of the town centre. A project took shape to overhaul Bolton's Victorian market hall, no more than 200 metres from Arndale's 1970s development, and erect a glamorous new shopping centre in the latest postmodern style on a site immediately adjacent to the market. This conjoined development of the Market Hall and Market Place (as the postmodern centre was called) became the linchpin of Bolton's 1980s regeneration, illustrating both what had changed in this era, and how much had remained the same. Most significant among the changes was the direct financial contribution of central government in the form of a £4.2 m award from the Urban Development Grant Programme. This grant scheme had been established by Michael Heseltine when he was Environment Secretary in 1982, as part of the government's response to the Merseyside riots a year earlier, and the award made to Bolton for its Market Place development was the largest sum given under the scheme so far.[44] Although not a particularly impressive sum given the overall costs involved in central area redevelopment (nor in relation to the general level of resources available to central government), this grant reinforced the long-standing presumption that the state would subsidise commercial property development in areas which were struggling economically. It was a mark of the declining capacities of local government that, by the

---

[43] Town & City Properties & Bolton Corporation, 'The Arndale Centre Bolton' (1971), development prospectus; 'Arndale Shopping Centre Supplement', *Bolton Evening News*, 29 September 1971. These documents, along with Shankland's 1964 Plan, at Bolton Local History Centre.

[44] See David Johnson, 'An Evaluation of the Urban Development Grant Programme', *Local Economy* 2:4 (1988), 251–270. Details of redevelopment in Bolton Environmental Education Project, *The Market Place: Bolton's New Shopping Centre* (1989), at Bolton Local History Centre.

1980s, these financial inducements increasingly had to come direct from central government.

If the sources of subsidy had shifted, the private sector partners remained very much the same. Indeed, the choice of developer for the Bolton Market Place scheme spoke to continuities in the structures of power, property and wealth in Britain which stretched back well beyond the post-war era. The project was undertaken by Grosvenor Developments, the property developing arm of the Duke of Westminster's enormously wealthy land and property holding company. In existence since 1677, the Grosvenor estate had profited dramatically in the eighteenth and nineteenth centuries through the elite residential development of its lands in Mayfair and Belgravia. In the post-1945 period, Grosvenor Estates continued to benefit from its fabulously expensive London properties along with its large rural estates, while also branching out into new commercial development activity both in Britain and beyond.[45] The cultural and commercial prestige of this connection seems to have been a real draw for Bolton, with the new centre hailed as bringing 'a touch of West End theatricality to shopping . . . in an upmarket, Oxford Street style setting'. The Duke himself – lauded in the local press as 'one of Britain's most successful businessmen' – told Bolton's Chamber of Commerce at a celebratory dinner that Grosvenor's £37 m investment in the Market Place scheme 'represents a major vote of confidence in the town'. Familiar narratives of civic rebirth facilitated by mutually beneficial partnerships were wheeled out, with Bolton's Labour council leader applauding the Market Place scheme as 'a good example of the cooperation between central and local government and the private sector' which 'puts the town amongst the front rank of shopping centres in the North West'. 'Once again', he concluded, 'we're putting Bolton firmly on the map'.[46]

The new facilities themselves were a flamboyant showcase for all the latest accomplishments in British retailing, commercial architecture and large-scale property development. The grade II listed Market Hall, completed in 1855, was extensively refurbished and restored 'to its true Victorian beauty' at a cost of £4 m. The former 'colour and chaos' of haphazard market stalls was replaced by a new arrangement of large, standardised kiosks, each decked out with a house style of 'Olde Worlde' décor ('reminiscent of fun pubs', as one critic put it), and heavily armoured by expensive security shutters.[47] If the Market Hall illustrated the verve for repackaged architectural heritage, the adjoining Market

---

[45] Marriott, *The Property Boom*, 90–93 & 193–194.
[46] These details in 'Bolton's Shopping Sensation', press supplement, *Bolton Evening News*, 23 March 1988.
[47] Chris Lethbridge, 'Architecture', *City Life*, August 1988.

Place represented the latest, quirkiest, fashions in postmodern retail design. Outside, a bizarre ensemble of towers, cupolas, oriental screens and textured facades amounted to what the critic Colin Amery called 'a powerful, if puzzling architectural statement'. Inside, a full panoply of postmodern pastiche was on display in faux 'Roman' mosaics, neoclassical columns and pediments and intricate 'art nouveau' ironwork, all aimed, of course, at visual and experiential spectacle. 'It's a spectacular experience', the new centre's manager explained; 'the aim is to put the fun back in shopping'. The 'jewel in the crown' of the new centre was a large 'visually exciting' Debenhams department store, which offered 70,000 square feet spread over three floors 'in which to display the best in fashion, eighties style'. Overall, Amery felt that the new shopping centre 'achieves a sense of retail theatre'. 'The new inner city creates fantasy worlds indoors that are exotic and nostalgic', he concluded, and 'architects are forced to follow the language of advertising and consumer desire'.[48]

Theatrical and exciting it may have been, but the public policy arguments which justified subsidising a development like this relied upon its purported role as a spur to broad-based local economic regeneration. Bolton's council was quick to claim success in this regard, arguing in 1989 that the centre had 'proved to be just the tonic that the town needed', and that, 'Bolton is now a thriving and dynamic town centre, enticing more and more private investment, producing badly needed jobs, prestige and prosperity and confirming its position as the major sub-regional centre'.[49] The development certainly did provide some new jobs in the area (around 750–1,000 was the most optimistic estimate), and there were government-funded retail training courses at Bolton College to help locals take advantage of these opportunities. Given the tens of thousands of jobs that the town had lost, however, such numbers barely scratched the surface. In 1988, the year of the Market Place's grand gala opening, unemployment in Bolton stood at 13 per cent, with 13,404 people out of work.[50] By the later 1980s, too, questions were beginning to be asked about the quality of jobs being provided by the booming retail sector. Part of what made this flagship industry of the 1980s so 'flexible' and 'dynamic' was the low wages and insecure contracts it offered its overwhelmingly female and predominantly part-time

---

[48] Colin Amery, 'Bolton Has the Latest Look', *Financial Times*, 12 December 1988, 23; also 'Bolton's Shopping Sensation', press supplement, 23 March 1988. Amery's designation of Bolton as 'inner city' is odd, and reflects the imprecision and multiple meanings that the term carried.
[49] Bolton Environmental Education Project, *The Market Place* (1989), 35.
[50] Charles Henn, 'Town by Town', *The Guardian*, 7 June 1988, 31.

labour force.[51] Both council and developer were keen to stress that the new development, and the revamped Market Hall in particular, was also providing new opportunities for local traders. Yet, in a story which had been repeated all over the country since the 1940s, the principal effect of such redevelopment was to exorbitantly hike shop rental levels, putting many of the existing traders out of business altogether. In Bolton the shops that had been trading out of council-owned units around the perimeter of the old Market Hall were offered new leases at dramatically higher rents once the development was complete. Rents of £1,600 per annum were raised to £8,000, for example, while others who had been paying £4,000 were now asked for £27,000 each year.[52]

The market limped on for a few years before it was ejected altogether in 2007, when the Market Hall was overhauled again to allow the private shopping centre to expand into the Victorian structure in place of the town's market. A further £30 m was spent converting Bolton's Market Hall into an extension to the adjacent shopping centre, in a move which was opposed by a petition that gathered more than 80,000 signatures. Despite this storm of public protest, here it might be argued, lay the real regenerative potential of the Market Place development; not in propping up outmoded and inefficient small traders, or in providing local employment, but in encouraging an influx of glamorous new retail businesses to the town, and thereby attracting more customers from a wider catchment area to spend their money in Bolton. Yet even on these terms, the centre was not a success. A familiar pattern of regular, costly and wasteful rounds of refurbishment every few years spoke to the limitations of the new centre's pulling power. In 2014, the Market Place's operators went into administration, by which time the centre was 40 per cent empty. The shopping centre, one journalist noted, 'tries to hide its problems as best it can', but the question remained of who would want to take on 'a half-empty shopping centre in a depressed northern English town'. Bolton's director of development and regeneration explained that the council 'felt deeply frustrated' and 'could see [the facility] deteriorating both in terms of occupancy and reputation'.[53]

The failure of Bolton's Market Place was certainly not for want of promotional effort. As with so many other centres up and down the country, the new facility was relentlessly publicised and promoted

[51] Carl Gardner & Julie Sheppard, *Consuming Passion: The Rise of Retail Culture* (London: Unwin Hyman, 1989), 14.
[52] See Bolton Metropolitan Borough, *Report on the Market Place to the Land Subcommittee* (1988).
[53] Sarah O'Connor, 'Bolton Retail Deal a Sign of Life in Regional Property', *Financial Times*, 24 February 2014, 4.

through press coverage, participatory events and attractions, and the obligatory public ceremonials of grand gala openings, as well as the regular renovation and rebranding of the centre itself. The first opening ceremony for 'Bolton's shopping sensation' took the form of a full day of celebration on 24 March 1988, which drew upon a familiar promotional panoply of performances, competitions and celebrity appearances. The TV personality Stuart Hall presided over the day's events, and there were music performances, an all-day live radio broadcast and a contest to win a £100 'shopping spree', overseen by 'special Market Place Hostesses'. 'The day really will have fun for all the family', promotional press coverage explained, with the ceremonial opening itself performed by Bolton's mayor, who was pictured riding the escalators with his chains of office. 'Today Bolton sees another great step forward', the mayor explained, 'presenting itself in its true light as a progressive town always endeavouring to meet the needs of both its citizens and the many visitors'.[54] Such sentiments echoed directly the pronouncements which had been made repeatedly by civic leaders at such events across the post-war decades, including at the opening of Bolton's previous shopping sensation, the Arndale development, just seventeen years earlier.

Nine months after this initial ceremony, a more prestigious affair was overseen by the Queen when she visited Bolton to give 'the royal seal of approval' to the new development. 'Booming Bolton and its shopping masterpiece received high praise from the highest in the land', local publicity explained, when the Queen accompanied the Duke of Westminster on a tour of the Market Place (Figure 7.4). Back in 1948, the young Princess Elizabeth had followed the same script when she cut the ribbon at Coventry's new shopping centre, telling the gathered crowds that the shopping district was 'as fine as modern taste and craftsmanship can build it and worthy of the great city of which it will be the centre'. Coventry's reconstructed shopping centre was, the Princess said, a product of the 'spirit of enterprise ... a spirit alive to the great opportunities of our day'.[55] Forty years later in Bolton, the Queen spoke again of the 'spirit of enterprise' that had produced the Market Place shopping centre and was 'encouraged today to see ... that "Made in Bolton" is still a hallmark of excellence'. The monarch felt 'sure that these buildings will not only make an important contribution to the life of your community but will also give lasting pleasure

---

[54] These details in 'Bolton's Shopping Sensation', *Bolton Evening News* promotional supplement, 23 March 1988. In 2013 Stuart Hall was convicted of multiple sexual offences against minors relating to the period between 1967 and 1986, in the wake of the scandal surrounding the TV personality Jimmy Saville after his death in 2011.

[55] As captured in the British Pathé newsreel, 'Princess Elizabeth at Coventry' (1948). Available online.

Figure 7.4 Queen Elizabeth II tours Bolton's new market place shopping centre in a gala opening event of 1 December 1988, accompanied by the lead developer, Gerald Grosvenor, the sixth Duke of Westminster. Source: Getty Images.

because of the quality of their design'.[56] In the end, though, Bolton's 1980s overhaul merely stood as yet another symbol of the paucity of social and cultural provision which such projects offered, along with their utter inadequacy as a means of bolstering ailing local economies and improving the material welfare of some of the country's most deprived populations.

Conclusion

The closing decades of the twentieth century saw some significant new developments in the management of cities and the consumer economy. A more permissive approach to major out-of-town developments was perhaps the most important of these; this created new ex-urban geographies of shopping, arranged around the national motorway network and dominated by behemothic new poles of consumer attraction serving

---

[56] 'Market Place First Anniversary', *Bolton Evening News* promotional supplement, 22 March 1989. Available at Bolton Local History Centre.

entire regions of the country. This was where the logics of rationalisation and concentration which had served the organised sections of the retail trade so well led to, as the scale of the retail economy outgrew the geographies and infrastructural capacities of traditional urban centres. The new regional centres offered retail managers the opportunity to apply their sales-maximising techniques of environmental and experiential management to an unprecedented degree, and the commercial potential of these facilities was such that they saw Britain's shopping geography subsumed into an incomprehensibly valuable market for global real estate investment. Also new in the 1980s was the rise of an urban policy agenda of 'regeneration', which focused heavily upon promoting physical redevelopment and encouraging private sector investment in less favoured locales. In comparison with earlier waves of 'urban renewal', 'regeneration' was steered more closely from the centre through development agencies and centrally controlled funding streams with which cash-strapped and brow-beaten local authorities were obliged to cooperate. Both of these developments – the rise of the regeneration agenda and the newly permissive approach to out-of-town retail developments – have been widely interpreted as emblems of the transformed politics of the Thatcherite age, in which private sector initiative, market sovereignty and 'enterprise culture' were to be prioritised above all else. This certainly accords with much of the rhetorical framing of these developments in urban policy and planning, but we should be careful not to overstate the novelty of these initiatives, or to understate the continued role for public governance in shaping the geographies of consumption and the political economy of urban redevelopment.

Alongside these changes there were also powerful strands of continuity in the planning, management and redevelopment of Britain's towns and cities which stretched right back to the early post-war period. There was nothing novel or distinctly Thatcherite about 'partnering' with the private development industry, which had been a hallmark of British urbanism since the 1940s. Nor was the overwhelming focus upon promoting local economic growth via new retail and property investment a new departure; as the case of Bolton clearly illustrates, many local authorities had been pursuing such aims through the planning system for decades, particularly where they were over-reliant on declining industries. It was also particularly notable how far post-war reconstruction, 1960s urban renewal and late-century urban regeneration all placed high-end shopping development at the centre of their developmental strategies. In the 1980s, personal consumption and 'retail culture' certainly took on a new political salience, as a symbol of the aspirational agendas of the age, but shopping, and the economic activity and commercial cultural forms it went along with, had been at the heart of public and private visions for urban improvement right across the second half of the twentieth century. The differences in the late century were more ones of degree rather than kind, as the consumer domain loomed ever larger in the cultural life of the nation and the overall structure of the economy. By 1998, consumer spending accounted for 60 per cent of Britain's GDP and, for councils looking to promote local economic growth, attracting such expenditure was the most obvious route to take.[57] And yet, what had also been clear right across the period was how fragile and finite consumer-driven prosperity was – always susceptible to economic downturns, and highly uneven in both its geographic distribution and its social reach. Within Britain's competitive system of local planning and redevelopment, enticing expensive retail development was consistently viewed as both a local developmental strategy and, more curiously, as a form of social policy, which could improve the lot of local populations. This was always highly questionable, and late-century regeneration efforts in places like Bolton and Glasgow were just as ineffective as earlier post-war projects in using subsidised shopping developments to promote broad-based local prosperity and socio-economic renewal.

[57] 'Singing in the Rain', *The Economist*, 7 November 1998, 33.

Conclusion

At the beginning of the twenty-first century, the position of the shopping city model at the heart of UK urban policy and planning seemed fully assured. The New Labour government elected in 1997 recast the urban regeneration agenda under a new rubric of 'urban renaissance', with a greater emphasis upon social provision and community initiatives, but the prevailing economic and developmental model for urban centres remained shopping-centred and property-led.[1] Indeed, the impetus provided by the renaissance agenda combined with a wider climate of economic optimism and expansion around the turn of the century to see a marked intensification of retail development activity in many cities. In Birmingham, for example, the Bull Ring shopping centre was levelled and rebuilt at a cost of £500 m, reopening in 2003 with a 'distinctive curved exterior' and a cladding of striking metallic discs that made it 'Birmingham's most photographed building'. The city council, meanwhile, purchased the adjacent Pallasades shopping centre located above Birmingham's New Street Station. This ensemble was redeveloped to create the new Grand Central shopping centre, which sold for £335 m in 2015. Once these two complexes were brought under single ownership, they made up the largest city-centre shopping centre in the country. Birmingham, it was reported, 'has recreated itself as a one-stop shop for fashionistas' and the ambition for the city council was 'for Birmingham to overtake Leeds and Glasgow as the leading shopping destination outside London'.[2] Or in the city of Liverpool, where the St. John's Precinct was being redeveloped in 2007 by one of the same companies involved in the Bull Ring's recreation. Indeed, the very same architectural practice was retained to fit a similarly dazzling exterior onto the 1960s complex 'to provide a modern shopping environment for

---

[1] Rob Imrie & Mike Raco (eds.), *Urban Renaissance? New Labour, Community and Urban Policy* (Bristol: The Policy Press, 2003).

[2] These details in: Liam Kennedy (ed.), *Remaking Birmingham: the Visual Culture of Urban Regeneration* (London: Routledge, 2004); John Murray Brown, 'Regeneration and Quality Woo Savvy Shoppers to Birmingham', *The Financial Times*, 28 September 2015.

Liverpool City Centre'.[3] Elsewhere in the city, the mammoth 'Liverpool ONE' project saw an entire district of forty-two acres remade by the Grosvenor Group (still the development vehicle for the Duke of Westminster's property interests) as the largest open-air shopping centre in the country. This project opened in 2008 at an overall cost approaching £1 bn and formed a much-vaunted centrepiece of 'the renaissance of Liverpool'; the city now touted its success as 'one of the fastest growing economies in Europe' with its rebirth 'clearly visible from the number of new landmark developments taking place'.[4]

Liverpool ONE in particular became a touchstone for much public criticism lamenting the privatisation and 'enclosure' of such a large portion of the city.[5] Indeed, both within the academy and within wider public commentary, the early years of the twenty-first century were a moment of deep intellectual concern about the private sector-dominated, retail-led remaking of cities, and much theorising of the entrepreneurial, neoliberal modes of urban governance that facilitated this.[6] It was also a high moment for critical commentaries on 'the consumer society and the postmodern city', as ideas from French and US scholarship came to occupy an increasingly familiar place within critiques of the post-industrial landscapes of 'pleasure and placelessness' in urban Britain.[7] Such criticisms became familiar enough to enter into mainstream commentaries and popular polemics on British urbanism, architecture and society.[8] Although there were ever more voices being raised ever more publicly in opposition to the shopping city and the political and economic forms that undergirded it, rather less attention was devoted to just how shaky the entire edifice really was. And yet, a decade later, this urban developmental model is in a state of crisis and collapse.

---

[3] Land Securities, 'The Vision for St. Johns', development prospectus (2007), available at Liverpool City Archives.

[4] 'Doing Business in Liverpool and the North West', *The Financial Times*, 25 October 2007, 1.

[5] See, for example, Anna Minton, *Ground Control: Fear and Happiness in the Twenty-First-Century City* (London: Penguin, 2009); Paul Kingsnorth, 'Cities for Sale', *The Guardian*, 29 March 2008.

[6] For example, Neil Brenner & Nik Theodore (eds.), *Spaces of Neoliberalism: Urban Restructuring in North America and Western Europe* (Oxford: Blackwell, 2002); Jamie Peck and Kevin Ward (eds.), *City of Revolution: Restructuring Manchester* (Manchester: Manchester University Press, 2002); Helga Leitner, Jamie Peck & Eric S. Sheppard (eds.), *Contesting Neoliberalism: Urban Frontiers* (London: The Guilford Press, 2007); David Harvey, *A Brief History of Neoliberalism* (Oxford: Oxford University Press, 2007).

[7] For example, Hannigan, *Fantasy City*; Clarke, *The Consumer Society and the Postmodern City*; Miles, *Spaces for Consumption*.

[8] For example, Owen Hatherley, *A Guide to the New Ruins of Great Britain* (London: Verso, 2010).

The most immediate cause of this collapse is the secular decline of town centre retailing whose share of total retail expenditure has declined steadily in recent decades, from 49.4 per cent in 2000 to 36.6 per cent in 2018. This long-term trend is tied to the rise of large-scale out-of-town shopping from the 1980s, but in recent years has been more directly attributable to the dramatic increase in the volume of online sales. The United Kingdom does more shopping online (as a percentage of total sales) than any other EU country, and more too than the United States, and the proportion is rising fast. In 2008 internet sales accounted for 5 per cent of the total; by 2019 internet sales accounted for 19 per cent of the total. These trends have had a marked effect on the commercial performance of town centre retailing. It is estimated that footfall in town centres has fallen by 17.4 per cent between 2009 and 2017. The number of physical stores in the country as a whole has also declined substantially, falling more than 15 per cent in the five years from 2012 to 2017. Store closures have become a widely reported issue as numerous well-known retail chains have gone into administration. In 2018, twenty-eight retail chains with multiple stores ceased trading, while more than 14,500 stores closed with the loss of more than 117,000 jobs. The British Retail Consortium declared 2019 to be the worst year on record for the sector with unprecedented levels of store closures, job losses and empty shops. The rate of vacant shops nationally is currently 1 in 10, but in many towns the figure is much higher, with around 20–30 per cent of shops standing empty. The Centre for Retail Research has also declared the sector to be 'in crisis', and attributed this to 'high costs, low profitability, and losing sales to online shopping'.[9] In 2020 the ongoing collapse of town centre retailing was deleteriously accelerated by the economic disruption and forced closures of the Coronavirus pandemic. Even the most successful retail firms – such as the high street leader John Lewis – now wavered. The John Lewis group recorded a £517 m loss for 2020 and is closing a third of its fifty stores nationwide; these stores were the most successful flagship attractions for many shopping centres and desperately courted by local authorities as linchpins of urban retail economies.

This crisis and contraction in the retail sector poses a fundamental challenge to towns and cities all over the country precisely because the prosperity and vitality of central areas has come to rely so heavily upon the

[9] These details in: House of Commons Library Briefing Paper SN06186, *Retail Sector in the UK* (2018); Institute of Place Management, *High Street 2030: Achieving Change* (2018); Daniel Thomas, 'Intu Faces Tough Task to Emerge in Better Shape for Investors', *The Financial Times*, 12 August 2019; Alistair Kefford, 'The Death of the High Street', *History & Policy* (2020), available online. See also British Retail Consortium [brc.org.uk] and Centre for Retail Research [retailresearch.org].

local retail economy. As has been seen, for many smaller urban centres the problems with this model had been building steadily across the later decades of the twentieth century, as larger cities and out-of-town shopping centres proved more attractive destinations for finite regional expenditures. Now though, the scale of the retail crisis nationwide is threatening the economic base of many major cities, as well as casting the out-of-town malls into a state of commercial free fall. In June 2020, 'Intu' – the shopping centre hegemon whose rise to dominance was detailed in Chapter 7 – went into administration. The firm is reportedly carrying £5 bn of net debt, as the value of its many mall complexes across the country tumbles. In a further sign of the entanglement of Britain's urban retail property within global systems of finance and investment, Intu's anxious creditors include the Bank of America, Barclays, Credit Suisse, HSBC, Lloyds, Natwest and UBS, as well as foreign, and state-linked, pension funds such as the Canada Pension Plan Investment Board, a Canadian Crown Corporation and one of the world's biggest private equity investors.[10] Recent analysis by the *Estates Gazette* suggests that overseas investors own almost a fifth of UK shops.[11] The major property groups like Intu and Hammerson which built, bought and operated Britain's outsize shopping centres are seeing the value of these facilities collapse, along with their share prices, and are struggling to secure the new borrowing they will need to stay afloat. Failing shopping centres are being demolished altogether in some places, as in Stretford and Nottingham, with owners and local authorities seeking investment to redevelop sites for alternative, non-retail purposes. And, just as in the post-war decades, many local authorities feel themselves obliged to step in and subsidise redevelopment in what are often key town centre locations and issues of 'confidence' for local economies; by 2020 it was estimated that councils had spent £1 bn in the previous four years buying up sites in shopping centres. At the national level, the Ministry of Housing, Communities and Local Government is distributing a £1 bn 'Future High Streets Fund' (part of an even larger £3.6 bn Towns Fund) to local authorities with the aim, again, of shoring up town centre economies with new public investment.

Given this dramatic contemporary context, it is a particularly opportune moment to consider the historical trajectory – the life and death – of the shopping city, and to ask how and why this model of organising urban

---

[10] Kate Burgess, 'Why a Midsummer Nightmare Ending Looms for Intu', *The Financial Times*, 23 June 2020; George Hammond, 'UK Shopping Centre Owner Intu Files for Administration', *The Financial Times*, 26 June 2020.

[11] Neil Lee & Polly Swan, *A High Street Revolution: How Private Developers can Support the Community Takeover of our Town Centres* (Power to Change, 2021).

space, society and economies came to be so comprehensively installed as the linchpin of British urban policy and development. Amidst all the force and flair of scholarly critiques of unfettered consumer capitalism, neoliberalisation or the cultural logics of postmodernity, it should be remembered how far the rise to dominance of the shopping-centred urban economic model was a product of the public planning system – its developmental aims and business-friendly operation – across the second half of the twentieth century. Beginning in the 1940s, the public planning apparatus placed supreme emphasis upon promoting private sector growth in the nation's urban centres and turned repeatedly to the most profitable and well-organised sections of the retail trade to furnish this. Even in the mid-century moment of reconstruction, British planners and officials saw high-value shopping as the favoured route towards future growth and prosperity and elevated leading retail chains and commercial property developers to the status of privileged partners in the remaking of urban Britain. The political economy of planning was shaped by these economistic, growth-ist imperatives, in which urban land – like any other national asset – should be put to work in the most productive and profitable manner.

Equally critical, though, both to planning's political complexion and to its concrete impacts upon Britain's towns and cities, was a continuous and unresolved tension around the appropriate role of the state in managing society, territory and the economy. Although the post-war era saw significant extensions of the remit of public government, the arena of planning remained marked by inconstancy and continued wrangles over the politics and purpose of new state powers. Certainly, many of planning's most passionate advocates entertained distinctly *dirigiste* ambitions and dreamed of wielding powerful new instruments of state to remould urban space and society according to their own visions of the public good. Yet this was not the flavour of British planning in practice, which was much more ambivalent and constrained. The British planning and redevelopment regime remained firmly coloured by a continuing faith in private enterprise, commercial freedoms and market forces, and by a corresponding reliance upon private interests and profit-driven actors to deliver urban transformation. Crucially, the vital question of 'betterment' – of who would collect the massive financial gains created by urban redevelopment – was never resolved in favour of the state; the real beneficiaries became Britain's booming property sector, along with the national and, increasingly, international financial systems in which it was rapidly absorbed.

Indeed, in the arena of retail and redevelopment, what is so striking about the post-war planning system is the way in which it endorsed and assisted commercially defined aims and projects by harnessing new state powers to favoured private interests. The retail sector itself was transformed and restructured through such measures, as public planning powers worked to reinforce the dominance of the most organised and profitable sections of the trade, while accelerating the demise of small and independent retailers. The remarkable growth in the scale and profitability of the property development sector, too, was inextricable from the working of the new planning system, as the public sector delivered unprecedented commercial opportunities to private property interests. The impact of such practices upon urban Britain was dramatic, as central areas were overhauled and reconfigured around extravagant and expensive new shopping facilities. Economically and experientially, such projects were transformative; they recast the commercial possibilities and economic geography of urban centres while also reshaping the basic infrastructures and experience of everyday urban life. Many scholars to date have emphasised either the democratic intent or the demotic flavour of post-war urban renewal, positioning such endeavours as part of the wider story of social democratic, welfare state Britain. While certainly not disavowing such influences and impulses, the history of urban transformation presented here draws out some rather different dynamics. The British experience of planning for affluence underlines forcefully how central new forms of commercial consumption became to the polity and its public culture in the second half of the twentieth century and also – despite the best endeavours of many reformist technocrats – how difficult it was in practice to marry the cultures and values of mass affluence with more welfarist, civic and collective visions of social development.

Paying close attention to the operation and impacts of planning and urban renewal in this era also forces us to confront some of the many constraints and compromises that characterised social democracy in Britain, and which operated both within and beyond the apparatus of public government. Responsibility for the management of cities and society was shared between the formal administrative apparatus of the state and a range of influential commercial forces and actors, many of whom fostered their own visions of the future and agendas for change. Inconsistency and ideological uncertainty from within the state produced an overall political economy of planning which relied heavily upon these commercial forces and actors, and allowed them to determine the physical forms and developmental trajectories that reconstruction, renewal and regeneration produced. Such politics and practices produced urban centres that were brash, gaudy and expensive, geared excessively around a particular vision of higher-end retailing and structured according to the commercial and financial logics of retail property investment. Even as such projects were taking shape, the demand and desire for them from the general public was questionable and unproven. Indeed, there were many groups and individuals in post-war society who remained actively and implacably opposed to this deeply commercial model of urban renewal.

It was also clearly the case that this competitive, commercially led system produced definite tendencies towards oversupply of expensive retail space and over-competition between urban centres. The dangers inherent in this were exposed whenever consumer spending flagged nationally, casting local retail economies in doubt, or when new developments struggled to live up to expectations or weather the storms of new poles of competition. The now pressing problems of 'dying' towns and high streets did not begin with the rise of online retailing in the twenty-first century, but were clearly evident in many locales as early as the 1970s. And the persistent efforts to deploy commercial redevelopment as an instrument of local economic regeneration were also always questionable. The British state, at both the local and the national level, supported and subsidised commercial retail development in struggling urban centres all over the country since the mid-twentieth century. At times these projects delivered modest local employment gains, or ground rents that bolstered local authority finances, but overall their value as drivers of local economic regeneration was decidedly limited, and certainly insufficient to mitigate the deep structural challenges facing many cities and regions across the second half of the twentieth century. The speed and scale of the current collapse of town centre economies is yet another indication of how fragile and uncertain a basis for local economies the shopping city model of urban development always was. Attending to these problematic dynamics within the public–private trajectory of urban transformation across the second half of the twentieth century can thus offer lessons for how we might meet the current crisis (and where we might avoid pouring more public funds into failing economic models). It should also bring alternatives more clearly into view. Just as many voices were raised against these developmental models in the post-war city, so today critiques of the physical, political and economic landscape of Britain's urban centres abound. Organising our cities around ever-expanding volumes of commercial retailing is now incontrovertibly unviable; it has long been dubious as a means of revitalising local economies and supporting local populations, and certainly damaging from an environmental perspective. Recovering the uncertainties and contested politics of such patterns of urban development serves as a useful reminder of their contingency and negotiability, at a moment when alternative visions of 'the urban' – of public space, public culture and economic life – seem to be sorely needed.

List of Archives and Abbreviations

TNA: The National Archives, Kew, UK Government Collections.
HLG: Housing and Local Government Collection, TNA.
RIBA: Royal Institute of British Architects, London, Architectural Library.
GMCRO: Greater Manchester County Record Office, Manchester Central Library, City Archive.
BLHC: Bolton Local History Centre, Bolton Library, Local Archive.
NMM: National Maritime Museum, Greenwich, P&O Business Archive.
WYAS: West Yorkshire Archive Service, Leeds, City Archive.
NRO: Nottinghamshire Archives, Nottingham, City Archive.
LRO: Liverpool Record Office, Liverpool, City Archive.
TWA: Tyne & Wear Archives, Newcastle, City Archive.
GCA: Glasgow City Archives, Glasgow.

Bibliography

Published Primary Sources

Association of Planning and Regional Reconstruction. *Maps for the National Plan: A Background to the Barlow Report, the Scott Report, the Beveridge Report* (London: Lund Humphries, 1945).

Association of Planning and Regional Reconstruction. *Town and Country Planning Textbook: An Indispensable Book for Town Planners, Architects, and Students* (London: The Architectural Press, 1950).

Beddington, Nadine. 'Shopping Environment: Efficiency and Fun', *Official Architecture and Planning* 33:1 (1970), 41–44.

Beddington, Nadine. *Design for Shopping Centres* (London: Butterworth, 1982).

Berbiers, John L. 'Canterbury: Reconstruction in the Central Area', *Journal of the Town Planning Institute* 47:2 (1961), 36–39.

Berbiers, John L., Gummer, C. W., Baker, G. & Grant, J. L. 'New Shopping Centre for Longmarket, Canterbury', *Official Architecture and Planning* 21:6 (1958), 266–267.

Bowley, A. S. 'The Police and the Planners', *The Police Journal* 46 (1973), 308–314.

Burns, Wilfred. *British Shopping Centres: New Trends in Layout and Distribution* (London: Leonard Hill, 1959).

Burns, Wilfred. *New Towns for Old: The Technique of Urban Renewal* (London: Leonard Hill, 1963).

Burns, Wilfred. *Newcastle: A Study in Replanning at Newcastle upon Tyne* (London: Leonard Hill, 1967).

Clark, Sergeant J. 'Security and the Development of a Town Centre', *The Police Journal* 41 (1968), 23–26.

Crosland, Anthony. *The Future of Socialism* (London: Jonathan Cape, 1956).

Crossman, Richard. *Labour in the Affluent Society* (London: The Fabian Society, 1960).

Dannatt, Trevor. *Modern Architecture in Britain: Selected Examples of Recent Building* (London: Batsford, 1959).

Darley, Gillian & Saunders, Matthew. 'A SAVE Report: Conservation and Jobs', *Built Environment Quarterly* 2:3 (1976), 211–226.

Darlow, Clive. *Enclosed Shopping Centres* (London: Architectural Press, 1972).

Davidson, A. W. & Leonard, J. E. (eds.). *The Property Development Process* (Centre for Advanced Land Use Studies, 1976).

Davies, Jon Gower. *The Evangelistic Bureaucrat: A Study of a Planning Exercise in Newcastle upon Tyne* (London: Tavistock, 1972).

Davies, R. L. 'Store Location and Store Assessment Research: The Integration of Some New and Traditional Techniques', *Transactions of the Institute of British Geographers* 2:2 (1977), 141–157.

Davies, Ross & Howard, Elizabeth. 'Issues in Retail Planning within the United Kingdom', *Built Environment* 14:1 (1988), 7–21.

Debord, Guy. *Society of the Spectacle* (London: Rebel Press, 2002). Ken Knabb, Trans. Original publication 1967.

Finer, Herman. *Municipal Trading: A Study in Public Administration* (London: George Allen & Unwin, 1941).

Galbraith, John Kenneth. *The Affluent Society* (London: Hamish Hamilton, 1958).

Galbraith, John Kenneth. *The New Industrial State* (Harmondsworth: Penguin, 1975).

Gibbon, Sir Gwilym. *Problems of Town and Country Planning* (London: George Allen & Unwin, 1937).

Gibson, B. H. 'Policing New Towns', *The Police Journal* 44 (1971), 340–345.

Gosling, David & Maitland, Barry. *Design and Planning of Retail Systems* (London: Architectural Press, 1976).

Green, F. H. W. 'Motor-bus Centres in South-West England Considered in Relation to Population and Shopping Facilities', *Transactions and Papers* 14 (1948), 59–68.

Green, Patricia M. 'Survey of a Local Shopping Centre: Planning for the Customer', *Official Architecture and Planning* 30:8 (1967), 1101–1104.

Gregg, Pauline. *The Welfare State: An Economic and Social History of Great Britain from 1945 to the Present Day* (London: Harrap, c. 1968 [undated]).

Haar, Charles M. 'Planning Law: Public v. Private Interest in the Land and the 1959 Act', in F. J. McCulloch et al. (eds.), *Land Use in an Urban Environment: A General View of Town and Country Planning* (Liverpool: Liverpool University Press, 1961), 95–124.

Hall, Margaret. *Distributive Trading: An Economic Analysis* (London: William Brendon and Son). Undated, c. 1948.

Hart, T. *The Comprehensive Development Area: A Study of the Legal and Administrative Problems of Comprehensive Land Development with Special Reference to Glasgow* (Edinburgh: Oliver & Boyd, 1968).

Healey & Baker. *Retail Report 1985* (Oxford: Nuffield Press, 1985).

Hornbeck, James S. *Stores and Shopping Centres* (London: McGraw-Hill, 1962).

Jefferys, James B. *The Distribution of Consumer Goods* (Cambridge: Cambridge University Press, 1950).

Johnson-Marshall, Percy. 'Coventry: Test-Case of Planning', *The Listener*, 17 April 1958, 654.

Jones, Colin S. *Regional Shopping Centres: Their Location, Planning and Design* (London: Business Books, 1969).

Lanchester, Henry Vaughan. *The Art of Town Planning* (London: Chapman and Hall, 1932).

Lavery, Patrick. 'The Demand for Recreation: A Review of Studies', *Town Planning Review* 46:2 (1975), 185–200.

Leeds City Council, Ministry of Transport & Ministry of Housing and Local Government. *Planning and Transport: the Leeds Approach* (London: HMSO, 1969).

Levy, Herman. *The Shops of Britain: A Study of Retail Distribution* (London: Kegan Paul, Trench, Trubner, 1947).

Lichfield, Nathaniel. 'The Evaluation of Capital Investment Projects in Town Centre Redevelopment', *Public Administration* 45:2 (1967), 129–148.

Liverpool City Centre Planning Group. *Liverpool City Centre Plan* (Liverpool, 1965).

MacFadyen, E. 'Retailers at the Crossroads', *Building with Steel* 10 (May, 1972).

Macmillan, Harold. *The Middle Way: A Study of the Problem of Economic and Social Progress in a Free and Democratic Society* (London: Macmillan, 1938).

Marcuse, Herbert. *One Dimensional Man: Studies in the Ideology of Advanced Industrial Society* (London: Routledge & Kegan Paul, 1964).

Maxwell, R. I. 'Planning for Increasing Leisure: Problems of Town and Country', *Royal Society of Health Journal* 82 (1962), 319–323.

Ministry of Housing and Local Government & Ministry of Transport. *Town Centres: Approach to Renewal* (London: HMSO, 1962).

Ministry of Town and Country Planning. *The Redevelopment of Central Areas* (London: HMSO, 1947).

Multiple Shops Federation. *The Planning of Shopping Centres* (London: Fosh & Cross, 1963).

Myles Wright, H. 'The First Ten Years: Post-war Planning and Development in England', *Town Planning Review* 26:2 (1955), 73–91.

National Economic Development Council. *The Growth of the Economy* (London: HMSO, 1964).

Neal, Lawrence. *Retailing and the Public* (George Allen & Unwin, 1933).

Nicholas, Rowland. *City of Manchester Plan* (London: Jarrold & Sons, 1945).

Northen, R. I. & Haskoll, Michael. *Shopping Centres: A Developer's Guide to Planning and Design* (Reading: Centre for Advanced Land Use Studies, 1977).

Northen, R. I. *Shopping Centre Development* (Reading: Centre for Advanced Land Use Studies, 1984).

Packard, Vance. *The Hidden Persuaders* (Harmondsworth: Penguin, 1960).

Parker, H. R. 'Suburban Shopping Facilities in Liverpool', *The Town Planning Review* 33:3 (1962), 197–223.

Parry Lewis, J. & Traill, A. L. 'The Assessment of Shopping Potential and the Demand for Shops', *Town Planning Review* 38:4 (1968), 317–326.

Paton Watson, J. & Abercrombie, Patrick. *A Plan for Plymouth* (Plymouth: Underhill, 1943).

Pickering, J. F. *Resale Price Maintenance in Practice* (London: George Allen & Unwin, 1966).

Pigg, D. R. 'Securing the Future of Town Centres', *Municipal Engineer* 93:4 (1992), 193–198.

Reilly, Charles & Aslan, N. J. *Outline Plan for the County Borough of Birkenhead* (Birkenhead, 1947).

Roskill, O. W. 'The Detailed Planning of Shopping Centres', *Official Architecture and Planning* 21:9 (1958), 414–416.

Royal Commission on the Distribution of the Industrial Population. *Report* (London: HMSO, 1940).

Scott, N. Keith. *Shopping Centre Design* (London: Van Nostrand Reinhold, 1989).

Seymour Harris, J. 'The Design of Shopping Centres', *Official Architecture and Planning* 24:6 (1961), 271–274.

Shankland, Graeme. 'Dead Centre – The Crisis of Planning and the Future of Our Cities', *Official Architecture and Planning* 20:3 (1957), 137–140.

Sharp, Evelyn. 'Town and Country Planning', *Public Administration* 26:1 (1948), 19–30.

Sheffield Town Planning Committee. *Sheffield Replanned* (Sheffield, 1945).

Shepherd, P. M. & Thorpe, D. *Urban Redevelopment and Changes in Retail Structure 1961–1971* (Manchester: Retail Outlets Research Unit, 1977).

Sigsworth E. M. & Wilkinson, R. K. 'Rebuilding or Renovation?', *Urban Studies* 4:2 (1967), 109–121.

Smailes, Arthur E. 'The Urban Hierarchy in England and Wales', *Geography* 29:2 (1944), 41–51.

Smailes, Arthur E. 'The Analysis and Delimitation of Urban Fields', *Geography* 32:4 (1947), 151–161.

Smailes, Arthur E & Hartley, G. 'Shopping Centres in the Greater London Area', *Transactions and Papers* 29 (1961), 201–213.

Smith, Geoffrey C. 'The Spatial Information Fields of Urban Consumers', *Transactions of the Institute of British Geographers* 1:2 (1976), 175–189.

Smith, Henry. *Retail Distribution: A Critical Analysis* (London: Oxford University Press, 1948).

Taylor, Tony. 'The British Council of Shopping Centres', *Planning Practice and Research* 8:3 (1993), 43–44.

Thomas, M. E. & Waide, W. L. 'Shopping Centres and Community Investment', *Official Architecture and Planning* 30:8 (1967), 1094–1100.

Titmuss, Richard M. *Essays on 'The Welfare State'* (London: Unwin University Books, 1963).

Tripp, H. Alker. *Town Planning and Road Traffic* (London: Edward Arnold, 1942).

Wardley, S. G. 'Partnership', in The Property Council, *The Property Developer* (London: 1964), 37–39.

Warnaby, Gary. 'Marketing UK Cities as Shopping Destinations: Problems and Prospects', *Journal of Retailing and Consumer Services* 5:1 (1998), 55–58.

Watkins, Millicent. 'Buildings in the Town Centre', *Town Planning Review* 25:2 (1954), 85–94.

Wilkinson R. & Sigsworth, E. M. 'A Survey of Slum Clearance Areas in Leeds', *Bulletin of Economic Research* 15:1 (1963), 25–51.

Wilson, L. Hugh. 'Civic Design and the Shopping Centre', *Official Architecture and Planning* 21:6 (1958), 271–274.

Secondary Literature

Abrams, Lynn, Kearns, Ade, Hazley, Barry & Wright, Valerie. *Glasgow: High-Rise Homes, Estates and Communities in the Post-War Period* (London: Routledge, 2020).

Allan, Charles M. 'The Genesis of British Urban Redevelopment with Special Reference to Glasgow', *Economic History Review* 18:3 (1965), 598–613.

Ambrose, Peter. *Whatever Happened to Planning?* (London: Methuen, 1986).

Ambrose, Peter & Colenutt, Bob. *The Property Machine* (Harmondsworth: Penguin, 1975).

Amin, Ash. 'Collective Culture and Urban Public Space', *City* 12:1 (2008), 5–24.

Andrews, Aaron. 'Multiple Deprivation, the Inner City, and the Fracturing of the Welfare State: Glasgow, c. 1968–78', *Twentieth Century British History* 29:4 (2018), 605–624.

Andrews, Aaron. 'Dereliction, Decay and the Problem of De-industrialization in Britain, c. 1968–1977', *Urban History* 47:2 (2020), 236–256.

Augé, Marc. *Non-Places: Introduction to an Anthropology of Supermodernity* (London: Verso, 2008) [original French ed., 1992].

Avermaete, Tom. 'A Thousand Youth Clubs: Architecture, Mass Leisure and the Rejuvenation of Post-War France', *Journal of Architecture* 18:5 (2013), 632–646.

Bailey, Peter. '"A Mingled Mass of Perfectly Legitimate Pleasures": The Victorian Middle Class and the Problem of Leisure', *Victorian Studies* 21:1 (1977), 7–28.

Bailkin, Jordanna. *The Afterlife of Empire* (Berkeley: University of California Press, 2012).

Baker, Alan & Billinge, Mark (eds.). *Geographies of England: The North-South Divide, Material and Imagined* (Cambridge: Cambridge University Press, 2004).

Baudrillard, Jean. *Simulacra and Simulation* (Ann Arbor: University of Michigan Press, 1994) [original French ed., 1981].

Beaumont, Caitríona. *Housewives and Citizens: Domesticity and the Women's Movement in England, 1928–64* (Manchester: Manchester University Press, 2013).

Benson, John. *The Rise of Consumer Society in Britain, 1880–1980* (London: Longman, 1994).

Bingham, Adrian. *Gender, Modernity, and the Popular Press in Inter-War Britain* (Oxford: Oxford University Press, 2004).

Black, Lawrence. '"Sheep May Safely Gaze": Socialists, Television and the People in Britain, 1949–64', in Lawrence Black (ed.), *Consensus or Coercion? The State, the People and Social Cohesion in Post-War Britain* (Cheltenham: New Clarion, 2001), 28–48.

Black, Lawrence. *The Political Culture of the Left in Affluent Britain, 1951–64: Old Labour, New Britain?* (Basingstoke: Palgrave Macmillan, 2003).

Black, Lawrence. *Redefining British Politics: Culture, Consumerism and Participation, 1954–70* (Basingstoke: Palgrave Macmillan, 2010).

Black, Lawrence & Pemberton, Hugh (eds.). *An Affluent Society? Britain's Post-War 'Golden Age' Revisited* (Aldershot: Ashgate, 2004).

Black, Lawrence, Pemberton, Hugh & Thane, Pat (eds.). *Reassessing 1970s Britain* (Manchester: Manchester University Press, 2013).

Boddy, Martin. *The Building Societies* (London: Macmillan, 1980).

Boddy, Martin. 'The Property Sector in Late-Capitalism: The Case of Britain', in Michael Dear & Allen J. Scott (eds.), *Urbanization and Urban Planning in Capitalist Society* (London: Routledge, 1981), 267–286.

Bogdanor, Vernon & Skidelsky, Robert (eds.). *The Age of Affluence 1951–1964* (London: Macmillan, 1970).

Borsay, Peter. *The English Urban Renaissance: Culture and Society in the Provincial Town 1660–1770* (Oxford: Clarendon Press, 1989).

Boughton, John. *Municipal Dreams: The Rise and Fall of Council Housing* (London: Verso, 2018).

Bowden, Sue & Offer, Avner. 'Household Appliances and the Use of Time: The United States and Britain since the 1920s', *Economic History Review* 47:4 (1994), 725–748.

Brenner, Neil, Marcuse, Peter & Mayer, Margit (eds.). *Cities for People Not for Profit: Critical Urban Theory and the Right to the City* (London: Routledge, 2012).

Brenner, Neil & Theodore, Nik (eds.). *Spaces of Neoliberalism: Urban Restructuring in North America and Western Europe* (Oxford: Blackwell, 2002).

Brückweh, Kerstin (ed.). *The Voice of the Citizen Consumer: A History of Market Research, Consumer Movements, and the Political Public Sphere* (Oxford: Oxford University Press, 2011).

Bullock, Nicholas. *Building the Post-War World: Modern Architecture and Reconstruction in Britain* (London: Routledge, 2002).

Burnett, John. *A Social History of Housing, 1815–1985* (London: Methuen, 1986).

Calder, Barnabus. *Raw Concrete: The Beauty of Brutalism* (London: William Heinemann, 2016).

Chapman, Tony & Hockey, Jenny (eds.). *Ideal Homes? Social Change and Domestic Life* (London: Routledge, 2002).

Cherry, Gordon E. *The Evolution of British Town Planning* (Leighton Buzzard: Leonard Hill, 1974).

Cherry, Gordon, 'George Pepler 1882–1959', in Gordon Cherry (ed.), *Pioneers in British Planning* (London: The Architectural Press, 1981), 131–149.

Cherry, Gordon E. *Town Planning in Britain since 1900: The Rise and Fall of the Planning Ideal* (Oxford: Blackwell, 1996).

Child, Phil. 'Landlordism, Rent Regulation and the Labour Party in Mid-Twentieth Century Britain, 1950–64', *Twentieth Century British History* 29:1 (2018), 79–103.

Christopher, Brett. *The New Enclosure: The Appropriation of Public Land in Neoliberal Britain* (London: Verso, 2019).

Clapson, Mark. *Invincible Green Suburbs, Brave New Towns: Social Change and Urban Dispersal in Post-War England* (Manchester: Manchester University Press, 1998).

Clapson, Mark & Larkham, Peter J. (eds.). *The Blitz and Its Legacy: Wartime Destruction to Post-War Reconstruction* (Farnham: Ashgate, 2013).

Clarke, David B. *The Consumer Society and the Postmodern City* (London: Routledge, 2003).

Coad, Roy. *Laing: The Biography of Sir John W. Laing, CBE, 1879–1978* (London: Hodder & Stoughton, 1979).

Cochrane, Alan. *Understanding Urban Policy* (Oxford: Blackwell, 2007).

Cohen, Lizabeth. *A Consumers' Republic: The Politics of Mass Consumption in Postwar America* (New York: Knopf, 2004).

Cowman, Krista. 'Play Streets: Women, Children and the Problem of Urban Traffic, 1930–1970', *Social History* 42:2 (2017), 233–256.

Crafts, Nicholas. 'The British Economy', in Francesca Carnevali & Julie-Marie Strange (eds.), *20th Century Britain: Economic, Cultural and Social Change* (London: Routledge, 2007), 7–25.

Crossick, Geoffrey & Jaumain, Serge (eds.), *Cathedrals of Consumption: The European Department Store, 1850–1939* (Aldershot: Ashgate, 1999).

Cullingworth, Barry & Nadin, Vincent. *Town and Country Planning in the UK* (London: Routledge, 2006).

Cupers, Kenny. *The Social Project: Housing Postwar France* (Minneapolis: University of Minnesota Press, 2014).

Daunton, Martin. *Just Taxes: The Politics of Taxation in Britain, 1914–1979* (Cambridge: Cambridge University Press, 2002).

Daunton, Martin J. & Rieger, Bernhard (eds.), *Meanings of Modernity: Britain from the Late-Victorian Era to World War II* (Oxford: Berg, 2001).

Davies, Aled. '"Right to Buy": The Development of a Conservative Housing Policy, 1945–1980', *Contemporary British History* 27:4 (2013), 421–444.

Davies, Aled. *The City of London and Social Democracy: The Political Economy of Finance in Britain, 1959–1979* (Oxford: Oxford University Press, 2017).

Davies, Aled. 'Pension Funds and the Politics of Ownership in Britain, c. 1970–1986', *Twentieth Century British History* 30:1 (2019), 81–107.

Davis, John. 'Rents and Race in 1960s London: New Light on Rachmanism', *Twentieth Century British History* 12:1 (2001), 69–92.

De Grazia, Victoria. *Irresistible Empire: America's Advance through Twentieth-Century Europe* (Cambridge, MA: Belknap, 2006).

Doyle, Barry M. 'The Structure of Elite Power in the Early Twentieth-Century City: Norwich 1900–35', *Urban History* 24:2 (1997), 179–199.

Doyle, Barry M. 'The Changing Functions of Urban Government: Councillors, Officials and Pressure Groups', in Martin Daunton (ed.), *The Cambridge Urban History of Britain, Volume 3: 1840–1950* (Cambridge: Cambridge University Press, 2001), 287–314.

Edgerton, David. *The Shock of the Old: Technology and Global History since 1900* (London: Profile Books, 2006).

Edgerton, David. *The Rise and Fall of the British Nation: A Twentieth-Century History* (London: Allen Lane, 2018).

Essex, Stephen & Brayshay, Mark. 'Boldness Diminished? The Post-War Battle to Replan a Bomb-Damaged Provincial City', *Urban History* 35:3 (2008), 437–461.

Fabian, Sina. 'Flights to the Sun: Package Tours and the Europeanisation of British Holiday Culture in the 1970s and 1980s', *Contemporary British History* 35:3 (2021), 417–438.

Fainstein, Susan S. *The City Builders: Property, Politics & Planning in London and New York* (Oxford: Blackwell, 1994).

Ferris, Paul. *The City* (London: Penguin, 1965).

Flinn, Catherine. *Rebuilding Britain's Blitzed Cities: Hopeful Dreams, Stark Realities* (London: Bloomsbury, 2018).

Francis, Matthew. '"A Crusade to Enfranchise the Many": Thatcherism and the "Property-Owning Democracy"', *Twentieth Century British History* 23:2 (2012), 275–297.

Gardner, Carl & Sheppard, Julie. *Consuming Passion: The Rise of Retail Culture* (London: Unwin Hyman, 1989).

Gilbert, David, Matless, David & Short, Brian (eds.), *Geographies of British Modernity: Space and Society in the Twentieth Century* (Oxford: Blackwell, 2003).

Giles, Judy. *The Parlour and the Suburb: Domestic Identities, Class, Femininity and Modernity* (Oxford: Berg, 2004).

Glendenning, Miles & Muthesius, Stefan. *Tower Block: Modern Public Housing in England, Scotland, Wales and Northern Ireland* (New Haven: Yale University Press, 1994).

Gold, John R. *The Practice of Modernism: Modern Architects and Urban Transformation, 1954–1972* (London: Taylor & Francis, 2007).

Goss, Jon. '"The "Magic of the Mall": An Analysis of Form, Function, and Meaning in the Contemporary Retail Built Environment', *Annals of the Association of American Geographers* 83:1 (1993), 18–47.

Goss, Jon. 'Modernity and Postmodernity in the Retail Landscape', in Kay Anderson & Fay Gale (eds.), *Cultural Geographies* (Australia: Longman, 1999), 199–220.

Gosseye, Janina & Avermaete, Tom (eds.). *Shopping Towns Europe: Commercial Collectivity and the Architecture of the Shopping Centre* (London: Bloomsbury, 2017).

Gottdiener, Mark (ed.). *New Forms of Consumption: Consumers, Culture and Commodification* (Oxford: Rowman & Littlefield, 2000).

Greenhalgh, James. 'Consuming Communities: The Neighbourhood Unit and the Role of Retail Spaces on British Housing Estates, 1944–1958', *Urban History* 43:1 (2016), 158–174.

Greenhalgh, James. *Reconstructing Modernity: Space, Power and Governance in Mid-Twentieth Century Cities* (Manchester: Manchester University Press, 2017).

Gunn, Simon. 'The Rise and Fall of British Urban Modernism: Planning Bradford, circa 1945–1970', *Journal of British Studies* 49:4 (2010), 849–869.

Gunn, Simon. 'The Buchanan Report, Environment and the Problem of Traffic in 1960s Britain', *Twentieth Century British History* 22:4 (2011), 521–542.

Gunn, Simon. 'People and the Car: The Expansion of Automobility in Urban Britain, c.1955–1970', *Social History* 38:2 (2013), 220–237.

Gunn, Simon. 'Ring Road: Birmingham and the Collapse of the Motor City Ideal in 1970s Britain', *The Historical Journal* 61:1 (2018), 227–248.

Gurney, Peter. '"The Curse of the Co-ops": Co-operation, the Mass Press and the Market in Interwar Britain', *English Historical Review* 130 (2015), 1479–1512.

Gurney, Peter. *The Making of Consumer Culture in Modern Britain* (London: Bloomsbury, 2017).

Gurney, Peter. 'Redefining "the Woman with the Basket": The Women's Co-operative Guild and the Politics of Consumption in Britain during World War Two', *Gender & History* 32:1 (2020), 189–207.

Haeussler, Mathias. 'The Popular Press and Ideas of Europe: The Daily Mirror, the Daily Express, and Britain's First Application to Join the EEC, 1961–63', *Twentieth Century British History* 25:1 (2014), 108–131.

Hamnett, Chris. 'The Church's Many Missions: The Changing Structure of the Church Commissioners Land and Property Holdings, 1948–1977', *Transactions of the Institute of British Geographers* 12:4 (1987), 465–481.

Hall, Peter. 'The Containment of Urban England', *The Geographical Journal* 140:3 (1974), 386–408.

Hall, Peter. *Cities of Tomorrow: An Intellectual History of Urban Planning and Design in the Twentieth Century* (Oxford: Blackwell, 2002).
Hall, Peter & Tewdwr-Jones, Mark. *Urban and Regional Planning* (London: Routledge, 2019).
Hall, Tim & Hubbard, Phil (eds.). *The Entrepreneurial City: Geographies of Politics, Regime and Representation* (Chichester: Wiley, 1998).
Hannigan, John. *Fantasy City: Pleasure and Profit in the Postmodern Metropolis* (London: Routledge, 1998).
Hardwick, M. Jeffrey. *Mall Maker: Victor Gruen, Architect of an American Dream* (Philadelphia: University of Pennsylvania Press, 2010).
Harling, Philip. *The Modern British State* (Cambridge: Polity, 2001).
Harrison, Ewan. '"Money Spinners": R. Seifert & Partners, Sir Frank Price and Public-Sector Speculative Development in the 1970s', *Architectural History* 61 (2018), 259–280.
Harvey, David. *The Urbanization of Capital* (Oxford, 1985).
Harvey, David. 'From Managerialism to Entrepreneurialism: The Transformation in Urban Governance in Late Capitalism', *Geografiska Annaler B* 71 (1989), 3–17.
Harvey, David. *The Condition of Postmodernity: An Enquiry into the Origins of Cultural Change* (Oxford: Blackwell, 1990).
Harvey, David. 'The Right to the City', *International Journal of Urban and Regional Research* 27:4 (2003), 939–941.
Harvey, David. *A Brief History of Neoliberalism* (Oxford: Oxford University Press, 2007).
Harwood, Elaine. *Space, Hope and Brutalism: English Architecture, 1945–1975* (New Haven: Yale University Press, 2015).
Hasegawa, Junichi. *Replanning the Blitzed City Centre* (Buckingham: Open University Press, 1992).
Hatherley, Owen. *A Guide to the New Ruins of Great Britain* (London: Verso, 2010).
Healey, Patsy, Davoudi, Simin, O'Toole, Mo, Tavsanoglu, Solmaz & Usher, David (eds.). *Rebuilding the City: Property-led Urban Regeneration* (London: E&FN Spon, 1992).
Heim, Carol E. 'The Treasury as Developer-Capitalist? British New Town Planning in the 1950s', *The Journal of Economic History* 50:4 (1990), 903–924.
Hetherington, Kevin. *Capitalism's Eye: Cultural Spaces of the Commodity* (London: Routledge, 2007).
Hilton, Matthew. 'The Female Consumer and the Politics of Consumption in Twentieth-Century Britain', *The Historical Journal* 45:1 (2002), 103–128.
Hilton, Matthew. *Consumerism in Twentieth-Century Britain: The Search for a Historical Movement* (Cambridge: Cambridge University Press, 2003).
Hilton, Matthew, Moores, Chris & Sutcliffe-Braithwaite, Florence. 'New Times Revisited: Britain in the 1980s', *Contemporary British History* 31:2 (2017), 145–165.
Howard, E. B. & Davies, R. L. *The Impact of Regional, Out-of-Town Retail Centres: The Case of the Metro Centre* (Oxford: Pergamon Press, 1993).
Hulme, Tom. *After the Shock City: Urban Culture and the Making of Modern Citizenship* (London: Royal Historical Society, 2019).

Imrie, Rob & Raco, Mike (eds.). *Urban Renaissance? New Labour, Community and Urban Policy* (Bristol: The Policy Press, 2003).

Jackson, Ben & Saunders, Robert (eds.). *Making Thatcher's Britain* (Cambridge: Cambridge University Press, 2012).

Jackson, Louise. '"The Coffee Club Menace": Policing Youth, Leisure and Sexuality in Post-war Manchester', *Cultural and Social History* 5:3 (2008), 289–308.

Jackson, Peter, Lowe, Michelle, Miller, Daniel & Mort, Frank (eds.). *Commercial Cultures: Economies, Practices, Spaces* (Oxford: Berg, 2000).

Jameson, Frederic. *Postmodernism, or, the Cultural Logic of Late Capitalism* (London: Verso, 1991).

Jefferys, James B. *Retail Trading in Britain, 1850–1950* (London: Cambridge University Press, 1954).

Jenkins, Simon. 'The Politics of London Motorways', *The Political Quarterly* 44:3 (1973), 257–270.

Jessop, Bob. 'The Narrative of Enterprise and the Enterprise of Narrative: Place Marketing and the Entrepreneurial City', in Tim Hall & Phil Hubbard (eds.), *The Entrepreneurial City: Geographies of Politics, Regime and Representation* (Chichester: Wiley, 1998), 77–102.

Johnson, David. 'An Evaluation of the Urban Development Grant Programme', *Local Economy* 2:4 (1988), 251–270.

Harriet Jones, '"This is Magnificent!"': 300,000 Houses a Year and the Tory Revival after 1945', *Contemporary British History* 14:1 (2000), 99–121.

Jones, Peter. 'Re-thinking Corruption in Post-1950 Urban Britain: The Poulson Affair, 1972–1976', *Urban History* 39:3 (2012), 510–528.

Jones, Phil & Evans, James. *Urban Regeneration in the UK* (Los Angeles: SAGE, 2013).

Joyce, Patrick. *The Rule of Freedom: Liberalism and the Modern City* (London: Verso, 2003).

Judt, Tony. *Postwar: A History of Europe since 1945* (London: Vintage, 2010).

Kärrholm, Mattias. *Retailising Space: Architecture, Retail and the Territorialisation of Public Space* (London: Routledge, 2012).

Kefford, Alistair. 'Disruption, Destruction and the Creation of "the Inner Cities": the Impact of Urban Renewal on Industry, 1945–1980', *Urban History* 44:3 (2017), 492–515.

Kefford, Alistair. 'Housing the Citizen-Consumer in Post-war Britain: The Parker Morris Report, Affluence and the Even Briefer Life of Social Democracy', *Twentieth Century British History* 29:2 (2018), 225–258.

Kefford, Alistair. 'The Death of the High Street', *History & Policy* (2020), online repository.

Kefford, Alistair. 'Actually Existing Managerialism: Planning, Politics and Property Development in Post-1945 Britain', *Urban Studies* 58:12 (2020), 2441–2455.

Keith-Lucas, Bryan & Richards, Peter G. *A History of Local Government in the Twentieth Century* (London: George Allen & Unwin, 1978).

Kennedy, Liam (ed.). *Remaking Birmingham: The Visual Culture of Urban Regeneration* (London: Routledge, 2004).

Kowinski, William Severini. *The Malling of America: An Inside Look at the Great Consumer Paradise* (New York: William Morrow, 1985).

Krugman, Paul. 'What's New About the New Economic Geography?', *Oxford Review of Economic Policy* 14:2 (1998), 7–17.

Kynaston, David. *Austerity Britain, 1945–1951* (London: Bloomsbury, 2007).

Kynaston, David. *Modernity Britain: A Shake of the Dice, 1959–62* (London: Bloomsbury, 2014).

Laermans, Rudi. 'Learning to Consume: Early Department Stores and the Shaping of the Modern Consumer Culture (1860–1914)', *Theory, Culture and Society* 10:4 (1993), 79–102.

Larkham, Peter J. & Lilley, Keith D. 'Plans, Planners and City Images: Place Promotion and Civic Boosterism in British Reconstruction Planning', *Urban History* 30:2 (2003), 183–205.

Larkham, Peter & Lilley, Keith. 'Exhibiting the City: Planning Ideas and Public Involvement in Wartime and Early Post-War Britain', *Town Planning Review* 83:6 (2012), 647–668.

Lawless, Paul. *Britain's Inner Cities: Problems and Policies* (London: Paul Chapman, 1989).

Lawrence, Jon. *Me, Me, Me: The Search for Community in Post-war England* (Oxford: Oxford University Press, 2019).

Lee, Neil & Swan, Polly. *A High Street Revolution: How Private Developers can Support the Community Takeover of our Town Centres* (Power to Change, 2021).

Leitner, Helga, Peck, Jamie & Sheppard, Eric S. (eds.), *Contesting Neoliberalism: Urban Frontiers* (London: The Guilford Press, 2007).

Ley, David. 'Waterfront Development', in Ilse Helbrecht & Peter Dirksmeier (eds.), *New Urbanism: Life, Work and Space in the New Downtown* (Farnham: Ashgate, 2011), 47–60.

Loney, Martin. 'The British Community Development Projects: Questioning the State', *Community Development Journal* 16:1 (1981), 55–66.

Low, Setha M. & Smith, Neil (eds.). *The Politics of Public Space* (London: Routledge, 2006).

Lowe, Michelle. 'From Victor Gruen to Merry Hill: Reflections on Regional Shopping Centres and Urban development in the US and UK', in Peter Jackson, Michelle Lowe, Daniel Miller & Frank Mort (eds.), *Commercial Cultures: Economies, Practices, Spaces* (Oxford: Berg, 2000), 245–260.

MacGregor, Susanne & Pimlott, Ben (eds.). *Tackling the Inner Cities: The 1980s reviewed, prospects for the 1990s* (Oxford: Clarendon, 1990).

Madgin, Rebecca. *Heritage, Culture and Conservation: Managing the Urban Renaissance* (Saarbrucken: VDM Verlag, 2009).

Maier, Charles S. 'Between Taylorism and Technocracy: European Ideologies and the Vision of Industrial Productivity in the 1920s', in Charles Maier (ed.), *In Search of Stability: Explorations in Historical Political Economy* (Cambridge: Cambridge University Press, 1987), 22–69.

Malpass, Peter. 'The Wobbly Pillar? Housing and the British Postwar Welfare State', *Journal of Social Policy* 32:4 (2003), 589–606.

Mandler, Peter. 'New Towns for Old: The Fate of the Town Centre', in Becky Conekin, Frank Mort & Chris Waters (eds.), *Moments of Modernity: Reconstructing Britain 1945–1964* (London: Rivers Oram, 1999), 208–227.

Mandler, Peter. 'Good Reading for the Million: The "Paperback Revolution" and the Co-Production of Academic Knowledge in Mid Twentieth-Century Britain and America', *Past & Present* 244:1 (2019), 235–269.

Marriott, Oliver. *The Property Boom* (London: Hamish Hamilton, 1967).

Martin, Ron. 'The Political Economy of Britain's North-South Divide', *Transactions of the Institute of British Geographers* 13:4 (1988), 389–418.

Marwick, Arthur. *British Society since 1945* (London: Penguin, 2003).

Mass, Sarah. 'Commercial Heritage as Democratic Action: Historicizing the "Save the Market" Campaigns in Bradford and Chesterfield, 1969-76', *Twentieth Century British History* 29:3 (2018), 459–484.

Mass, Sarah. 'Cost-benefit Break Down: Unplannable Spaces in 1970s Glasgow', *Urban History* 46:2 (2019), 309–330.

Matless, David. *Landscape and Englishness* (London: Reaktion Books, 1998).

Matrix. *Making Space: Women and the Man-Made Environment* (London: Pluto, 1984).

McConnell, Allan. 'The Recurring Crisis of Local Taxation in Post-war Britain', *Contemporary British History* 11:3 (1997), 39–62.

McWilliam, Rohan. *London's West End: Creating the Pleasure District, 1800–1914* (Oxford: Oxford University Press, 2020).

Meller, Helen. *Towns, Plans and Society in Modern Britain* (Cambridge: Cambridge University Press, 1997).

Miles, Steven & Paddison, Ronan, 'The Rise and Rise of Culture-led Urban Regeneration', *Urban Studies* 42:5/6 (2005), 833–839.

Miles, Steven. *Spaces for Consumption: Pleasure and Placelessness in the Post-Industrial City* (London: SAGE, 2010).

Miller, Daniel, Jackson, Peter, Thrift, Nigel, Holbrook, Beverly & Rowlands, Michael (eds.). *Shopping, Place and Identity* (London: Routledge, 1998).

Miller, Peter & Rose, Nikolas. 'Mobilizing the Consumer: Assembling the Subject of Consumption', *Theory Culture Society* 14:1 (1997), 1–36.

Millward, Robert. 'The Rise of the Service Economy', in Roderick Floud & Paul Johnson (eds.), *The Cambridge Economic History of Modern Britain: Structural Change and Growth, 1939–2000* (Cambridge: Cambridge University Press, 2004), 238–266.

Minton, Anna. *Ground Control: Fear and Happiness in the Twenty-First-Century City* (London: Penguin, 2009).

Mitchell, Don. *The Right to the City: Social Justice and the Fight for Public Space* (New York: The Guilford Press, 2003).

Morelli, Carlo. 'Increasing Value? Modern British Retailing in the Late Twentieth Century', in Richard Coopey & Peter Lyth (eds.), *Business in Britain in the Twentieth Century: Decline and Renaissance?* (Oxford: Oxford University Press, 2009), 271–295.

Mort, Frank. 'The Commercial Domain: Advertising and the Cultural Management of Demand', in Peter Jackson, Michelle Lowe, Daniel Miller & Frank Mort (eds.), *Commercial Cultures: Economies, Practices, Spaces* (Oxford: Berg, 2000), 35–53.

Mort, Frank & Thompson, Peter. 'Retailing, Commercial Culture and Masculinity in 1950s Britain: The Case of Montague Burton, the "Tailor of Taste"', *History Workshop Journal* 38:1 (1994), 106–128.

Mort, Frank. *Cultures of Consumption: Masculinities and Social Space in Late Twentieth-Century Britain* (London: Routledge, 1996).

Mort, Frank. 'Fantasies of Metropolitan Life: Planning London in the 1940s', *Journal of British Studies* 43:1 (2004), 120–151.

Mort, Frank. 'On Tour with the Prince: Monarchy, Imperial Politics and Publicity in the Prince of Wales's Dominion Tours 1919–20', *Twentieth Century British History* 29:1 (2018), 25–57.

Nixon, Sean. 'Understanding Ordinary Women: Advertising, Consumer Research and Mass Consumption in Britain, 1948–67', *Journal of Cultural Economy* 2:3 (2009), 301–323.

Nixon, Sean. *Hard Sell: Advertising, Affluence and Transatlantic Relations, c. 1951–69* (Manchester: Manchester University Press, 2013).

Oatley, Nick. *Cities, Economic Competition and Urban Policy* (London: Paul Chapman, 1998).

Offer, Avner, *Property and Politics 1870–1914: Landownership, Law, Ideology and Urban Development in England* (Cambridge: Cambridge University Press, 1981).

Offer, Avner. 'British Manual Workers: From Producers to Consumers, c. 1950–2000', *Contemporary British History* 22:4 (2008), 537–571.

Oldenziel, Ruth & Zachmann, Karin (eds.). *Cold War Kitchen: Americanization, Technology, and European Users* (Cambridge, MA: MIT Press, 2009).

Ortolano, Guy. 'Planning the Urban Future in 1960s Britain', *The Historical Journal* 54:2 (2011), 477–507.

Ortolano, Guy. *Thatcher's Progress: From Social Democracy to Market Liberalism through an English New Town* (Cambridge: Cambridge University Press, 2019).

Otter, Chris. *The Victorian Eye: A Political History of Light and Vision in Britain, 1800–1910* (Chicago: University of Chicago Press, 2008).

Owens, Edward. *The Family Firm: Monarchy, Mass Media and the British Public, 1932–53* (London: Royal Historical Society, 2019).

Pacione, Michael. 'Housing Policies in Glasgow since 1880', *Geographical Review* 69:4 (1979), 395–412.

Parker, Simon. 'The Leaving of Liverpool: Managed Decline and the Enduring Legacy of Thatcherism's Urban Policy', *LSE British Politics and Policy* (2019) online repository.

Peden, G. C. *British Economic and Social Policy: Lloyd George to Margaret Thatcher* (Oxford: Philip Allan, 1991).

Pemberton, Hugh. 'The Transformation of the Economy', in Paul Addison and Harriet Jones (eds.), *A Companion to Contemporary Britain 1939–2000* (Oxford: Blackwell, 2007), 180–202.

Pendlebury, John. 'Alas Smith and Burns? Conservation in Newcastle upon Tyne City Centre, 1959–1968', *Planning Perspectives* 16:2 (2001), 115–141.

Porter, Bernard. '"Though not an Historian Myself . . . " Margaret Thatcher and the Historians', *Twentieth Century British History* 5:2 (1994), 246–256.

Quilley, Steve. 'Entrepreneurial Turns: Municipal Socialism and After', in Jamie Peck and Kevin Ward (eds.), *City of Revolution: Restructuring Manchester* (Manchester: Manchester University Press, 2002), 76–94.

Rappaport, Erika Diane. *Shopping for Pleasure: Women in the Making of London's West End* (Princeton: Princeton University Press, 2000).

Rappaport, Erika, Trudgen Dawson, Sandra & Crowley, Mark J. (eds.). *Consuming Behaviours: Identity, Politics and Pleasure in Twentieth-Century Britain* (London: Bloomsbury, 2015).

Ravetz, Alison. *Council Housing and Culture: The History of a Social Experiment* (London: Routledge, 2001).

Ritschel, Daniel. *The Politics of Planning: The Debate on Economic Planning in Britain in the 1930s* (Oxford: Oxford University Press, 1997).

Robinson, Emily, Schofield, Camilla, Sutcliffe-Braithwaite, Florence & Thomlinson, Nathalie. 'Telling Stories about Post-war Britain: Popular Individualism and the "Crisis" of the 1970s', *Twentieth Century British History* 28:2 (2017), 268–304.

Robson, Brian T. *Those Inner Cities: Reconciling the Economic and Social Aims of Urban Policy* (Oxford: Clarendon, 1988).

Rosevear, Stephen. 'Balancing Business and the Regions: British Distribution of Industry Policy and the Board of Trade, 1945–51', *Business History* 40:1 (1998), 77–99.

Saint, Andrew. *Towards a Social Architecture: The Role of School-Building in Post-war England* (New Haven: Yale University Press, 1987).

Saumarez Smith, Otto. 'Central Government and Town-Centre Redevelopment in Britain, 1959-1966', *The Historical Journal* 58:1 (2015), 217–244.

Saumarez Smith, Otto. *Boom Cities: Architect Planners and the Politics of Radical Renewal in 1960s Britain* (Oxford: Oxford University Press, 2019).

Saumarez Smith, Otto. 'The Lost World of the British Leisure Centre Boom', *History Workshop Journal* 88 (2019), 180–203.

Saumarez Smith, Otto. 'Action for Cities: The Thatcher Government and Inner-City Policy', *Urban History* 47:2 (2020), 274–291.

Robert Saunders, '"Crisis? What Crisis?" Thatcherism and the Seventies', in Ben Jackson & Robert Saunders (eds.), *Making Thatcher's Britain*, (Cambridge University Press, 2012), 25–42.

Schofield, Camilla. *Enoch Powell and the Making of Postcolonial Britain* (Cambridge: Cambridge University Press, 2013).

Scott, James C. *Seeing Like a State: How Certain Schemes to Improve the Human Condition Have Failed* (New Haven: Yale University Press, 1998).

Scott, Peter. 'Learning to Multiply: The Property Market and the Growth of Multiple Retailing in Britain', *Business History* 36:3 (1994), 1–28.

Scott, Peter. *The Property Masters: A History of the British Commercial Property Sector* (London: E&FN Spon, 1996).

Scott, Peter. 'The Worst of Both Worlds: British Regional Policy, 1951–64', *Business History* 38:4 (1996), 41–64.

Scott, Peter, 'Industrial Estates and British Industrial Development 1897–1939', *Business History* 43:2 (2001), 73–98.

Scott, Peter. *Triumph of the South: A Regional Economic History of Early Twentieth Century Britain* (Aldershot: Ashgate, 2007).

Scott, Peter. *The Making of the Modern British Home: The Suburban Semi and Family Life between the Wars* (Oxford: Oxford University Press, 2013).

Scott, Peter. *The Market Makers: Creating Mass Markets for Consumer Durables in Inter-war Britain* (Oxford: Oxford University Press, 2017).

Scott, Peter M. & Walker, James T. 'The Impact of "Stop-Go" Demand Management Policy on Britain's Consumer Durables Industries, 1952–65', *Economic History Review* 70:4 (2017), 1321–1345.

Shapely, Peter. 'Civic Pride and Redevelopment in the Post-war British City', *Urban History* 39:2 (2012), 310–328.

Shaw, Gareth, Curth, Louise & Alexander, Andrew. 'Selling Self-Service and the Supermarket: the Americanisation of Food Retailing in Britain, 1945–60', *Business History* 46:4 (2004), 568–582.

Simmonds, Alan G. V. 'Conservative Governments and the New Town Housing Question in the 1950s', *Urban History* 28:1 (2001), 65–83.

Simmons, Colin & Caruana, Viv. 'Enterprising Local Government: Policy, Prestige and Manchester Airport, 1929–82', *Journal of Transport History* 22:2 (2001), 126–146.

Steedman, Carolyn. *Landscape for a Good Woman* (London: Virago, 1986).

Stephenson, Gordon. *Compassionate Town Planning* (Liverpool: Liverpool University Press, 1994).

Stevenson, John. 'Planners' Moon? The Second World War and the Planning Movement', in Harold L. Smith (ed.), *War and Social Change: British Society in the Second World War* (Manchester: Manchester University Press, 1986), 58–77.

Stocks, Nigel. 'The Greater Manchester Shopping Enquiry: A Case Study of Strategic Retail Planning', *Land Development Studies* 6:1 (1989), 57–83.

Sutcliffe-Braithwaite, Florence. *Class, Politics and the Decline of Deference in England, 1968–2000* (Oxford: Oxford University Press, 2018).

Tallon, Andrew. *Urban Regeneration in the UK* (London: Routledge, 2009).

Thane, Pat. *Divided Kingdom: A History of Britain, 1900 to the Present* (Cambridge: Cambridge University Press, 2018).

Thomas, Amy. 'Prejudice and Pragmatism: The Commercial Architect in the Development of Postwar London', *Grey Room* 71 (2018), 88–115.

Tichelar, Michael. *The Failure of Land Reform in Twentieth-Century England* (London: Routledge, 2018).

Tiratsoo, Nick. 'The Reconstruction of Blitzed British Cities, 1945–55: Myths and Reality', *Contemporary British History* 14:1 (2000), 27–44.

Todd, Selina. *The People: The Rise and Fall of the Working Class 1910–2010* (London: John Murray, 2014).

Todd, Selina. 'Phoenix Rising: Working-Class Life and Urban Reconstruction, c. 1945–1967', *Journal of British Studies* 54:3 (2015), 679–702.

Tomlinson, Jim. *The Politics of Decline: Understanding Post-war Britain* (Harlow: Longman, 2000).

Tomlinson, Jim. 'Managing the Economy, Managing the People: Britain c.1931–70', *Economic History Review* 58:3 (2005), 555–585.

Trainor, Richard H. 'The "Decline" of British Urban Governance since 1850: A Reassessment', in Robert J. Morris & Richard H. Trainor (eds.), *Urban Governance: Britain and Beyond since 1750* (Aldershot: Ashgate, 2000), 28–46.

Trentmann, Frank. 'Bread, Milk and Democracy: Consumption and Citizenship in Twentieth-Century Britain', in Martin Daunton & Matthew Hilton (eds.), *The Politics of Consumption: Material Culture and Citizenship in Europe and America* (Oxford: Berg, 2001), 129–164.

Trentmann, Frank (ed.). *The Making of the Consumer: Knowledge, Power and Identity in the Modern World* (Oxford: Berg, 2006).

Tyson, John R. (ed.), *Charles Wesley: A Reader* (Oxford: Oxford University Press, 1989).

Vernon, James. 'Heathrow and the Making of Neoliberal Britain', *Past & Present* 252:1 (2021), 213–247.

Wakeman, Rosemary. *Practicing Utopia: An Intellectual History of the New Town Movement* (Chicago: University of Chicago Press, 2016).

Waller, P. J. *Town, City and Nation: England 1850–1914* (Oxford: Oxford University Press, 1983).

Walton, John. 'Urban Sociology: Critical Essays. By C.G. Pickvance', *American Journal of Sociology* 83:3 (1977), 799–803.

Walton, John K. *The British Seaside: Holidays and Resorts in the Twentieth Century* (Manchester: Manchester University Press, 2000).

Wannop, Urlan. 'The Evolution and Roles of the Scottish Development Agency', *Town Planning Review* 55:3 (1984), 313–321.

Ward, Stephen V. 'Public-Private Partnerships', in Barry Cullingworth (ed.), *British Planning: 50 Years of Urban and Regional Policy* (London: Athlone Press, 1999), 232–249.

Ward, Stephen V. *Planning the Twentieth-Century City: The Advanced Capitalist World* (Chichester, Wiley, 2002).

Ward, Stephen V. 'Gordon Stephenson and the "Galaxy of Talent": Planning for Post-war Reconstruction in Britain 1942–1947', *Town Planning Review* 83:3 (2012), 279–296.

Ward, Stephen V. *The Peaceful Path: Building Garden Cities and New Towns* (Hatfield: Hertfordshire, 2016).

Watson, Nigel. *Arnold Ziff: The Making of a Great Yorkshireman* (London: Valentine Mitchell, 2005).

Weaver, Michael. 'The Birmingham Bull Ring Riots of 1839: Variations on a Theme of Class Conflict', *Social Science Quarterly* 78:1 (1997), 137–148.

Weber, Rachel. 'Extracting Value from the City: Neoliberalism and Urban Redevelopment', *Antipode* 34:3 (2002), 519–540.

Wetherell, Sam. 'Freedom Planned: Enterprise Zones and Urban Non-Planning in Post-war Britain', *Twentieth Century British History* 27:2 (2016), 266–289.

Wetherell, Sam. *Foundations: How the Built Environment Made Twentieth-Century Britain* (Princeton: Princeton University Press, 2020).

Weiler, Peter. 'The Rise and Fall of the Conservatives' "Grand Design for Housing", 1951–64', *Contemporary British History* 14:1 (2000), 122–150.

Weiler, Peter. 'Labour and the Land: From Municipalization to the Land Commission, 1951–1971', *Twentieth Century British History* 19:3 (2008), 314–343.

Wildman, Charlotte. 'A City Speaks: The Projection of Civic Identity in Manchester', *Twentieth Century British History* 23:1 (2012), 80–99.

Wildman, Charlotte. *Urban Redevelopment and Modernity in Liverpool and Manchester, 1918–1939* (London: Bloomsbury, 2016).

Williams, Gwndaf. *The Enterprising City Centre: Manchester's Development Challenge* (London: Spon Press, 2003).

Winstanley, Michael. 'Concentration and Competition in the Retail Sector c.1800-1990', in Maurice W. Kirby & Mary B. Rose (eds.), *Business Enterprise in Modern Britain: From the Eighteenth Century to the Twentieth Century* (London: Routledge, 1994), 236–262.

Zukin, Sharon. 'The Postmodern Debate over Urban Form', *Theory, Culture and Society* 5:2–3 (1988), 431–446.

Zukin, Sharon. *Landscapes of Power: From Detroit to Disneyworld* (Berkeley: University of California Press, 1991).

Zweiniger-Bargielowska, Ina. *Austerity in Britain: Rationing, Controls and Consumption, 1939–1955* (Oxford: Oxford University Press, 2000).

Zweiniger-Bargielowska, Ina. *Women in Twentieth-Century Britain: Social, Cultural and Political Change* (London: Routledge, 2001).

Index

For EU product safety concerns, contact us at Calle de José Abascal, 56–1°,
28003 Madrid, Spain or eugpsr@cambridge.org.

www.ingramcontent.com/pod-product-compliance
Ingram Content Group UK Ltd.
Pitfield, Milton Keynes, MK11 3LW, UK
UKHW020401140625
459647UK00020B/2585